CAMBRIDGE C

MW01074009

P. 256
30
257

STATIUS

SILVAE

BOOK II

EDITED BY

CAROLE E. NEWLANDS

Professor of Classics, University of Colorado Boulder

CAMBRIDGE
UNIVERSITY PRESS

CAMBRIDGE UNIVERSITY PRESS

Cambridge, New York, Melbourne, Madrid, Cape Town, Singapore,
São Paulo, Delhi, Dubai, Tokyo, Mexico City

Cambridge University Press
The Edinburgh Building, Cambridge CB2 8RU, UK

Published in the United States of America by Cambridge University Press, New York

www.cambridge.org
Information on this title: www.cambridge.org/9780521666237

First published 2011

Printed in the United Kingdom at the University Press, Cambridge

A catalogue record for this publication is available from the British Library

ISBN 978-0-521-66187-4 Hardback
ISBN 978-0-521-66623-7 Paperback

For
Alexander Graham Newlands
and
Georgina Elizabeth Newlands

CONTENTS

PREFACE

My interest in Statius' *Siluae* began many years ago when, as an undergraduate at St Andrews University, Scotland, I attended a series of brilliant lectures on these poems taught by Chris Carter. He conveyed to me his excitement about the novelty of the *Siluae*, their bold experimentation with language and poetic convention. Later, at the start of graduate school at UC Berkeley, the medieval scholar Alain Renoir ordered me to start my studies by reading Statius, who was not at that time of first order of importance for classicists. However, a positive shift in interest in this Flavian poet has taken place, and in this edition I have been able to take advantage of the important textual and literary critical work done on the *Siluae* in recent decades. In keeping with the aims of the series, I have tried to explain the cultural context of the seven poems of book 2 as well as elucidate Statius' text. It is my hope that this edition will make Statius' *Siluae* more accessible by contributing to an appreciation of their innovations in style, theme and genre; and by helping elucidate Roman culture in the age of Domitian and Statius' sophisticated engagement with it. Statius, who was born and raised in Naples, wrote the *Siluae* shortly after the eruption of Vesuvius; his *Siluae* provide rare, important social testimony to the culture of which the art and artefacts from Pompeii and Herculaneum give us tantalising glimpses.

The genesis of this commentary was a conversation with Elaine Fantham, who has offered sound advice and warm encouragement over the years. Summer research grants from the Graduate School of the University of Wisconsin Madison, and a fellowship from the Loeb Classical Foundation, gave me much-needed time, during four years as chair at UW Madison, to work on the commentary; a term at the School of Historical Studies at the Institute for Advanced Study, Princeton gave me wonderful resources and a peaceful environment to pursue my research. Finally Clare Hall and the Faculty of Classics in the University of Cambridge provided welcome support in the last stages of composition; I am deeply grateful to all these institutions. Many colleagues in the field have helped by reading portions of the commentary at various stages, and to them I owe a large debt of gratitude: Kathleen Coleman, Bruce Gibson, Alex Hardie, John Miller, Silvia Montiglio, Sara Myers. Kris Ehrhart at UW Madison provided valuable research assistance. I particularly want to thank Jim McKeown for his patience and insight on reading my early drafts, and Philip Hardie, who read and commented on several versions of the commentary with characteristic incisiveness; from both of them I learned a great deal. Michael Sharp at the Press has helped guide the production of this commentary with great professionalism and care.

Boulder, Colorado　　　　　　　　　　　　CAROLE E. NEWLANDS
July 2010

INTRODUCTION

1. LIFE

Our evidence for St.'s life comes mainly from the *Siluae*, particularly 3.5, an epistle to his wife, and 5.3, the poem on his father's death.[1] St. was a poet of two cities and two cultures. He was born around 50 CE in Naples, 'practically a Greek city' (*quasi Graecam urbem*, Tac. *Ann.* 15.33), where Hellenic culture was supported by Roman wealth and power.[2] The city celebrated Greek-style games founded by Augustus;[3] Greek and Latin, and probably Oscan, were spoken in the city, with Greek remaining the language of cultural prestige in many official contexts.[4] St. was the son of an eminent *grammaticus* and Greek professional poet who, composing in a tradition of extemporaneous poetry, won prizes at the major Greek games and was honoured with a statue in the Athenian agora.[5] St. was doubly privileged: born in a city with a rich cultural heritage, he was taught a demanding curriculum in Greek literature by his father in a period when such knowledge was crucial for social advancement.[6]

At some point in St.'s youth father and son moved to Rome where St. senior had a successful career as *grammaticus* to the Roman elite and probably also to the imperial family.[7] He enjoyed too the great honour of reciting his poem on the civil war of 68–9 in the temple of Jupiter Optimus Maximus on the Capitol (5.3.199–204). The father thus may have been closer to the imperial court than the son.[8] Although St. won first prize in poetry at Domitian's Alban games, he did not win at the more important Capitoline games, possibly in the same year, 90 CE.[9] His property at Alba, near Domitian's summer palace (3.1.161–4), often believed to have been a gift to St. from the emperor, was probably given by Vespasian to St.'s father, who was buried there (5.3.35–40); St. received from Domitian only the water rights, which from the time of Augustus were a common

---

[1] On 5.3 and St.'s career see Hardie 1983: 5–14.

[2] Leiwo 1994: 40–1 comments that for the Romans the positive side of Hellenism was cultural: literature, arts, architecture. St. idealises Naples as a place where Roman and Greek traditions harmoniously mingle (3.5.93–4).

[3] Leiwo 1994: 45–6.

[4] On the Greek character of Naples see D'Arms 1970: 142–3; Hardie 1983: 2–4; Leiwo's 1994 survey of the epigraphic use of Greek and Latin in Naples concludes that the city stands out in Campania in its use of Greek as the language of bureaucracy, though often in a hybrid form, until the end of the third century CE.

[5] On the success of St. senior as a *grammaticus* see McNelis 2002; on the tradition of Greek professional poets see Hardie 1983: 16–30; on the statue see Clinton 1973.

[6] McNelis 2002: 79.   [7] Hardie 1983: 10–11; Gibson on 5.3.178–80.

[8] As Coleman 1986: 3105 notes, 'st. nowhere boasts of familiarity with the emperor'. When once invited to an imperial banquet he was one of more than 1,000 guests (4.2.33).

[9] 3.5.32–3; 4.2.65–7; 5.3.225–30. On the disputed date of St.'s victories see Coleman on *Silu.* 4 pp. xvii–xviii.

1

imperial grant (Fron. *Aq.* 99.3, 105.1).[10] The social status of father and son remains unclear; possibly they never reached equestrian rank. St. died probably in 96 CE, the same year as Domitian's assassination.

In addition to the five books of *Siluae* St. wrote an early poem on Domitian's wars, *De bello Germanico*, of which only four lines survive,[11] and the epic poems *Thebaid* and the *Achilleid*, the latter incomplete. Juvenal, perhaps spuriously, suggests that St. also wrote a pantomime script *Agaue*.[12] Martial, Pliny and Quintilian do not mention St.[13] Silius and St. knew one another's poetry but it is impossible to determine priority in any allusion.[14] Juvenal is the only near-contemporary author to mention St.; his condemnatory sketch of St. prostituting his *Thebaid* by public recitation (7.82–7) has provided a persistent image of St. as the literary hack, his epic a 'whore' that he tries to market to the Roman people through public recitation. The *Siluae* create an image of a poetic self and of a literary culture that is quite different. 5.3.215–19, for instance, records his father's pride at the son's recitations before an elite gathering of senators.[15] St. did not have Pliny's advantage of noble birth and elite connections; undoubtedly it was important for him to keep his work and his own presence in the public eye.

We should look to the *Siluae* not so much for biographical facts as for St.'s representation of his career. In 5.3 St. models his life on that of Horace, whose father also was a powerful influence (*S.* 1.6). St. shows traditional filial piety but emphasises the literary rather than moral education his father gave him.[16] 5.3 thus also promotes the genius of the son as an experimenter with Roman literary traditions from his special vantage point of biculturalism. In Rome St. found a cultural environment responsive to his new style of poetry. Extemporaneous composition was one of the high-profile events at Domitian's Capitoline games.[17] The degree to which 'the virtuoso skills of the epideictic performer had already penetrated the cultural life at the capital'[18] is demonstrated by the grave monument of the eleven-year-old Q. Sulpicius Maximus, who acquitted himself with honour among the Greek poets at the Capitoline games of 94 CE. His affectionate

[10]   See Eck 1983: 72–3; Rodgers 2004 on Fron. *Aq.* 99.3, *Aq.* 105.1; Peachin 2004: 127–30 provides the startling statistics that in the late first century CE only about 9 per cent of Rome's aqueduct system was publicly available for the city's non-elite population; the rest received water by imperial grant. On imperial *beneficia* see Millar 1977: 135–9.

[11]   The idea that Juv. 4 parodies the council of the gods in St.'s *De bello Germanico* goes back to the Vallan scholia (Courtney on Juv. pp. 195–200).

[12]   See Courtney on Juv. 7.87.

[13]   White 1993: 63 suggests that the silence may be owing to St.'s low social status; Roman poets are silent on Greeks and *grammatici*. In addition, Roman authors do not usually refer to their contemporaries unless to write their obituaries, as Pliny does for Martial and Silius in *Ep.* 3.5 and 3.7 respectively.

[14]   On the relationship between Silius and St. see Hutchinson 1993: 121–3.

[15]   Markus 2000: 163–8; 171–5.

[16]   Nagel 2000: 47–50; the filial modesty is closely connected with his literary modesty.

[17]   On the Capitoline games see Caldelli 1993: 53–120; Hardie 2003a: 126–34.

[18]   Hardie 2003a: 133–4.

parents had the boy's extemporaneous competition verses inscribed above the Latin epitaph, proof of the complex cultural milieu in which St. worked and over which Domitian presided, one that encouraged public, extemporaneous performance, whether at the official games or in the recitation hall.[19] In the *Siluae* St. cultivates a double vision of himself as both Roman and Neapolitan, a poet who introduced the epideictic and improvisational features of Greek professional poetry to a Roman audience, to Roman literary traditions, and to book form.

2. THE CHARACTER OF THE *SILVAE*

The *Siluae* are epideictic poetry. They describe and celebrate contemporary Flavian culture, its literary and political figures, its villas and works of art, its entertainments, its families and its court. They were written and published between 89 and 96 CE, in the latter part of the reign of Domitian (81–96), last of the Flavians. Books 1–3 were published as a set early in 93, shortly after publication of the *Thebaid* in 92, and book 4 was published two years later; a fifth book appeared posthumously.[20]

There is nothing else quite like the *Siluae* in extant Roman literature.[21] Paradox is their basic aesthetic and intellectual mode. They are playful and earnest, intimate and elevated, improvisational and learned; they challenge generic distinctions between 'high' and 'low' poetic forms, between epic and epigram; the shortest poem of book 2 is the most epicising in style (2.5). In the stylistic extremes of haste and elevation they are profoundly anti-Callimachean; but in their learning and their interest in 'minor' themes and characters they are closely tied to Hellenistic poetic traditions. They are thus experimental poetry trying out new styles and themes (e.g. the villa); vividly descriptive, they have powerful visual and imaginative appeal. The prefaces which introduce each book emphasise the novelty of the *Siluae* with a mixture of pride and modesty;[22] this is new work by that renowned epic poet St., the first preface claims,[23] yet they are only short, amusing pieces, *libellos* (1 *pr.* 2), a word that calls to mind Catullus' refined and superbly wrought *little* poetry book, *lepidum nouum libellum | arido modo pumice expolitum* (1.1–2). Such claims to modesty were a conventional means of drawing attention to one's literary prowess, while guarding against critical attack.[24]

We do not know whether the individual poems were actually performed on the spot.[25] Certainly the published text cultivates the *fiction* of improvisation and

---

[19] *CIL* VI. 33976; see Rawson 2003: 17–20.
[20] On the dating see Coleman on *Silu.* 4 pp. xvi–xx; Gibson on *Silu.* 5 pp. xxviii–xxx.
[21] Lucan wrote ten books of *Siluae*, completely lost; see 2.7.54–72n.
[22] Hutchinson 1993: 36.   [23] Well known throughout Italy (*Theb.* 12.814–15).
[24] See Fowler 1995: 211 on modesty as a 'generic pretence'.
[25] St. claims that his poems were dashed off hastily in the heat of the moment (1 *pr.* 2–4 *hos libellos, qui mihi subito calore et quadam festinandi uoluptate fluxerunt*). A few however required

performance. In the prose prefaces St. talks of extemporisation both as a fault, meaning that the *Siluae* were unpolished,[26] and as a virtue, meaning that they show the poet's virtuosity in swift composition.[27] The prefaces' play with modesty thus gives only a limited idea of the poems themselves.[28] The *Siluae* moreover were presumably revised before being published in a poetry book; publication *after* the original occasion allowed the poems to assume new meaning and a new coherent form.[29] Beginning his preface to book 1 St. claims that he hesitated a long time (*diu multumque dubitaui*) before he collected the poems for publication, thus establishing from the start a tension between the (seemingly) spontaneous original occasion and the laboured process of (re)collection and publication.[30]

Indeed, 'haste of composition' is a literary strategy that puts the *Siluae* in witty dialogue with the newly completed *Thebaid* (1 *pr.* 6–7); each of the *Siluae* claims to have been produced in two days or less, whereas the *Thebaid* was the product of twelve years of careful labour.[31] Yet since St. was already a published epic poet, the *Siluae* are works of poetic maturity, though St. teasingly calls them 'foreplay' (1 *pr.* 9 *praeluserit*), like the *Batrachomyomachia* ascribed to Homer or the *Culex* ascribed to Virgil.[32] Under a show of modesty St. places himself in the rank of Homer and Virgil. Indeed, given the publication of the *Thebaid*, *praeluserit* hints at further great works, specifically another epic, to come, so that St. will in fact surpass the achievement of Virgil and rival Homer.

The *Siluae* however have lagged behind the *Thebaid* in critical reputation. As praise poetry written for friends and the emperor, they have been regarded as the decadent product of a decadent regime,[33] either nauseous flattery, or at best subversion, of a tyrannical emperor.[34] Art historians and archaeologists have recently helped give a more balanced view of Domitian's reign; for example, after Augustus Domitian engaged in the most extensive rebuilding of the city.[35] And he by no means dominates the *Siluae*. Out of the first publication of seventeen poems only two directly address the emperor (1.1, 1.6). None of the books of the *Siluae* is dedicated to Domitian, although St. acknowledges the emperor's authority by starting books 1 and 4 with poems in his honour.[36] In book 2 only 2.5 acknowledges

more thought, e.g. St. consulted with Polla about the poem for Lucan's anniversary (2 *pr.* 22–6); he took a long time in writing the poem on Earinus (3 *pr.* 15–20); 3.5 is a letter to his wife and thus not originally 'performed'.

[26] Cf. 2 *pr.* 7–9 *huius amissi recens uulnus . . . epicedio prosecutus sum adeo festinanter ut excusandam habuerim affectibus tuis celeritatem*. He fears too the scrutiny of 'a too harsh file' (10 *asperiore lima*).

[27] Cf. 1 *pr.* 13 *gratiam celeritatis.*   [28] Hutchinson 1993: 36.

[29] Henderson 1998: 113: the '*Siluae* challenge us to respond to their rewriting'.

[30] Henderson 1998: 102–4.   [31] 1 *pr.* 13–14; *Theb.* 12.811–12.

[32] *praeludo* occurs in classical Latin poetry only here and at the start of the *Achilleid.*

[33] Full of 'kitsch' (Conte 1994: 483).

[34] E.g. Plin. *Pan.* 48; cf. Dio 67.9; 11–13. Discussion in Newlands 2002: 18–27.

[35] E.g. D'Ambra 1993; Darwall-Smith 1996. Syme 1930 prepared the way for the revisionist historical views of Jones 1992; Flower 2006: 266–71.

[36] Cf. 1 *pr.* 16–17 *sumendum enim erat 'a Ioue principium'*; 4 *pr.* 2–4 with Coleman.

Domitian at its close. As Rimell points out of Martial, there are no easy answers to the question of the Flavian poets' political beliefs; the personal style of St.'s and Martial's poetry puts interpretation ultimately with the readers, 'the ultimate device for sliding loose of incrimination'.[37] Yet certainly the early 90s, the time of publication of the *Siluae* and *Thebaid*, were deeply troubled by high-profile executions and expulsions; after the mutiny of Saturninus in 89 Domitian's reign seems to have entered a period of increased paranoia, if not terror.[38] The *Siluae* were undoubtedly shaped by the political turmoil of Domitian's last years to the extent that especially in book 2 they emphasise friendship and withdrawal from public life and boldly transfer political paradigms to the private sphere. As praise poetry they are devoted to finding new terms of excellence for the Flavian culture of leisure and friendship.

One of the most controversial features of the *Siluae* is the frequent use of myth. Myth is a sign not of the essential artifice of these poems but of their close reflection of contemporary culture where art as well as literature provided Romans on a daily basis with an expanded emotional and intellectual lexicon.[39] In the *Siluae* St. uses myth to illustrate arguments, to console, move, and delight, often in an encomiastic or playful context. He frequently enters into competition with the mythological world, claiming for instance that Pollius Felix is superior to the legendary poets of antiquity (2.2.60–2). Such hyperbole is often not to modern taste.[40] But it is underwritten by the need to find an appropriate vocabulary for new poetic themes, here the villa and its architect whose outstanding qualities call for the poet to respond with inventive hyperbole; it is also underwritten by wit, for this is poetry written in the first instance for cultured friends who would enjoy the conceit that Pollius as engineer/architect could effortlessly 'charm' nature. The ludic quality of the *Siluae* should not be underestimated; their very playfulness was the feature singled out for attack by their first critics.[41] They thus pivot on a dual aesthetic of exuberant splendour and informal occasionality, seriousness and humour.

Hinds has observed that one of the most famous and enduring tales of Roman literary history is that of Silver Age decline and decadence, and he points to St.'s statement of deference to Virgil at the end of the *Thebaid* as the verses that have perhaps been the most influential in keeping post-Augustan epic out of the modern literary canon.[42] Yet the *Siluae* show that this view of the *Thebaid* is contingent and partial; in 4.7.25–8 St. expresses his pride in having successfully

---

[37] Rimell 2008: 13–14.   [38] Jones 1992: 119–25, 147–9, 160–92.

[39] Zanker 2004: 36–42. Szelest 1972 comments that a unique feature of the *Siluae* was the intermingling of humans and deities in a contemporary setting; but the Romans would encounter 'gods' on a daily basis through public and private works of art.

[40] Van Dam on 2.1.88–102; Damon 2002.

[41] Cf. 1 *pr.* 9 *stilo remissiore praeluserit.* But critics have objected to their playfulness from their very first publication (4 *pr.* 29–30 *exerceri autem ioco non licet.' 'secreto' inquit*).

[42] Hinds 1998: 91–8.

challenged the *Aeneid* with his 'bold lyre'. The *Siluae* thus are important for understanding St.'s epics as the epics in turn are important for understanding the *Siluae*. Most of our literary sources for Domitian's reign postdate it. All the more reason then to study the *Siluae* for, along with Martial's *Epigrams*, they offer vivid, contemporary testimony to the social, intellectual and political culture of Domitian's Rome and the poet's role within it.

3. TITLE/TITLES

i. Siluae

The title is the poet's own, first occurring at 3 *pr.* 7 *tertius hic Siluarum nostrarum liber ad te mittitur*.[43] Metaphorical titles for literary collections were a Hellenistic convention, attacked by Pliny the Elder who preferred the plain *Historia Naturalis* to 'Honeycomb' or 'Meadow' (*Nat.* 1.24–8). *Siluae* acknowledges a debt to Hellenistic aesthetics, and surely also to Lucan's now lost ten books of *Siluae*.

But why *Siluae*?[44] *silua* has the literal meaning of 'wood' and the metaphorical meaning of 'raw material'. Quintilian uses the term in its sense of 'raw material' to describe a hastily produced literary work or rough draft (*Inst.* 10.3.17).[45] However, he is writing of oratory, not of poetry; he uses *silua* in the singular, not the plural, and St. only uses *Siluae* in the plural. Problematic also is Aulus Gellius' use of *Siluae* in the preface to the *Noctes Atticae* (*pr.* 5–6) to connote 'variety within unity', for he has in mind a long prose miscellany, not poetry books.[46]

Recently Wray has argued that the title *Siluae* is a sophisticated calque on Greek ὕλη, which means 'wood' in the literal senses of 'forest' and the 'material' from which objects are crafted, and 'poetic material' in a metaphorical sense.[47] The Greek term used figuratively was subject to slippage between singular and plural; hence we can understand *Siluae* as a polysemous term, a collective plural meaning 'Wood/Woods' and 'poetic material' (to be crafted into interesting forms).[48] The title reflects St.'s fondness for etymological play in the *Siluae*, including with Greek words; typically its artfulness exists in tension with notions of a hastily produced work or of random variety that the term *silua/ae* also connotes. The idea of 'trees' also then remains in play; their long figurative association with poetry is expressed, for instance, at Cic. *Leg.* 1.1: both live a long time and are sown, one by the farmer's art, the other by the imagination. The title also surely refers to Virgil's programmatic use of the word *siluae* in the

---

[43] Cf. also 4 *pr.* 24.
[44] See Bright 1980: 20–42 for detailed discussion of the various possible meanings; also Coleman on *Silu.* 4 pp. xxii–xxiv.
[45] Cf. also Cic. *Orat.* 12.
[46] Bright 1980: 34. Gellius here debates with Pliny the Elder over titles; see Krevans 2005: 87–8.
[47] Wray 2007.
[48] Coleman on *Silu.* 4 p. xxiii notes that Suetonius uses ὕλη to describe the encyclopedic (800 book) *commentarii* of L. Ateius Praetextatus and this may be its title.

Eclogues.[49] The connection with the *Eclogues* gives an attractive symmetry to St.'s poetic corpus; in his *Thebaid* he acknowledges the importance of the *Aeneid* (*Theb.* 12.816–17), and in the *Siluae* he makes literary homage to the *Eclogues* which, like St.'s poems, strikingly intermingle naturalism and artifice, fantasy and politics.

To sum up, the title marks out the *Siluae* as a planned poetry book that, in common with Hellenistic poetry books (such as Meleager's *Garland*), draws upon the natural world for its title. The title cannot be reduced to one single meaning. While it plays upon the notions of extemporaneous composition and variety articulated by Quintilian and Gellius respectively, Greek etymological play and the connection with Virgil's *Eclogues* suggest a high degree of literary sophistication.

ii. tituli

M transmits to us titles for each of the poems but we do not know if these are the poet's own. They seem to be early, possibly the work of late antique grammarians, for Sidonius knew them (*Epist.* (*Carm.* 22) 6). The strongest argument for authenticity lies in their transmission of names not mentioned in the body of the work: Atedius (2.1 and 2.3), Felix (3.1) and Nouius (4.6). But critics have felt these names could have been deduced from the *Siluae* and that titles are unnecessary, given the naming of the addressees; moreover, apart from Martial's *Xenia* and *Apophereta* there is no precedent for titles, which would be a Statian innovation. On the other hand titles would be in keeping with the experimental character of the *Siluae*. Then again they can be misleading; for instance the title to 2.6 calls Philetos a *puer delicatus*, though the poem emphasises his manliness. Arguments either way are inconclusive.[50] St. was the son of a grammarian and, as his prefaces show, he was deeply concerned with preserving the original structure and contents of his poetry books.[51] Equally however the titles could be the work of an editor responding not long after St.'s time to the poet's evident fears that in transmission the order of the poems would be confused and their addressees and occasions, many familiar only to a contemporary readership, would be misunderstood.[52]

4. THEMES OF BOOK 2

i. *Overview*

Paradox is a favourite stylistic trope of the *Siluae*. Not surprisingly therefore book 2 is constructed around two paradoxical themes: the destructiveness of death,

---

[49] A suggestion made by Hardie 1983: 76. Cf. Virg. *Ecl.* 1.1–5; 4.3.

[50] The best discussions to date are Coleman on *Silu.* 4 pp. xxviii–xxxii; Schröder 1999: 180–9.

[51] Newlands 2009a.

[52] As indeed happened even with the *tituli*; M gives 'via Domitiana' as the title of 3.5.

an ineluctable natural force, and the power of art to tame nature and confer immortality.

Consolatory poems make up the bulk of book 2 (1, 4, 5, 6, 7); it may therefore seem somewhat monochromatic by comparison with the highly varied first book, which has no consolatory poems. Hardie referred to book 2 as 'lightweight, eschewing the political and public themes which appear in Book 1'.[53] True, the dedicatee is the elderly Melior, not the up and coming Stella of book 1 who was among those in charge of Domitian's Secular games.[54] And whereas book 1 begins and ends with poems to Domitian (1.1 and 1.6), only 2.5 refers to the emperor, and then only in its conclusion (27–30). Yet premature death is hardly 'lightweight'. Melior dominates the collection with three poems (1, 3, 4), and the book, St. claims, is oriented towards his interests (2 pr. 4), hence its literary and domestic preoccupations.[55] In its elevation of private life it forms a significant counterpoint to book 1. It boasts two new kinds of poem, the villa poem (2.2) and the posthumous birthday poem (2.7), while the creative, witty imitation of Ovid in 2.3 and 2.4 and of Martial in 2.5, along with the close engagement with Lucan in 2.7, reveals the book's concern with literary history and poetics. The tension between art and nature provides a dynamic theme throughout, appearing overtly in 2.2 but also in various forms from the start; for example 2.1 promotes the advantages of nurture over nature, a conclusion then scrutinised in the mock-heroic 2.5. From its long first poem on the original theme of a foster child's death to the final poem on the death of the epic poet Lucan book 2 advertises the experimental quality of the *Siluae* as a new literary work.

The fact that none of the addressees of book 2 was particularly prominent or powerful in Flavian society makes this book also socially interesting.[56] It reflects new attitudes towards traditional aristocratic values concerning kinship and wealth. Book 2 reveals a thematic shift away from the idea that virtue is based on inherited family prestige, perhaps not a surprising idea under the Flavian dynasty which expanded the senatorial and equestrian orders to bring in capable administrators and create a new elite based on talent rather than ancient family glory.[57] The fame of Pollius Felix, a Neapolitan businessman and retired philosopher, rests squarely on virtue, not ancestry (2.2.146n.).

Also to be queried is the assumption that book 2 is not concerned with political themes. Some critics have argued that the retirement from public life of the main addressees of book 2, Melior and Pollius Felix, was politically motivated.[58] But retirement to one's estate was perfectly usual for an elderly, wealthy Roman. All the same, as was argued above, the book's emphasis on the virtues of withdrawal may well be a comment on current political conditions. Throughout the book

---

[53] Hardie 1983: 67.   [54] Hardie 1983: 68.
[55] Bright 1980: 58. In book 3 only 3.1 is addressed to its dedicatee, Pollius Felix, and the book strikes a balance between private and public figures and themes.
[56] On the addressees of book 2 see section 6.iii.
[57] Mellor 2003; Bernstein 2008: 18–29.   [58] See on Melior in 6. iii below.

St. takes the language of public discourse and applies it to private virtues, thus elevating the life of cultured withdrawal as an alternative to political life. A concern with the relationship between emperor and poet is also evident in the book, expressed obliquely in 2.4 and 2.5 and more overtly in 2.7. This middle book in the first collection of *Siluae* is largely domestic in theme, but it challenges the powerful hierarchies of politics and literary genres.

ii. *Lament and consolation*

Background

As in the *Thebaid*, premature death figures prominently in the *Siluae*, but their focus is consolation rather than lament. In the ancient world the death of a child or youth was regarded as particularly tragic since it meant not only the loss of future promise but a reversal of the natural order whereby the young looked after the old.[59] St. bridges the emotional gap between consoler and consoled by sharing in the mourner's grief; with only words left to rely on he creates a literary memorial for the deceased, using abundant mythological comparisons, wordplay and puns, elaborate descriptions of the funerals, and an overall epicising style.[60]

The Roman tradition of literary consolation basically developed from two main sources, the Roman funeral oration, the *laudatio funebris*, which marked the climax of the Roman funeral,[61] and Greek verse epigram, though the poetic tradition traced its origins to the episode in the *Iliad* when Priam and Achilles weep together for Hector (Hom. *Il.* 24.507–51). Social factors also influenced the development of consolatory literature in Rome in the early imperial period. The virtual demise of the Republican funeral pageant with its public parade through the city and its display of ancestor masks (Plb. 6.53–5) led to a new interest in graveside posthumous rituals and in new forms of artistic, commemorative expression.[62] Tombs increasingly became objects of artistic display; carved mythological scenes first appeared at the end of the first century CE as an important type of funerary art.[63] In literature praise of the dead was transferred to the more private prose epistle and elegy with a new emphasis on consolation. Cicero's poetic self-consolation on the death of his daughter Tullia is lost, but much of the thought remains in his *Tusculan Disputations* 1 and 3 and in the letter of Sulpicius Severus to Cicero (*Fam.* 4.5).[64] St.'s epicising, mythological poems of consolation can be seen as textual counterparts to the elaborately decorated

---

[59] Griessmair 1966; Lattimore 1962: 184–98; Fedeli on Prop. 3.7.2.
[60] Hardie 1983: 86.
[61] Only fragments of such speeches remain (Flower 1996: 128–58). Scourfield 1993: 15–26 reviews the tradition of consolatory literature, both poetry and prose. Also Durry xxiii–xxxiv; N–H I 280–1; Gibson on *Silu.* 5 pp. xxxi–xxxiv.
[62] See Bodel 1999: 270–1; Zanker 2004: 33–6, 65.
[63] See Koortbooijan 1995; Zanker 2004.
[64] See Scourfield 1993: 18–20; Wilcox 2005: 246–8.

tombs appearing at this time; in both art and text myth displayed or elevated the social rank of the deceased and the bereaved, while providing a common emotional language for coming to terms with death.[65]

That the literary tradition of consolation is 'rich in banality' is a fairly common view;[66] the *Siluae* have often been regarded as rhetorical exercises along the prescriptive lines of the treatise of Menander Rhetor (*c.* 300 CE), the earliest extant work on epideictic theory.[67] But while the experience of death is universal, its expression can vary widely according to the particular circumstances and the importance and character of those involved. Indeed, literary consolations pose particular challenges for poets in their attempt to defy death by memorialising a person's life. Davis argues that the consolatory poem, which typically moves from lament to consolation proper, can be a particularly dynamic form: 'The mood of lament is rebellion . . . the mood of consolation is reconciliation after curse.'[68] Indeed, recent scholarship on poetry of lament and consolation has argued for a more flexible approach to the genre that emphasises its potential for eclecticism.[69]

St.'s contribution to the genre

Book 2 reveals St. as an important innovator in literary consolation; the *Siluae* provide us with more poems of this type than does any other body of Roman literature (2.1, 2.4, 2.5, 2.6, 2.7, 3.3, 5.1, 5.3, 5.5). They experiment with the various generic affiliations of lament and consolation, including pastoral, elegy, and especially epic, and they range widely over different occasions; for instance the book begins with a poem on the death of a child set at the pyre and ends with a poem on the poet Lucan written for his birthday anniversary; with mock-heroic *élan*, 2.4 and 2.5 lament a parrot and a lion; 2.6 applies an epic theme, the tragic death of an ephebic warrior, to a beloved slave.

2.1 announces the novelty of the poet's approach to consolation with its lengthy commemoration of a child and son of freed slaves, Melior's beloved foster son, to be sure, but without lineage. The earlier Roman poetic models for consolation (barring Ovid's poem on the death of Corinna's parrot, *Am.* 2.4) concerned elite figures.[70] True, Martial laments the untimely deaths of slave children but in

---

[65] Zanker 2004: 32–6, 63–5.   [66] Russell and Wilson 332.

[67] On Menander's date see Russell and Wilson xxxiv–xl. They also caution against the 'hypostasizing of generic patterns' (xxxiii) in poetry from rhetorical theory many centuries later. See also Zablocki 1966: 309–10; Hardie 1983: 103–9; Gibson on *Silu.* 5 pp. xxxi–l.

[68] Davis 1967: 119.

[69] Thévenaz 2002 argues that Mart. 5.34, 5.37, 10.61 (on Erotion) use the original occasion to display a creative engagement with literary genre; see also Fedeli on Prop. 3.7 pp. 229–32.

[70] McKeown III 109 groups 2.1 with Hor. *Carm.* 1.24 (Horace's and Virgil's friend Quintilius), Virg. *A.* 6. 868–86 (the emperor's nephew Marcellus), Prop. 4.11 (the aristocratic Cornelia), Ov. *Am.* 3.9 (Tibullus), *Epicedion Drusi* (Livia's son).

epigram, not in long poems such as 2.1.[71] Horace displays the social and literary hierarchy of mourning by chiding his friend Valgius in *Carm.* 2.9 for his excessive grief for a slave boy; yet he opens *Carm.* 1.24 on the death of the aristocratic Quintilius by acknowledging that there can be no limit to grief (1–2). In writing a poem that endorses profound grief for a low-born child, St. boldly adapts to a Roman social context Hellenistic poetry's interest in humble characters and children,[72] thus making good his commitment to the ideals of 'minor poetry'.[73] A poem on Domitian's equestrian statue opens book 1; a poem on a child and his foster father opens book 2, thus programmatically announcing its preoccupation with new approaches to personal themes.

By writing in hexameters instead of the more usual elegiacs and by doing so at such length in 2.1, St. dissolves the traditional polarities between elegy and epic. The hexameter heroises both the dead child and the bereaved. As Rosati argues, in writing in hexameter St. gives elegy a new dignity.[74] 2.4 and 2.5, the poems on the deaths of tamed animals, can be read as playful variations on consolatory themes and epic tropes. 2.4, a witty expansion of Catullus' and Ovid's 'bird poems', offers some light relief to Melior; 2.5 is a mock-heroic play on *exitus* literature and on Martial's 'arena' epigrams.[75] While both these poems are underwritten by serious themes, they show the poet's delight in experimentation with genre and various literary models.

Another significant feature of St.'s consolatory poems is his challenge to the traditional notions that grief was unmanly. His poems provide a useful counterweight to the philosophical teachings of Seneca, for instance, which counsel restraint in grief for both the bereaved and the consoler.[76] The choice of hendecasyllables for 2.7, the book's final poem, is surprising, yet can be seen in part as a response to 2.1, which drew on epic to elevate a dead child and his foster father's grief; writing of an actual epic poet, known moreover for his passionate style, St. rather wittily modulates his commemoration in a lower key;[77] here too he creates a new consolatory type, the posthumous birthday poem.

---

[71] Mart. 1.88, 101, 5.34, 37, 6.28, 29, 10.61, 11.91. Plin. *Ep.* 5.16 on the death of a Minicia Marcella, a girl close in age to Glaucias, emphasizes her elite status.

[72] E.g. Molorchus (Call. *Aet.* 3 frs. 54–9 Pf.; *Silu.* 3.1.29 *pauperis . . . Molorchi;* 4.6.51). Callimachus at the start of the *Aetia* is like a 'child' unrolling the poem (fr. 1.5–6 Pf.).

[73] 2.1 is also influenced by the Hellenistic aesthetic interest in idealised children that is expressed in the visual arts through the Roman fondness for the depiction of young children and cherubs in domestic decoration. See Slater 1974: 135.

[74] Rosati 1999: 163: 'il conclut l'aventure de l'élégie, la reconduit vers l'ordre, en lui imposant une nouvelle contenance et une nouvelle dignité'.

[75] Herrlinger 1930: 70–1, 87–90 sees 2.5 as a serious poem, in contrast to 2.4. On links between these two poems and animal fable see Newlands 2005. On *exitus* literature see introd. to 2.5.

[76] Cf. Sen. *Ep.* 63, 99; *Dial.* 6, 11, 12; Kassel 1958: 51–2; Manning 1978: 258–9; Wilson 1997; Markus 2004. Seneca however should not be taken as entirely representative of Roman practice; see MacMullen 1980.

[77] Cf. 2 *pr.* 25–6n.

iii. *Art and nature: the villa and garden*

2.2 on Pollius' villa, and 2.3 on Melior's garden, are likewise new types of poem, the latter a blend of the villa and birthday poem, a new hybrid literary form.[78] In 2.2 and 2.3 the domestication of nature assumes social and political relevance as the villa and the garden offer significant alternatives to Rome, the site of uncertain ambition. The theme is given more quixotic treatment in 2.4 and 2.5, where animals provide a more oblique way of exploring issues involving patronage and artistic freedom.[79] 2.4 moreover wittily parodies not only consolatory themes but the grand architectural description of 2.2.[80]

There are no true Greek precedents for the Roman luxury villa; it is a striking Roman innovation, a major cultural institution of the imperial age for which St. was the first significant poet.[81] In the first century CE, an era of limited opportunities for self-promotion given the emperor's broad control of visual media, at least within Rome, the country villa developed as an important site of personal and family display and commemoration.[82] Moreover, devotion to literature and the contemplative life became desirable even for men of political standing as a way of creating distance from potential or actual civic difficulties.[83] Leisure thus became in the empire 'a powerful mode of aristocratic self-definition' and the villa its chief visual expression.[84] In *Silu.* 1.3, 2.2 and 3.1 the villa is not only a marvel of architecture and technology,[85] it also represents the virtues of the owners – typically their learning, fine artistic taste, great wealth and pursuit of philosophical moderation, the latter not a contradiction since St. redefines *wealth* as a good when used wisely.[86] The poet's propertied patrons of book 2, Atedius Melior and Pollius Felix, were moreover elderly and retired from public affairs and thus at the stage of life for cultivating their estates; as Pliny remarks to Pomponius Bassus (*Ep.* 4.23.3–4), *otium* represents the final reward of a well led career: *nam et prima uitae tempora et media patriae, extrema nobis impertire debemus, ut ipsae leges monent, quae maiorem annis otio reddunt . . . istud pulcherrimae quietis exemplum.*

Although Pollius' villa is located on the Bay of Naples, 2.2 makes no reference to the area's recent devastation by the eruption of Vesuvius in 79 CE. But unlike in the first villa poem, 1.3, where nature and art are essentially in harmony, 2.2

---

[78] See 1.3 and 3.1.   [79] See esp. introd. to 2.5.   [80] See 2.4.11–15n.
[81] Wallace-Hadrill 1998: 46; on the moralists' attack on the villa as the *locus* of luxury see introd. to 2.2.
[82] Bodel 1997; Myers 2005 discusses the new positive attitude to the villa and leisure displayed in Pliny and St.; St. praises the villa owner Vopiscus for *docta otia* (1.3.108), Pollius for his 'learned poetry' (*doctamque . . . chelyn*, 2.2.119–20); cf. Plin. *Ep.* 1.22.11 *studiosum otium.*
[83] For Stoics such as Seneca *otium* is the goal of the *sapiens*, a concept to be distinguished from *ignauia* in that cultivation of the contemplative life provided a secure refuge from the tempest of politics and the corruption of the state. Cf. Sen. *Ep.* 55.4 *multum autem interest, utrum uita tua otiosa sit an ignaua*; Sen. *Dial.* 8.3.4; Griffin 1976: 328–34; Woodman on Vell. (1983) pp. 239–45; Myers 2000: 123–5; Newlands 2002: 154–63.
[84] See Connors 2000: 493–5; Myers 2005: 105.
[85] Pavlovskis 1973.   [86] Newlands 2002: 127–38; 154–63.

depicts the building of Pollius' villa as an epic struggle against a chiefly harsh and resistant nature.[87] At the same time, although much of the language is georgic, the Virgilian farmer's constant struggle against nature is replaced by swift, decisive mastery, in part a reflection of the poet's fluent, rapid style in the *Siluae*. Nature, tamed, becomes in harmony with human needs. 2.2 provides not a blueprint for architectural design but rather an invitation to enter an idealised world predicated on social unity and ethical balance; the villa is troped to reflect a distinctive Epicurean praxis.

2.2 is also a self-conscious reflection on this new type of poem; only the finest writer can do justice to Pollius' villa (36–44). The description of a great building, so Lucian argues, requires the application of intellect to vision (*Dom.* 6). St. pulls out all the stops for his learned, philhellenic patron and audience. The density of mythological allusions and Graecisms in 2.2, compared to the other poems in this book, represents an attempt to reflect in style both the marvellous villa, filled with Greek works of art, and the owner, culturally sophisticated and dedicated to Epicurean philosophy. The poet is thus very visible throughout. With frequent second-person address he invites his imagined readership to join him on a tour of the villa in the mind's eye, sharing in his wonder; he describes the villa in stages as he gradually ascends from the low-lying shore to the cliff top villa (an ascent to the Epicurean heights), then to inside the villa, and thence to the highest, most beautiful room (1–94). Unlike Pliny, who locates luxury outdoors in his gardens,[88] St. emphasises the wealth and beauty within. This upward and inward movement is aesthetic as well as social and philosophical; with the gorgeous 'catalogue' of marbles, rich in geographical and mythological associations (85–94), St. reaches descriptive heights, matching style to theme.

Unlike the description of a work of art, describing a building means movement through space. 2.2 does not offer a 'road map' through the villa but rather shifting perspectives from adjacent locations. The poem adapts to the contemporary villa the common Roman rhetorical metaphor of the house whose rooms are depositories of memory through which the orator moved in the various stages of his oration.[89] Thus for all the 'Greekness' of the villa, this ecphrasis is also a very Roman literary construct. As he moves through Pollius' villa, St. fixes the various points of interest in the reader's memory, thus honouring and memorialising his hosts, directing his readers towards an aesthetic and moral interpretation, and displaying his poetic originality in a dazzling new literary form.

The 'garden' poem is in important ways a corollary to the villa poem, with the Caelian hill in 2.3 replacing the Bay of Naples; in Rome too by the first century CE the aristocratic mansion and park had essentially replaced the public places and buildings of the Republican city for social interaction among family, friends, and patrons and clients.[90] Even here in the heart of Rome Melior's estate, like

---

[87] Cf. 1.3.16–17 *non largius usquam | indulsit natura sibi.*   [88] E.g. Plin. *Ep.* 5.6.36–40.
[89] Cf. Quint. *Inst.* 11.2.11–22; Yates 1966: 1–26.   [90] Eck 1997: 78–9.

Pollius' villa, is an idealised, alternative world remote from Roman politics. Yet 2.3 makes also a strong contrast with 2.2 through the absence of luxury; those who stayed in Rome did not have the latitude for architectural self-display enjoyed by those outside the capital.[91] Thus St. does not describe Melior's house. Moreover, unlike Pliny's gardens with their elaborate displays of topiary, statuary and fountains – typically Roman gardens were artistic repositories of mythological allusion – Melior's garden is a plain ensemble of tree and lake, given lustre only by the poet's new 'Roman' myth which celebrates not civic virtues, traditionally tied to public duty and performance, but order and self-governance apart from a communal setting.[92] 2.3 creates through words a garden with mythological and moral origins and celebrates an ethical, safe enclave for the cultivation of poetry, friendship and virtue within the capital city.

In its fusion of Ovidian myth, epideictic and birthday celebration 2.3 is perhaps St.'s most important demonstration of epigram's 'generic mobility' taken to a higher level.[93] Generally 2.3 has been seen as a key example of 'mannerist' aesthetics, with reflection being the central trope.[94] It has also been interpreted as a political allegory.[95] Melior's politics must remain speculation; the urban garden however always had a political edge from its proximity to imperial property.[96] The safety of Melior's garden in the heart of Rome can be understood as a particular virtue late in Domitian's reign. In echoing at the start of 2.3 the poem on Domitian's equestrian statue in Rome (1.1–2), St. draws a strong contrast between public and private space.[97]

In this regard, the choice of a plane tree in 2.3 is particularly significant. A popular garden tree, it was also closely associated with philosophy since Plato set the *Phaedrus* beneath a plane tree by a babbling brook (229a–b, 230b).[98] By the late Roman Republic serious political and philosophical discussion had been transferred to the villa, but trees continued to play an important role; for example, the debate in Cicero's *De oratore* over the role of oratory in a changed world lacking Republican freedoms takes place under a plane tree on Crassus'

[91] Bodel 1997: 18.
[92] Connolly 2007: 267 defines Republican citizenship as 'the practice of spectacular virtue in the course of an active life in the setting of a political community'.
[93] Cf. 157–8; 2 pr. 14–18; Thomas 1998: 205.
[94] See Cancik 1965: 48–56 on the poem's symmetrical structure; Pederzani: 151–4 on the allegorical mirroring of the aetiological myth in the final encomium of Melior; Hardie 2005 on the poem's key tropes of reflection and rebirth.
[95] Vessey 1981.
[96] Beard 1998 argues that gardens are contested space in that they function as both part of, and apart from, the activity of the city, politics, public life, the Palatine.
[97] Martial returns the 'plane tree' to the public realm with his epigram on a plane planted by Julius Caesar. Compare esp. 2.3.1 and Mart. 9.61.5–6; 1.3.59 and Mart. 9.61.5; 1.3.61 and Mart. 9.61.20.
[98] The plane tree's connection with philosophy and intellectual debate was perhaps helped by the punning association between Plato's name and πλάτανος/*platanus*, verbal play that was exploited at the very least by Seneca, *Ep.* 55.6. See Henderson 2004: 81.

Tusculan estate, and many of Cicero's dialogues are set in the shade of trees on villa estates.[99] Melior's plane tree is rooted then in a tradition of philosophical debate; but isolated and picturesque, it is now associated with the contemplative life, not with Ciceronian ideas of the importance of virtue aimed at the public good.[100] The plane represents a cultural shift whereby virtue, detached from civic ambition, could be most safely cultivated within private space.

The plane tree was also a poet's tree, long associated in antiquity with the Muses and their shrines;[101] the statue honouring the Hellenistic poet Philitas, for instance, depicted him under a plane.[102] In 2.3 the plane tree is the source of the poet's inspiration; it provides him with the 'material' for his mythic narrative.[103] Drawing an explicit analogy between his poem and the tree, St. hopes that both will endure to a great age, *ingenti forsan uictura sub aeuo* (63). As the plane tree reaches for the heights (40 *iturus in aethera uertex*), so too the poem aims for immortality.

Modest and playful though 2.3 may be on the surface, the plane tree, double in shape and elusive in reflection, is a symbol of the 'Silvan' aesthetic, exemplifying this poetry's love of paradox and literary allusion, and the frequent interplay of epic, elegy and epigram. Through its long literary history the tree is also closely associated with some of the key cultural values of the *Siluae*, in particular their endorsement of the cultured life as a blueprint for virtue, as an alternative to the perils of a public career, and, for some, as the pathway to the Muses.

This is a very Ovidian poem in many ways, not least in its creative transgression of Ovidian norms. While St. departs from the erotic paradigms offered by the *Metamorphoses* and the *Fasti* and offers a 'rape narrative' without violence or physical metamorphosis, Ovid provides him with a metaphorical way for talking about his poetry, not with a grove in an allegorical landscape (as in *Am.* 3.1), but with a single, richly evocative, tree in his patron's Roman garden. 'Trees are like people'[104] but so too are poems which, when planted by the imagination, will outlive the oldest trees; cf. Cic. *Leg.* 1.1 *nullius autem agricolae cultu stirps tam diuturna quam poetae uersu seminari potest.*

5. THE STRUCTURE OF BOOK 2

The weak canonic status of St. has caused him to be generally overlooked in discussions of poetry books. The structure of book 2 however reflects conscious

---

[99] See Linderski 1989. On the influence of the *Phaedrus* on later literary topography see A. Hardie 1997: 28–30.

[100] Zetzel 2003 points out that the setting of *De oratore*, which makes the plane part of a villa estate, exemplifies Cicero's ambivalent use of Greek culture and his argument for the importance of social over philosophical wisdom.

[101] A. Hardie 1997, esp. 27–30. Plato was buried in the Mouseion at Athens, probably near a grove of plane trees; see also Hardie 2003b: 33.

[102] Hermesianax fr. 7.75–8 P; see A Hardie 1997: 24–6, 32–3.

[103] See Wray 2007.   [104] Nisbet 1995a: 202.

authorial design.[105] Key for St. was the preface, a Flavian innovation,[106] for it allowed him not only to summarise the book's contents but, by listing the individual poems, also to fix the order in which they are to be read, thereby presumably attempting to forestall future editorial interventions.[107] The book has a clearly articulated frame, opening and closing in a symmetrical fashion with poems on premature death (2.1, 2.7); three short 'epigrammatic' poems (2.3, 2.4 and 2.5), as St. points out in the preface (14–18), form a coherent central cycle that is essentially humorous in tone and is flanked by pairs of longer, more serious poems (2.1, 2.2, 2.6, 2.7). This arrangement is not purely formal but shows significant thematic patterning.[108] For instance the poems of the central cycle are linked through their play upon the relationship between art and nature[109] and their sustained, overt engagement with particular poetic models, Ovid and Martial. But 2.3, the poem on Melior's garden, is also closely linked with 2.2, the poem on Pollius' villa, and, as a birthday poem, with 2.7, the anniversary poem for Lucan.[110] Such interconnections cross the boundaries of a strictly formal arrangement and invite shifting perspectives on the book's major themes. The preface thus presents book 2 as an artistic unit whose full meaning emerges only from its complex narrative patterning.

Book 2 is the middle book of the first published collection of *Siluae*; it thus looks forward and backwards to the themes of the previous and following books. Pollius Felix and Naples, the topic of 2.2, play a major role in book 3, providing its frame (3.1, 3.5). Book 1 ends with a demonstration of imperial power, a poem on the games for the Saturnalia organised by Domitian, who changed the date of the festival to 1 December.[111] At the end of book 2 St. likewise manipulates time by adding to the calendar a new date, 3 November, Lucan's birthday.[112] The winter season and the themes of death and commemoration bring book 2 appropriately to a close; hendecasyllables are a closural metre in the *Siluae*.[113] Yet despite St.'s

---

[105] So too Martial's poetry books, following Hellenistic precedent; see Barchiesi 2005: 320–30.
[106] See introd. to preface.
[107] On the plasticity of the poetry book in antiquity and its reshaping by subsequent editorial, or readerly, interventions, see Barchiesi 2005: 337–9.
[108] Thus Newmyer 1979: 125–6. He claims three principles of book structure (55): metrical variation, chronological ordering, and alternation of long and short poems. Chronology is of little help with St.; structuring by metre plays a significant role only in book 4; see Coleman on *Silu.* 4 pp. xx–xxii. Newmyer notes (57–8) that alternation of poem length is particularly striking with book 2. 2.3, 2.4, 2.5 = 144 lines; thus comparable to 2.2 (155 lines) and 2.7 (135 lines).
[109] Bright 1980 60–3 claims that 2.3 is also about death, arguing wrongly that Pholoe perished in the waters; see also Cancik 1965: 20.
[110] A connection generally overlooked; e.g. Newmyer 1979: 126 sees 2.7 (along with 2.2) as an anomaly in the book. 2.1 and 2.6, on the deaths of beloved young dependents, are also linked with one another and with 2.7 through the theme of premature death.
[111] Cf. 1.6; 1. *pr.* 31; Newlands 2002: 236–7.
[112] On the date of Lucan's birthday see Vacca (Hosius p. 334.12–14).
[113] Hendecasyllabic poems also end books 1 (1.6) and 4 (4.9).

mainly literary historical focus in 2.7, as a commemorative poem for a 'martyred' Roman poet it forms a provocative conclusion to a book whose themes have, with the exception of the short 2.5, been largely domestic and private.[114] Its concluding praise of a poet who boldly wrote of the perils of autocracy and of the corruption of imperial power, its challenge to the dominance of Virgil in literary history,[115] and its novel development of the birthday poem,[116] all these features give vigour to encomium and mark the originality of St. as poet. Lucan provides the conduit through which St. can articulate his own distinct poetics and bolster his claim to be Lucan's as well as Virgil's successor. The book ends on a high note with a celebration of literary immortality as St. demonstrates, with an eye to his own posterity, how and why poets should be remembered.

6. PATRONS AND PATRONAGE

i. *Patronage in the Flavian age*

At the start of the *Siluae* St. compliments Manilius Vopiscus for being foremost in rescuing from decay the parlous current state of literature (1 *pr.* 24–5 *qui praecipue uindicat a situ litteras iam paene fugientes*). Patronage then, whatever negative connotations it might evoke today of flattery or penury, was crucial for the Flavian poet and provided an anchor amidst the uncertainties of book publication.

The poems of St. and Martial offer valuable insight into the conditions for the production and dissemination of poetry in an imperial context. Each of the four books of *Siluae* published in St.'s lifetime is dedicated to a patron and comes with a 'cover letter' or prose preface, an innovation of St. and Martial that allows them to honour their patrons and advertise their published work to the wider public;[117] all of the individual poems of book 2 likewise have personal addressees with the exception of 2.5, which was presented to Domitian.[118] In receiving the honour of a poem or a poetry book, the patron, generally a man of letters, would be expected to reciprocate by promoting the poet's verse; the very receiving of the gift gave it the patron's *imprimatur*, thus presumably helping also in the work's dissemination. Often too the patron read the poet's work first in a draft; sometimes he provided the physical as well as the artistic conditions for poetic composition. St. thanks Pollius Felix for providing him both with literary stimulus and a place to work (3 *pr.* 3–4): *cum scias multos ex illis in sinu tuo subito natos*; *sinu* is the 'bay' of Naples where Pollius lived and also a metaphor for the patron's protection.

---

[114] In the Empire celebrating the birthday of famous men of the past could be a capital offence. E.g. Salvius Cocceianus, who celebrated the birthday of Otho, was put to death by Domitian (Suet. *Dom.* 10). On the political manipulation of birthdays under Augustus see Courtney on Juv. 5.36–7; Feeney 2007: 155–6.

[115] 2.7.79–80n.   [116] Introd. to 2.7.

[117] See Johannsen 2006; Newlands 2008.   [118] Cf. 2 *pr.* 16–18.

As White argued, 'patron' in a Roman context is an anachronistic term. The relationship between 'patron' and poet was preferably characterised by terms of 'friendship', *amicitia*, which did not convey clear distinctions of status although, as Saller points out, patronage was in fact characterised by asymmetrical social relationships.[119] St. levels the social gap between himself and the wealthier recipients of his poems by addressing them in affectionate terms as his friends, similarly involved in literary studies. St. never mentions money paid for poems or direct commissions, though Nauta believes some poems were written to order under the cover of the patron's 'initiative'.[120] But even in these cases the language of 'request' is not straightforward.[121] 'Exchange' figures prominently in the poet's language of personal relationships; economic metaphors are a common feature of the polite code of *amicitia* and need not be taken literally to refer to substantial material gifts.[122] Book 2 is presented to Melior as a gift; in return St. received the status of being Melior's *amicus* and also his support in promoting the work.

In the Flavian period there was no one single literary circle dispensing patronage, or a dominant authority figure like Maecenas.[123] Each book of the *Siluae* is dedicated to a different patron. This may well be a sign of a difficult literary environment where writers had to struggle to find support; Juvenal's seventh *Satire* offers a portrait of a literary society with few and stingy patrons, and many starving poets. But St. does not complain about lack of attention from his patrons; his main problem seems to have been lack of recognition from Domitian. His disappointment at not winning at the Capitoline games, a recurrent theme in the *Siluae*, suggests that though Domitian encouraged the arts through his new Alban and Capitoline games, these represented the official arm of imperial patronage; imperial rewards were not otherwise forthcoming from this 'cruel and ungrateful Jove' (3.5.32–3),[124] hence the need for varied sources of private patronage.[125] That none of the poems describing imperial events (1.1, 1.6, 2.5, 3.4, 4.1, 4.2, 4.3) is directly addressed to the emperor can be read as setting him apart as a godlike being; but it can also suggest that the emperor and his court were not at the centre of St.'s social world in the *Siluae*; this is particularly true for book 2.

There were certain advantages however to a more diffuse network of patronage. For instance, the Flavian poet was less dependent than was Horace on a

---

[119] White 1978: 81–2; Saller 1982: 1. See also Rühl 2006: 15–31.
[120] Nauta 2002: 244–8, singling out 1.2, 2.7 and 3.4; see also 27–30, 87–90. He argues that a fiction of 'sincerity' often made a text seem unsolicited.
[121] Cf. 2 *pr.* 24n.
[122] Roller 2001: 131–3; Coffee 2006: 421–7. White 1978: 86–8 emphasises that there is no evidence for poets receiving large sums of money for poems. Most Roman poets were at least knights (though probably not St.) and thus possessed at least 400,000 sesterces.
[123] White 1975: 300.
[124] On the importance of victory at the Capitoline games, particularly with recognition by the emperor (who crowned the winners), see Caldelli 1993: 53–120, esp. 104–8; on St.'s failure there see p. 1.
[125] On Domitian's active patronage of the arts see Coleman 1986.

single person's interests and needs. The presence of several patrons in a poetry book moreover must have put subtle pressure on the dedicatee to live up to the honour of being the 'supreme' patron of the work; writing for several patrons made the poet more powerful than an ordinary client, especially important since St. was of relatively humble background, and put him in a strong position for negotiating an exchange in terms of the promotion of his work.[126] The patrons of book 2, Melior, Ursus and Polla in Rome, Pollius Felix on the Bay of Naples, are evidence of a lively literary culture where varied sources of support meant to some extent greater flexibility, and greater opportunities perhaps for promotion of one's work; Pollius Felix was St.'s 'anchor' in the Bay of Naples. Through his prefaces St. introduces the wider public to his ' friends', a special community of readers with shared cultural interests who in turn form an ideal model for the wider readership of posterity. All the same, the patrons of book 2 were not politically powerful people like Maecenas; their *imprimatur* on a poetry book would not have had comparable weight in sustaining *litteras fugientes*.[127]

ii. *Recitation*

The cultural environment in which the *Siluae* were produced was receptive to performance, or the fiction of performance, not only through grand occasions like the Alban and Capitoline games, but through recitation, that is public, or semi-public, readings; these were virtually institutionalised in the Roman world by the Flavian age.[128] Juvenal suggests that St. is so lacking in patronage that he has to prostitute his talent by the public reading of a dramatic script (7.82–7).[129] Yet recitation was crucial to the dissemination of texts and took place in a variety of contexts: the poet might recite to a few friends and patrons who would give him crucial feedback; he might enter a contest; he might give a non-dramatic performance; or he might give a theatrical performance.[130] Recitation allowed a poet to supplement the patron's support by trying out his work in a larger arena, thus catching the public eye. Although Pliny complains that there is scarcely a day in April without a public reading (*Ep.* 9.17), he often participated in readings before friends.[131] Despite its imperial detractors

---

[126] Nauta 2002: 27–8 rejects as too extreme Zetzel's (1982: 101) view that by the end of the first century BCE the patrons had become the clients; rather *amicitia* created a balanced system of exchange between poet and patron.

[127] The dedicatees of books 1 and 4 were fairly prominent though both were young: Stella was one of the *xv uiri sacris faciundis* involved in the running of the Secular games of 88 CE; Vitorius Marcellus was the dedicatee of Quintilian's *Institutio oratoria*. See Hardie 1983: 68, 164–5.

[128] On recitation see Markus 2000.

[129] See Courtney ad loc.; Tandoi 1969.   [130] Small 1997: 35–8.

[131] See e.g. *Ep.* 9.34, where Pliny, concerned about making a good impression and fearing he reads badly, chose a freedman to read for him in front of friends.

then,[132] recitation was an important element in the production and circulation of poetry, a key preliminary stage of a poem's or poetry book's exposure to the outside world. It allowed the poet to claim the authoritative literary presence that was potentially endangered by the proliferation of his writing through unscrupulous copyists and booksellers.[133] St.'s claim to have given a public reading of his work to an elite body of senators (5.3.215–17) suggests moreover that for social outsiders like himself recitation was crucial to gaining recognition.

The grave monument of the eleven-year-old Q. Sulpicius Maximus, inscribed with his competition Greek verses, gives us some idea of the high esteem in which poetic performance was held in this period.[134] Yet despite his success as improviser, the boy is depicted as holding a scroll, proof of the ultimate importance of publication in St.'s world. Thus we should not place undue emphasis on formal recitation as a way of attracting readers, and possibly also patrons, at least not at the expense of publication.[135]

iii. *The patrons of book 2*[136]

Atedius Melior (preface, 2.1, 2.3, 2.4): the poems of St. and Martial are our only source of information about Atedius Melior, the dedicatee of book 2.[137] According to Martial, Melior was a generous, popular host (2.69.7); elegant and rich (4.54.8), he made wise use of his wealth (8.38). St. adds that Melior was elderly (2.1.69) and suggests also that he was unmarried and childless; he praises him as a valued, close friend and discriminating literary critic (2 *pr.* 2–3 *in iudicio litterarum . . . tersissime*). St. and Martial mention that Melior was a friend of a certain Blaesus, who was deceased by the time of St.'s poems; he may have been the Iunius Blaesus who took the anti-Flavian side in the civil wars of 68/9 CE but was murdered by Vitellius;[138] Hardie suggests that Melior's public career may have been damaged because of his friendship with this Blaesus.[139] Vessey argues that Melior was a suspect in the Saturninus conspiracy of 88/9 CE and thus had to withdraw from public life.[140] But Melior may simply, like Pollius Felix, have retired to his estate because of old age; he did not moreover flee Rome but remained on the Caelian hill. White assumes that because St. speaks more effusively of Melior than does Martial, St. occupied a higher position than Martial in Melior's hierarchy

---

[132] E.g. Tac. *Dial.* 9.4 attacks public reading as producing only *clamorem uagum et uoces inanes et gaudium uolucre*. Cf. Suet. *Poet.* 2.26–9, which praises Virgil as a master-performer, reading the *Georgics* to Augustus for four days straight.

[133] Habinek 1998: 107.   [134] See section 1 above, pp. 2–3.

[135] See Hutchinson 1993: 146–8; Fowler 1995: 204–21 responding to White 1974, for whom the 'the poet's published books represent only the last and least important means of presenting poems to patrons' (40). On the poetry book as the 'icon of chic communication' see Barchiesi 2005: 321–4.

[136] Fundamental on St.'s circle of patron friends are White 1975; Nauta 2002.

[137] White 1975: 272–5; Grewing 211; Nauta 2002: 226–7, 239; Rühl 2006: 293–6.

[138] 2.1.191–2n.   [139] Hardie 1983: 66–7.   [140] Vessey 1981: see 2.3.15–16n.

of friends.[141] But it is difficult to make such a distinction given the brevity of epigram. Melior dominates book 2, both as its dedicatee and as the recipient of three of its seven poems, including the longest in the book (2.1).

Pollius Felix (2.2): our evidence for the life of Pollius Felix is again internal. He had been an important local dignitary of two major cities on the Campanian coast, Naples and Puteoli (2.2.133–7; 3.1.91–2). D'Arms argued that he was the son of a freedman, a claim subsequently disputed by Hardie and Nisbet, who think it more likely that he was a member of the local aristocracy.[142] He was extremely wealthy: in addition to the estate at Surrentum described in 2.2 he had three other properties in Italy (2.2.107–11). His wife Polla may have been the former wife of Lucan (called Polla Argentaria), of high birth therefore; such a marriage would have elevated Pollius' family line.[143] But there is no positive proof for this identification; see on Polla below. Pollius Felix is the dedicatee of book 3 and the addressee of its first poem.

Flauius Ursus (2.6): again we know nothing of Ursus beyond what St. tells us in the preface and in this poem, namely that he was young, rich and hardworking; he owned substantial property and may have been a lawyer (2.6.61–8, 95). An Ursus held the suffect consulship under Domitian but we lack the evidence to identify him or associate him through family connections with St.'s friend.[144] The poem on the death of his beloved slave is much shorter than 2.1 on the death of Melior's foster son, suggesting perhaps that St. was not on such intimate terms with Ursus.[145]

Polla Argentaria (2.7): Lucan's widow was an active patron of the arts; Martial wrote three epigrams on the occasion of her husband's birthday (7.21, 22, 23) and compliments her as a reader of his poetry (10.64).[146] Otherwise nothing is certain. She was possibly the granddaughter of the Greek rhetorician M. Argentarius, famed for his declamations in Latin (Sen. *Con.* 9.3.12). Critics have long speculated that she may be the same person as the Polla who is the wife of Pollius Felix.[147] The banking terminology of 2.2.151–4, describing Polla's prudent management of the household accounts, may pun upon the association between *Argentaria* and *argentarius* 'banker.'[148] Intriguingly too Sidonius in *Carm.* 23.165–6 refers to Lucan's widow as having been twice-married to poets – *quid quos duplicibus iugata taedis | Argentaria Polla dat poetas?* – lines which could apply to

---

[141] White 1975: 273.   [142] D'Arms 1974: 111; Hardie 1983: 67–8; Nisbet 1995b: 33–4.
[143] Zeiner 2005: 174–5.   [144] Hardie 1983: 218 n. 92; *RE* VI 2730.
[145] Rühl 2006: 289.   [146] White 1975: 280–6.   [147] Nisbet 1995b: 31–46.
[148] Nauta 2002: 223–5 accepts Nisbet's identification 'as a plausible hypothesis, but not as fact'. Hemelrijk 1999: 132–5 argues that it is unlikely that the Polla of 2.7, widow of a member of a highly distinguished senatorial family, would have married downwards; but she assumes that Pollius was a former slave, whereas his social status is unknown. The Polla of 2.2 is described solely within a domestic context, not a social one of litterati such as might be expected of Lucan's widow; but the context of 2.2, Epicurean retirement, determines the nature of Polla's praise.

Pollius Felix, an enthusiastic poet,[149] though they gave rise in the Middle Ages to the erroneous speculation that she married St. after Lucan's death.[150] In the *Siluae* she appears as actively involved in promoting her husband's memory.[151] By marriage Polla was connected not only to Lucan but to the Senecas. Ferri suggests that Polla was the head of a circle that included members associated with the exterminated Annaei line.[152] White argues that St. was on closer terms with Polla than was Martial; St. praises her formally in 2.7 (81–9) and compliments her as *rarissima uxorum* (2 *pr.* 23), whereas Martial uses no complimentary epithets.[153] But again Martial's restraint could be simply ascribed to the brevity of epigram.

7. MARTIAL AND STATIUS

Martial and St. were contemporaries. They moved in the same cultural circles, sharing six of the same literary friends, and composing poems on six of the same occasions; even the choice of words at times is similar.[154] They also share and promote similar cultural attitudes towards luxury and the aestheticisation of power.[155] Book 2 begins and ends with poems whose themes had also inspired Martial: 2.1 on the death of Glaucias (= Mart. 6.28, 29), and 2.7 on the anniversary of Lucan's death (= Mart. 7.21–3); 2.5 plays upon Martial's 'arena' epigrams.[156] Yet neither poet refers directly to the other.[157]

Henriksén has rightly challenged Heuvel's theory of poetic enmity modelled on the supposed quarrel between Callimachus and Apollonius of Rhodes; according to Heuvel, Martial and St. tried to correct one another.[158] Nauta has suggested that the similarities are simply owing to the fact that both poets moved in the same milieu and obtained the same information from their patrons. But he concurs that on at least one occasion St. corrects Martial: at 1.5.35 St. claims onyx and ophites are used in Etruscus' baths, contrary to Mart. 6.42.14–15.[159]

'Rivalry' is perhaps a more appropriate term than 'enmity', for it does not necessarily entail hostility or embitterment. Martial and St. wrote in a competitive literary climate where they looked to patrons to read and promote their verse and sought imperial recognition at the two great festivals instituted by Domitian. It would be surprising if Martial and St. did not respond to one another in their

---

[149] Cf. 2.2.112–20.
[150] His wife's name was Claudia (3 *pr.* 21); Van Dam 1984: 454–5.
[151] See 2 *pr.* 22–6.   [152] Ferri 26.
[153] Mart. 10.64 addresses Polla as *regina*, a word with either demeaning or bitter connotations in the context of patronage, suggesting at the very least an uncertain and distant relationship; see White 1975: 285.
[154] E.g. 2.1.71n.; Heuvel 1936–7: 303–5.   [155] Rosati 2006.
[156] Outside book 2, 1.2 corresponds to Mart. 6.21, 1.5 to Mart. 6.42, 3.4 to Mart. 9.11–13, 16, 17, 36, 4.6 to Mart. 9.43–4. See White 1975; Nauta 2002: 88–9.
[157] Full discussion of their relationship in Henriksén 1998.
[158] Heuvel 1936–7; Henriksén 1998, esp. 81–2.
[159] Nauta 2002: 246–8. See also Coleman on 4 *pr.* 24.

poetry. True, neither names the other; but then Roman poets rarely refer to their contemporaries.[160] In 2 *pr.* 14–18 St. perhaps challenges Martial by claiming that the central portion of his poetry book consists of poems that are like epigrams; indeed 2.5 adopts an important theme of Martial's epigrams, 'the lion in the arena'.[161] Martial's 'lion and hare' cycle celebrates the lions' trick of letting hares play safely around them;[162] but in producing several variations on this theme Martial laid himself open to the charge of repetitiveness.[163] St. avoids a possibly jaded audience and jaded reception by describing a new 'wonder' involving the lion in the arena that made riveting theatre for the audience, an unscripted event that would appeal to the extemporaneous poet and show that the 'arena' poem was not exhausted.[164] At the same time St. does not compete directly with Martial on his own ground; instead he adapts epigrammatic themes to hexameter verse.[165] And whereas Martial rejects mythological themes, St. often views contemporary life through a mythological lens.[166] It is impossible to say what the personal relationship between Martial and St. might have been; their literary relationship seems to have been one of creative, stimulating exchange.

8. STYLE

i. *Language and syntax*

The style of the *Siluae* has a ludic quality, ranging in tonality from epic solemnity to humour and playfulness. All the same the diction is fairly traditional and for the most part elevated, sometimes with mock-heroic resonance; for instance only a few neologisms occur in Book 2, and they are formed on traditional lines (2.1.95 *fluctiuagus*; 2.3.60 *Phoebeia* (of Diana); 2.7.74 *Maroniani* (of Virgil));[167] prosaic words (e.g. 2.1.58 *bilis*) are few. But St. is both bold and nuanced in his use of diction, showing a fondness for striking metaphors, frequent wordplay (especially with etymologies, both Roman and Greek), paradox and oxymora, and mythological and literary allusions; there is especially frequent intertextual engagement with Horace, Lucan, Lucretius, Martial, Ovid and the younger Seneca as well as with

---

[160] See n. 13 above.

[161] Most of the poems on shared themes are of similar date, except for 2.5; Martial's *Liber spectaculorum* was published early in Domitian's reign (Coleman 2006: lxii–lxiv), book 1, which contains many poems on the arena, between 85 and 88 CE (Howell on Mart. 1 pp. 5–6).

[162] Mart. 1.6, 14, 22, 48, 51, 60, 104.

[163] Cf. Mart. 1.44 with Howell; Lorenz 2002: 131–2.

[164] Mart. *Sp.* 21, on the tigress who attacked a wild lion, comes closest to the incident that St. describes; Martial emphasises its novelty: *res noua, non ullis cognita temporibus* (4).

[165] Bright 1980: 10–11.

[166] E.g. Mart. 10.4, whose opening lines (1–3) seem to make a specific dig at the *Thebaid*.

[167] See Dewar on *Theb.* 9.305. Compound adjectives ending in -*fer* and -*ger* are particularly a feature of Ovid's epic style adopted by St.; e.g. 2.1.181 *anguifer*; 2.1.217 *imbrifer*; 2.2.77 *armiger*; 2.3.12 *belligerum*; 2.6.86 *odoriferos*.

Virgil. Emphatic second-person address, apostrophe and exclamation at the same time lend a personal quality to the poetry; frequent repetition of words conveys an improvisational tone while also sometimes emphasising a particular poetic theme. In short in the *Siluae* St. artfully modulates the learned sophistication of a neo-Callimachean with the intimacy of personal, occasional poetry. The following analysis of four lines from 2.6 makes no claims to be comprehensive but focuses on some of the significant stylistic features in book 2:

> . . . non talem Cressa superbum
> callida sollicito reuocauit Thesea filo,
> nec Paris Oebalios talis uisurus amores
> rusticus inuitas deiecit in aequora pinus (2.6.25–8).

Here the deceased young slave Philetos is compared to mythological heroes on the grounds that, unlike them, Philetos would have made the perfect bridegroom. Mythological comparisons are a prominent feature of the *Siluae*, possibly influenced by their encomiastic use in elegiac poetry.[168] In this excerpt the two heroes Theseus and Paris are presented as lovers, and St. gives his hexameters an elegiac cast by devoting one distich to each, thus imitating the self-containment of the elegiac couplet;[169] the effect of a distich is enhanced by the alternation of trisyllabic and disyllabic words at the end of each line. Each example is characterised by dramatic compression. The poet's command of vivid, arresting detail is shown in the vignettes depicting moments of personal crisis: Ariadne bringing Theseus back from the labyrinth with the thread, and Paris setting off on his momentous voyage to Helen and leaving his Oenone behind. Not only do the heroes fall short as potential bridegrooms, they also fall short in the loyalty that is Philetos' particular virtue.[170] Their pairing is particularly pointed, for Theseus preceded Paris in abducting Helen; a larger narrative pattern of betrayal links the two comparisons.[171]

Each exemplum is introduced by *talis*, a formula that derives from the Hesiodic *Catalogue of Women* (*talis* = οἷος) and marks the elevated register;[172] the spondaic opening *non talem*, occurring after the strong caesura, is emphatic. The case and construction are varied (acc., nom., *non*, *nec*), as is the use of names. A high proportion of Greek proper names and patronymics characterise the personal poems of the *Siluae*, occurring less frequently in the poems concerning Domitian.[173] Though fairly traditional, they contribute to the sensuous quality

---

[168] McKeown on Ov. *Am.* 1.10.1–8.   [169] Likewise 2.6.30–3 (Achilles and Troilus).
[170] See 2.6.10.   [171] Knox on Ov. *Ep.* 5.172; Kenney on Ov. *Ep.* 16.153.
[172] McKeown on Ov. *Am.* 1.10.1–2.
[173] For instance there are no Greek names or epithets at all in 2.5; by contrast 2.2 praising Pollius' Greek-style villa is full of Graecisms.

of the style and its curious blend of elevation and intimacy.[174] Here in 2.6 Theseus' name is in the elevated Greek form of the accusative.[175] The women are not directly named but are called after their country of origin. Ariadne is 'the Cretan', an Ovidian epithet;[176] Helen is Paris' 'Oebalian [i.e. Spartan] love'. St. here reveals his fondness for etymological wordplay, an important feature of the style of the *Siluae* that allows for expansion of meaning;[177] *callida* glosses *Cressa*, since the Cretans were known for their devious behaviour, *mendax . . . Creta* (Ov. *Ars* 1.298).

The first two lines are characterised by a favourite device, hyperbaton. Line 27 has the appearance of a Golden Line, two epithets and two nouns frame a verb;[178] but *callida*, misleadingly echoed by *Thesea* in the second part of the line, modifies *Cressa* in the previous line, while *sollicito* modifies *filo* as a transferred epithet, for it can describe either Ariadne, anxious on her lover's behalf, or Theseus, anxious that he will not escape from the labyrinth. *superbum*, which modifies Theseus, is separated from its noun by two intervening epithets and a verb. The word order is deceptive, like the windings of the labyrinth which the thread has to negotiate.

Both Theseus and Paris are given ambiguous epithets that subtly mock their heroic status. *superbum*, emphatically placed at the end of line 25, often, but not always, has negative connotations.[179] Here it suggests various levels of meaning: Theseus is 'proud' in his courage; 'proud in his beauty'; or 'too proud' in that he will exploit and discard Ariadne; this range of possibilities is encapsulated in the one epithet, which invites us to evaluate Theseus' character. Paris is called *rusticus*, a reference to his status as shepherd at the time of the Judgment and his departure for Sparta. But enjambment draws attention to the epithet's pejorative meaning of 'boorish'; as Kenney notes on Ov. *Ep.* 16.222, *rusticus* in Ovid connotes 'lack of amatory *savoir-faire*'. St. wittily contradicts Ov. *Ars* 2.369 (of Paris) *non rusticus hospes*. Here the juxtaposition of *rusticus* and the mellifluous Greek epithet *Oebalios* ironically contrasts the shepherd lover and the most beautiful woman in the world, the exotic 'Oebalian'. St. also probably hints at the story that is elided here, Paris' love affair with Oenone whom, according to Ov. *Ep.* 5. 41–52, he leaves with false protestations of love.[180] Paris' 'boorish' character is perhaps also conveyed by the violent haste with which he casts his ship into the water

---

[174] Mayer 1982: 318 argues that imperial poets regarded the Augustan, rather than the Hellenistic poets, as 'classics'. He however underplays the importance of Greek poets to the *Siluae*, even if there is no one dominant model.

[175] Typically, like Ovid, St. prefers Greek inflections of Greek names such as the acc. -*n*; the acc. -*a* is used for Greek names in -*eus*; e.g. 2.1.89 *Pelea*.

[176] *Cressa* first appears in Latin poetry at Virg. *G.* 3.345 (of a quiver); Ovid is the first to use it of Ariadne (*Am.* 1.7.16).

[177] Barney 1998. For instance St. puns on the names of all his addressees (Nisbet 1995b); he is fond of etymological play with Greek words, esp. in 2.2 (e.g. 2.2.23–4n.; 2.2.58n).

[178] Wilkinson 1963: 215.   [179] Tellingly perhaps SB omits translating *superbum*.

[180] She claims that she was his wife when he was content with shepherding; cf. Ov. *Ep.* 5.80 *nulla nisi Oenone pauperis uxor.*

(deiecit). Again, the epithet for the male lover is complex and invites an evaluation of Paris' character. Typically St. adds drama to the scene by personifying the ship;[181] spondaic *inuitas* not only evokes the common trope of sailing as a moral outrage but also suggests the ship's resistance to Paris' intended adultery as well as to a journey that will result in the destruction of Troy.

As Micozzi comments, St.'s style is characterised by density rather than by abundance;[182] these epithets demonstrate the frequently enigmatic quality of St.'s diction and style. There is no excess here but rather sophisticated, pointed compression, learning and also wit. Nor is this mythological excursus irrelevant to the main theme of 2.6. The failings of great heroes illustrate the main point of St.'s encomium, namely that virtue is independent of social status; though a slave, Philetos is the morally superior figure. The artful style and nuanced diction treat myth not as inert but as full of dramatic psychological possibilities.

Roberts has convincingly argued that the *Siluae* are crucial texts in the development of the late antique 'jeweled style' of poetry, a term derived from Sidonius Apollinaris' metaphorical description of the *Siluae* as *gemmea prata siluularum* (*Carm.* 9.229), a phrase which captures the poems' interplay between *ars* and *natura*.[183] Indeed, Roberts claims that the poet's attention to visual and architectural detail, and the interplay of smallness of literary scale with brilliance and colour, make the *Siluae* 'late antique poetry before its time'.[184]

However, the style of the *Siluae* has commonly been characterised as 'mannerist', an art historical term introduced to literary studies by Curtius and generally associated with literary decadence.[185] Art historians themselves however disagree over the meaning and applicability of the term.[186] Gombrich for instance argued that 'postclassical', a term that embraces the literature as well as the visual arts, is more appropriate for a style that experiments with classical tradition and norms.[187] As an epithet for St.'s style, Gombrich's 'postclassical' seems apt; with his nuanced, innovative approach to classical diction and themes St. invites new perspectives on the ancient world. Or, as Poliziano so eloquently claims, *elocutionis autem ornamenta atque lumina tot tantaque exposuit, ita sententiis popularis, uerbis nitidus, figuris iucundus, tralationibus magnificus, grandis resonansque carminibus esse studuit* ('he displayed so many wonderful ornaments and beauties of style, and he strove

---

[181] St. makes frequent and varied use of personification in the *Siluae*; e.g. (of death) 2.1.121–2; 2.6.77–9; (of a porticus) 2.2.30–1.

[182] Micozzi 16–17.   [183] Roberts 1989: 50–65.

[184] Roberts 1989: 62. On the influence of St. on the late antique poets Ausonius, Claudian, Prudentius and Fortunatus see Hill 2002; Roberts 2009: 6–102.

[185] Curtius 1953: 277; Vessey 1973: 7–14.

[186] On the problems with the term see e.g. Shearman 1967: 15–22. He defines 'mannerism' as *style* in the sense of the utmost sophistication, while acknowledging that others see it as 'an expression of the unrest, anxiety, and bewilderment generated by the process of alienation of the individual from society'. Still others are dissatisfied with the term's associations with superficiality that overlook deeper meanings within an intellectual framework; see e.g. Kaufmann 1993: 102.

[187] Gombrich 1996: 407. See also Criado 2000.

to be so attractive in his pronouncements, polished in his diction, pleasing in his figures of speech, magnificent in his metaphors, grand and resonant in his poetry', *Oratio super Fabio Quintiliano et Statii Siluis*).[188]

ii. *Versification*

The metrical patterns of St.'s hexameters are virtually the same in the *Siluae* as in the epics.[189] They are fairly fluent, falling between Virgil and Ovid in the proportion of dactyls in the first four feet and in the use of elisions.[190] Monosyllabic endings are rare, occurring in book 2 only at 2.1.123, and 2.3.66. 2.1 displays two hypermetric lines (212, 220) modelled on Virgilian practice. Nevertheless St. sometimes gives his hexameter lines an elegiac cast in keeping with amatory or consolatory themes (e.g. 2.1.152n.).

All the poems of book 2 are in dactylic hexameters, apart from 2.7, which is in hendecasyllables.[191] Normally a swift and relatively informal metre, St.'s hendecasyllables achieve a certain grandeur with polysyllabic names such as *Hyperionis* (25) and Greek rare epithets such as *Hyantiae* (8), the short *i* for metrical convenience. Usually hendecasyllabic lines are self-contained, but St. daringly employs enjambment at 10–11, 46–7, 121–2, 128–9, 130–1. Contrary to Catullan practice, elision in St.'s hendecasyllables is fairly infrequent, but there is a double elision at 83, a special line honouring Polla. Normally the caesura occurs in the hendecasyllabic line at the fifth or sixth syllable; but St. achieves grand effects by delaying the caesura to the seventh or eighth syllable after or before grand names or polysyllabic words at 25, 32, 69, 93. Whereas for Catullus the hendecasyllabic line could start with a trochee or a spondee, St., like Martial, always begins the line with a spondee.

9. TEXT AND RECEPTION OF THE *SILVAE*

There is little direct evidence for the influence of the *Siluae* on later poetry. Three ancient citations of the *Siluae* – Serv. *G.* 4.125 (citing 3.2.10 *Oebalidae fratres*) and Sidonius Apollinaris, *Carm.* 9.228–9 and *Epist.* (*Carm.* 22) 6 – suggest that they were greatly admired in late antiquity. But their influence probably ran much deeper than these few surviving citations suggest. Pliny's *Epistles* for instance are in a sense a continuation of the *Siluae* in prose, for they too cultivate the occasional; the descriptions of Pliny's villas are indebted to St.,[192] and the influence of St.'s epistolary prefaces is also deeply felt.[193]

However, although in the Middle Ages St. was one of the most famous ancient authors, celebrated for his two epics and chosen by Dante as a guide in the

---

[188] Garin 1952: 872. [189] See Duckworth 1967: 102–4. [190] See Dewar xxxiv.
[191] On St.'s hendecasyllables see Raven 136–7. [192] Myers 2005.
[193] Pagàn 2010. On the considerable influence of the *Siluae* on late antique epideictic poetry see p. 26 above.

Purgatorio, it remains uncertain whether the *Siluae* continued to be known after late antiquity.[194] Some of the themes of the *Siluae* – descriptions of buildings such as baths, the *ubi sunt* lament – became popular medieval topoi. Yet we lack manuscript evidence for the *Siluae*, with one important exception. 2.7, the poem on Lucan, appears in a ninth-century German copy (Firenze BML plut. 29.32); this is our earliest manuscript not just of the *Siluae* but of any of St.'s works. It seem however to have had only limited influence on medieval poets.[195] It was not until the fifteenth century that the *Siluae* certainly became known once again to the literary world.[196] In 1417 Poggio Bracciolini, on a papal mission, discovered in an unspecified location near Constance (possibly the famous monastery of Reichenau) a manuscript containing Silius Italicus, St.'s *Siluae* and Manilius' *Astronomica*. Poggio had the manuscript transcribed by someone whom he subsequently blamed as 'the most ignorant of scribes'. It is this corrupt transcription, M, now in Madrid (= Madrid Biblioteca Nacional, MS 3678) that has survived and forms the basis of all subsequent manuscripts.[197] Hence the text of the *Siluae* has provided a field day for textual critics, the recent Loeb (2003) by Shackleton Bailey with its more than 250 emendations being a case in point.

The diffusion of the poems was slow, but certainly by the end of the fifteenth century the *Siluae* were widely known and popular in Italy, with many manuscripts and printed editions in circulation.[198] The *editio princeps* of the *Siluae* was printed in 1472. The commentary of Domitius Calderini was published in 1475;[199] in 1480–1 the humanist scholar Poliziano, who had direct access to M, lectured on the *Siluae* in his introductory lectures at Perugia.[200] The lectures had wide impact within Florentine culture and beyond.[201] Poliziano also published four poems gathered together as *Siluae*, which are modelled on the Roman poet's stylistic principles of learned variety and improvisation, though they are quite different in theme;[202] Poliziano prefaces his first poem by apologising for publishing *carmen . . . inconditum, inemendatum*.[203]

The discovery of the exemplar M caused a revolution in thinking about St., not necessarily to his advantage. The Middle Ages believed the author of

---

[194] Anderson 2000: xxi; Courtney, *Silu.* pp. v–viii. Pavlovskis 1965 argues for the influence of 1.2 (an epithalamium) upon medieval poetry. Courtney, *Silu.* pp. vii–viii adds weight to the theory that there may have been a circle of poets in Padua of the thirteenth or fourteenth century who had access to a MS of the *Siluae* now lost to us.

[195] Anderson 2000: xx argues that as it does not seem to have been copied, it had no influence on medieval tradition. But see n. 194 above.

[196] Reeve 1983: 397–9 on the history of the text of the *Siluae*.

[197] Reeve 1977: 201–6, 220–1; Gibson on *Silu.* 5 pp. l–lii.   [198] Anderson 2000: xxi.

[199] The product of his lectures *c*. 1470–3; see Reeve 1977: 217; Martinelli 1978.

[200] Martinelli 1978: xiv–xvi; Courtney 1992: xi–xx.

[201] See *Ep.* 4 to Beroaldo (*Politiani: opera omnia*, ed. I Maïer, Turin 1970–1); Martinelli 1978: xiii–xiv.

[202] Poliziano takes his fourth title, *Nutricia*, from St.'s *Soteria* (1.4); but the poems are influenced rather by late antique and Petrarchan models; see Bausi 1996: xxvii–xxviii.

[203] See the introduction of Bausi 1996: xiv–xvi.

the *Thebaid* and *Achilleid* was a rhetorician from Toulouse,[204] but now he was discovered to be a poet from Naples in southern Italy.[205] As a result, the literary and scholarly community received not only a new body of work from St.; they also received a new perception of him as a Neapolitan, closely tied therefore to the Epicurean and Greek traditions of that region of Italy; his poetic repertory along with his social connections was much more complex than had hitherto been recognised.

The 'Greekness' of certain of the *Siluae* as well as their praise of Domitian may well have been factors in their swift loss of popularity; the corrupt state of the text certainly militated against their widespread diffusion and adoption as a school text. Although Poliziano vigorously defended the *Siluae* over the epics as unique poems to be commended for their brilliance and richness of style, Scaliger, in a judgment that proved influential, found them inflated compared to the *Thebaid*.[206] They did have considerable impact on vernacular poetry, but among learned authors. For example in sixteenth/early seventeenth-century England[207] the most well-known exponent of the *Siluae* is Ben Jonson, who composed two collections of poetry entitled the *Forrest* and the *Underwood*, the latter prefaced by a discussion of the term *silua*.[208] The former contains the first 'country house poem' or 'estate poem' in English literature, 'To Penshurst',[209] directly inspired by St.'s villa poems.[210] But by then the reputation of the *Siluae* was waning. Active scholarship on the *Siluae* in the sixteenth and seventeenth centuries culminated in Gronovius' 1653 commentary, a publication which followed upon that of the school text of the *Siluae* by Thomas Stephens (1651), which, despite mounting a vigorous defence of Statius as an unjustly neglected author wrongly accused of an inflated style, did not inspire other such efforts.[211]

Until recently the *Siluae* have generally languished on the margins of the classical canon; a penchant for similar titles flourished, but not poetic imitations, the most well-known perhaps being Whitman's *Leaves of Grass*.[212] By the nineteenth century the *Siluae* were largely dismissed as 'mannerist' and decadent.[213] Despite

---

[204] Suet. *Rhet.* fr. 3; see Kaster 331–2.

[205] St.'s Neapolitan origins were often noted in the early manuscripts, as if this were surprising; see Reeve 1977: 225, n. 101.

[206] See Reeve 1977; Van Dam 1996: 315–16.

[207] On the development of a vernacular tradition of occasional poetry in Spain see Laguna 39–44. In France Ronsard's *Bocage* was indebted to the *Siluae*; see Fowler 1982: 164; 1994: 12.

[208] See Patterson 1984: 143–4.

[209] Fowler 1994: 1 prefers the term 'estate poem' as more accurately incorporating the land and the house.

[210] See Newlands 1988; Fowler 1994: 11–13.

[211] For the eighteenth century there is only Markland's important 1728 commentary. On the history of the text and editions of the *Siluae* see SB 7–10; also Vessey 1996.

[212] See Fowler 1982: 165–6.

[213] A low point for the reception of the *Siluae* was M. Nisard's influential *Études sur les poètes latins de la décadence* (Paris 1849), which portrayed St. as a mincing flatterer and fop, the ultimate example of social, moral and literary decadence. See Vessey 1996: 8–10.

the earlier critical work on the poems, the instability of the text and the perceived difficulty of the style continued to militate against their wide acceptance and their incorporation, for instance, into the classroom. The first English translation of the *Siluae* was not till 1908.[214] The stabilisation of the text thanks to the work of Vollmer (1898), Courtney (1992) and now Shackleton Bailey (2003), along with the commentaries of Van Dam (1984), Coleman (1988) and Gibson (2006), has fostered increased interest in the *Siluae* as important social and cultural as well as literary productions; it has also made possible the recent translation of Nagle (2004) and the vivacious 'versions' of Howell and Shepherd (2007), which have helped begin the process of removing the taint of fustian from the *Siluae*, making them more broadly accessible.[215]

One final example will show that, despite their relative obscurity as 'learned' poetry and their uneven fortunes in reception, the *Siluae* have been valued at times not only for their descriptive power and their generic experimentation but also for their emotional and psychological range. In De Thou's early seventeenth-century *Historia universalis* the author pauses to reflect on the most terrible moment he has to record in French history, the St Bartholomew Day massacres of 1572. To express his horror at the event, he quotes his father's thoughts on that day, drawn from 5.2. 88–90.[216] The De Thous were famous for their library and their learning; father and son were members of the French literary elite. Yet the use of the *Siluae* at a moment of crisis suggests a recognition of the poetry's emotional and political potential. De Thou senior takes St.'s lines, referring to a domestic tragedy, and applies them to a political context, allowing them to speak for the moment; St. would have approved.

10. A NOTE ON THIS COMMENTARY

The first English commentary on *Siluae* 2 was published by H.-J. Van Dam in 1982. Since then Courtney's Oxford text (1990, rev. 1992) and Shackleton Bailey's Loeb edition (2003) have done much to improve the text of the *Siluae*, while a revival of interest in all St.'s works as well as in the Flavian period has done much to improve our understanding of this poet and his social and cultural context.

This commentary on *Siluae* 2 attempts to take account of the new developments in scholarship in the *Siluae* and in St.'s poetry. The text is based on Courtney's OCT (1992) but incorporates several of SB's emendations;[217] see the list in 'Textual changes'.

---

[214] By D. A. Slater (Oxford).
[215] For a survey of scholarship on the *Siluae* to 2002 see Coleman 2003. On Howell and Shepherd see Newlands 2009b.
[216] De Thou, *Historia sui temporis*, Paris 1607 III, book 52, p. 21.
[217] See the exchange between Courtney (2004) and Shackleton Bailey (2004). Thanks to Professor Courtney for allowing me to use his OCT text as a basis.

TEXTUAL CHANGES

Differences from Courtney's OCT text, with reference to Shackleton-Bailey's Loeb edition:

locus	Newlands	Courtney	SB
2.1.20	*(scelus heu!)*	*scelus et*	*(scelus heu!)*
2.1.34	*quem, Natura, patrem!*	*(quem, Natura!) patrem*	*quem, Natura, patrem!*
2.1.51	*bracchia quo*	*bracchiaque [et]*	*bracchia quo*
2.1.67	*muta domus, fateor*	*muta domus †fateor†*	*muta domus, fateor*
2.1.128	*uestes*	*telas*	*uestes*
2.1.48	*mixta*	*†mixta†*	*mulsa*
2.1.223	*meruitue*	*renuitue*	*meruitue*
2.2.14	*curuae*	*curuas*	*curuae*
2.2.35	*Lechaeo*	*Lyaeo*	*Lechaeo*
2.2.38	*sedet*	*se det*	*se det*
2.2.59	*intrantesque*	*intrantemque*	*intrantesque*
2.3.3	*<in>curuata*	*curuata*	*<in>curuata*
2.4.15	*augusti*	*angusti*	*angusti*
2.5.1	*monstrata*	*constrata*	*constrata*
2.5.4	*quid quod*	*quid, quod*	*quid quod*
2.5.12	*clausis . . . portis*	*clausas . . . portas*	*clausis . . . portis*
2.6.6	*alte tamen aut*	*†ad te tamen at†*	*alte tamen aut*
2.6.16	*sibique*	*sibi †que†*	*sibique*
2.6.22	*sed*	*spe*	*sed*
2.6.39	*quales*	*quales*	*quales*
2.6.42	*bellus*	*liber*	*bellus*
2.6.70	*margine*	*†carmen†*	*margine*
2.6.79	*quinto . . . ortu*	*quinta . . . Oeta*	*quinto . . . ortu*
2.6.104	*dabis*	*dabit*	*dabis*
2.6.105	*monstrabis*	*monstrabit*	*monstrabis*
2.6.105	*docebis*	*docebit*	*docebis*
2.6.105	*amorem*	*amori*	*amorem*
2.7.79	*quid maius loquar?*	*quid? maius loquar*	*quin maius loquar*
2.7.134	*dolorque festus*	*dolorque festus,*	*dolorque festus*

P. PAPINI STATI SILVARVM
LIBER SECVNDVS

P. PAPINI STATI SILVARVM
LIBER SECVNDVS

STATIVS MELIORI SVO SALVTEM

Et familiaritas nostra qua gaudeo, Melior, uir optime nec
minus in iudicio litterarum quam in omni uitae colore tersissime, et ipsa opusculorum quae tibi trado condicio sic posita est
ut totus hic ad te liber meus etiam sine epistula spectet. primum
enim habet Glauciam nostrum, cuius gratissima infantia et   5
qualem plerumque infelices sortiuntur †apud te complexus
amabam iam non tibi†. huius amissi recens uulnus, ut scis,
epicedio prosecutus sum adeo festinanter ut excusandam
habuerim affectibus tuis celeritatem. nec nunc eam apud te
iacto qui nosti, sed et ceteris indico, ne quis asperiore lima   10
carmen examinet et a confuso scriptum et dolenti datum, cum
paene superuacua sint tarda solacia. Polli mei uilla Surrentina
quae sequitur debuit a me uel in honorem eloquentiae eius
diligentius dici, sed amicus ignouit. in arborem certe tuam,
Melior, et psittacum scis a me leues libellos quasi epigrammatis   15
loco scriptos. eandem exigebat stili facilitatem leo mansuetus,
quem in amphitheatro prostratum frigidum erat sacratissimo
imperatori ni statim tradere. ad Vrsum quoque nostrum,
iuuenem candidissimum et sine iactura desidiae doctissimum,
scriptam de amisso puero consolationem super ea quae ipsi   20
debeo huic libro libenter inserui, quia honorem eius tibi
laturus accepto est. cludit uolumen genethliacon Lucani, quod
Polla Argentaria, rarissima uxorum, cum hunc diem forte
†consuleremus†, imputari sibi uoluit. ego non potui maiorem
tanti auctoris habere reuerentiam quam quod laudes eius   25
dicturus hexametros meos timui.

haec qualiacumque sunt, Melior carissime, si tibi non
displicuerint, a te publicum accipiant; si minus, ad me reuertantur.

1

Qvod tibi praerepti, Melior, solamen alumni
improbus ante rogos et adhuc uiuente fauilla

ordiar? abruptis etiamnunc flebile uenis
uulnus hiat magnaeque patet uia lubrica plagae.
cum iam egomet cantus et uerba medentia saeuus   5
confero, tu planctus lamentaque fortia mauis
odistique chelyn surdaque auerteris aure.
intempesta cano; citius me tigris abactis
fetibus orbatique uelint audire leones.
nec si tergeminum Sicula de uirgine carmen   10
affluat aut siluis chelys intellecta ferisque,
mulceat insanos gemitus. stat pectore demens
luctus et admoto latrant praecordia tactu.
nemo uetat; satiare malis aegrumque dolorem
libertate doma. iam flendi expleta uoluptas,   15
iamque preces fessus non indignaris amicas?
iamne canam? lacrimis en et mea carmine in ipso
ora natant tristesque cadunt in uerba liturae.
ipse etenim tecum nigrae sollemnia pompae
spectatumque Vrbi (scelus heu!) puerile feretrum   20
produxi; saeuos damnati turis aceruos
plorantemque animam supra sua funera uidi,
teque patrum gemitus superantem et bracchia matrum
complexumque rogos ignemque haurire parantem
uix tenui similis comes offendique tenendo.   25
et nunc heu uittis et frontis honore soluto
infaustus uates uersa mea pectora tecum
plango lyra; †et diu† comitem sociumque doloris,
si merui luctusque tui consortia sensi,
iam lenis patiare precor: me fulmine in ipso   30
audiuere patres; ego iuxta busta profusis
matribus at<que> piis cecini solacia natis
et mihi, cum proprios gemerem defectus ad ignes
quem, Natura, patrem! nec te lugere seuerus
arceo, sed confer gemitus pariterque fleamus.   35
   iamdudum dignos aditus laudumque tuarum,
o merito dilecte puer, primordia quaerens
distrahor. hinc anni stantes in limine uitae
ac me forma rapit, rapit inde modestia praecox
et pudor et tenero probitas maturior aeuo.   40
o ubi purpureo suffusus sanguine candor
sidereique orbes radiataque lumina caelo
et castigatae collecta modestia frontis

ingenuique super crines mollisque decorae
margo comae? blandis ubinam ora arguta querelis 45
osculaque impliciti uernos redolentia flores
et mixtae risu lacrimae penitusque loquentis
Hyblaeis uox mixta fauis, cui sibila serpens
poneret et saeuae uellent seruire nouercae?
nil ueris affingo bonis. heu lactea colla 50
bracchia quo numquam domini sine pondere ceruix!
o ubi uenturae spes non longinqua iuuentae
atque genis optatus honos iurataque multum
barba tibi? cuncta in cineres grauis intulit hora
hostilisque dies; nobis meminisse relictum. 55
quis tua colloquiis hilaris mulcebit amatis
pectora, quis curas mentisque arcana remittet?
accensum quis bile fera famulisque tumentem
leniet ardentique in se deflectet ab ira?
inceptas quis ab ore dapes libataque uina 60
auferet et dulci turbabit cuncta rapina?
quis matutinos abrumpet murmure somnos
impositus stratis, abitusque morabitur artis
nexibus aque ipso reuocabit ad oscula poste?
obuius intranti rursus quis in ora manusque 65
prosiliet breuibusque umeros circumdabit ulnis?
muta domus, fateor, desolatique penates
et situs in thalamis et maesta silentia mensis.
    quid mirum, tanto si te pius altor honorat
funere? tu domino requies portusque senectae, 70
tu modo deliciae, dulces modo pectore curae.
non te barbaricae uersabat turbo catastae,
nec mixtus Phariis uenalis mercibus infans
compositosque sales meditataque uerba locutus
quaesisti lasciuus erum tardeque parasti. 75
hic domus, hinc ortus, dominique penatibus olim
carus uterque parens atque in tua gaudia liber,
ne quererere genus. raptum sed protinus aluo
sustulit exsultans ac prima lucida uoce
astra salutantem dominus sibi mente dicauit 80
amplexusque sinu tulit et genuisse putauit.
fas mihi sanctorum uenia dixisse parentum,
tuque, oro, Natura, sinas, cui prima per orbem
iura animis sancire datum: non omnia sanguis

proximus aut serie generis demissa propago   85
alligat; interius noua saepe ascitaque serpunt
pignora conexis. natos genuisse necesse est,
elegisse iuuat. tenero sic blandus Achilli
semifer Haemonium uincebat Pelea Chiron,
nec senior Peleus natum comitatus in arma   90
Troica, sed claro Phoenix haerebat alumno.
optabat longe reditus Pallantis ouantis
Euander, fidus pugnas spectabat Acoetes,
cumque procul nitidis genitor cessaret ab astris
fluctiuagus uolucrem comebat Persea Dictys.   95
quid referam altricum uictas pietate parentes?
quid te post cineres deceptaque funera matris
tutius Inoo reptantem pectore, Bacche?
se secura sati Tuscis regnabat in undis
Ilia, portantem lassabat Romulus Accam.   100
uidi ego transertos alieno in robore ramos
altius ire suis. et te iam fecerat illi
mens animusque patrem, necdum moresue decorue;
tu tamen et uinctas etiamnunc murmure uoces
uagitumque rudem fletusque infantis amabas.   105
    ille, uelut primos exspiraturus ad austros
mollibus in pratis alte flos improbus exstat,
sic tener ante diem uultu gressuque superbo
uicerat aequales multumque reliquerat annos.
siue catenatis curuatus membra palaestris   110
staret, Amyclaea conceptum matre putares
(Oebaliden illo praeceps mutaret Apollo,
Alcides pensaret Hylan); seu gratus amictu
Attica facundi decurreret orsa Menandri,
laudaret gauisa sonum crinemque decorum   115
fregisset rosea lasciua Thalia corona;
Maeonium siue ille senem Troiaeque labores
diceret aut casus tarde remeantis Vlixis,
ipse pater sensus, ipsi stupuere magistri.
scilicet infausta Lachesis cunabula dextra   120
attigit, et gremio puerum complexa fouebat
Inuidia; illa genas et adultum comere crinem
et monstrare artes et uerba infigere, quae nunc
plangimus. Herculeos annis aequare labores

coeperat assurgens, sed adhuc infantia iuxta; 125
iam tamen et ualidi gressus mensuraque maior
cultibus et uisae puero decrescere uestes,
cum tibi quas uestes, quae non gestamina mitis
festinabat erus? breuibus constringere laenis
pectora et angusta nolens artare lacerna, 130
enormes non ille sinus sed semper ad annos
texta legens, modo puniceo uelabat amictu,
nunc herbas imitante sinu, nunc dulce rubenti
murice; tum uiuis digitos incendere gemmis
gaudebat; non turba comes, non munera cessant; 135
sola uerecundo derat praetexta decori.
    haec fortuna domus. subitas inimica leuauit
Parca manus. quo, diua, feros grauis exseris ungues?
non te forma mouet, non te lacrimabilis aetas?
hunc nec saeua uiro potuisset carpere Procne 140
nec fera crudeles Colchis durasset in iras,
editus Aeolia nec si foret iste Creusa;
toruus ab hoc Athamas insanos flecteret arcus;
hunc quamquam Hectoreos cineres Troiamque perosus
turribus e Phrygiis flesset missurus Vlixes. 145
septima lux, et iam frigentia lumina torpent,
iam complexa manu crinem tenet infera Iuno.
ille tamen Parcis fragiles urguentibus annos
te uultu moriente uidet linguaque cadente
murmurat; in te omnes uacui iam pectoris efflat 150
reliquias, solum meminit solumque uocantem
exaudit, tibique ora mouet, tibi uerba relinquit
et prohibet gemitus consolaturque dolentem.
gratum est, Fata, tamen quod non mors lenta iacentis
exedit puerile decus, manesque subibit 155
integer et nullo temeratus corpora damno,
qualis erat. quid ego exsequias et prodiga flammis
dona loquar maestoque ardentia funera luxu,
quod tibi purpureo tristis rogus aggere creuit,
quod Cilicum flores, quod munera graminis Indi, 160
quodque Arabes Phariique Palaestinique liquores
arsuram lauere comam? cupit omnia ferre
prodigus et totos Melior succendere census
desertas exosus opes, sed non capit ignis

inuidus, atque artae desunt in munera flammae.   165
horror habet sensus. qualem te funere summo
atque rogum iuxta, Melior placidissime quondam,
extimui! tune ille hilaris comisque uideri?
unde animi saeuaeque manus et barbarus horror
dum modo fusus humi lucem auersaris iniquam,   170
nunc toruus pariter uestes et pectora rumpis
dilectosque premis uisus et frigida lambis
oscula. erant illic genitor materque iacentis
maesta, sed attoniti te spectauere parentes.
quid mirum? plebs cuncta nefas et praeuia flerunt   175
agmina, Flaminio quae limite Muluius agger
transuehit, immeritus flammis dum tristibus infans
traditur et gemitum formaque aeuoque meretur;
talis in Isthmiacos prolatus ab aequore portus
naufragus imposita iacuit sub matre Palaemon,   180
sic et in anguiferae ludentem gramine Lernae
rescissum squamis auidus bibit ignis Ophelten.
    pone metus letique minas desiste uereri.
illum nec terno latrabit Cerberus ore,
nulla soror flammis, nulla assurgentibus hydris   185
terrebit; quin ipse auidae trux nauita cumbae
interius steriles ripas et adusta subibit
litora, ne puero dura ascendisse facultas.
    quid mihi gaudenti proles Cyllenia uirga
nuntiat? estne aliquid tam saeuo in tempore laetum?   190
nouerat effigies generosique ardua Blaesi
ora puer, dum saepe domi noua serta ligantem
te uidet et similes tergentem pectore ceras.
hunc ubi Lethaei lustrantem gurgitis oras
Ausonios inter proceres seriemque Quirini   195
agnouit, timide primum uestigia iungit
accessu tacito summosque lacessit amictus,
inde †magis† sequitur; neque enim magis ille trahentem
spernit et ignota credit de stirpe nepotum.
mox ubi delicias et rari pignus amici   200
sensit et amissi puerum solacia Blaesi,
tollit humo magnaque ligat ceruice diuque
ipse manu gaudens uehit et, quae munera mollis
Elysii, steriles ramos mutasque uolucres

porgit et obtunso pallentes germine flores.   205
nec prohibet meminisse tui, sed pectora blandus
miscet et alternum pueri partitur amorem.
  hic finis rapto. quin tu iam uulnera sedas
et tollis mersum luctu caput? omnia functa
aut moritura uides; obeunt noctesque diesque   210
astraque, nec solidis prodest sua machina terris.
nam populus mortale genus, plebisque caducae
quis fleat interitus? hos bella, hos aequora poscunt;
his amor exitio, furor his et saeua cupido,
ut sileam morbos; hos ora rigentia brumae,   215
illos implacido letalis Sirius igni,
hos manet imbrifero pallens autumnus hiatu.
quicquid init ortus, finem timet. ibimus omnes,
ibimus; immensis urnam quatit Aeacus umbris.
  ast hic quem gemimus felix hominesque deosque   220
et dubios casus et caecae lubrica uitae
effugit, immunis fatis. non ille rogauit,
non timuit meruitue mori: nos anxia plebes,
nos miseri, quibus unde dies suprema, quis aeui
exitus incertum, quibus instet fulmen ab astris,   225
quae nubes fatale sonet. nil flecteris istis?
sed flectere libens. ades huc emissus ab atro
limine, cui soli cuncta impetrare facultas,
Glaucia (nil sontes animas nec portitor arcet
nec durae comes ille serae); tu pectora mulce,   230
tu prohibe manare genas noctesque beatas
dulcibus alloquiis et uiuis uultibus imple
et periisse nega, desolatamque sororem,
qui potes, et miseros perge insinuare parentes.

2

Est inter notos Sirenum nomine muros
saxaque Tyrrhenae templis onerata Mineruae
celsa Dicarchei speculatrix uilla profundi,
qua Bromio dilectus ager collesque per altos
uritur et prelis non inuidet uua Falernis.   5
huc me post patrii laetum quinquennia lustri,
cum stadio iam pigra quies canusque sederet

puluis, ad Ambracias conuersa gymnade frondes,
trans gentile fretum placidi facundia Polli
detulit et nitidae iuuenilis gratia Pollae,   10
flectere iam cupidum gressus qua limite noto
Appia longarum teritur regina uiarum.
   sed iuuere morae. placido lunata recessu
hinc atque hinc curuae perrumpunt aequora rupes.
dat natura locum montique interuenit unum   15
litus et in terras scopulis pendentibus exit.
gratia prima loci, gemina testudine fumant
balnea et e terris occurrit dulcis amaro
nympha mari. leuis hic Phorci chorus udaque crines
Cymodoce uiridisque cupit Galatea lauari.   20
ante domum tumidae moderator caerulus undae
excubat, innocui custos laris; huius amico
spumant templa salo. felicia rura tuetur
Alcides; gaudet gemino sub numine portus:
hic seruat terras, hic saeuis fluctibus obstat.   25
mira quies pelagi: ponunt hic lassa furorem
aequora et insani spirant clementius austri;
hic praeceps minus audet hiems, nulloque tumultu
stagna modesta iacent dominique imitantia mores.
inde per obliquas erepit porticus arces,   30
urbis opus, longoque domat saxa aspera dorso.
qua prius obscuro permixti puluere soles
et feritas inamoena uiae, nunc ire uoluptas;
qualis, si subeas Ephyres Baccheidos altum
culmen, ab Inoo fert semita tecta Lechaeo.   35
   non, mihi si cunctos Helicon indulgeat amnes
et superet Piplea sitim largeque uolantis
ungula sedet equi reseretque arcana pudicos
Phemonoe fontes uel quos meus auspice Phoebo
altius immersa turbauit Pollius urna,   40
innumeras ualeam species cultusque locorum
Pieriis aequare modis. uix ordine longo
suffecere oculi, uix, dum per singula ducor,
suffecere gradus. quae rerum turba! locine
ingenium an domini mirer prius? haec domus ortus   45
aspicit et Phoebi tenerum iubar, illa cadentem
detinet exactamque negat dimittere lucem,

cum iam fessa dies et in aequora montis opaci
umbra cadit uitreoque natant praetoria ponto.
haec pelagi clamore fremunt, haec tecta sonoros   50
ignorant fluctus terraeque silentia malunt.
his fauit natura locis, hic uicta colenti
cessit et ignotos docilis mansueuit in usus.
mons erat hic ubi plana uides, et lustra fuerunt
quae nunc tecta subis; ubi nunc nemora ardua cernis   55
hic nec terra fuit: domuit possessor, et illum
formantem rupes expugnantemque secuta
gaudet humus. nunc cerne iugum discentia saxa
intrantesque domos iussumque recedere montem.
iam Methymnaei uatis manus et chelys una   60
Thebais et Getici cedat tibi gloria plectri;
et tu saxa moues, et te nemora alta sequuntur.
    quid referam ueteres ceraeque aerisque figuras,
si quid Apellei gaudent animasse colores,
si quid adhuc uacua tamen admirabile Pisa   65
Phidiacae rasere manus, quod ab arte Myronis
aut Polycliteo iussum est quod uiuere caelo,
aeraque ab Isthmiacis auro potiora fauillis,
ora ducum ac uatum sapientumque ora priorum,
quos tibi cura sequi, quos toto pectore sentis   70
expers curarum atque animum uirtute quieta
compositus semperque tuus? quid mille reuoluam
culmina uisendique uices? sua cuique uoluptas
atque omni proprium thalamo mare, transque iacentem
Nerea diuersis seruit sua terra fenestris: 75
haec uidet Inarimen, illinc Prochyta aspera paret;
armiger hac magni patet Hectoris, inde malignum
aera respirat pelago circumflua Nesis;
inde uagis omen felix Euploea carinis
quaeque ferit curuos exserta Megalia fluctus;   80
angitur et domino contra recubante proculque
Surrentina tuus spectat praetoria Limon.
una tamen cunctis, procul eminet una diaetis
quae tibi Parthenopen derecto limite ponti
ingerit: hic Grais penitus desecta metallis   85
saxa, quod Eoae respergit uena Syenes,
Synnade quod maesta Phrygiae fodere secures

per Cybeles lugentis agros, ubi marmore picto
candida purpureo distinguitur area gyro;
hic et Amyclaei caesum de monte Lycurgi   90
quod uiret et molles imitatur rupibus herbas;
hic Nomadum lucent flauentia saxa Thasosque
et Chios et gaudens fluctus aequare Carystos;
omnia Chalcidicas turres obuersa salutant.
macte animo quod Graia probas, quod Graia frequentas   95
arua, nec inuideant quae te genuere Dicarchi
moenia: nos docto melius potiemur alumno.
    quid nunc ruris opes pontoque noualia dicam
iniecta et madidas Baccheo nectare rupes?
saepe per autumnum iam pubescente Lyaeo   100
conscendit scopulos noctisque occulta sub umbra
palmite maturo rorantia lumina tersit
Nereis et dulces rapuit de collibus uuas.
saepe et uicino sparsa est uindemia fluctu
et Satyri cecidere uadis nudamque per undas   105
Dorida montani cupierunt prendere Panes.
    sis felix, tellus, dominis ambobus in annos
Mygdonii Pyliique senis nec nobile mutes
seruitium, nec te cultu Tirynthia uincat
aula Dicarcheique sinus, nec saepius istis   110
blanda Therapnaei placeant uineta Galaesi.
hic ubi Pierias exercet Pollius artes
(seu uoluit monitus quos dat Gargettius auctor,
seu nostram quatit ille chelyn, seu dissona nectit
carmina, siue minax ultorem stringit iambon),   115
hinc leuis e scopulis meliora ad carmina Siren
aduolat, hinc motis audit Tritonia cristis.
tunc rapidi ponunt flatus, maria ipsa uetantur
obstrepere, emergunt pelago doctamque trahuntur
ad chelyn et blandi scopulis delphines aderrant.   120
uiue, Midae gazis et Lydo ditior auro,
Troica et Euphratae supra diademata felix,
quem non ambigui fasces, non mobile uulgus,
non leges, non castra terent, qui pectore magno
spemque metumque domas uoto sublimior omni,   125
exemptus fatis indignantemque refellens
Fortunam, dubio quem non in turbine rerum

deprendet suprema dies, sed abire paratum
ac plenum uita. nos, uilis turba, caducis
deseruire bonis semperque optare parati,   130
spargimur in casus: celsa tu mentis ab arce
despicis errantes humanaque gaudia rides.
tempus erat cum te geminae suffragia terrae
diriperent celsusque duas ueherere per urbes,
inde Dicarcheis multum uenerande colonis,   135
hinc ascite meis, pariterque his largus et illis
ac iuuenile calens rectique errore superbus.
at nunc discussa rerum caligine uerum
aspicis. illo alii rursus iactantur in alto,
sed tua securos portus placidamque quietem   140
intrauit non quassa ratis. sic perge, nec umquam
emeritam in nostras puppem demitte procellas.
tuque, nurus inter longae ∗ ∗ ∗ ∗   147
∗ ∗ ∗ ∗ praecordia curae,
non frontem uertere minae, sed candida semper
gaudia et in uultu curarum ignara uoluptas;   150
non tibi sepositas infelix strangulat arca
diuitias auidique animum dispendia torquent
fenoris: expositi census et docta fruendi
temperies. non ulla deo meliore cohaerent
pectora, non alias docuit Concordia mentes   155
                    ∗ ∗ ∗ ∗ ∗
discite securi, quorum de pectore mixtae   143
in longum coiere faces sanctusque pudicae
seruat amicitiae leges amor. ite per annos
saeculaque et priscae titulos praecedite famae.   146

                          3

STAT quae perspicuas nitidi Melioris opacet
arbor aquas complexa lacus; quae robore ab imo
<in>curuata uadis redit inde cacumine recto
ardua, ceu mediis iterum nascatur ab undis
atque habitet uitreum tacitis radicibus amnem.   5
quid Phoebum tam parua rogem? uos dicite causas,
Naides, et faciles (satis est) date carmina, Fauni.
nympharum tenerae fugiebant Pana cateruae;

ille quidem it cunctas tamquam uelit, it tamen unam
in Pholoen. siluis haec fluminibusque sequentis   10
nunc hirtos gressus, nunc improba cornua uitat.
iamque et belligerum Iani nemus atraque Caci
rura Quirinalesque fuga suspensa per agros
Caelica tesca subit; ibi demum uicta labore,
fessa metu, qua nunc placidi Melioris aperti   15
stant sine fraude lares, fluxos collegit amictus
artius et †niueae† posuit se margine ripae.
insequitur uelox pecorum deus et sua credit
conubia; ardenti iamiam suspiria librat
pectore, iam praedae leuis imminet. ecce citatos   20
aduertit Diana gradus, dum per iuga septem
errat Auentinaeque legit uestigia ceruae.
paenituit uidisse deam, conuersaque fidas
ad comites: 'numquamne auidis arcebo rapinis
hoc petulans foedumque pecus, semperque pudici   25
decrescet mihi turba chori?' sic deinde locuta
depromit pharetra telum breue, quod neque flexis
cornibus aut solito torquet stridore, sed una
emisit contenta manu laeuumque soporem
Naidos auersa fertur tetigisse sagitta.   30
illa diem pariter surgens hostemque proteruum
uidit et in fontem, niueos ne panderet artus,
sic tota cum ueste ruit, stagnisque sub altis
Pana sequi credens ima latus implicat alga.
quid faceret subito deceptus praedo? nec altis   35
credere corpus aquis hirtae sibi conscius audet
pellis et a tenero nandi rudis. omnia questus,
immitem Brimo, stagna inuida et inuida tela,
primaeuam nisu platanum, cui longa propago
innumeraeque manus et iturus in aethera uertex,   40
deposuit iuxta uiuamque aggessit harenam
optatisque aspergit aquis et talia mandat:
'uiue diu nostri pignus memorabile uoti,
arbor, et haec durae latebrosa cubilia nymphae
tu saltem declinis ama, preme frondibus undam.   45
illa quidem meruit, sed ne, precor, igne superno
aestuet aut dura feriatur grandine; tantum
spargere tu laticem et foliis turbare memento.

tunc ego teque diu recolam dominamque benignae
sedis et illaesa tutabor utramque senecta,   50
ut Iouis, ut Phoebi frondes, ut discolor umbra
populus et nostrae stupeant tua germina pinus.'
sic ait. illa dei ueteres imitata calores
uberibus stagnis obliquo pendula trunco
incubat atque umbris scrutatur amantibus undas.   55
sperat et amplexus, sed aquarum spiritus arcet
nec patitur tactus. tandem eluctata sub auras
libratur fundo rursusque enode cacumen
ingeniosa leuat, ueluti descendat in imos
stirpe lacus alia. iam nec Phoebeia Nais   60
odit et exclusos inuitat gurgite ramos.
    haec tibi parua quidem genitali luce paramus
dona, sed ingenti forsan uictura sub aeuo.
tu cuius placido posuere in pectore sedem
blandus honos hilarisque tamen cum pondere uirtus,   65
cui nec pigra quies nec iniqua potentia nec spes
improba, sed medius per honesta et dulcia limes,
incorrupte fidem nullosque experte tumultus
et secrete palam quod digeris ordine uitam,
idem auri facilis contemptor et optimus idem   70
promere diuitias opibusque immittere lucem;
hac longum florens animi morumque iuuenta
Iliacos aequare senes et uincere persta
quos pater Elysio, genetrix quos detulit annos.
hoc illi duras exorauere sorores,   75
hoc, quae te sub teste situm fugitura tacentem
ardua magnanimi reuirescet gloria Blaesi.

4

PSITTACE, dux uolucrum, domini facunda uoluptas,
humanae sollers imitator, psittace, linguae,
quis tua tam subito praeclusit murmura fato?
hesternas, miserande, dapes moriturus inisti
nobiscum, et gratae carpentem munera mensae   5
errantemque toris mediae plus tempore noctis
uidimus. affatus etiam meditataque uerba
reddideras. at nunc aeterna silentia Lethes

ille canorus habes. cedat Phaethontia uulgi
fabula: non soli celebrant sua funera cycni.   10
   at tibi quanta domus rutila testudine fulgens
conexusque ebori uirgarum argenteus ordo
argutumque tuo stridentia limina cornu
et querulae iam sponte fores! uacat ille beatus
carcer, et augusti nusquam conuicia tecti.   15
   huc doctae stipentur aues quis nobile fandi
ius natura dedit; plangat Phoebeius ales
auditasque memor penitus demittere uoces
sturnus et Aonio uersae certamine picae
quique refert iungens iterata uocabula perdix   20
et quae Bistonio queritur soror orba cubili.
ferte simul gemitus cognataque ducite flammis
funera, et hoc cunctae miserandum addiscite carmen:
'occidit aeriae celeberrima gloria gentis
psittacus, ille plagae uiridis regnator Eoae,   25
quem non gemmata uolucris Iunonia cauda
uinceret aspectu, gelidi non Phasidis ales
nec quas umenti Numidae rapuere sub austro,
ille salutator regum nomenque locutus
Caesareum et queruli quondam uice functus amici,   30
nunc conuiua leuis monstrataque reddere uerba
tam facilis, quo tu, Melior dilecte, recluso
numquam solus eras. at non inglorius umbris
mittitur: Assyrio cineres adolentur amomo
et tenues Arabum respirant gramine plumae   35
Sicaniisque crocis, senio nec fessus inerti
scandet odoratos phoenix felicior ignes'.

5

QVID tibi monstrata mansuescere profuit ira,
quid scelus humanasque animo dediscere caedes
imperiumque pati et domino parere minori?
quid quod abire domo rursusque in claustra reuerti
suetus et a capta iam sponte recedere praeda   5
insertasque manus laxo dimittere morsu?
occidis, altarum uastator docte ferarum,
non grege Massylo curuaque indagine clausus,

non formidato supra uenabula saltu
incitus aut caeco foueae deceptus hiatu, 10
sed uictus fugiente fera. stat cardine aperto
infelix cauea, et clausis circum undique portis
hoc licuisse nefas placidi tumuere leones.
tum cunctis cecidere iubae, puduitque relatum
aspicere, et totas duxere in lumina frontes. 15
at non te primo fusum nouus obruit ictu
ille pudor: mansere animi, uirtusque cadenti
a media iam morte redit, nec protinus omnes
terga dedere minae. sicut sibi conscius alti
uulneris aduersum moriens it miles in hostem 20
attollitque manum et ferro labente minatur,
sic piger ille gradu solitoque exutus honore
firmat hians oculos animamque hostemque requirit.
magna tamen subiti tecum solacia leti,
uicte, feres, quod te maesti populusque patresque, 25
ceu notus caderes tristi gladiator harena,
ingemuere mori, magni quod Caesaris ora
inter tot Scythicas Libycasque et litore Rheni
et Pharia de gente feras, quas perdere uile est,
unius amissi tetigit iactura leonis. 30

6

SAEVE nimis, lacrimis quisquis discrimina ponis
lugendique modos. miserum est primaeua parenti
pignora surgentesque (nefas!) accendere natos;
durum et deserti praerepta coniuge partem
conclamare tori, maesta et lamenta sororum 5
et fratrum gemitus; alte tamen aut procul intrat
altius in sensus maioraque uulnera uincit
plaga minor. famulum (quia rerum nomina caeca
sic miscet Fortuna manu nec pectora nouit),
sed famulum gemis, Vrse, pium, sed amore fideque 10
has meritum lacrimas, cui maior stemmate cuncto
libertas ex mente fuit. ne comprime fletus,
ne pudeat; rumpat frenos dolor iste, deisque
si tam dura placent * * * *
* * * hominem gemis (ei mihi, subdo

ipse faces), hominem, Vrse, tuum cui dulce uolenti　　　15
seruitium, cui triste nihil, qui sponte sibique
imperiosus erat. quisnam haec in funera missos
castiget luctus? gemit inter bella peremptum
Parthus equum fidosque canes fleuere Molossi
et uolucres habuere rogum ceruusque Maronem.　　　20
quid si nec famulus? uidi ipse habitusque notaui
te tantum cupientis erum; sed maior in ore
spiritus et tenero manifesti in sanguine mores.
optarent multum Graiae cuperentque Latinae
sic peperisse nurus. non talem Cressa superbum　　　25
callida sollicito reuocauit Thesea filo,
nec Paris Oebalios talis uisurus amores
rusticus inuitas deiecit in aequora pinus.
non fallo aut cantus assueta licentia ducit:
uidi et adhuc uideo, qualem nec bella cauentem　　　30
litore uirgineo Thetis occultauit Achillem,
nec circum saeui fugientem moenia Phoebi
Troilon Haemoniae deprendit lancea dextrae.
qualis eras, procul en cunctis puerisque uirisque
pulchrior et tantum domino minor! illius unus　　　35
ante decor, quantum praecedit clara minores
luna faces quantumque alios premit Hesperos ignes.
non tibi femineum uultu decus oraque supra
mollis honos, quales dubiae quos crimina formae
de sexu transire iubent: torua atque uirilis　　　40
gratia nec petulans acies blandique seuero
igne oculi, qualis bellus iam casside uisu
Parthenopaeus erat, simplexque horrore decoro
crinis et obsessae nondum primoque micantes
flore genae; talem Ledaeo gurgite pubem　　　45
educat Eurotas, teneri sic integer aeui
Elin adit primosque Ioui puer approbat annos.
nam pudor ingenuae mentis tranquillaque morum
temperies teneroque animus maturior aeuo
carmine quo patuisse queant? saepe ille uolentem　　　50
castigabat erum studioque altisque iuuabat
consiliis; tecum tristisque hilarisque nec umquam
ille suus, uultumque tuo sumebat ab ore,
dignus et Haemonium Pyladen praecedere fama

Cecropiamque fidem. sed laudum terminus esto 55
quem fortuna sinit: non mente fidelior aegra
sperauit tardi reditus Eumaeus Vlixis.
  quis deus aut quisnam tam tristia uulnera casus
eligit? unde manus Fatis tam certa nocendi?
o quam diuitiis censuque exutus opimo 60
fortior, Vrse, fores! si uel fumante ruina
ructassent dites Vesuuina incendia Locroe
seu Pollentinos mersissent flumina saltus
seu Lucanus Acir seu Thybridis impetus altas
in dextrum torsisset aquas, paterere serena 65
fronte deos, siue alma fidem messesque negasset
Cretaque Cyreneque et qua tibi cumque beato
larga redit Fortuna sinu. sed gnara dolorum
Inuidia infelix animi uitalia uidit
laedendique uias. uitae modo margine adultae; 70
nectere temptabat iuuenum pulcherrimus ille
cum tribus Eleis unam trieterida lustris.
attendit toruo tristis Rhamnusia uultu
ac primum impleuitque toros oculisque nitorem
addidit ac solito sublimius ora leuauit, 75
heu misero letale fauens, seseque uidendo
torsit et inuidit, mortisque amplexa iacenti
iniecit nexus carpsitque immitis adunca
ora uerenda manu. quinto uix Phosphoros ortu
rorantem sternebat equum: iam litora duri 80
saeua, Philete, senis dirumque Acheronta uidebas,
quo domini clamate sono! non saeuius atros
nigrasset planctu genetrix tibi salua lacertos
nec pater, et certe qui uidit funera frater
erubuit uinci. sed nec seruilis adempto 85
ignis: odoriferos exhausit flamma Sabaeos
et Cilicum messes Phariaeque exempta uolucri
cinnama et Assyrio manantes gramine sucos
et domini fletus; hos tantum hausere fauillae,
hos bibit usque rogus; nec quod tibi Setia canos 90
restinxit cineres, gremio nec lubricus ossa
quod uallauit onyx, miseris acceptius umbris
quam gemitus. sed et ipse uetat. quid terga dolori,
Vrse, damus? quid damna foues et pectore iniquo

uulnus amas? ubi nota reis facundia raptis? 95
quid caram crucias tam saeuis luctibus umbram?
eximius licet ille animi meritusque doleri,
soluisti. subit ille pios carpitque quietem
Elysiam clarosque illic fortasse parentes
inuenit, aut illi per amoena silentia Lethes 100
forsan Auernales alludunt undique mixtae
Naides, obliquoque notat Proserpina uultu.
pone, precor, questus; alium tibi Fata Phileton,
forsan et ipse dabis, moresque habitusque decoros
monstrabis gaudens similemque docebis amorem. 105

7

Lvcani proprium diem frequentet
quisquis collibus Isthmiae Diones
docto pectora concitatus oestro
pendentis bibit ungulae liquorem.
ipsi quos penes est honor canendi, 5
uocalis citharae repertor Arcas
et tu, Bassaridum rotator Euhan,
et Paean et Hyantiae sorores,
laetae purpureas nouate uittas,
crinem comite, candidamque uestem 10
perfundant hederae recentiores.
docti largius euagentur amnes
et plus, Aoniae, uirete, siluae,
et, si qua patet aut diem recepit,
sertis mollibus expleatur umbra. 15
centum Thespiacis odora lucis
stent altaria uictimaeque centum
quas Dirce lauat aut alit Cithaeron.
Lucanum canimus, fauete linguis;
uestra est ista dies, fauete, Musae, 20
dum qui uos geminas tulit per artes,
et uinctae pede uocis et solutae,
Romani colitur chori sacerdos.
   felix heu nimis et beata tellus,
quae pronos Hyperionis meatus 25
summis Oceani uides in undis

stridoremque rotae cadentis audis;
quae Tritonide fertiles Athenas
unctis, Baetica, prouocas trapetis:
Lucanum potes imputare terris.   30
hoc plus quam Senecam dedisse mundo
aut dulcem generasse Gallionem.
attollat refluos in astra fontes
Graio nobilior Melete Baetis;
Baetim, Mantua, prouocare noli.   35
    natum protinus atque humum per ipsam
primo murmure dulce uagientem
blando Calliope sinu recepit.
tum primum posito remissa luctu
longos Orpheos exuit dolores   40
et dixit: 'puer o dicate Musis,
longaeuos cito transiture uates,
non tu flumina nec greges ferarum
nec plectro Geticas mouebis ornos,
sed septem iuga Martiumque Thybrim   45
et doctos equites et eloquente
cantu purpureum trahes senatum.
nocturnas alii Phrygum ruinas
et tardi reduces uias Vlixis
et puppem temerariam Mineruae   50
trita uatibus orbita sequantur:
tu carus Latio memorque gentis
carmen fortior exseres togatum.
ac primum teneris adhuc in annis
ludes Hectora Thessalosque currus   55
et supplex Priami potentis aurum,
et sedes reserabis inferorum;
ingratus Nero dulcibus theatris
et noster tibi proferetur Orpheus.
dices culminibus Remi uagantes   60
infandos domini nocentis ignes.
hinc castae titulum decusque Pollae
iucunda dabis allocutione.
mox coepta generosior iuuenta
albos ossibus Italis Philippos   65
et Pharsalica bella detonabis,

quo fulmen ducis inter arma diui
     * * * * *
libertate grauem pia Catonem
et gratum popularitate Magnum.
tu Pelusiaci scelus Canopi   70
deflebis pius et Pharo cruenta
Pompeio dabis altius sepulchrum.
haec primo iuuenis canes sub aeuo
ante annos Culicis Maroniani.
cedet Musa rudis ferocis Enni   75
et docti furor arduus Lucreti
et qui per freta duxit Argonautas
et qui corpora prima transfigurat.
quid maius loquar? ipsa te Latinis
Aeneis uenerabitur canentem.   80
   nec solum dabo carminum nitorem
sed taedis genialibus dicabo
doctam atque ingenio tuo decoram,
qualem blanda Venus daretque Iuno
forma, simplicitate, comitate,   85
censu, sanguine, gratia, decore,
et uestros hymenaeon ante postes
festis cantibus ipsa personabo.
   o saeuae nimium grauesque Parcae!
o numquam data longa fata summis!   90
cur plus, ardua, casibus patetis?
cur saeua uice magna non senescunt?
sic natum Nasamonii Tonantis
post ortus obitusque fulminatos
angusto Babylon premit sepulchro;   95
sic fixum Paridis manu trementis
Peliden Thetis horruit cadentem;
sic ripis ego murmurantis Hebri
non mutum caput Orpheos sequebar.
sic et tu, rabidi nefas tyranni,   100
iussus praecipitem subire Lethen,
dum pugnas canis arduaque uoce
das solacia grandibus sepulchris,
(o dirum scelus, o scelus!) tacebis.'
   sic fata est leuiterque decidentes   105

abrasit lacrimas nitente plectro.
    at tu, seu rapidum poli per axem
famae curribus arduis leuatus,
qua surgunt animae potentiores,
terras despicis et sepulchra rides;   110
seu pacis merito nemus reclusi
felix Elysii tenes in oris,
quo Pharsalica turba congregatur,
et te nobile carmen insonantem
Pompei comitantur et Catones   115
(tu magna sacer et superbus umbra
nescis Tartaron et procul nocentum
audis uerbera pallidumque uisa
matris lampade respicis Neronem);
adsis lucidus et uocante Polla   120
unum, quaeso, diem deos silentum
exores: solet hoc patere limen
ad nuptas redeuntibus maritis.
haec te non thiasis procax dolosis
falsi numinis induit figura,   125
ipsum sed colit et frequentat ipsum
imis altius insitum medullis;
at solacia uana subministrat
uultus, qui simili notatus auro
stratis praenitet incubatque somno   130
securae. procul hinc abite, Mortes:
haec uitae genitalis est origo.
cedat luctus atrox genisque manent
iam dulces lacrimae, dolorque festus
quicquid fleuerat ante, nunc adoret.   135

COMMENTARY

Preface to book 2

Epistolary prose prefaces were a Hellenistic development, beginning possibly with the letters that Archimedes attached to most of his scientific works (Janson 1964: 19–21). Parthenius' prose Ἐρωτικὰ παθήματα provides the first extant epistolary preface attached to a non-scientific work; by honouring the poet Gallus as dedicatee, it thus promotes the value of the book (Lightfoot 222–4). The practice of putting an epistolary prose preface at the start of a Roman *poetry* book seems however to have been a Flavian innovation (Janson 1964: 107–12). Martial does this selectively (books 1, 2, 8, 9, 12), St. with all four books of the *Siluae* published in his lifetime; the posthumous book 5 has a prefatory letter for 5.1 only. The preface to book 2 is in the conventional form of a letter to the dedicatee (cf. 4 *epistula*), with a salutary phrase at the start (*Statius Meliori suo salutem*); the prefaces for books 3 and 4 have both opening salutation and concluding *uale*.

This preface dedicates the book to Atedius Melior, who receives the presentation copy. The preface has many functions beyond summarising the book's contents (thus Van Dam 55): it honours Melior and publicly affirms his friendship with St.; it also honours the addressees of the individual poems and, in keeping with the book's generally domestic character, it emphasises their emotional ties with St. (Johannsen 2006: 268–71). Through the preface St. enters a contractual relationship with his dedicatee and his public: Melior's acceptance of the new work guarantees its value to the wider readership and compliments those who can help to promote it (cf. Plin. *Nat. pr.* 6–11).

The preface also provides a guard against the vagaries of transmission: it names the addressees; it fixes the order and number of the poems, presenting them as a carefully arranged poetry book; this strategic 'table of contents' also offers a broader narrative structure for the book and invites readers to consider the thematic and aesthetic relationships between the poems. The preface thus provides an interpretive as well as expository guide to the poetry book, offering comment on the poet's artistic practices in the *Siluae* and defending, for instance, their speed and improvisational character. (Mart. 2 *pr.* 4–5 claims his prefaces derive from the polemical prologues of Roman drama.) Improvisation thus is offset by collection for publication (cf. 1 *pr.* 4–5 *singuli de sinu meo . . . congregatos ipse | dimitterem*). The dedicatory preface gives the poetry a seriousness that belies St.'s reference to the *Siluae* as *opuscula* (3). As an epistle, the preface mediates between the private and public worlds, the poet's time and posterity. It confers immortality on both the poet and his honorand.

Further reading: on the conventions of the Latin prose preface see Janson 1964; on the prose prefaces of St. see Coleman on *Silu.* 4 pp. 53–5; Newlands 2002:

32–6; 2009; on those of Martial and St. see Johannsen 2006; on those of St. and Pliny see Pagán 2009.

1–4 Although an epistle is often an intimate conversational prose form, the opening period is elegant and formal as befits a dedication. The compound subject, *familiaritas nostra . . . | et ipsa opusculorum . . . condicio*, each part modified by a relative clause (*qua gaudeo, quae tibi trado*), is separated by a lengthy apostrophe to Melior. On the formal style of St.'s prefaces see Van Dam 54.

1 familiaritas nostra: *nostra* suggests a mutual regard. The language of 'friendship' helps erase social distinctions between poet and patron (White 1978: 78–82).   **Melior, uir optime:** an irresistible pun on Atedius Melior's *cognomen*; cf. 2.3.70; Mart. 8.38.7 (*bonus*). *optimus* often suggests moral excellence. St. puns on the names of all his addressees (2.2.23n., 2.6.10n., 2.7.1n.; Nisbet 1995b), often towards the start.

2–3 in iudicio litterarum . . . tersissime 'very sophisticated in your literary taste'. *tersus* often describes refinement of literary style (*OLD* 3), rarely of persons; cf. Quint. *Inst.* 10.1.94 *est tersior ac purus magis Horatius*. St. promotes book 2 by presenting Melior as the ideal reader of the *Siluae*, a literary connoisseur. St.'s dedicatees are discriminating men of letters: Stella is a poet (1.2.256–9); Pollius Felix is a poet and critic (2.2.112–20, 3 *pr.* 1–7); Vibius Maximus supported the publication of the *Thebaid* (4.7.25–8).

2 in omni uitae colore 'in every style of life'; cf. Hor. *S.* 2.1.60 *quisquis erit uitae scribam color*; also *Ars* 86, 236. The allusion perhaps suggests the affinity of the *Siluae* with satire and 'minor poetry'. 'Colour' suits the splendour of Melior's life (cf. Mart. 4.54 *nitido . . . Meliore*); as a common rhetorical term for brilliant embellishment (*TLL* III 1720.43–72; Ov. *Pont.* 4.13.3–4 *color huc . . . | et structura mei carminis*), *color* also suggests St.'s skill in the poetic 'colouring' of his patrons.

3 et ipsa opusculorum . . . condicio 'and the very character of my little works' (*OLD condicio* 8). The use of diminutives to refer to one's work is a form of modesty conventional in prefaces (Janson 1964: 145); cf. 1 *pr.* 1–15. Its effect (cf. 4 *pr.* 3 *opusculum*) is offset by the distinction of the work's recipient.   **quae tibi trado:** given the formal letter and careful arrangement of the collected poems, St. presumably is not handing over a draft for Melior's comments but rather the first published copy as part of the dedication; cf. Cat. 1.   **sic posita est** 'is of such a type' (that . . .) (*OLD pono* 12a).

4 ut totus hic ad te liber meus . . . spectet: a result clause often taken as suggesting that Melior provides a unifying structure for the book. But since only three of the seven poems are addressed to Melior, such a claim cannot be sustained (Bright 1980: 58). Hardie 1983: 66–7 proposes that Melior's poems 'set the tone' of the new book – genial and apolitical; it also suits Melior's cultural interests. The title *Siluae* is not used until 3 *pr.* 7 and again at 4 *pr.* 25.

4–12 St. begins a summary of each of the poems in order, naming the individual recipients. 2.1 is given most attention as the first and longest poem in the collection (234 lines), written moreover for Melior on the premature death of his foster son Glaucias.

4 primum: either an adjective referring to *opusculorum* (3), thus 'the first poem', or an adverb 'in the first place', with *liber* understood as the subject of *habet*.

5 Glauciam nostrum: i.e. the poem on Glaucias. 'Our' suggests the close relationship between Melior and St., united in their affection for Glaucias (1n.).   **cuius gratissima infantia** 'whose infancy most pleasing [to us]'; the text may be corrupt (6–7n.). *infantia*, lit. the state of 'not speaking', conveys pathos, for Glaucias was well beyond infancy. The Romans had no special word for 'baby'; *infans* was often used loosely to refer to a young child with or without the ability to speak (Dixon 1992: 104).

5–6 et qualem plerumque infelices sortiuntur 'and such as generally the ill-fated have as their lot', a parenthetical reference to the topos that those who die prematurely are the most pleasing to us. *infelix* is often applied to children or adolescents who died young and thus were seen as esp. 'ill-fated' (*OLD* 3).

6–7 †apud te complexus amabam iam non tibi†: St., while staying with Melior, came to love Glaucias also. But it is unclear whether *complexus* is a noun (acc. pl.) or participle (nom. sing.); if the latter, *eum* understood could supply the object for both *complexus* and *amabam*; *gratissima infantia* (5) however would still be without a verb and an obvious connection to the rest of the sentence. *iam non tibi* is also problematic. There may be a lacuna in the text after *amabam*; but the ending of a colon with the heroic clausula (as at the end of hexameter verse) is highly unusual in epistles (Quint. *Inst.* 9.4.75). SB (Appendix p. 388) suggests (1) adopting at line 5 Calderini's emendation *gratissimam infantiam* as the object of participial *complexus*; (2) integrating the obscure *iam non tibi* with *amabam*. But his translation 'whose charming infancy . . . I took in my arms in my home and loved, no longer just for your sake', is strained; *infantia* in the sense of 'infant' is highly unusual. The colon should be obelised.

7–12 An apology for the haste in writing the poem almost immediately upon Glaucias' death – a sign that the poem was St.'s own initiative. He highlights a leitmotiv of his 'Silvan' poetics, speed of composition (8n., 8–9n., 10n.). He glosses over the much later *publication* of the poem, probably by two years (introd. to 2.1; Henderson 1998: 102–7).

7 recens uulnus: a 'wound' is a frequent metaphor for the pain of bereavement (2.1.3–4n.). *recens* 'fresh' suggests St.'s promptness in writing a consolatory poem.

8 epicedio: St. introduces this Greek word to Latin literature, using it only here to suggest the polish, learning and innovation that he brings to this literary form in its adaptation to Roman culture. Strictly speaking the *epicedion* was a song performed before the cremation or burial of the corpse; cf. Serv. *Ecl.* 5.14 *nam epicedion est, quod dicitur cadauere nondum sepulto, ut extinctum nymphae crudeli funere Daphnin; epitaphion autem post completam sepulturam dicitur, ut Daphnis ego in siluis hinc usque ad sidera notus. epicedion* is used slightly loosely of 2.1, which is set at the ashes of the funeral pyre, just after the cremation therefore (2.1.1–3). But as a literary form the *epicedion* soon acquired greater flexibility and came to mean a funeral panegyric in verse (Durry xxx–xxxi).   **festinanter:** cf. 1 *pr.* 2–4 *hos libellos qui . . . quadam festinandi uoluptate fluxerunt.*

8–9 excusandam habuerim affectibus tuis celeritatem 'I thought I owed your feelings an apology for my speed of composition'; *habere* takes the predicative gerundive (*OLD* 17); for *excusare* in the sense of 'apologise' cf. Mart. 1 *pr.* 10 *lasciuam uerborum ueritatem, id est epigrammaton linguam, excusarem, si meum esset exemplum; TLL* v.2 1303.14–59. St. went against the general wisdom that some delay in composition of a *consolatio* was generally more beneficial for the bereaved (11–12n.). *celeritas* occurs only in prose, which gave St. access to a semi-technical vocabulary metrically impossible in verse; cf. 1 *pr.* 11–14 *sed apud ceteros necesse est multum illis pereat ex uenia, cum amiserint quam solam habuerunt gratiam celeritatis.* Quint. *Inst.* 10.3.17 condemns *silua* (a literary draft) for speed of composition. But *celeritas* also connotes literary fluency (*OLD* 2c), a necessary attribute of the orator; cf. Quint. *Inst.* 4.107, 12.10.65.

9–10 eam . . . iacto: sc. *celeritatem*; St. has no need to 'air' (*OLD iacto* 10b) his distinctively swift style among his friends.

10 qui nosti: i.e. *qui scis quam celeriter scripserim*; cf. 7 *ut scis.*   **sed et ceteris indico:** St. writes not for Melior alone but for a wider public.   **asperiore lima:** the file for smoothing the rough side of a book roll is a neoteric figure for careful revision of a literary work; cf. Hor. *Ars* 291 *limae labor*, with Brink; Coleman on 4.7.26 *Thebais multa cruciata lima.* Paradoxically this file is 'rather rough', for the metaphor unusually refers to the reader's, not the writer's, critical acumen; cf. Mart. 5.80.13–14 *censoria . . . | lima.* St. fears a harsh critic (*OLD asper* 12b).

11 carmen . . . et a confuso scriptum et dolenti datum 'a poem . . . both written by a man troubled with grief and given to one in mourning'. An elegantly balanced colon structured by *et . . . et* with alliteration and assonance; *confuso*, connoting a person troubled in mind, is virtually synonymous with *dolenti*. St. suggests that he did not revise the poem for publication but that it reflects the immediacy of grief; the swift response is a virtue in consolation as well as in style. Such statements should not necessarily be taken at face value; in his prefaces St. articulates a rhetoric of 'occasionality' that draws attention to his skill in recreating the past moment.   **examinet** 'should criticise' (*OLD* 4).

11–12 cum paene superuacua sint tarda solacia: a claim contrary to Stoic belief that consolation is effective only *after* a period of time, such as a year; cf. Sen. *Dial.* 12.1.2 *dolori tuo dum recens saeuiret sciebam ocurrendum non esse, ne illum ipsa solacia irritarent et accenderent, nam in morbis quoque nihil est perniciosius quam immatura medicina*; Cic. *Tusc.* 3.76; Sen. *Ep.* 99.1; Kassel 1958: 23. Yet 2.1 was published around two years after Glaucias' death, and 5.1 was written at least a year after Priscilla's death (Gibson on 5.1.16). 2.1 provides an instance of how poems change in meaning and function after collection and publication (introd. to 2.1). Hor. *Carm.* 2.20.24 introduced *superuacuus* to poetry, with reference to the futility of funerary monuments; St. may acknowledge, like Horace, the more lasting importance of a literary memorial.

12–14 2.2 on the villa of Pollius Felix at Sorrento on the Bay of Naples. St. apologises again for his haste in writing, without here explaining the circumstances.

12 Polli mei: the affectionate possessive acknowledges Pollius as a close friend (14 *amicus*) of St. in particular, not of Melior; cf. 18 *Vrsum . . . nostrum*.

13 quae sequitur: such statements (cf. 4 *primum*) underline the importance to the author of preserving the order of the poems in the collection.   **uel in honorem eloquentiae eius** 'if only in honour of his eloquence' (*OLD uel* 6); cf. 2.2.9 *placidi facundia Polli*. Pollius too wrote poetry (2.2.112–20); in complimenting Pollius' literary skills, St. confirms his good taste in accepting his poem.

14–18 The three shortest poems are grouped together: 2.3, 2.4, 2.5.

14–15 in arborem . . . tuam . . . et psittacum 'upon your tree and upon the parrot'.

15 leues libellos: St. uses the term *libellus* consistently to mean a single poem (1 *pr.* 2, 16, 27; 3 *pr.* 2, 11, 23); *liber* refers to the individual book as at line 4 (cf. also 2 *pr.* 21; 3. *pr.* 7; 4 *pr.* 1, 3–4, 34). White's 1974 claim that *libelli* are relatively unpolished, unpublished drafts was countered by Fowler 1995 on the grounds that *libellus* does not necessarily connote lack of careful composition (cf. Cat. 1.1 *lepidum nouum libellum*); at work is the topos of modesty. *leuis* is a programmatic term for non-epic poetry; cf. Mart. 7.8.9 (on his epigrams) *iocos leuioraque carmina*; N–H on Hor. *Carm.* 2.1.40.

15–16 quasi epigrammatis loco scriptos 'written as it were like epigram'; *loco* with gen. suggests manner (*OLD* 18c). The poems are short, witty and influenced by funerary and amphitheatrical epigram. St. perhaps implicitly challenges Martial in this genre. But he appropriates 'epigram' in his own way, using the hexameter, not the elegiacs traditional to epigram, and exceeding epigrammatic brevity.

16 stili facilitatem: ease or fluency of style is a virtue both of mature oratory (Quint. *Inst.* 10.1.111) and of swift, improvisational verse (Quint. *Inst.* 10.7.18).

17–18 quem in amphitheatro prostratum frigidum erat sacratissimo imperatori ni statim tradere 'whom it would have been flat to hand over to our most sacred emperor if not immediately, when the lion lay flat out in the amphitheatre'. St. claims the poem was written and delivered to the emperor on the spot. *quem* blurs the division between the lion and the poem about the lion. Imperf. indicative *erat* is used in the apodosis of an unreal conditional clause to indicate action that was foiled or interrupted by the event stated in the negative protasis, here *ni statim* [*tradidissem*]. See *NLS* 200; the verb of the protasis is omitted as in Greek (*ni statim* = εἰ μὴ αὐτίκα); Smyth 2345–6.

17 prostratum frigidum: cf. Mart. *Sp.* 8.1 *prostratum . . . leonem*, with Coleman: *prostratum* conveys 'the sprawling inertness of the corpse'. Its juxtaposition with *frigidum* puns on the latter's dual meaning of 'physically cold' (*OLD* 6) and 'dead and flat' of style (8b), in contrast to a key virtue of the *Siluae*, *calor* (1 *pr. 3 subito calore*). The poem was written quickly while the lion was still warm – hot material for a poem; the poet's art will wittily 'reanimate' the lion.   **sacratissimo**: cf. 1 *pr.* 16 (of Domitian) *primus libellus sacrosanctum habet testem. sacratus* of the emperor is Ovidian, suggesting veneration for Augustus in the context of the developing imperial cult (Börner on Ov. *Fast.* 2.60); St. first uses the superlative form, suggesting Domitian's closeness to divinity (Coleman on 4 *pr.* 6). Although an emperor at Rome could not claim divine status while alive, from the time of Augustus there were cults of the living emperor in Italy and in the provinces; these were promoted by Vespasian, seeking legitimacy for his new dynasty (Price 1987: 84–5; Fishwick 1987: 295–300; Ando 2003). Domitian esp. cultivated the idea of Flavian divinity through deification of family members; cf. 1.1.74 *magnorum proles genitorque deum* (Scott 1936: 61–82; Sauter 1934:105–16; Clauss 1999: 119–32; Newlands 2002: 11–13).

18 tradere: as at 3 *tradere* refers to a formal presentation. St. says nothing about Domitian's reaction to the gift of the poem, a gift now transferred to Melior.

18–22 2.6 on the premature death of the young slave of Flavius Ursus.

18 Vrsum quoque nostrum: cf. 1 *familiaritas nostra*; the personal pronoun suggests Ursus too was Melior's friend, though not perhaps a close one (21–2n.). Although Ursus was a regular Roman *cognomen*, his poem, following directly upon one about a lion – with the bear the stock large animal of the amphitheatre – seems to be wittily placed.

19 iuuenem candidissimum: *candidus* has a range of meanings and here probably suggests Ursus' youthful beauty (*OLD* 5; cf. 2.6.34–7), good fortune (*OLD* 7; cf. 2.6.60–8), and moral probity (*OLD* 8). He is the only young man among the addressees.   **sine iactura desidiae doctissimum** 'a most learned young man who does not waste his leisure time'. Ursus was not retired like Melior and Pollius but had a career, probably in law (2.6.95n.). In his free time, St. implies, he pursues literary interests.

20 consolationem 'a poem of consolation', first at Cic. *Tusc.* 1.65–6, 76, with reference to his poem on his daughter's death. The Latin *consolatio* distinguishes 2.6 from 2.1 which, delivered at the pyre, is more properly an *epicedion* (8n.).

20–1 super ea quae ipsi debeo: St. paid one of his unspecified debts to Ursus by including the consolatory poem in book 2: Ursus will acquire prestige from the appearance of his poem in the latest book by a fashionable author. Financial language, in particular the discharging and payment of debts, becomes prominent towards the end of the preface (21–2n., 24n.). Such language had ethical connotations, implying socially beneficial behaviour; St. seeks not a cash advance but strengthened friendship ties that will promote his poetry and support his career. On Roman 'economic morality' in general see Roller 2001: 131–3; in St. see Coffee 2006, esp. 421–7.

21 huic libro . . . inserui: cf. 4 *pr.* 22–3 *huic uolumini inserui*, with Coleman; *insero* is a quasi-technical term for including material in a literary work.

21–2 honorem eius tibi laturus accepto est 'he will credit the prestige gained from his poem to you [i.e. Melior]'. The relationship between Melior and Ursus is also described in economic terms: *accepto ferre* means 'to credit someone with'. Ursus will be pleased at the additional prominence gained by appearing in a book dedicated to Melior, but he thus will be in Melior's debt (as well as St.'s); see Nauta 2002: 242–3.

22–6 2.7, an encomiastic birthday poem written for Polla in honour of her deceased husband, the poet Lucan, the only prominent historical figure in the book.

22 uolumen: the book roll containing *Siluae* 2; cf. 4. *pr.* 22–3.   **genethlia-con:** sc. *carmen* 'a birthday poem'; the Greek adjective occurs only here in Roman literature. The Greek titles *epicedion* and *genethliacon* frame book 2, suggesting the poet's philhellenism.

23 Polla Argentaria: Lucan's widow.   **rarissima uxorum:** cf. Prop.1.8.42 *Cynthia rara mea est!* – a poem that, like 2.7, honours enduring love but, by contrast with 2.7, within the ephemeral elegiac context.

23–4 cum hunc diem forte †consuleremus†: a vague reference to Polla's part in the origin of the poem; unlike 2.1, it seems, 2.7 was planned in advance, probably for delivery on Lucan's birthday anniversary (*hunc diem*), and then included in the poetry book. Ordinarily *consulo* with acc. means 'consult' (typically a person) not 'consult about' which makes however better sense here. White 1975: 281–3 proposed Skutsch's emendation *coleremus*: St. was celebrating Lucan's birthday with Polla when she asked him on the spot for a poem. *forte* however, which must be taken with the verb, in that case is problematic: commemoration of the deceased's birthday was never a 'chance' event, and on such a ritual, planned occasion Polla's wish for a poem is unlikely to have been 'by chance' or on the spot. *forte* suggests the element of spontaneity associated with the composition of improvisational, occasional poetry. Mozley's somewhat loose 'when we happened to be considering the celebration of the day' conveys the probable sense.

24 imputari sibi uoluit 'she wished [the poem] to be charged to her': *imputare*, a bookkeeping term (cf. 4 *pr.* 15, with Coleman; Mart. 5. 80.2), perhaps puns on the name Polla *Argentaria* (Nisbet 1995b). As at 22 (*laturus accepto*) the verb implies a reciprocal debt towards St.: Polla's involvement in St.'s poem paid dividends in the renown that she (and Lucan) gained, while he expects of her, as perhaps his most prominent addressee, promotion of his poetry. Nauta 2002: 244–8 argues that this is one of only three instances (also 1.2 and 3.4) where St. suggests that the patron commissioned the poem; see also Hardie 1983: 70. But *uoluit* implies only that Polla wished prestige from the poem; her degree of involvement in its composition or publication is unknown. The financial language need not imply that actual payment was involved; the poem created a 'moral debt' (White 1975: 282). See 20–1n.

25–6 laudes eius dicturus hexametros meos timui: a variation in prose of the poetic *recusatio*; about to write Lucan's praise in hexameters, the poet changed metre (to hendecasyllables). The acc. with *timui* in the sense 'I feared' rather than 'I feared for' (cf. 1 *pr.* 6–7 *pro Thebaide mea . . . timeo*) rules out the sense that his hexameters would not meet Lucan's standards. On the other hand Gibson's (on *Silu.* 5 p. xxi) suggestion that St. fears his hexameters might surpass Lucan's is contrary to the encomiastic context; *timui* is linked with the fear inherent in *reuerentiam* (25). St. perhaps rather suggests that the magnitude of composing an encomium on Lucan would have made his hexameters, had he written in that metre, so powerful as to be in the wrong register for the *Siluae* and thus to be feared as violating the book's decorum. Martial's epigrams on Lucan's birthday (7.21, 22, 23) likewise avoid the hexameter, opting for elegiacs. Hendecasyllables were a popular metre in the Flavian period; first associated with scurrilous verse, they came to encompass a wide range of themes (Plin. *Ep.* 4.4.3–4) and were not without prestige.

27–8 haec qualiacumque sunt . . . reuertantur: St. politely implies that the decision for publication is up to Melior; cf. 4 *pr.* 34–5 *hunc tamen librum tu, Marcelle, defendes, si uidetur, hactenus sin minus, reprehendemur.* As part of his strategy of modesty, he transfers some of the responsibility for the work's success to Melior (Janson 1964: 106–8, 141–2). *haec* emphasises book 2 as a distinct unit.

27 Melior carissime: cf. 4 *pr.* 1 *Marcelle carissime.* The brevity of the address (cf. the effusiveness of 1–3) signals the conclusion of the dedication.

28 publicum 'public notice'. St. asks Melior for a boost to his poetry book by bringing it to public attention through personal endorsement. Unlike Martial, St. in his dedicatory epistles emphasises publication, the defining moment in the occasional poet's relationship with his public (White 1974: 56–61). On the mechanics of publication in the Roman world see Small 1997: 26–40. **si minus** 'if not'; i.e. *at si displicuerint*; cf. *4 pr.* 35 *sin minus*, with Coleman ('an urbanely mild negative'). *si minus* occurs with two conditional clauses when the verb is to be supplied from the context (L–H–S 454–5). **reuertantur:** return implies failure and the wrong sort of exchange – unlikely in a social and literary context in which St.'s patrons have clearly incurred the poet's debt.

Siluae 2.1

This first poem takes a theme integral to St.'s epics, premature death; St. consoles Melior for the death of his young foster son Glaucias. Mart. 6.28 and 6.29 also commemorate Glaucias' death. Since Martial's book 6 was published in 90 CE, Grewing on Mart. 6 pp. 210–1 assigns the date of composition of 2.1 to late 89 CE/early 90 CE. But the first collection of *Siluae* was not published before 92 CE, thus at least two years after the child's death. 2.1 avoids the question of the effectiveness of the occasional poem, esp. since St. claims it was written quickly to console Melior while his pain was still raw (2 *pr.* 7–12); cf. Ov. *Pont.* 4.11.17–18 *temporis officium est solacia dicere certi, | dum dolor in cursu est et petit aeger opem.* Inevitably a poem loses some of its immediacy when published in a collection, yet it assumes new functions as a vivid, enduring memorial of Glaucias and as a gift of friendship to Melior; as the first poem of book 2 it also has a programmatic function in its bold adaptation of elegiac themes to hexameter poetry. Antiquity offers few literary parallels for commemorating the death of a child; Glaucias moreover was of low status, the son of freed slaves (introd. 10–11). In contrast to book 1, which has no consolatory poems and begins and ends with poems to the emperor, 2.1 thematically establishes the importance of Roman family life and of the private cult of memory in Roman culture; it challenges the Roman gendered approach to grief as unmanly; and it provides rare, charming descriptions of a child's life which support recent research on the Roman family (e.g. Rawson 2003) demonstrating a new sentimentality towards children in the imperial era. Finally it offers insight into fosterage, a sparsely documented aspect of Roman family relationships which was characterised by close emotional bonds. The poem reflects contemporary Roman thought on the social assets acquired through education and loving fosterage rather than innate nobility; see Bernstein 2008, esp. 106–9.

Literary allusions offer a variety of perspectives on premature death. The solemn theme and elevated style are mediated by the poet's emphasis on his love for Melior and Glaucias, which complements the poem's promotion of emotional over blood ties. St. shares Melior's grief; the poem is part self-consolation. The poem too is full of Lucretian echoes, as St. engages with that great Roman poem about death and counters to some extent its Epicurean message of detachment.

Further reading: on the tradition of poetic consolation Gibson on *Silu.* 5 pp. xxxi–l. On foster children Nielsen 1987, 1997, 1999; Rawson 2003: 251–5. On 2.1 Vessey 1986: 2765–84; Bernstein 2005; Zeiner 2005: 160–71; Rühl 2006: 288–9.

1–18 St. creates a fiction of raw immediacy; he stands with Melior before the still smoking funeral pyre. The poet's claim of participation in the funeral is conventional but gives authenticity to his poem (cf. *Epic. Drusi* 85, 202) and here suggests St.'s close friendship with Melior (cf. *2 pr. 1 familiaritas nostra*). Although philosophical tradition counselled against extravagance in mourning, weeping and other physical expressions of grief were expected at the funeral (Sen. *Ep.* 99.15–16).

1–3 quod tibi . . . solamen . . . | ordiar? 'what consolation shall I begin for you?' The opening question is despairing in tone, solemn and formal in diction; cf. Hor. *Carm.* 1.24.1–2 *quis desiderio sit pudor aut modus | tam cari capitis? solamen* is an elevated poetic noun coined by Virgil (Harrison on Virg. *A.* 10.493–4). *ordiri*, here highlighted by enjambment and a following sense-pause, is a formal verb for the start of a (usually prose) literary work (*OLD* 2b); cf. Sil. 1.1 *ordior arma*, with Feeney 1982. A series of sympathetic rhetorical questions to Melior punctuate the poem (Rühl 2006: 288).

1 Melior: St. honours his patron by naming him in the centre of the first line. By contrast Glaucias, like the slave Philetos at 2.6.81, is not named until the poem's end; see 229n.   **praerepti . . . alumni:** *rapere* is a common metaphor for death's rapacity (*OLD* 5; Brelich 1937: 20; Lattimore 1962: 153–4); cf. *Epic. Drusi* 372 *illa* [*Fortuna*] *rapit iuuenes*. But *praereptus* is rare in the required sense of 'snatched away before his time' and is possibly St.'s innovation (*OLD* 1c; Vessey 1986: 2766); cf. 2.6.4 *praerepta coniuge. alumnus* is a precise term for a 'foster child'; Mart. 6.28.1 more formally refers to Glaucias as *libertus*. As it carries emotional weight, *alumnus* often appears in St. at line end; cf. *Theb.* 5.501 (of Opheltes); Micozzi on *Theb.* 4.148–9.

2 improbus: a surprising adjective emphasised by enjambment; cf. (in the same metrical position) Virg. *G.* 1.145–6 *labor omnia uincit | improbus.* Here it means 'presumptuous' (SB) rather than 'relentless' (Van Dam) or 'heartless(ly)' (Mozley), for the attempt at consolation, while the child's ashes are still warm, is premature. St. is fond of *improbus* in a wide range of meanings (Dilke on *Ach.* 1.41).   **rogos:** pl. for sing. as commonly in St.   **adhuc uiuente fauilla** 'as the embers still smoulder'; cf. Ov. *Fast.* 4.553 *uiuente fauilla*, of Ceres' failed attempt to immortalise Triptolemus by placing him in the fire (Ov. *Fast.* 4.503–62). The story is part of the myth of Prosperpina (*Fast.* 4.417–618); the allusion thus provides a double narrative reminder of the powerlessness of even the gods when confronted by death. But the paradoxical juxtaposition of *fauilla* with *uiuente* hints at the life that the poet can potentially bring to the dead. Sing. *fauilla* for 'embers' or collective 'ash' is conventional (Bömer on Ov. *Fast.* 2.523). The poem's dramatic setting confirms its definition as an *epicedion*, a poem delivered at the pyre (2. *pr.* 8n.).

3–4 abruptis etiamnunc flebile uenis | uulnus hiat magnaeque patet uia lubrica plagae 'with the arteries slit the wound, still weeping, gapes, and the slippery passage of the huge gash lies open', a graphic use of the conventional medical imagery of grief (Gibson on 5.1.30).

3 abruptis . . . uenis: *uenas abrumpere* describes a common means of suicide, slitting the arteries (Van Dam; *uena* means either 'vein' or 'artery'); cf. Tac. *Ann.* 15.63.6 *Seneca . . . crurum quoque et poplitum uenas abrumpit*; *Ann.* 6.29.1, 15.59.5, 16.9.2. The arteries were regarded as the seat of deep emotion (Pease on Virg. *A.* 4.2). Melior is metaphorically 'killing himself' with grief.   **flebile** stresses that the wound is still moist and thus not yet healed. In this sense of 'weeping' *flebilis* normally applies only to persons (*OLD* 4; *Theb.* 6.245 *flebilis infans*); but cf. Sen. *Ag.* 395 *stat nunc Sipyli uertice summo flebile saxum. flebilis* is often found on funeral inscriptions (N–H on Hor. *Carm.* 1.24.9; cf. Ov. *Am.* 3.9.3 *flebilis Elegia*).

4 lubrica uia: a rare use of *lubricus* suggesting both the flow of blood and tears and the mental instability caused by grief; for this latter sense see 221n.; *TLL* VII 2.1689.39–40.   **plagae:** a 'gash' (*OLD* 2) is a common figure for the blow of ill fortune or untimely death (*OLD* 1 b); cf. 2.6.7–8 *maioraque uulnera uincit | plaga minor*; Ov. *Pont.* 2.7.41–2 *Fortunae uulneror ictu, | uixque habet in nobis iam noua plaga locum.*

5–6 egomet . . . | confero, tu . . . mauis: adversative asyndeton, emphasised by the personal pronoun with enclitic -*met*, now sharply distinguishes St. and Melior. M reads *consero*, easily interchanged with the more appropriate *confero*, a formal word used especially of funeral tributes; cf. 35; 3.3.42 *et ipse tuli quos nunc tibi confero questus.* Here it has conative force ('I am trying to bring').

5 iam: cf. *adhuc* (2), *etiamnunc* (3), temporal adverbs stressing the present moment at the pyre.   **cantus et uerba medentia** 'songs of healing words' (hendiadys); poetic consolation is the 'cure' for grief and the poet is the 'doctor'; cf. 5.1.16 *medicina dolori*, with Gibson.   **saeuus** 'cruel' (in trying to console when grief is so fresh).

6 planctus lamentaque fortia: not quite synonyms; *planctus* can refer to the physical striking of the breast as opposed to the vocal manifestations of grief (*lamenta*); cf. Tac. *Hist.* 4.45 *planctum et lamenta. fortia* means 'loud' as at *Theb.* 6.590 *forti . . . plausu* (*OLD* 3b), with the ironic overtone of 'brave'; Melior's persistence in grief is a form of courage. St. contradicts the moralists' feminisation of grief;

e.g. Sen. *Ep.* 99.1 *epistulam quam scripsi Marullo cum filium paruulum amisisset et diceretur molliter ferre misi tibi.*

7 odistique chelyn: music was believed to have therapeutic power, soothing or at least distracting from suffering (e.g. Hom. *Od.* 4.594–8). But Melior is so grief-stricken that he cannot be easily reached through the senses (7–13); cf. 5.5.32–3 *amens | scindo chelyn*; E. *Alc.* 342–7. *chelys*, a Greek borrowing, appears in Roman poetry first at [Ov.] *Ep. Sapph.* 181 (*TLL* III 1005.75–8); of all subsequent poets St. shows a marked preference for *chelys* (*TLL* III 1006.4–16) over *lyra*, using it twenty-two times in the *Siluae*. It appears only four times in the *Thebaid*, but has programmatic weight at *Theb.* 1.33 *nunc tendo chelyn* and *Theb.* 8.374 *maiorque chelyn mihi tendat Apollo.*   **surdaque auerteris aure:** an unusual reflexive use of *auerto* with abl. of manner. The absence of its normal direct object emphasises, perhaps, Melior's refusal to hear words of consolation; cf. Sil. 13.393 *odit solacia luctus.* The idea of deafness anticipates the Sirens (10–11) and Odysseus (13), who provide a mythological goad to Melior: while Odysseus' men turned deaf ears to the Sirens' song, Odysseus had the courage to listen.

8 intempesta 'unseasonable [songs]', a rare epithet used only here in the *Siluae;* cf. *Theb.* 10.79 *intempesta somni dulcedine captos.* Consolation seems too soon for Melior.

8–9 citius me tigris abactis | fetibus orbatique uelint audire leones: tigers and lions were proverbially savage and thus often paired in literature (Dewar on *Theb.* 9.15–16). The female of each species was regarded as very protective of its young and hence esp. ferocious; cf. Luc. 1.327 *utque ferae tigres numquam posuere furorem*; Ov. *Met.* 13.547 (of Hecuba) *utque furit catulo lactente orbata leaena.* The unconventional masc. *orbatique* facilitates the comparison with Melior; cf. V. Fl. 6.346–7 *ceu saeptus . . . | leo*, a unique parallel. Taming wild beasts was the civilising achievement of Orpheus (Hor. *Ars* 391–3); but the old ways of conquering wildness and passion exemplified by the legendary singer falter in the face of Melior's terrible grief (10–12n.). Competitive comparison is a particular feature of St.'s *Siluae* (23n.; Van Dam on 8–12).

10–12 nec si . . . | affluat . . . | mulceat : pres. unreal condition, with *nec* modifying *mulceat* (12) in the apodosis. The most mesmerising poetry – the songs of the Sirens and of Orpheus – could not ameliorate Melior's grief.

10 tergeminum Sicula de uirgine carmen 'the threefold song from the Sicilian maiden', i.e. from the Sirens; *uirgine* is collective sing. The elevated *tergeminus* is used of supernatural beings, esp. Hecate, who has three aspects (Virg. *A.* 4.511 *tergeminamque Hecaten*, with Pease; *Theb.* 10.366), and Cerberus, the triple-headed dog who guards the Underworld (Prop. 4.7.52 *tergeminusque canis*; Gibson on Ov. *Ars* 3.321–2); at 1.1.92 St. uses it of forked lightning. St. uniquely uses *tergeminus* for the three Sirens, here as a transferred epithet; cf. 3.4.83 (of the three Graces) *hunc bona tergemina pectebat Gratia dextra.* Homer mentions only two

Sirens (*Od.* 12.52, 167); the tradition that there were three seems to derive from Hellenistic poetry; cf. Lyc. 712 κούρας . . . τριπλᾶς. St. here locates the Sirens off Sicily, but at 2.2.10 and 116 he follows an alternative tradition that placed their rocky islands just off Sorrento in Italy.

11 affluat 'should stream from', the only use of *affluo* for poetry (Vessey 1986: 2768), but a fitting image for the song of the sea-dwelling Sirens. **siluis chelys intellecta ferisque** 'the lyre understood by woods and wild beasts' belongs to Orpheus, a conventional figure in consolations as a bereaved husband and the poet whose song could conquer death (Virg. *G.* 4.453–527; Ov. *Met.* 10.1–77; N–H on Hor. *Carm.*1.24.13). But here Orpheus illustrates the limits of poetic consolation; his lyre could soothe wild nature but not Melior's wild grief. Elsewhere St. reinterprets Orpheus as a figure of artistic failure; cf. 5.1.23–29; at 5.1.202–4 grief silences him (Lovatt 2007). St. emphasises the artistic challenge of writing poetic consolations (Gibson on 5.1.203). *intellecta* here takes the dat. of agent; cf. *Theb.* 5.614–15 *et murmura soli | intellecta mihi*.

12 insanos gemitus: cf. 5.5.23 *tanta est insania luctus*. Madness was seen as the concomitant of grief (Gibson on 5.1.22).

12–13 stat pectore demens | luctus: monosyllabic *stat*, highlighted by fourth-foot strong caesura, emphasises the fixity of Melior's grief, settled deep in his heart; see 2.3.1–2n. In contrast to *insanus*, *demens* occurs sparingly in St.'s work and is used only here to describe grief. Its appearance may be explained by the etymological link between *carmen* and *(de)mens* or *(a)mens*; such literary play on *carmen* and *mens* goes back to Cat. 68.7–8 and Lucr. 1.143–4. 'Out of his mind' Melior cannot apply himself to poetry; the key words *carmen* (10) and *demens* (12) occupy line end as etymological markers; cf. 5.5.32–4 *amens | scindo chelyn. iuuat heu, iuuat inlaudabile carmen | fundere*, with Hardie 2005b: 82–3. *luctus*, emphasised by enjambment, first appears as a personified emotion at Virg. *A.* 6.273–4, occupying the threshold of the Underworld; for subsequent poets 'Grief' belongs to Hades itself (Austin ad loc.). Grief's residence in Melior's heart suggests that he is metaphorically 'in hell'.

13 latrant praecordia 'his heart barks'. St. imitates a bold Homeric metaphor (*Od.* 20. 13 κραδίη δέ οἱ ἔνδον ὑλάκτει) describing Odysseus' inner rage but self-control, 'the only instance of ὑλακτεῖν in the Homeric corpus used metaphorically' (Rose 1979: 216). The metaphor is first rendered directly at Enn. *Ann.* 481 Sk. *animusque in pectore latrat*, then by St. here and, with transitive use, at *Theb.* 2.338 *magnas latrantia pectora curas*. The rare epic metaphor ennobles Melior's grief while also hinting that he should follow Odysseus' example and cultivate endurance; see Fowler 2002 on Lucr. 2.17. **admoto . . . tactu** 'when touch has been applied', a metaphor for administering comfort; cf. *Ach.* 1.343 (a literal use) *et admoto non distat comere tactu*; 5.1.30 *nunc etiam attactus refugit iam plana cicatrix*; *Theb.*

2.338–9 *magnas latrantia pectora curas | admota deprendo manu*; Cic. *Tusc.* 4.61 *alia . . . sit ad eum admouenda curatio*. St. continues the healing imagery introduced at line 5.

14 nemo uetat 'nobody forbids [you to grieve]', a prescriptive approach to grief and a blunt rejection of restraint (Vollmer ad loc; Markus 2004: 127–30); cf. 5.5.62–4 *potius fugientia ripas | flumina detineas, rapidis aut ignibus obstes, | quam miseros lugere uetes*.   **satiare malis** 'take your fill of woes', deponent imperative with abl. noun. Philosophical tradition advocated moderation in grief (Baltussen 2009: 78–9). St.'s language is Lucretian, but not the thought; cf. Lucr. 3.906–7 *at nos . . . insatiabiliter defleuimus*; rather at death the wise man should be 'sated' with life, like a contented dinner guest; cf. Lucr. 3.960 *satur ac plenus*, with Kenney; Lucr. 3.938. St. by contrast asserts the validity of grieving; yet the allusion also subtly begins the work of consolation by introducing alternative paradigms for confronting loss (2n., 13n.).   **aegrumque dolorem:** cf. Lucr. 3.905 (the fortunate state of the deceased) *priuatu' doloribus aegris*; Lucr. 3.933–4 *quod nimis aegris | luctibus indulges*? The allusion to the Epicurean view of death as 'freedom from cares' again points towards consolation.

14–15 aegrumque dolorem | libertate doma 'tame bitter sorrow by giving it free course' (SB), an apt oxymoronic expression for the psychological release of emotional pain.

15 iam flendi expleta uoluptas (sc. *est*) 'has the pleasure of weeping now been satisfied?' The first of three short questions; repetition of *iam* (16, 17) in initial line position creates a sense of urgency – and futility, for Melior is not ready for consolation; cf. 208n. The possibility that pleasure can be found in grief is Epicurean and is attacked by Seneca (*Ep.* 99.25–9; cf. *Ep.* 63.5–7), though he finds acceptable the pleasure found in *remembrance* of the deceased (*Ep.* 99.18–19; Wilson 1997: 57, 62; Montiglio 2008; Baltussen 2009: 89–90). St. continues the alimentary metaphor (*OLD expleo* 3; 14n.); cf. Ov. *Tr.* 4.3.37–8 *est quaedam flere uoluptas; | expletur lacrimis egeriturque dolor*. On ancient belief in the therapeutic power of tears see Stroh 1971: 32 n. 72.

16 fessus: more frequent in epic than *lassus* (cf. 2.2.26–7n.) and preferred by St. in all his works (Van Dam); again St. elevates Melior's grief.

17 iamne canam? the brief question makes a surprising climax to the apparently 'rising' tricolon, its intensity drawing attention to a major issue of 2.1, the efficacy of poetry. Repetition at the beginning of two units (16–17) is a poetic pattern often associated with grief for a child, conveying special pathos (Wills 138–42).

17–18 lacrimis en et mea carmine in ipso | ora natant 'look how my face too swims with tears in the course of my song'. This is a generally accepted emendation for M's *mea carmina in ipso | ore natant* ('my songs swim with tears in my mouth'), which would mean 'my songs are choked in my mouth by tears' (*OLD nato* 3). Such a metaphor would be unique, though the conceit that the poet's tears make song difficult is related to the predicament of the elegiac heroine such as Ovid's Briseis, who produces elegant song in the midst of tears (*Her.* 3.1–4). Although eyes rather than lips or the face more usually 'swim' with tears (cf. *Epic. Drusi* 94 *lumina caerulea iam iamque natantia morte*), the same striking metaphor of 'the face swimming with tears' occurs at *Theb.* 2.337–9 (alluded to at 13n.) *quotiens haec ora natare | fletibus . . . | deprendo?*; cf. *Theb.* 11.558 *cerno graues oculos atque ora natantia leto*. The postponement of *en* is unusual (Bömer on Ov. *Met.* 3.605) and harsh with the following *et*, but its abruptness conveys the poet's distress (cf. 26–9, 34–5). The idea that sorrow should be shared was a consolatory convention derived from the meeting of Achilles and Priam (Hom. *Il.* 24.507–70); cf. Cic. *Fam.* 4.5.1 *grauiter molesteque tuli communemque eam calamitatem existimaui*; *Fam.* 5.16; N–H I 280–1.

18 tristesque cadunt in uerba liturae: a programmatic moment; the 'blot' is a hallmark of the Ovidian elegiac epistle, signifying the author's sorrow and difficulty in writing; cf. Ov. *Tr.* 3.1.15–16 *littera suffusas quod habet maculosa lituras | laesit opus lacrimis ipse poeta suum*; *Tr.* 1.1.13. Ovid adopted the motif from love poetry; cf. Prop. 4.3.4; Ov. *Ep.* 3.3, 11.1–2. *tristes* suggests esp. Ovid's exile poetry; cf. 3.5.14 (a letter to St.'s wife on 'exile' to Naples) *cur hoc triste tibi?* By referring to *written* lament St. breaks here the illusion of extemporaneous composition at the pyre.

19–35 A description of Glaucias' funeral, resumed at 158–78.

19 ipse etenim tecum: the pronouns emphasise the poet's closeness to Melior as an active, sympathetic participant at the funeral. Postponement of the connective *etenim* derives from Hellenistic usage (Austin on Virg. *A.* 1.333). The period (19–25) is loosely coordinated; -*que* occurs five times at line start (20, 22, 23, 24), an elevated form of polysyndeton suggesting a rapid, distressing sequence of events.   **nigrae sollemnia pompae:** *niger* is the colour of mourning and of the Underworld (N–H on Hor. *Carm.* 1.24.18); dark clothes were worn by the bereaved (Flower 1996: 102). *sollemnia* in the sense of 'religious ceremony' (*OLD* 1) is often plural. How probable is it that the child Glaucias had the grand funeral that St. now describes? In Roman society children were traditionally buried quietly at night without grand ceremony (Flower 1996: 96–7). Yet evidence now suggests that in imperial times some display, even by day, had become acceptable; children in this period had assumed greater visibility in various media (20n.; Rawson 2002: 277–90). The account of Glaucias' funeral is also influenced by epic tradition, esp. the *Thebaid* with the funeral of the infant Opheltes (*Theb.* 6.1–237). It is difficult to separate the historical from the literary. Plin. *Ep.* 4.2 offers a near-contemporary instance of the epic style funeral of Regulus' young son. Whether or not Melior gave Glaucias a funeral on an epic scale, St. memorialised it as such.

20 spectatumque Vrbi (scelus heu!) puerile feretrum 'the child's bier (alas, the crime!) watched by the city'; cf. Mart. 6.28.1–2 *libertus Melioris ille notus | tota qui cecidit dolente Roma*, with Grewing. The crowd of spectators at a funeral is a common hyperbole in epitaphs, starting from the scene at Hector's funeral (Hom. *Il.* 24.707–804); cf. 5.1.216–17 (with the bereaved the sole focus of attention) *toto spectatur in agmine coniunx*. The idea was not purely literary. Traumatic events, such as untimely death, often arouse extraordinary reactions in the populace. The funeral of Marcianus, a child prodigy, seemingly drew huge crowds (*CIL* VI 7578; Rawson 1999: 83–5, 97). *feretrum* is an elevated word of Greek origin (φέρετρον) for 'bier'; *puerile feretrum* (cf. *Theb.* 6.55 of Opheltes) has an oxymoronic quality.   (**scelus heu!**): M reads *scelus et*, printed by Courtney as hendiadys with *feretrum* 'the crime of the bier'. But the abstract 'crime' goes oddly with the active *produxi* (21) as one of its objects. SB follows Ker in emending *et* to *heu* and treating the phrase as a parenthetical exclamation of horror at the child's bier, a tragic 'crime' in that it contravenes nature's laws. Though *scelus heu* occurs nowhere else in St., he may echo its rare, and highly pathetic, appearance at Virg. *Ecl.* 9.17 (though across a line break).

21 produxi: a technical term for conducting a corpse or funeral procession to the grave or pyre (*OLD* 6c); cf. Virg. *A.* 9.486–7 *nec te, tua funera, mater | produxi*. St. assigns himself a privileged position in the funeral procession; cf. *ipse* (19), *uidi* (22), *tenui* (25). The heavily spondaic line emphasises the solemnity of the occasion.   **saeuos damnati turis aceruos:** incense was burned on funeral pyres as perfume and as an offering to the gods (Virg. *A.* 6.225 *turea dona*); it is 'doomed' because it shares the boy's fate; cf. *Theb.* 6.55 *damnatus flammae torus*. *aceruos* suggests Melior's lavishness, but piles of incense also helped burning (Noy 2000: 38), hence they are 'cruel.' The Romans practised cremation (Tac. *Ann.* 16.6 *mos Romanus*) until at least the time of Hadrian, who may have been the first emperor to have been inhumed (Morris 1992: 31–69). On the Roman funeral pyre see Noy 2000.

22 plorantemque animam supra sua funera 'the soul wailing over its corpse'. *funus* in the poetic pl. often means 'corpse' in St. (*OLD* 2b; Williams on *Theb.* 10.7); cf. 158; *Theb.* 1.36–7 *tumulisque carentia regum | funera*. *plorare* does not occur in epic but belongs to lyric-elegiac style (Axelson 28–9). The idea of the soul lamenting its untimely fate originates in literature with the deaths of Patroclus and Hector (Hom. *Il.* 16.856–7 and 22.362–3); see Vermeule 1979: 1–23, esp. fig. 5, p. 10 and fig. 14, p. 19. But the idea of the mourner *seeing* the deceased soul lamenting at its own funeral is unparalleled; the closest instance occurs at *Theb.* 12.55–6, where the Argives lament because they remain unburied, barred from the funeral pyre. On the varied Greek and Roman ideas of what happened to the soul after death see Lattimore 1962: 21–48.

23 teque patrum gemitus superantem et bracchia matrum: Melior mourns Glaucias more than parents mourning a son. St. often introduces the idea of competitiveness in mourning, thus contesting philosophical wisdom on restraint; cf. 174, 2.6.85, 2.7.124–5. Surpassing the parents in grief is esp. relevant to the poem's elevation of foster parents; see esp. 82–105. Bruising one's arms was a conventional gesture of feminine mourning, though not confined to women in St.; cf. *Theb.* 6.133–4 (of Hypsipyle) *liuida . . . | bracchia*; 2.6.82–4 (of parents); 3.3.176–7 (of Claudius Etruscus).

24 complexumque rogos: cf. 3.3.9 *complexumque rogos incumbentemque fauillis.* The desire for a shared death (*iuncta mors*) by throwing oneself upon the body or the pyre developed as a literary motif from the wish of Patroclus' ghost that Achilles' bones be buried with his (Hom. *Il.* 23.83–92); see Hardie on Virg. *A.* 9.444. It is a prominent motif in the *Thebaid*; cf. *Theb.* 6.174–6 (Eurydice), 10.439– 48 (Dymas), 12.800–2 (Evadne). St. elevates his friend's grief by assimilating it to epic models (Manning 1978: 254–60). But literature may have also influenced social practice; the freedman P. Catienus Philotimus threw himself on his patron's pyre despite having been made his heir (Plin. *Nat.* 7.122); for other examples of suicide on the pyre see Noy 2000: 31.   **ignemque haurire parantem:** cf. Quint. *Inst.* 6 *pr.* 12 *tuum corpus frigidum exsangue complexus animam recipere auramque communem haurire amplius potui.* The idea of capturing the beloved's last breath was conventional (Pease on Virg. *A.* 4.684), but St. gives it a new twist: Melior wishes to consume the funeral fire itself. In so doing, he literalises the erotic metaphor of Ov. *Met.* 10.252–3 *miratur et haurit | pectore Pygmalion simulati corporis ignes.* Melior is cast as a tragic Pygmalion who has lost near-perfection.

25 uix tenui similis comes offendique tenendo: the motif of the restraining comrade occurs frequently in St.'s depictions grief; cf. 5.1.200 *uix retinent comites*, with Gibson; *Theb.* 6.35–7 *lacerasque super procumbere nati | reliquias ardet totiensque auulsa refertur. | arcet et ipse pater*; *Theb.* 6.203. The resumption of a verb by a participle or gerund (*tenui . . . tenendo*) is esp. Ovidian and here intensifies the effort involved in preventing Melior from taking his life (Wills 326–7). The lengthy separation of the object *teque* (23) from its verbs also suggests the difficulty of restraint.   **similis comes:** in the Republic *comes* generally denoted a friend of slightly lesser rank or age (Hellegouarc'h 56–60); thus it delicately acknowledges the difference between St. and Melior in age and wealth, while *similis* stresses their bond in grief.

26 et nunc heu: the same phrase expresses Creon's grief at his son's pyre (*Theb.* 12.80).   **uittis et frontis honore soluto** 'now that the headband, my forehead's badge of honour, has been cast off' (abl. abs., the nouns ἀπὸ κοινοῦ with *soluto*); *honos* has the sense here of adornment; cf. *Theb.* 9.705–6 *frontis seruat honorem | ira decens*, with Dewar. Physical disarray was a sign of grief; cf. *Theb.* 6.30–1 (Opheltes' father) *sedet ipse exutus honoro | uittarum nexu genitor.* The undoing of the poet's *uittae* specifically symbolises poetic incapacity; cf. 5.3.7–8 *fugere meos Parnasia crines | uellera*; 5.5.28–9 *sed nec solitae mihi uertice laurus | nec fronte uittatus honos.* That grief robs one of words is a convention of the consolatory genre (e.g. Sen. *Dial.* 12.1); that it also destroys poetic inspiration is a theme first expressed in

Roman literature at Cat. 65.1–4. The failure of one's art is also a motif of erotic elegy (cf. Tib. 1.4.82 *deficiunt artes*) and of Ovid's exile poetry. See 11n. *uittae* were properly worn by priests (*OLD* 2a) and indicate the poet's quasi-sacral authority in his role as 'priest' of the Muses; cf. *Ach.* 1.10–11 *neque enim Aonium nemus aduena pulso | nec mea nunc primis augescunt tempora uittis.*

27 infaustus uates: a paradox, for the *uates* composes poetry of the highest order whereas *infaustus* is fiercely negative, 'ill-starred' (*OLD infaustus* 1; cf. 120). In the *Thebaid* St. uses *uates* most often in the sense of 'prophet', in the *Siluae* most often in the sense of 'poet', with reference to himself at 1.4.25, 2.1.26, 4.4.10 (Lovatt 2007: 145–8).

27–8 uersa mea pectora tecum | plango lyra 'along with you I beat my breast, my lyre upturned'; cf. Ov. *Am.* 3.9.7 (Cupid's quiver on the death of Tibullus) *euersamque pharetram.* This striking image for poetic incapacity derives from Roman funerary practice, which involved the inversion of social norms (Morris 1992: 9–10): magistrates wore mourning at a funeral, and the symbols of office and rank were reversed, e.g. the *fasces* at Drusus' funeral (*Epic. Drusi* 141–2, with Schoonhoven); cf. Luc. 8.734–5. Children's sarcophagi depicted cupids with torches turned upside down (Huskinson 1996: 14). Beating the breast is generally associated with female lamentation, e.g. *Theb.* 3.126; but cf. Sil. 13.389 (of Scipio) *pulsato . . . pectore*; see 23n.

28–30 †et diu† comitem sociumque doloris . . . | iam lenis patiare precor 'now I beg you be calm and suffer me as the companion and ally of your grief', i.e. St. asks Melior to try to listen to him. M's *et diu* is metrically impossible and does not make sense in the context of a prospective wish. Van Dam lists the main conjectures, the most plausible being Housman's *crudi* (accepted by SB), an epithet uniquely used by St. of raw pain (*OLD* 8), e.g. *Theb.* 3.335 *crudosque . . . dolores*; and Markland's *duri*, which is close to *diu* but seems 'lame' to Van Dam; but cf. Virg. *A.* 5.5 *duri magno sed amore dolores.* Although St. never uses *durus* as a descriptive epithet for *dolor* elsewhere, he frequently uses it to express death's inexorability; cf. 2.1.230, 2.6.4, 14, 80. *precor* governs *patiare* (second-person sing. pres. subj.) in a final noun-clause, with *ut* omitted (*NLS* 130, 146).

29 si merui luctusque tui consortia sensi 'if I have so deserved and have felt partnership in your grief'. *consortium* is largely prosaic, occurring in Latin poetry first in the Flavian period (*TLL* IV 488.32–71).

30 fulmine in ipso 'at the unexpected deadly blow of fate', a dramatic metaphor for the shock of sudden death; cf. 225; Gibson on 5.5.50; Schoonhoven on *Epic. Drusi* 11.

30–2 St.'s claim, restated at 5.5.38–41, that he has already written poems consoling fathers, mothers and sons, is problematic, for none of the extant *Siluae* qualify apart from 3.3, which consoles the son of Claudius Etruscus for his father's death.

St. perhaps refers to unpublished poems, or poems not selected for the editions of *Siluae* (Nauta 2002: 285). The claim at very least is self-promoting. *solacia* are 'poems of consolation', as at 2 *pr.* 12, in this sense more common in Latin poetry than *solamen* (1–3n.).

31 iuxta busta: St. stresses the immediacy of his other poems of consolations, delivered by the *bustum*, technically the burnt-out pyre; cf. Serv. *A.* 11.201 *pyra est lignorum congeries; rogus cum iam ardere coeperit dicitur; bustum uero iam exustum uocatur.*

31–2 profusis | matribus: an unusual use of *profusus* in the sense 'prostrate with grief' (*OLD* 7b), inspired perhaps by the more common *profusis lacrimis* 'with flowing tears' (e.g. Ov. *Met.* 7.91, 9.680).

33 et mihi: St.'s poem of self-consolation on the loss of his father (5.3); he too is a *pius natus*. St. saves his own loss for last.   **defectus** 'in a state of total collapse'; cf. 5.5.40–2 *ille ego lugentum mitis solator . . . | deficio.*

33–4 cum . . . gemerem . . . | quem, Natura, patrem! 'when I lamented, o Nature, what a father!' (SB). *quem* here = *qualem* indicating praise of St.'s father; see Pease on Virg. *A.* 4.10–11. Courtney prints (*quem, Natura!*), treating the phrase as a parenthetical exclamation 'when I lamented (whom, o Nature!), alas, my own father!' He follows Håkanson 1969: 49, who argues that when St. apostrophises *Natura* in the context of death, he is always thinking of the *near*-relationship between the deceased and the survivor, not of the former's qualities; but he adduces only two examples and the sense is strained. This line offers one of the few certainties about the date of the death of St. senior, for which we have only internal evidence – it happened before the publication of the *Siluae* in 92/3 CE (Hardie 1983: 13–14; Nauta 2002: 195–8; Gibson on *Silu.* 5 pp. 260–6).

34 nec . . . seuerus: i.e. St. writes not as a stern philosopher but sympathetically. His personal experience of loss lends authority to the *consolatio.*

35 sed confer gemitus pariterque fleamus 'but mingle your groans with mine and let us weep together'; St. establishes emotional 'parity' with his patron.

36–68 Praise of Glaucias' beauty and character. A child's perfection was closely tied to the theme of *mors immatura* and was a common epitaphic theme for children (40n.); cf. Sen. *Dial.* 6.23.3 *quicquid ad summum peruenit, ab exitu prope est.* Recall of pleasant memories of the deceased conveys pathos but also has therapeutic value; remembrance was an important aspect of consolation; cf. Sen. *Ep.* 63.3–7, 99.19–24; *Silv.* 2.3.15n.

36–8 iamdudum dignos aditus laudumque tuarum | . . . primordia quaerens | distrahor: St. brings the boy back to life, as it were, by direct address; *tuarum*, indicating the emotional shift to Glaucias (cf. 34 *te* of Melior), imparts a note of quasi-informality, but otherwise the langue is stately: *aditus* suggests a formal beginning (cf. Sen. *Dial.* 6.4.3 *hic . . . aditus illi [consolanti] fuit, hoc* *principium*); *primordia* is an even grander term for the beginning of a literary work and is Lucretius' favourite word for atoms (Bailey on Lucr. 1.55 *rerum primordia pandam*; *TLL* x 2.1270.12–29); cf. *Theb.* 1.4 *gentisne canam primordia dirae?*; St. thus suggests that his description of Glaucias will be detailed, *quaerens* adding a semi-scientific note. The claim of the difficulty in knowing where or how to begin is conventional; cf. 2.2.44–5, 2.6.48–50; *Rhet. Her.* 3.6.11.

36 iamdudum 'for a long time now' is not part of the vocabulary of improvisational composition; it draws attention to the temporal shifts involved in the formalisation of 'consolation' as a published work.

37 o merito dilecte puer: cf. Ov. *Met.* 3.500 (of Narcissus) *heu frustra dilecte puer.* The allusion compliments Glaucias' beauty; substitution of *merito* for *frustra* emphasises that, unlike Narcissus, he had a better character. Gibson on *Silu.* 5 pp. xxxix–xl argues that praise of physical beauty is an erotic feature absent from 5.5 (on the death of St.'s foster son), which is thus solely paternal in tone; but 5.5 is fragmentary, and comparison is tentative at best. The allusion need not imply that Glaucias had a sexual relationship with Melior, for Narcissus symbolises *untouched*, if highly eroticised, beauty; moreover, that the deceased was 'dear to the master' was a common epitaphic expression (Citroni on Mart. 1.101.2). Myth elevates Glaucias to a state of perpetual beauty and virtue; he remains a cultural and emotional asset to Melior (Bernstein 2005). Though *puer* hints at his servile status (*OLD* 5), in 2.1 *puer* generally emphasises the child over the slave; cf. 121, 127, 188, 192, 201; Grewing on Mart. 6.28.9.

38 distrahor 'I am torn in different directions' (*OLD* 8) over whether to describe the boy's beauty first or his character. The division of praise into physical and moral attributes was an ancient classification; cf. Men. Rh. 11.420; *Rhet. Her.* 3.6.10. St. however also assigns moral significance to physical attributes; see 43n.

38–9 hinc anni stantes in limine uitae | ac me forma rapit, rapit inde modestia praecox: in place of Courtney's *ac* SB prints *hinc*, an old conjecture for M's *hic*; he thus recognises three possibilities, youth, beauty and character. This is unnecessary. St. is undecided over whether to praise first youth *and* beauty, or moral qualities; initial *hinc* 'on the one hand' *inde* 'on the other hand', neatly separate the two groups (Courtney 1966: 98). Adjacent gemination of indicative verbs (*rapit, rapit*) is esp. characteristic of Senecan drama and lends intensity to St.'s uncertainty about how to proceed (Wills 102–4, 392–3). Cf. *Theb.* 12.794 *rapit huc, rapit impetus illuc.*

38 anni stantes in limine uitae: the metaphor 'the threshold of life' is Homeric (e.g. *Il.* 22.60), introduced to Roman poetry by Lucretius (along with the more common *leti limen*); cf. Lucr. 3.681 *uitae cum limen inimus*, with Kenney; Virg. *A.* 6.427–8 *in limine primo . . . uitae*, with Norden; *Theb.* 5.535 (of Opheltes) *uix prima ad limina uitae.* With pl. *anni* and the omission of *primus* St. adapts the metaphor from infancy to adolescence; Glaucias was on the verge of puberty (52, 124).

39 modestia praecox: St. often favours oxymora in praise of character; see 2.3.65n. Though precocious, Glaucias was the opposite of boastful (74n.).

40 pudor 'modesty' (*OLD* 2b); cf. Mart. 6.28.6 (Glaucias) *integer pudore.* **tenero probitas maturior aeuo:** cf. 2.6.49 *teneroque animus maturior aeuo. tener* in both instances means 'young' and is often used by St. of beautiful boys (cf. *Theb.* 5.443 *tener . . . Hylas*). That those who died young were wise beyond their years was a frequent epitaphic theme for children and a consolatory commonplace (Kleijwegt 1991: 123–31; Sens 2002–3: 114; Rawson 2003: 17–21); cf. Quint. *Inst.* 6 *pr.* 10 (on his nine-year-old son) *probitatis, pietatis, humanitatis, liberalitatis*; Plin. *Ep.* 8.16.2 (on a twelve-year-old girl) *anilis prudentia, matronalis grauitas . . . et tamen suauitas puellaris cum uirginali uerecundia.* 'Probity' was an important social as well as moral quality involving respect for family and friends (Hellegouarc'h 285–6).

41–55 A catalogue of a beloved's physical charms was conventional (N-H on Hor. *Carm.* 2.4.21). Here, structured as an *ubi sunt* lament for beauty's loss, it has a melancholy cast; cf. *Theb.* 5.613 (of Opheltes) *heu ubi sidereique uultus? ubi uerba?* The lament is structured around three emotional rhetorical questions, *o ubi* (41), *ubinam* (45), *o ubi* (52). Although the direct addressee remains Glaucias (36–8n.), such universalising laments implicitly address the survivors rather than the deceased.

41 o ubi: initial hiatus conveys particular pathos. **purpureo suffusus sanguine candor** 'your milky-white complexion suffused with a rosy flush'. *purpureus* 'implies the bright glow of youth and health' (Austin on Virg. *A.* 1.159); cf. Virg. *A.* 11.819 (of Camilla) *purpureus quondam color*, with Horsfall. In Graeco-Roman society rosy tones combined with white represented outstanding physical beauty; cf. Tib. 3.4.29–30 (of Apollo) *candor erat . . . | et color in niueo corpore purpureus*; Ov. *Met.* 3.491 (of Narcissus) *et neque iam color est mixto candore rubori.*

42 sidereique orbes radiataque lumina caelo 'eyes shining like stars, their light gleaming with heavenly radiance'. Stars were frequent metaphors in antiquity for beauty (Harrison on Virg. *A.* 10.180), both in lovers (cf. Ov. *Am.* 3.3.9 *radiant ut sidus ocelli*) and in children; cf. Hom. *Il.* 6.401 (Astyanax, another tragic model of a short-lived child) ἀλίγκιον ἀστέρι καλῷ̃ι; *Theb.* 5.613 (Opheltes) *sidereique uultus.* The eyes were also commonly regarded as interpreters of the soul (e.g. Cic. *Orat.* 60). *radiata* means 'furnished with rays', an unusual epithet for eyes, but cf. Ov. *Met.* 4.192–3 *quid nunc, Hyperione nate, | forma colorque tibi radiataque lumina prosunt* (itself an allusion to Lucr. 5.462 *radiati lumina solis*). Like Ovid, St. plays on the dual meaning of *lumen* ('eye' or 'light'). *radiata* alludes to ancient theories of optics according to which vision occurs when rays emanate like fire from the eye (Vitr. 6.2.3; Morales 2004: 15–16). *caelo* however is unclear and, along with the unusual *radiata*, has caused editors to suspect corruption; the phrase is perhaps best taken in the hyperbolic sense of 'furnished with rays by heaven', with an active sense of *radiata* deduced from the passive – Glaucias' eyes are beautifully radiant like the sun and stars.

43 castigatae collecta modestia frontis 'the tidy modesty of his taut brow', a union of the abstract with the concrete; i.e. his brow was unwrinkled, his hair tidy. *castigatus* is a rare epithet; cf. Ov. *Am.* 1.5.21–2 *castigato planus sub pectore uenter*, with McKeown; Dewar on *Theb.* 9.687–8. St. puns on the aural association between *castigatae* and *castus* ('chaste'), essentially glossing *modestia*, which can mean 'chastity' (*OLD* 3); cf. Mart. 6.28.6 (Glaucias) *castus moribus*; Luc. 8.156 *pudor... probitas castique modestia uoltus*. On the topos that youth is smooth-faced, age wrinkled, see N–H on Hor. *Carm.* 2.11.6 *leuis iuuentas*; on the moral significance of the clear brow see Gleason 1995: 71–2.   **collecta:** Ov. *Am.* 1.11.1 first uses *colligere* to mean 'tidy the hair'. Neat hair was a sign of moral restraint; on the semiotics of hair see Oliensis 2002.

44 ingenuique ... crines 'hair such as would suit the freeborn,' i.e. 'soft and fine'; cf. Ov. *Am.* 1.7.50 *ingenuas... genas*, with McKeown, a similar play on the two senses of *ingenuus* 'freeborn' (2.6.48n.) and 'delicate' (*OLD* 2 and 3 respectively).

44–5 mollisque ... | margo: *margo* in the sense of 'fringe of hair' is unusual; at *Theb.* 6.723–4 it describes the edge of fur round a tiger skin.

45 blandis ... ora arguta querelis 'the chattering mouth with charming complaints'; cf. 74 on the glib speech of foreign child slaves. *blandus* frequently describes the winsomeness of children; cf. 1.2.19 (Cupid); *Theb.* 6.161 (Opheltes); *Ach.* 1.196 (the child Achilles). But here St. echoes Lucr. 6.1245 on the plaints of plague victims – *blandaque lassorum uox mixta uoce querelae* – a grim subtext that suggests the brevity of the boy's charm and the inexorability of fate.

46 osculaque impliciti uernos redolentia flores 'your kisses redolent of spring flowers when you were embraced'; cf. Mart. 5.37.9 (on the slave girl Erotion) *fragrauit ore quod rosarium Paesti*. 'Spring flowers' evoke Glaucias' early death; metaphors of the 'flower of youth' were often used in funerary contexts for the young (106–7n.; Lattimore 1962: 195–7); cf. Hor. *Carm.* 2.11.9–10 *non semper idem floribus est honor | uernis*. *implicitus* can have the active sense of 'embracing' (Van Dam); here gen. *impliciti*, referring to Glaucias, retains its passive force; cf. V. Fl. 1.258 *impliciti Peleus rapit oscula nati*.

47 et mixtae risu lacrimae: the juxtaposition of tears and laughter expresses a child's changeable emotions. The oxymoron derives from Hom. *Il.* 6.484 δακρυόεν γελάσασα, of Andromache fearing the loss of both infant son and husband; cf. *Theb.* 6.166 (of Opheltes) *tuos questus... lacrimososque risus*. The Homeric passage provides another paradigm for untimely death (42n.) as well as another model of consolation in Hector's injunction against mourning, since none can escape fate (Hom. *Il.* 6.486–93).

47–8 penitusque loquentis | Hyblaeis uox mixta fauis 'the boy's voice as he spoke was thoroughly mixed with Hyblaean honeycomb', a pleasing variation on the more common 'voice sweeter than honey' (Hom. *Il.* 1.249 μέλιτος γλυκίων . . . αὐδή); *penitus* modifies *mixta*. To avoid the close repetition with *mixtae* (47), SB adopts Housman's *mulsa* 'sweetened'. But this is an unpoetic word (*OLD mulsus* 2). Close repetition is a feature of the improvisational style and also creates thematic unity within a poem; see 128–9n.; Van Dam on 2.2.69.

48 Hyblaeis: a Virgilian epithet (*Hyblaeus*) coined from Hybla, a Sicilian town on Aetna's slopes famous for honey proverbial for its sweetness (Clausen on Virg. *Ecl.*1.54).

48–9 cui sibila serpens | poneret et saeuae uellent seruire nouercae 'for which the serpent would set aside its hissing and which cruel stepmothers would wish to serve'. *cui*, referring to *uox*, does double duty as dat. of advantage with *poneret* and dat. object of intransitive *seruire*, the latter a strong word in the context of a child of slave origins. Repeated *-et* suggests an improvisational style (Van Dam; cf. 47–8n.), here conveying wonder: Glaucias was so beautiful that he would cause the impossible to happen in the natural and social world (*if* he were still alive, hence the imperf. subj. implying a pres. unreal condition); cf. 5.2.79–80 (of the youthful Crispinus) *qui uoce praeuertere morsus | serpentum atque omnes uultu placare nouercas*, with Gibson; [Sen.] *Oct.* 170–1 (of Britannicus) *saeua cui lacrimas dedit | etiam nouerca*. The stepmother was a conventional symbol of evil (Watson 1995). Snakes, stepmothers and childhood feature in the myth of Hercules attacked in his cradle. Snakes also associate Glaucias with Opheltes, killed by a snake (181n.; *Theb.* 5.505–604), but Glaucias' voice, so St. implies, would have charmed it. Sigmatism here suggests serpentine hissing.

50 nil ueris affingo bonis 'I make no false additions to true virtues', the poet's only use of *affingo* (*OLD* 3). This emphatic claim comes right after an unlikely mythological comparison, a witty hint that fiction can encode important truths; see 2.6.29n.   **heu lactea colla:** the same detail describes the Gauls engraved on Aeneas' shield at Virg. *A.* 8.660; cf. *A.* 10.134–8, esp. 137 (of Ascanius' jewel-like beauty) *ceruix . . . lactea*, with Harrison; Mart. 1.31.6. Glaucias was like a gleaming work of art; *heu* conveys the poet's emotional involvement in the description. *candidus* is a more usual epithet for a beautiful neck (McKeown on Ov. *Am.* 1.5.10).

51 bracchia quo numquam domini sine pondere ceruix: M unmetrically reads *bracchiaque*; emendation of *que* to *quo*, relative adjective modifying *pondere*, gives the literal sense 'the arms without which (whose) weight his master's neck never was', i.e. 'the arms ever weighing upon your master's neck'

(SB's translation and text, following Van Dam and others). Courtney's *bracchiaque [et] numquam domini sine pondere ceruix* is a less extreme instance of hyperbaton but suggests that the boy's neck bears the weight of his master, a cruel burden for the child and an uncomfortable posture for the adult; Courtney's (1971: 96) examples of 'leaning on another person' do not address the age and size differential here. There are many parallels for children hanging upon their parents' necks as a loving gesture; e.g. 1.2.103–4 *tenera matris ceruice pependit* | *blandus*; Virg. *A.* 1.715 *complexu Aeneae colloque pependit*; V. Fl. 1.258 *caraque diu ceruice pependit*; Plin. *Ep.* 5.16.3 *ut illa patris ceruicibus inhaerebat*. Melior is here first named *dominus* 'master of slaves'; see 70, 80.

52 o ubi: emotional hiatus at the end of the *ubi sunt* lament as at its start (41n.).   **uenturae spes non longinqua iuuentae** 'the not long distant hope of approaching manhood'; *iuuenta* marks the period when a youth grows his first beard (Lucr. 5.888–9), confirmation in Roman society of the successful arrival at manhood. Death just before the first beard, a sign of readiness for marriage and thus an esp. tragic time to die, was a common epitaphic theme (Griessmair 1966: 60–2; Lattimore 1962: 192–8). 'Hope' commonly appears on funerary inscriptions for the young, lamenting their promise; e.g. *AP* VII 453.2 (on a twelve-year-old son) τὴν πολλὴν ἐλπίδα; Dewar on *Theb.* 9.49.

53 atque genis optatus honos 'the longed-for bloom upon his cheeks', a periphrasis for the first beard. The more poetic, archaic form *honos*, preferred by Virgil to *honor* (Austin on Virg. *A.* 4.4), stresses the importance of this event for the young Roman male, who dedicated the cuttings from his first shave in a religious ceremony. On the *depositio barbae* cf. 3.4.1–11, 78–98; Dio 48.34.3 (on Octavian); Petr. 29.8; Suet. *Nero* 12; Carcopino 2003: 160–2. The desirability of Glaucias' first beard argues against a sexual relationship between him and Melior – in a pederastic relationship the beard marked the end of a boy's physical attractiveness (Richlin 1992: 35–6, Williams 1999: 26, 73–4).

53–4 iurataque multum | barba tibi? *tibi* is dat. of agent, but to whom does it refer? The most obvious person is Glaucias, the addressee of the *ubi sunt* lament (36–8n.) who, it seems, swore oaths to the gods on the promise of his growing a beard. But several commentators have claimed that *tibi* means Melior, for fathers too can swear such oaths; Van Dam cites Lycurgus who swore to vow his own hair to Jupiter when his son Opheltes dedicated his first beard (*Theb.* 6.193–200); on children as the object of their fathers' prayers see Gibson on 5.3.146. Certainly St. can make free and sometimes obscure changes of address with the second-person pronoun (Håkanson 1969: 43). Yet to assume that the addressee has shifted to Melior here is unnecessarily complicated. Melior is clearly the addressee at 56, *after* the conclusion of the *ubi sunt* lament; St. prepares the way for the switch to Melior by *nobis* at 55, but *tibi* here still refers to Glaucias. See Courtney 1971: 96.

On swearing on parts of the body (one's own or another's) see Hardie on Virg.
A. 9.300.

54 cuncta in cineres grauis intulit hora: 'the stern hour' is a solemn
expression for death; cf. Luc. 6.415 (the battle of Pharsalia) *summique grauem
discriminis horam. inferre* is commonly used of burying a corpse (*OLD* 5). Harsh alliteration and assonance emphasise that time, personified, has borne all loveliness
to the grave.

55 hostilisque dies: cf. Lucr. 3.898 *dies infestus* (of the day of death). *hostilis*
is a unique epithet in this context (*OLD* 3), the militaristic overtones suggesting
death's inexorable power. Caesura after *dies* at sentence end makes a strong sense
pause and metrically reproduces the sudden, decisive break in Glaucias' young
life.   **nobis meminisse 'relictum:'** sc. *est.* The *ubi sunt* lament ends with
a pointed, elliptical *sententia*; memory alone offers compensation for the cruelty
of death and time, a fitting, consolatory conclusion; cf. Sen. *Ep.* 99.24 *meminisse
perseueret, lugere desinat*; cf. also Plut. *Mor.* 610E–F (on the value of remembering the
happy years spent with a child who died young); 36–68n. Verbs of 'remembering'
are infrequent in St.'s *consolationes*; *meminisse* in the sense of 'remembering the dead'
occurs in the *Siluae* only here and at 151 and 206. *nobis* means Melior and St., a
change in pronouns full of pathos; see 53–4n.

56–68   The addressee shifts to Melior (56 *tua*) along with a new rhetorical strategy, a series of direct questions recalling Glaucias' charming behaviour; repetition
of interrogative *quis* (56, 57, 58, 60, 62, 65) cumulatively emphasises Melior's loss.
St. describes here the strong emotional underpinnings of an *alumnus* relationship: spontaneous embraces and pleasing prattle are common themes in Roman
descriptions of childhood and reveal the semantic overlap between the language
of erotic and parental love; cf. Virg. *A.* 1.715–19; Ov. *Ep.* 8.91–4; *Theb.* 5.608–19;
Nielsen 1997: 189.

56–7 quis tua colloquiis hilaris mulcebit amatis | pectora 'who will
cheerfully soothe your breast with his beloved conversation?'; cf. Virg. *A.* 1.130
(the ideal statesman) *ille regit dictis animos et pectora mulcet.* The allusion, wittily
adapted to a domestic context, suggests that Glaucias was wise beyond his years;
hilaris, not found in Virgil, makes an amusing contrast with Virgil's statesman
(*A.* 1.151 *pietate grauem*). Cheerfulness is a positive value in Melior's household; cf.
2.3.65 *hilaris . . . uirtus.*

56 colloquiis: pl. in its three occurrences in St. and connoting *pleasing* conversation. *amatus* 'beloved' is a unique epithet for this noun (*TLL* III 1652.50).

57 curas mentisque arcana: cf. Luc. 8.279 (of Pompey after Pharsalia)
curarum . . . arcana mearum. Even the weightiest cares could be alleviated by Glaucias, though there may be a hint here of Melior's public (and possibly troubled)
past (introd. 20).

58 accensum quis bile fera famulisque tumentem: cf. Hor. *Carm.* 1.13.4 *feruens difficili bile tumet iecur*, a unique lyric precedent for the prosaic *bilis*, which occurs otherwise in satire and Plautus (Grewing on Mart. 6.64.24). Bile was associated with sensations like burning (cf. Mart. 6.24.24 *nostrae bilis inusserit ardor*) and hence with strong emotions, e.g. jealousy, as in Horace's ode, or anger, as here; *tumeo* likewise describes a state of anger (*OLD* 3a), with dat. of the object; cf. *Theb.* 11.378–9 *tumentem | placaui tibi saepe patrem*. The shift in tonal register lightly ridicules Melior's anger, though fear and violence were common means of social control of Roman slaves (Sen. *Ep.* 47.17–20; Bradley 1984: 113–17).

59 ardentique in se deflectet ab ira? 'and [who] will divert [you] from your burning anger to himself?'; i.e. who will provide a soothing and merry distraction as Glaucias used to do? The poet's concern is not the protection of the slaves from their master's anger but rather the protection of Melior from destructive passions.

60–1 inceptas quis ab ore dapes libataque uina | auferet et dulci turbabit cuncta rapina?: like Melior's parrot (2.4.4–7), Glaucias engaged in playful tricks at table. The ritual of dinner was an occasion for the display of special slaves whose appearance represented their master's values (Rawson 2003: 263). The echoing of terminal 'a' at the end of 60 and 61 (*uina, cuncta rapina*) suggests childish levity; see also the lilting cadences of 70–2. Van Dam calls play with food the 'normal pleasantries of lovers', but the playfulness of children at mealtime emerges as a literary topos as early as Hom. *Il.* 9.485–93: the infant Achilles, unable to handle utensils, soaks Phoenix's shirt with wine. On children at Roman dinners see Roller 2006: 157–79. The playfulness of children was an important theme of their sarcophagi (Huskinson 1996: 16–17). Quint. *Inst.* 1.1.20 encouraged play as a healthy activity for the young (Rawson 2003: 126–30).

60 libataque uina: tasting the same wine cup as your lover was an erotic topos; cf. Ov. *Am.* 1.4.31–2; *Ars* 1.577–8. But Glaucias playfully *removes* the wine Melior has sipped.

61 dulci . . . rapina: a characteristic oxymoron, as frequently with St.'s use of *dulcis* (Van Dam); cf. 71 *dulces . . . curae*, of the bittersweet nature of a parent's love.

62 quis matutinos abrumpet murmure somnos?: cf. Mart. 14.125 *matutinos . . . somnos*, of sleep missed by the client seeking the dole. *matutinus*, pertaining to things that happen in the early morning like the client's greeting (*TLL* VIII 506.18–36; cf. Sen. *Ep.* 95.47 *turba matutinae salutationis*), is largely poetic, occurring only here in St. *murmur* describes soft, babyish speech or sounds; cf. *Theb.* 5.613–15 (Opheltes) *ubi uerba ligatis | imperfecta sonis risusque et murmura soli | intellecta mihi?* Glaucias, Melior's first 'client', gently greets him. But the charming scene has a solemn edge; cf. Virg. *G.* 3.530 *nec somnos abrumpit cura salubris*, an idealised picture of rural life tragically set within an account of plague, an extreme version of death's inexorability.

63–4 artis | nexibus: cf. Ov. *Met.* 6.242 *arto . . . nexu*, of the tragic embrace of two of Niobe's sons, killed as they playfully wrestled. Such tragic allusions provide a form of consolation by integrating Glaucias into a literary/mythological canon of the premature dead; Melior too joins the cast of the famous bereaved.

64 ad oscula: St. recalls the motif of children's farewell kisses at Lucr. 3.894 *nec dulces occurrent oscula nati praeripere*. Children's kisses are the index of a virtuous home: cf. Virg. *G.* 2.523–4 *dulces pendent circum oscula nati, | casta pudicitiam seruat domus.*

66 breuibusque umeros circumdabit ulnis: cf. Ov. *Ep.* 8.93 (of the child Hermione) *breuibus . . . lacertis*. Here there is additional pathos from the double sense of *breuis* 'physically short' (*OLD* 1) and 'short-lived' (*OLD* 7). Both senses are in play at Mart. 6.28.3 *cari deliciae breues patroni*; cf. Mart. 6.29.7 *immodicis breuis est aetas. ulnis* is synecdoche for 'arms'; cf. 3.1.90 *blandisque uirum complectitur ulnis*; *Ach.* 1.172.

67 muta domus: Melior's house is silent like the Underworld (204n.).   **fateor:** Courtney's obelus of this verb seems overly cautious. Though its primary meaning 'I confess' is too strong here, parenthetical *fateor* generally has a weakened sense equivalent to *quidem* or *profecto* (cf. 3.4.39; *Ach.* 1.775); Austin on Virg. *A.* 2.134 describes it as 'a conversational turn'. Here it acknowledges St.'s sympathy with Melior: 'yes, I agree, I know you are grief-stricken'; see SB 109 n.9.   **desolatique penates:** quite rare in Roman poetry, *desolatus* has here the new sense of 'bereaved' (*TLL* v 735.6–10) rather than 'left alone'; the entire household is in grief.

68 et situs in thalamis et maesta silentia mensis: evocative details describing the bereaved house from Melior's point of view; the two main places in the house where Glaucias entertained Melior, linked here by internal rhyme at the strong caesura, are now still and silent. *thalami*, poetic pl., is a Greek poetic borrowing for 'bedroom', with a more formal ring than Roman *cubiculum* (Leach 2004: 47); it can also be a private room without marital connotations (2.2.73–4n.). *silentia*, exclusively pl. in St. and always in the fifth foot (Van Dam), contrasts pointedly with *mensis*, the usual site of animated conversation. Sigmatism brings the series of questions to a hushed close.

69–75 St. explains Glaucias' social status, born at home of slave parents who were freed by Melior. The address switches again to Glaucias (69 *te*).

69 quid mirum: wonder is characteristic of St.'s encomiastic strategies, conveying the exceptionality of the occasion and of those praised. Here he perhaps makes delicate allusion to Glaucias' low social status as a child born of slaves.   **altor** 'foster father'. Its derivation from *alo* suggests Melior's attentive care for his *alumnus* – which improved his prospects in life (Nielsen 1987: 145).

70 funere 'at his funeral' (*OLD* 1).   **tu domino requies portusque senectae:** an elegant chiasmus; cf. Virg. *A.* 9.481–2 (the lament of Euryalus' mother) *tune ille senectae | serae meae requies*, with Hardie. Melior seems not to have had biological or surviving children but raised Glaucias to cheer his old age. No mention is made of a Mrs Melior. The disruption of the natural and social order when a child died before the parents was a common epitaphic theme (Lattimore 1962: 187–94). *domino*, occurring shortly after *altor* (69), suggests the ambiguous status of Glaucias as a son of ex-slaves and a minor under his foster father's protection.

71 tu modo deliciae 'you were now his delight'; cf. 2.1.200; Mart. 6.28.3 *cari deliciae breues patroni. deliciae* is often taken as synonymous with *delicati* (thus Van Dam), i.e. boys used for (chiefly homosexual) sex (*TLL* v 1.447.78–448.210; Isid. *Orig.* 20.2 *deliciae nuncupatae quod his delectantur homines*); cf. Cat. 6.1, 32.1; Prop. 2.34.74; Pollini 2003: 150. But *deliciae* can also serve as a general or parental term of endearment; cf. Cic. *Att.* 1.5.8 (of his beloved daughter) *Tulliola, deliciae nostrae*; *Att.* 1.8.3. On the semantic overlap between erotic and parental language see 56–68n.; on the non-erotic use of *deliciae* see Laes 2003: 305; Nielsen 1987: 145.   **dulces modo pectore curae** 'now his sweet heart-felt charge'. *modo . . . modo* suggests an equivalence between *deliciae* and *curae*, emphasised by internal rhyme; note too the end rhyme of 70–2. While *cura* can refer to the beloved in a sexual relationship (*TLL* IV 1475.42–60), *curae* does not have erotic connotations but has the sense of 'responsibility' or 'charge' (*TLL* IV 1466.1–81, esp. 57–81). There is no need for the emendation *dulcis . . . cura* (thus Vollmer and Van Dam, wishing to enforce a sexual interpretation and avoid the rhyme). *dulcis* was a common epithet for young children, in particular foster children, expressing the emotional character of fosterage (Nielsen 1997: 188–90).

72 barbaricae . . . catastae: cf. Tib. 2.3.60 *barbara . . . catasta* (the first literary occurrence of *catasta*); Mart. 6.29.1–2 *non de plebe domus nec auarae uerna catastae | sed domini sancto dignus amore puer*, with Grewing. By contrast with the foreign slave, Glaucias was born at home and thus did not suffer the degradation of the slave market, exposed on the platform (*catasta*) where slaves were put up for sale, stripped for inspection (Sen. *Ep.* 80.9). Internal rhyme, emphasised by harsh *c* assonance, gives an unpleasant tenor to this line; *barbaricae*, rarer than *barbarus* for 'non-Greek' and here denoting the sale of Egyptian slaves (73n.), adds to the pejorative tone.   **non te . . . uersabat turbo:** the meaning is uncertain, given our limited knowledge of ancient slave marts. If *turbo* is taken to describe a spinning motion (*OLD* 4), the platform perhaps revolved, though we have no ancient evidence for this (*catasta*, the term for the grill on which Lawrence was martyred (Prud. *Perist.* 2.399), is stationary). Alternatively, if *turbo* is taken in the sense of 'whirlwind' or 'whirlpool' (*OLD* 2 and 3 respectively), then it is a figure for the constant turning round of the slave so that prospective buyers could have a good look from all sides.

73–5 nec . . . erum tarde parasti: Glaucias did not acquire his master late like a foreign child, who first had to be transported from Egypt and sold; rather Melior acknowledged him as his foster son at birth (78–81). *erus* means 'a master of household slaves'. St. emphasises Glaucias' ethnic and cultural origins within the *Roman* family, which facilitate his social and emotional assimilation to elite values; though lacking ancestry, Glaucias has the ethical virtues of a Roman (Bernstein 2005: 269).

73 mixtus Phariis uenalis mercibus infans 'as a tiny child put up for sale amidst Egyptian merchandise'. Commercial language treats the foreign slave, though very young, as a commodity (*OLD merx* (pl.) 1a); *uenalis* is the technical term for a slave on sale (*OLD* 1b). Cf. 5.5.66–9 *non ego mercatus Pharia de puppe loquaces* | *delicias doctumque sui conuicia Nili* | *infantem lingua nimium salibusque proteruum* | *dilexi*, with Gibson. *Pharius* 'belonging to Pharos' first occurs at Tib. 1.3.32 (Maltby ad loc.) and is favourite poetic shorthand of St. for 'Egyptian'; cf. 161, 2.5.29, 2.6.87, 2.7.71.

74 compositosque sales 'contrived witticisms' (*TLL* III 2121.32–47); cf. 5.5.66–9 cited above; Tib. 1.1.22 (lover's guile) *blandaque compositis abdere uerba notis*. St. contrasts Glaucias' innocent spontaneity (cf. 45–9, 56–66) with the calculated behaviour of the foreign child slave. 'Witticisms' (*OLD sal* 6b) are the mark of a sophisticated style (cf. Mart. 3.30.9 *lepore tinctos Attico sales*), but signs of unnatural forwardness and insincerity in children; cf. Quint. *Inst.* 1.2.7. **meditataque uerba** 'rehearsed words', unlike Glaucias' spontaneous speech; for this sense of *meditari* see Quinn on Cat. 62.12. The past participle of deponent *meditor* is used frequently in the passive sense. This phrase is repeated at 2.4.7, but what pleases in a parrot is suspect in a human.

76 hic domus, hinc ortus 'here your house, hence your origin' (SB), i.e. 'here in Rome' (by contrast with Egypt); St. need not imply that he himself is at Melior's house (thus Vollmer) rather than by the pyre.

76–7 dominique penatibus olim | carus uterque parens: the unusual ending of line 76 with an adverb emphasises that Glaucias' parents, who were still alive (234n.), had been 'long . . . dear' (SB) to Melior. Mention of both parents suggests that Glaucias was not the product of a sexual union between Melior and one of his slaves.

77–8 in tua gaudia liber | ne quererere genus 'made free for your happiness, so that you would not complain of your lineage'. *in* + acc. expresses purpose (*NLS* 151.6). Glaucias was a freedman (Mart. 6.28.1 *libertus Melioris ille notus*; cf. 6.29.4), thus freed some time after birth, perhaps at the same time as his parents, who may have been freed to enhance their son's social status. St. gave freedom to his own foster son in infancy; see Gibson on 5.5.73. The status of the children of ex-slaves and of foster children was often complex; a foster relationship in itself was no indicator of social or legal status nor of the possibility for inheritance (Nielsen 1987; Weaver 1991).

78–9 raptum sed protinus aluo | sustulit exsultans 'exulting he raised you as soon as you were snatched from the womb'; cf. 1.2.109–10 (Venus' acceptance of Violentilla as her 'foster child') *tellure cadentem | excepi fouique sinu*; 5.5.69–70 (of St.'s foster son) *tellure cadentem | excepi*. According to Roman birthing procedures a child was often born on or near the ground (Shaw 2001: 43). But there is no legal evidence that *tollere liberum* refers to a formal ritual accepting the child into a family, as has been widely believed (e.g. Nielsen 1999: 256; Zeiner 2005: 164–5). Rather Shaw 2001: 31–56 has argued that the phrase often simply means 'to raise a child' as in our English metaphor. Yet here Melior's presence at the birth and his lifting of the newborn shows at least an emotional commitment to the child; see 2.7.36–8n. Postposition of *sed*, a feature of neoteric style, occurs only here and at 2.7.126; lacking adversative force, it emphasises *protinus*.

79–80 ac prima lucida uoce | astra salutantem: the boy with starlike eyes (42) greets the shining stars with his first sound; yet there is a hint too that with his first cry sent heavenward Glaucias is not long for the physical world.

80 sibi mente dicauit 'in his mind he committed you to himself', a solemn expression of Melior's dedication to Glaucias, despite the formal lack of blood and legal ties in the foster relationship. *dicare* connotes serious devotion to a person or purpose (e.g. of marriage at 2.7.82; cf. Virg. *A.* 1.73); cf. 2.7.41 (of Lucan) *puer o dicate Musis*.

81 amplexusque sinu tulit et genuisse putauit: embracing an infant in one's lap, a sign of both affection and quasi-parental authority, has a long literary heritage; Phoenix recalls dandling Achilles on his knee (Hom. *Il.* 9.488; cf. *Od.* 16.443–4). St. comments on the psychological effect of the embrace; in act and in thought Melior is like a biological father; cf. 2.7.38 (of baby Lucan) *blando Calliope sinu recepit*; 4.8.13–14; 5.5.80–1.

82–105 St. advocates foster parenting with arguments stressing its superior emotional and moral value.

82 fas mihi sanctorum uenia dixisse parentum 'with the pardon of venerated parents it is right for me to say this'. St. begins with a *captatio beneuolentiae* to biological parents; *sanctorum* acknowledges the importance of heredity; *parentum* here includes ancestors (*OLD* 2). Etymological play between *fas* (derived from *fari* (Var. *L.* 6.29)) and *dixisse* emphasises the poet's authority. The perfect infinitive without preterite sense after impersonal constructions (such as *licet*) is an Augustan poetic practice (L–H–S 193a).

83 tuque, oro, Natura, sinas: a play upon Natura's etymology from *nascor* (O'Hara 1996: 266–7); she is asked to permit the poet's privileging of socially constructed over 'natural' ties. On the omission of *ut* in a final noun-clause for emotional emphasis see 28–30n.

83–4 cui prima per orbem | iura animis sancire datum (sc. *est*) 'to whom it was granted to sanction throughout the world the first laws for human souls'. *animis*, an early conjecture for M's *animus*, in the sense of 'people' or 'human lives/souls' is unprecedented in St., though 5.2.87 offers a possible parallel; hence other conjectures *homini* (SB) or *hominum* (Van Dam). *animis* perhaps adds to the Lucretian flavour of the invocation of Natura, *anima/animus* being a leitmotiv of his book 3.

84–6 non omnia sanguis | proximus . . . | alligat: i.e. the closest blood ties do not always forge a deep emotional bond.

85 serie generis demissa propago 'offspring descended from a family line'. *demissa* has here the specialised connotation of 'descent by race or birth (from)' (*OLD demitto* 12b). *series*, 'a line of ancestors or descendants' (*OLD* 3), makes *generis* redundant, but the pleonastic phrase emphasises the weight of Roman tradition.

86–7 interius noua saepe ascitaque serpunt | pignora conexis: foster or adopted children often create stronger emotional ties than biological offspring. *pignora*, lit. 'pledges', commonly means 'children' (*OLD* 4); *noua* refers to foster children, for they have no previous connections; *ascita* means 'adopted', a legal Roman term frequent in imperial literature (*OLD ascisco* 1c). *conexis* is a unique poetic use of a prose term for 'kindred' (*TLL* IV 167.78–84), here abl. of comparison with *interius*.

86 serpunt: this image of plant growth (*OLD* 2b) subtly naturalises the incorporation of non-biological children into the Roman family; cf. 85 *propago*, also an agricultural figure ('plant shoot' *OLD* 1), applied there to biological children.

87–8 natos genuisse necesse est, | elegisse iuuat 'giving birth to sons is a necessity, but choosing them is a pleasure'. A pithy concluding *sententia* whose sentiment reflects contemporary imperial discourse about the political advantages of adoption, selecting the best person for the job as opposed to the 'necessary' patriarchal pressures to perpetuate the family line; cf. Tac. *Hist.* 1.16 *loco libertatis erit quod eligi coepimus . . . nam generari et nasci a principibus fortuitum . . . adoptandi iudicium integrum*; Plin. *Pan.* 89. Glaucias is all the more special for having been singled out (Nielsen 1999: 256).

88–105 A series of mythological *exempla* illustrates the superiority of foster to biological parenting. Foster fathers with their charges are listed first (88–96), followed by foster mothers (97–100); Melior forms a climactic coda (102–5). The *exempla* are organised in antithetical couplets that contrast the deficient natural parent with the loving foster parent; proper names frequently occur at line end to emphasise the parallels (88, 89, 93, 95, 98, 100). Two Golden Lines (89, 95) stress at the stylistic level the superiority of the foster relationship; cf. *Theb.* 6.61–7, where Opheltes' mother complains of her child's attachment to her foster mother. Van Dam (on 88–102) claims that this display of mythological learning is excessive. Yet St. wittily gives here a new slant to familiar figures from mythology by emphasising their part in an *alumnus* relationship – thus implicitly complimenting Melior as foster father. Mythology too gives Glaucias the distinguished 'genealogy' that he lacked.

88 tenero sic . . . Achilli: *sic* starts the comparisons with Achilles, hero *par excellence* of St.'s future epic and a frequent figure in the *Siluae*; he earns four lines to the others' two. Here, with a touch of oxymoron (McKeown on Ov. *Am.* 2.18.1 *iratum . . . Achillem*), he is a 'tender youth' (40n.; cf. 98n.); his foster father Chiron is old (*Ach.* 1.106 *longaeuum*).   **blandus:** a contrast with Chiron's semi-bestial form; likewise at *Ach.* 1.124 *blandus* characterises Chiron's gentle demeanour towards Thetis after a wild gallop in welcome.

89 semifer '[though] half beast', Lucretian of centaurs (Lucr. 2.702 *semiferas hominum species*; Lucr. 4.739–40; 5.878–81), of Chiron first in Ovid; cf. *Met.* 2.633, with Bömer. Though *semifer* is often deprecatory, here it begins a Golden Line (Wilkinson 1963: 215–16) honouring Chiron; cf. *Ach.* 1.868 (of Achilles) *tu semiferi Chironis alumnus*. On Chiron as a bridge between St.'s social world and mythological poetry see Fantham 1999: 66–70.   **Haemonium . . . Pelea:** an elevated reference to Achilles' father Peleus (Greek form of the acc.), king of Thessaly (*Ach.* 1.90–1, 921–2); cf. Tib. 1.5.45, with Maltby. 'Haemonian' first appears in Augustan poetry at Prop. 1.13.21 as a poeticism for 'Thessalian' from Haemon, father of Thessalus. The epithet hints at Peleus' propensity for fighting (i.e. αἷμα 'blood'; O'Hara 1996: 29) in contrast to the gentle Chiron (*blandus*) who taught his spirited pupil the peaceful arts such as music; see Gibson on 5.3.194.   **uincebat:** sc. *pietate*.

90–1 Tradition granted Achilles two foster parents, Chiron and the Homeric hero Phoenix; both are mentioned together at 5.3.192–4; cf. 5.2.150–1, with Gibson. Here as in the *Achilleid* Chiron's role is primary (Heslin 2005: 170–3). In Homer Phoenix took charge of Achilles when the boy went to Troy (*Il.* 9.430–605) and also looked after him as an infant (*Il.* 9.485–93), a role later assigned to Chiron (perhaps first at Pi. *I.* 8.42).

90 senior Peleus: cf. *Ach.* 1.440 *senior Peleus nec adhuc maturus Achilles*. Phoenix was also elderly (Hom. *Il.* 9.432; *Il.* 17.561); he is paired with Nestor at *Il.* 19.311.

91 haerebat has physical and emotional sense; Phoenix lovingly kept to Achilles' side; cf. *Theb.* 9.808 *haerebat iuueni deuinctus amore pudico*, with Dewar.   **alumno:** cf. 1 *alumni*, likewise at line end, emphasising the parallel with Glaucias.

92–3 King Evander put the elderly Acoetes, his armour bearer, in charge of his son Pallas when he went to war with Aeneas (Virg. *A*. 11.30–3, 85–7); cf. Virg. *A*. 11.33 *caro . . . alumno*. The contrast between Evander and Acoetes is marked by the paratactic style.

92 optabat longe 'longed for from a distance', a sign of the psychological as well as physical remoteness of the father, tied up with affairs of state, from his son's daily life.   **reditus Pallantis ouantis** 'the return of Pallas in military triumph' (*OLD ouo* 1), a tragically unfulfilled wish.

93 fidus pugnas spectabat Acoetes: an astute psychological contrast between father and carer, emphasised by the line's framing with their names. The ambitious parent wanted glory for his son while Acoetes was faithfully present at the day-to-day fighting; imperf. *spectabat* suggests constant watching and care. The end of this line, *spectabat Acoetes*, is metrically parallel to the end of line 91 *haerebat alumno*, emphasising the parity of Phoenix and Acoetes as devoted foster parents of young heroes.

94–5 Perseus, son of Danae and Jupiter (Hom. *Il*. 14.319–20; Ov. *Met*. 4.611), was cast with his mother to the waves in a chest by his grandfather, king Acrisius. Dictys found them as he fished from the isle of Seriphos and raised the boy as his own (Hyg. *Fab*. 63).

94 cumque procul nitidis genitor cessaret ab astris 'and when his father was slow to come down to earth from the distant shining stars'; *ab* implies the ellipsis of an infinitive. *procul* intensifies *ab astris*: Jupiter was very far away indeed; cf. *Ach*. 1.121 *procul de litore* 'from the distant beach'. On Jupiter's exalted position in the sky cf. Virg. *A*. 1.223–6. Mention of Jupiter forms a climax of sorts to the list of fathers, but he is also the most negative example here; far more so than Evander (92n.), he keeps an extreme distance from his son. *cessaret* also carries the sense of 'being remiss' (*OLD* 3), further suggesting that Jupiter, called here 'parent' rather than 'god', fell short as a father.

95 fluctiuagus: a neologism with Lucretian resonance; Lucretius coined *montiuagus* (Lucr. 1.404, 597, 1081; cf. *Theb*. 1.581; *Ach*. 1.450), and *fluctifrago* (Lucr. 1.305). *fluctiuagus* appears five times in St.'s poetry but then not until late Latin (Laguna on 3.1.84; Dewar on *Theb*. 9.305); cf. Sil. 14.572 *undiuagus*. 'Wave-wandering' better suits the chest containing Perseus and Danae; but the grand epithet, when applied to the humble fisherman, elevates him for his selfless acts; Dictys earns a Golden Line (cf. 89).   **uolucrem . . . Persea:** Perseus wore winged shoes to enable him to fly; cf. Ov. *Met*. 4.616, with Barchiesi and Rosati; *Met*. 4.665–7.   **comebat** 'tended him'; cf. 1.2.110–12 (Venus' adornment of Violentilla) *nec colla genasque | comere . . . cessauit*; *Ach*. 1.343 (Thetis' attention to Achilles' female disguise) *ammoto non distat comere tactu*. The word's basic meaning 'adorn' (*TLL* III 1991.41–1992.48) suggests Dictys' quasi-maternal care of the boy. The second half of this line, *comebat Persea Dictys*, is metrically similar to the second half of line 89, *uincebat Pelea Chiron*, linking the first example and the last of mythological foster fathers and creating an overarching parallelism; see 93n.

96 quid referam altricum uictas pietate parentes?: a transitional line: the shift to feminine gender (*uictas*) introduces notable foster mothers. *quid referam* occurs several times in the *Siluae* (1.3.64, 1.5.57, 2.2.63, 5.3.246) to mark a transition, usually with an admiring inflection – the subject is so important, it is hard to find the words (Cancik 1965: 34; McKeown on Ov. *Am.* 1.5.23–4).

97–8 Ino, queen of Thebes and Bacchus' nurse after the death of his mother Semele (Ov. *Met.* 3.313–14), is first, perhaps to mark her importance in St.'s poetry (179–80n.).

97 te: i.e. Bacchus. St. varies the exempla with direct address, which gives an emotional tone to this tragic myth.   **post cineres deceptaque funera matris:** Juno, jealous of Semele, Jupiter's paramour, tricked her into asking that he appear to her in full majesty; as a result she was killed by his lightning bolt (Ov. *Met.* 3.256–315). The transferred epithet *decepta* highlights Juno's treachery while creating sympathy for her victims (Jupiter and Bacchus as well as Semele); see Dewar on *Theb.* 9.425 *deceptaque fulmina.* The ambiguity of *funus* 'death' (*OLD* 3) or 'funeral' (*OLD* 1) comes into play here as Semele's form of death, reduced to ashes by the thunderbolt, becomes her funeral pyre.

98 reptantem: 'crawling' is first used to describe an infant's movements by Seneca (*Her. F.* 218 *reptabat infans*); *reptare* is not otherwise common in this sense in either prose or poetry outside St., who uses it frequently; see Vollmer on 1.2.262; Dewar on *Theb.* 9.427; cf. *Ach.* 2.96 *et in teneris et adhuc reptantibus annis.*   **Inoo:** the recondite neoteric adjective *Inous* ('of Ino') was introduced to Latin poetry at Virg. *G.* 1.437 *Inoo Melicertae* under the influence of Callimachus and Parthenius (Thomas ad loc.; Lightfoot on Parth. fr. 3); cf. 2.2.35; Virg. *A.* 5.823 *Inousque Palaemon.*

99–100 Rome provides the climax with its founding myth of Romulus and Remus. Acca Larentia, wife of the shepherd Faustulus, raised the twins after their rescue by the wolf (Ov. *Fast.* 3.9–58); their mother meanwhile, having been cast out by her uncle, was married to the river god Anio (Ov. *Am.* 3.6.45–82). The tradition that Acca was a prostitute (*lupa*; Bömer on Ov. *Fast.* 3.55f.) is countered here by Acca's age. St. takes a novel approach to the well-known legend; see 100n.

99 se secura sati: Courtney's emendation for M's *iam secura patris*, since Ilia, once wedded to the river god Anio, had nothing to fear from her own father Numitor or indeed from her sons' father Mars; the context moreover requires mention of a son (Courtney 1968: 52). *satus* is poetic for 'son' (Horsfall on Virg. *A.* 7.656), here appropriate for the divine Romulus; *se* is abl. of origin; cf. *Theb.* 2.1

Maia satus aliger. Ilia was 'free from care for her son' either because she was 'sure of her child' (*OLD securus* 3) knowing that he was in good hands, or because she was 'negligent' (*OLD* 4); both senses could be in play here – her peace of mind about her child was a form of carelessness; cf. with similar ambiguity *Theb.* 4.800 (of Opheltes) *uitae multum securus.* If this emendation is correct, St. depicts Ilia unusually as an indifferent mother. At the very least *secura* contrasts Ilia sharply with Horace's characterisation of her as *nimium querenti* (*Carm.* 1.2.17). **Tuscis regnabat in undis:** cf. Ov. *Met.* 14.223 (of Aeolus) *Tusco regnare profundo.* Ilia became 'queen' by marrying the Etruscan river god Anio (N–H on Hor. *Carm.* 1.2.17). Sigmatism evokes Ilia's new watery realm.

100 portantem lassabat Romulus Accam: cf. Ov. *Fast.* 3.55–6 *tantae nutrix Larentia gentis,* with Bömer. The slow spondaic verbs suggest Acca's age and Romulus' weight, proof of his future greatness as ruler and god. As at 92–3 parataxis heightens the contrast between the behaviour of the natural and foster parents; while Ilia, carefree, queens it in the river, Acca bears the physical and metaphorical burden of Rome's future.

101–2 uidi ego transertos alieno in robore ramos | altius ire suis 'I have seen branches grafted on alien stock grow higher than its own'; cf. Virg. *G.* 2.32–3 *et saepe alterius ramos impune uidemus | uertere in alterius,* with Thomas. St. returns to the natural world and georgic language (cf. 85, 86) for final 'proof' of the success and 'naturalness' of foster parenting. SB argues that *suis* refers to the branches of the alien tree. Though more of a syntactic stretch, the branches of the parent tree better suit the case of Glaucias who, 'grafted' onto his foster family, far outranks his origins. *transertos* is an unusual agricultural term for 'grafted', found only in Cato (*Agr.* 133.3) and here. The archaic tone lends authority to the claims of personal observation.

102–3 et te iam fecerat illi | mens animusque patrem: a return to addressing Melior, the climactic *exemplum*; he is first called *pater* here. *mens animusque* is a frequent Lucretian pairing. Strictly speaking *animus* includes the emotions, while *mens* is rational (Kenney on Lucr. 3.94). Although Glaucias' character and beauty were not yet evident, nonetheless in 'mind and heart' Melior became a father to Glaucias.

104 uinctas etiamnunc murmure uoces 'words still fettered by the baby's babbling', i.e. sounds that are not yet proper words; cf. Luc. 9.1008 (of indistinct speech) *incerto turbatas murmure uoces.* On *murmur* in the sense of 'babble' see 62n. Some editors (e.g. Van Dam) emend *uinctas* to *iunctas* on analogy with *Theb.* 5.613–15 *uerba ligastis | imperfecta sonis.* But St. has a propensity for bold metaphors; *uinctas* plays upon the literal meaning of *infans* 'not speaking' (2 *pr.* 5n.).

105 uagitumque rudem: St. combines two senses of *rudis,* 'of tender years' (*OLD* 3) and 'not yet taught' (*OLD* 5), hence 'innocent' (SB).

106–36 Praise of Glaucias' precocity, displayed in his schooling and swift physical growth, but overshadowed by the certainty of *mors immatura*; on the exceptional talents of those who die young see 40n. Sen. *Ben.* 3.21.2 claims that education is a nice 'plus' that a master can bestow on a slave but not an essential such as food and clothing. Though the son of ex-slaves, Glaucias atypically receives the education of the *ingenui* (the free-born elite), in particular physical and rhetorical training; cf. Theoc. 24.103–31 on a similar elite training for the young Heracles. On the education of slaves in the ancient world see Mohler 1940, Forbes 1955; on the education of children in general see Kleijwegt 1991: 75–133; Rawson 2003: 146–209.

106–7 ille, uelut ... | ... flos improbus exstat: the simile of the dying flower expresses the deep pathos of premature death, beginning with Hom. *Il.* 8.306–7; Cat. 11.21–4 extended the simile's range by applying it to blighted love; Virg. *A.* 9.435–7 (Euryalus) and Ov. *Met.* 10.190–5 (Hyacinthus) combined the two themes. St. also extended the simile's range, e.g. applying it to a mother's early death (3.3.127–30). Here, in contrast to his models where the flower has already been cut, the flower briefly challenges death by facing the elements, a symbol of the brevity of life that is the price of exceptional beauty. On the lyric and epic models of the 'dying flower' simile see Hardie on Virg. *A.* 9.435–7.

106 exspiraturus 'destined to die'. St. often uses the fut. participle predicatively in the context of death to emphasise its tragic inevitability (Van Dam on 2.1.52; L–H–S 390); cf. Virg. *A.* 2.660 *perituraeque ... Troiae.*   **primos ... ad austros** 'at the first south-west winds'. The *Auster* brought rain (Pl. *Mer.* 876 *auster imbricus*) and also disease; cf. Virg *Ecl.* 2.58–9 *floribus Austrum | perditus et liquidis immisi fontibus apros*; Hor. *S.* 1.6.18; Prop. 2.16.56. At Virg. *A.* 9.436–7 rain destroys the flower; here wind is the threat. In a delicate compliment to Glaucias, the flower evokes the anemone, the 'wind flower' that commemorates Adonis, the archetype of beautiful tragic youth; cf. Ov. *Met.* 10.737–9 *breuis est tamen usus in illo; | namque male haerentem et nimia leuitate caducum | excutiunt idem, qui praestant nomina, uenti.*

107 mollibus in pratis 'in lush meadows', a Virgilian phrase; cf. Virg. *Ecl.* 10.42 (a futile invitation to Gallus' beloved Lycoris) *hic mollia prata*, probably in imitation of the λειμῶνες μαλακοί of Calypso (Hom. *Od.* 5.72; Mynors on Virg. *G.* 2.283). This recall of life's youthful pleasures strengthens the simile's pathos.   **improbus:** a surprising epithet in this context; see 2n. By 'standing out tall', the flower is tragically 'presumptuous', a variation on the traditional notion that those who excel among their peers are the first to die (Hes. *Op.* 3–8); cf. *Theb.* 4.319 (of Parthenopaeus) *teneroque unde improba pectore uirtus?*; Sen. *Dial.* 6.23.5.

108–9 tener ante diem uultu gressuque superbo | uicerat aequales 'though a delicate child, he was ahead of his years and had surpassed his peers in appearance and proud gait'. St. often uses *tener*, here with concessive force, of short-lived boys; see 88n. The contrast of the child's physical delicacy with his manly ambitions is conventional (Micozzi on *Theb.* 4.319); *ante diem* conveys particular pathos, suggesting both precocity and untimely death.

110–11 catenatis curuatus membra palaestris | staret: *palaestra* 'a place for wrestling' (always pl. in St.) is a Greek borrowing meaning by extension the activity of that place; cf. Virg. *A.* 3.281 *exercent...palaestras*; *A.* 6.642; *G.* 2.531. The wrestler's bent-limb stance (*curuatus*), often shown in vase painting, allowed for stability; *catenatis* 'enchained' is a metaphor for the sport's interlocking moves ('wrestler's lock' SB). Quint. *Inst.* 1.11.15 recommends physical training as well as book learning for the young; see Gibson on 5.2.111–24. On ancient wrestling see Miller 2004: 46–50. Harsh alliteration and assonance contrast starkly with the physical delicacy implied by the flower simile.

111 Amyclaea: a common term in Latin poetry for 'Spartan', from Amyclae, a Spartan town, and often shorthand for the proverbially fit. The Greek epithet and form of the acc. give a strong Hellenising tone to this section (see also 112, 113). The adjective also evokes Hyacinthus (106–7n., 112n.), who was worshipped at Amyclae; see Bömer on Ov. *Met.* 10.162.

112–13 Two further mythological parallels in parenthesis: had they known Glaucias, Apollo and Hercules would have exchanged him for the youths they loved (and lost), Hyacinthus and Hylas. Such homoerotic comparisons, with their emphasis on the ephemeral nature of beauty, provide a tragic undercurrent that also elevates Glaucias as a form of cultural as well as emotional capital; the compliment to Glaucias extends to Melior, implicitly in the company now of heroes and gods; see 88–105n.

112 Oebaliden: a patronymic for Hyacinthus, descended from the Spartan Oebalus; cf. Ov. *Met.* 10.196 *Oebalide*; Dilke on *Ach.* 1.20; Dewar on *Theb.* 9.690. **illo:** i.e. 'for Glaucias'. **praeceps...Apollo:** the god is 'impetuous' *(OLD* 3) since he would have rushed to exchange boys, and since his throw of the discus killed Hyacinthus (Ov. *Met.* 10.162–219); cf. *Theb.* 7.611 *praeceps...Tydeus*, with a similar negative valence. **mutaret** 'would have exchanged', imperf. subj. in an unreal condition (also 113, 115; *NLS* 121).

113 Alcides...Hylan: Hylas was Hercules' young squire on the Argo (*Theb.* 5.441–4) who was abducted by water nymphs (A. R. 1.1187–1362; Prop. 1.20; V. Fl. 3.481–725). **pensaret** 'would have bartered', an economic metaphor *(OLD* 3). **seu gratus amictu:** wrestlers were nude (Virg. *G.* 2.531); thus the cloak marks a shift to literary studies. Glaucias studied with a *grammaticus* (the profession of St.'s father; 5.3.146–94), who taught the art of speaking correctly (the mark of the educated Roman elite) and the interpretation of Greek and Latin poetry (Quint. *Inst.* 1.4.2, 1.8.4–12; Kaster 1988: xxvii–xxix; McNelis 2002;

Gibson on 5.3.148–58). Highly gendered, this system of education connected purity of body and of speech (Bloomer 2006). SB follows Van Dam in reading *Graius amictu* ('Greek in dress'), in keeping with Glaucias' Greek-style education; but Greek texts were central to Roman education and *gratus* suggests that he was pleasing to hear and watch. Children who died young were often represented as young scholars (40n.; Rawson 1999: 81). The grave monument of the eleven-year-old Q. Sulpicius Maximus, competitor in the Capitoline games of 94 CE, is inscribed with his competition poem and depicts him holding a scroll; see Rawson 1997: 222–3, 237; Hardie 2003a: 128, 133–4. Girls too were praised as scholars; cf. Plin. *Ep.* 5.16.3 (on Minicia Marcella) *quam studiose, quam intelligenter lectitabat!*

114 Attica facundi . . . orsa Menandri: as a model of eloquence for the young pupil Quintilian recommends Menander, the writer of Greek New Comedy (*Inst.* 1.8.7–8). He joins Homer and Euripides as the poets most studied at this level (McNelis 2002: 68).   **decurreret:** cf. 5.3.149 (of Homeric style) *decurrere uersu*, with Gibson. The verb suggests the boy's fluency (and ability to learn quickly).

115–16 laudaret gauisa sonum crinemque decorum | fregisset rosea lasciua Thalia corona 'wanton Thalia would have praised his voice in delight and would have crowned his beautiful hair with a wreath of roses'. In unreal conditions St. sometimes uses the pluperf. subj. interchangeably with the imperf. subj. (Vollmer on 1.1.60). The conventional theme of the Muse's reward to a poet here includes the precocious reciter.

116 fregisset: an unusual verb for crowning the hair with the rose garland; (*de*)*premere* is more usual for pressing down on hair; cf. Ov. *Am.* 1.10.6 *cum premeret summi uerticis urna comas. frangere* occurs in prose specifically of styling hair in curls or waves, a contemporary Flavian fashion; cf. Sen. *Con.* 1. *pr.* 8 *capillum frangere et ad muliebres blanditias extenuare . . . uocem*; Quint. *Inst.* 1.6.44 *comam in gradus frangere* ('to wave the hair tightly'); *TLL* VI 1.1245.64–7. St. may mean that the rose crown creates an extra layer to Glaucias' hair, so that it takes its place within the décor of his curls; arguably the line-end parallelism of *decorum* and *corona* (cf. *Theb.* 4.112–13) suggests the merging of hair and crown in a layered unity.   **rosea . . . corona:** the *corona* was a common emblem of poetic and athletic achievement; rose crowns in particular symbolised dedication to the Muses; cf. Prop. 3.3.36 (of a Muse) *at illa manu texit utraque rosam*; Hardie 2005a: 17–20. The rose was also known as very short-lived (N–H on Hor. *Carm.* 2.3.13–14). Thus the rose crown also anticipates the boy's death: the Romans celebrated a spring festival to the dead, the Rosaria, and roses commonly appeared in funerary art (Zanker 2004: 33–4).   **Thalia:** this Muse was associated with non-epic poetry and comedy, hence *lasciua*; cf. Virg. *Ecl.* 6.1–2 *prima Syracosio dignata est ludere uersu | nostra neque erubuit siluas habitare Thalia*, with Clausen; 5.3.98; Mart.

7.17.3 *lasciuae . . . Thaliae.* Her ancient assocation with θάλλω and hence with plant and human 'flourishing' also make her a poignant presence for a boy in the 'flower of youth'. On Thalia's associations with the cycle of life see Hardie 2005a: 25–7.

117 Maeonium . . . senem: Homer, commonly believed to be the son of Maeon (Graziosi 2002: 100); Hor. *Carm.* 1.6.2 introduced 'Maeonian', a Hellenistic coinage, to Roman poetry (N–H ad loc.). On the primacy of Homer in the curriculum of the *grammaticus* cf. 5.3.148–50; Quint. *Inst.* 1.8.5; McNelis 2002: 78–9; 114n. **Troiaeque labores:** the *Iliad*, so fundamental to Roman education that even Trimalchio claims he read Homer as a young slave (Petr. 48.7–8; cf. 59.4–5).

118 aut casus tarde remeantis Vlixis: periphrasis for the *Odyssey*. St. follows the order of his father's curriculum; cf. 5.3.148 *quis casus Troiae, quam tardus Vlixes.* In the *Siluae* Ulysses is always 'late' home; cf. 2.6.57, 2.7.49, 4.2.4; Ov. *Ep.* 1.1 *lento tibi . . . , Vlixe,* with Knox. *remeare* 'to go back home' is a Plautine word adopted by Virgil for epic (Austin on Virg. *A.* 2.95). Following Ovid, St. always uses the gen. *Vlixis* in place of Virgil's *Vlixi* (Austin on Virg. *A.* 2.7).

119 ipse pater sensus, ipsi stupuere magistri: after the subjunctives of 110–18, the indicative *stupuere,* along with asyndeton and assonance, emphasises the admiration of Glaucias' father and teachers. *stupeo* registers wonder at exceptional deeds or beauty, a feature of St.'s encomia; cf. 1.2.91, 1.5.43, 2.1.119, 2.3.52, 3.1.17, 4.2.20, 5.2.109, 117, 5.3.136. *sensus* suggests that Glaucias spoke with understanding of the words (rather than by rote) in his oral rendition of poetry. On *pater* see 102–3n. To ensure a son's proper education was an important paternal obligation; cf. 5.3.146–7. Since Roman literate education was aimed at training the citizen elite (Morgan 1998, esp. 226–36), Melior offered his foster son the opportunity to compensate perhaps for his humble origins.

120 scilicet . . . Lachesis: a sombre note after the triumph of Glaucias' recital; from birth he was marked out for a short life by Lachesis, one of the three *Parcae* ('Fates'), who spun 'the thread' of life (Hyg. *Fab.* 171; Clausen on Virg. *Ecl.* 4.47). First named at Hes. *Th.* 905, the Fates were later individualised by function; traditionally Clotho began the thread at birth, Lachesis drew it out, and Atropos cut it, but authors were not always consistent (Eden on Sen. *Apoc.* 4.1.1–2). Unlike Virgil, who never names the *Parcae* individually, St. often does so (Snijder on *Theb.* 3.68). The *Parcae* regularly appear on tombs; Zanker 2004: 66–7 discusses a child's sarcophagus depicting one of the *Parcae,* who stands behind the newborn holding a horoscope on which his short life span is already inscribed.

120–1 cunabula . . . | attigit: Roman etymology derived *Parcae* either from *a partu* 'from birth' (they were Roman birth goddesses before being linked to the

Greek Fates), or from *a non parcendo* 'from their inexorability' (Maltby s.v. *Parca*); cf. 3.3.186–7 *nec flectere Parcas | . . . datur*. These two ideas are grimly combined with Lachesis' evil touch of the cradle; cf. *Theb.* 2.249 *Lachesis . . . dura*. The touch of a supernatural being had powerful properties; cf. Ov. *Met.* 2.798–9 (Envy) *pectusque manu ferrugine tincta | tangit*. Venus bore the malformed Priapus because Hera, jealous of her rival's pregnancy, touched her belly with a curse (*RE* xxii 2.1916.60–1918.19).

120 infausta . . . dextra: a striking oxymoron, suggestive of a malignant deity, for the right hand usually brings good luck, but *infausta* has the active sense of 'bringing ill fortune' (*OLD* 2); cf. 5.1.141 (of 'Envy') *saeua . . . dextra*; 27n. St. may have been influenced by Cat. 64.311–13, where the left hand of the *Parca* holds the distaff but the right hand holds the thread and thus determines the child's fate. The portrayal of the Fate as malicious accords with epitaphic rather than literary convention (Lattimore 1962: 148–9, 156–8; Brelich 1937: 20–1, 27–9); cf. Cat. 64.303–83; Virg. *Ecl.* 4.46–7.

121–2 et gremio puerum complexa fouebat | Inuidia: Virgil, influenced by Callimachus, introduced Envy as a personification to Roman poetry; cf. Virg. *G.* 3.37–9 with Thomas; Ov. *Met.* 2.760–805. Envy is a rare figure in epitaphs, yet as a negative emotion aimed at those with the most promise it is commonly linked with the Fates, who cut short brilliant young lives; cf. 2.6.69; *Theb.* 10.384 *inuida fata piis*; Mart. 10.53.3 *inuida . . . Lachesis*; Quint. *Inst.* 6 *pr.* 10–11; Lattimore 1962: 157; Gibson on 5.1.137–44. Envy's clasp of Glaucias grimly contrasts with Melior's embraces (81 *amplexusque*).

122 illa: i.e. Envy, a perverse teacher who made the boy so talented and beautiful that he would be the greater cause for lament.   **genas et adultum comere crinem:** *comere* 'adorn' (95n.) properly refers here to the hair, not the cheeks, and thus is an instance of zeugma, a type of ellipsis in which one part of the expression must be supplied from the other part (Kenney on Lucr. 3.614); Lachesis made Glaucias' cheeks beautiful, presumably with the blush of youth, since he never grew a beard (52–4). *adultus* 'grown up, mature' is used of hair in the rare sense of 'fully grown' (*OLD* 5) and thus, as 115–16n. suggests, 'abundant'. The historical infinitive seldom appears singly (*NLS* 21); *comere* is followed by *monstrare, infigere* (123), giving emotional intensity to the duplicitous actions of *Inuidia*.

123 et monstrare artes et uerba infigere: instead of initial *et* SB reads Baehrens' *haec*, meaning 'the latter' (i.e. *Inuidia*); thus *illa* (122) means 'the former' (Lachesis). But Glaucias' beauty as well as intelligence surely both fall prey to *Inuidia*, whose essence is 'seeing' and who makes Glaucias desirable to herself as well as others; cf. Ov. *Met.* 2.780 (of Envy) *uidet . . . intabescitque uidendo*, with Barchiesi. *monstrare* means 'to teach' (2.4.31–2n.). By implanting (*infigere*) words in the boy's mind, Envy taught him to memorise and thus become fluent of speech.

123–4 quae nunc | plangimus: the two monosyllables at line end (see also 2.3.66) draw attention to the tragic contrast between past promise and present reality.

124–5 Herculeos annis aequare labores | coeperat assurgens: a controversial periphrasis for Glaucias' age shortly before his death. Mart. 6.28.8–9 claims the boy was twelve when he died (*bis senis modo messibus peractis | uix unum puer applicabat annum*, with Grewing); and Van Dam understands St. to mean that Glaucias' twelfth birthday had already passed. But the expression 'he had begun to equal Hercules' labours' suggests that Glaucias was *almost* twelve years old when, shortly before his death, he began to shoot up. But since he could have lived to his twelfth birthday, there is probably no discrepancy between Martial and St. over Glaucias' age at death.   **assurgens** 'as he was growing (up)', a plant metaphor (*OLD assurgo* 3b) for the 'flower of youth' (46n.).   **Herculeos . . . labores:** a Homeric imitation from Hor. *Carm.* 1.3.36, an ode on death's unpredictability (N–H ad loc.).

125 sed adhuc infantia iuxta 'and infancy was still close at hand'. *iuxta* is adverbial and temporal; cf. *Theb.* 8.610 *nec mala quae iuxta* 'not recent evils'. For the Romans, 'infancy' could last till age seven (Quint. *Inst.* 1.1.18; Grewing on Mart. 6.38.6).

126–7 mensuraque maior | cultibus 'his height was greater than his clothing'.

128–9 cum tibi quas uestes, quae non gestamina mitis | festinabat erus? 'when what clothes, what adornments did your kind master not hurry to acquire for you?'; *non* is ἀπὸ κοινοῦ with *quas* and *quae*. Courtney 1968: 53–4 emends *uestes* to the more difficult *telas* 'cloth woven on a web', transposed from 130, on the grounds that *uestes* already occurs at the end of 127. But as Vollmer suggests, the close repetition of *uestes* emphasises the speed of replacement (*festinabat*). *gestamina*, a grand, poetic word for stately objects such as shields and sceptres (first at Virg. *A.* 3.286 *clipeum, magni gestamen Abantis*), is humorously used for 'the trappings' for a small boy's clothes.

129–30 breuibus constringere laenis | pectora et angusta nolens artare lacerna 'not wishing to constrict his chest with short mantles or confine it with a tight cloak'. Courtney replaced M's *telas* (see 128–9n.) with *nolens* (cf. Courtney 2004: 450, who proposes *uitans*); otherwise these lines would suggest Melior's cruelty in constricting the boy in tight garments for fashion's sake rather than his considerate choice of clothing (131–2). Assonance of *a* humourously replicates the sound of distress from the constriction of a too tight garment. *laena* and *lacerna* are virtually synonyms, though the former has epic resonance as the only cloak mentioned by Virgil (Austin on Virg. *A.* 4.262–3). The *lacerna* appears frequently in Martial's epigrams as a rich, handsome garment; Mart. 8.10.1 refers to a *lacerna* costing ten thousand sesterces. On these two types of cloak see Wilson 1938: 112–25.

131–2 enormes non ille sinus sed semper ad annos | texta legens: Melior chose 'age appropriate' clothing, not garments with huge folds that would constrict movement.

132–3 modo puniceo uelabat amictu: *puniceus* 'the Phoenician colour' was deep scarlet, an expensive dye; the spectrum of reds was highly prized (Mart. 8.10.1–2; Plin. *Nat.* 9.124–38). St. may hint that Glaucias wore clothes similar in rich colour to the purple-striped *praetexta* of the nobly born, for he was noble in all but origin; see 136n.   **modo . . . nunc** signifies repetitive actions (Vollmer on 2.1.170; 2.4.30n.).

133 nunc herbas imitante sinu: green was a highly unusual colour in clothing, associated with bad taste and sexual deviancy in men, though Ovid finds it comely for women (Gibson on Ov. *Ars* 3.181; Hopman 2003: 563, 569–70). Here the analogy with grass (133) associates the garment's colour with the vigour of youth.

133–4 nunc dulce rubenti | murice: cf. Virg. *Ecl.* 4.43–4 *suaue rubenti | murice*. The neuter acc. adjective used adverbially is a Graecism cultivated probably first by Catullus (42.8, 51.5, 61.7) and favoured by St.; e.g. 226, 2.2.137, 3.1.40; *Theb.* 4.833. As the most expensive purple of all, the dye from the shellfish *murex* was morally suspect (Gibson on Ov. *Ars* 3.170 and 172). But Virgil's association of a boy's idealised youth with harmless luxuries, a sign of Golden Age renewal, gives positive value to Glaucias' rich cloak. Dress communicates and constitutes personal identity. Like the gorgeous furnishings of Pollius' villa (2.2.85–93), Glaucias' dress also attests to Melior's generosity, taste, and high social status.

134–5 tum uiuis digitos incendere gemmis gaudebat 'then he [*sc.* Melior] delighted to see his [*sc.* the boy's] fingers blaze with sparkling gems'. *uiuis* refers to the gems' apparent emission of fiery sparks (*OLD* 5b); *incendere* suggests their fiery brilliance; cf. *Theb.* 10.60 *purpura . . . mixtoque incenditur auro*. Expensive rings were a regular part of a Roman male's adornment (Quint. *Inst.* 11.3.142).

135 non turba comes . . . cessant: Glaucias had a constant throng of slaves and teachers; cf. Plin. *Ep.* 5.16.2 (of twelve-year-old Minicia Marcella) *ut nutrices, ut paedagogos, ut praeceptores pro suo quemque officio diligebat!*

136 sola uerecundo derat praetexta decori: *derat* is syncopated (= *deerat*). Glaucias was worthy of wearing purple but not the *praetexta*, the purple-bordered tunic worn by boys of noble family or at least free birth (Gibson on 5.3.119; Wilson 1938: 130) – a delicate acknowledgment of social distinction in dress. *uerecundo . . . decori* ('modest finery', SB) links dress to a familiar set of Roman ethical values based on moderation; cf. *Plin. Ep.* 5.16.2 (on Minicia Marcella) *suauitas puellaris cum uirginali uerecundia.*

137–45 Graphic personification animates the complaint against fate, a standard topos of *consolationes*; a third set of mythological parallels follows (cf. 88–100, 112–13).

137–8 subitas inimica leuauit | Parca manus: a puzzling gesture of raising the hands. Van Dam suggests it means a direct attack upon the boy, for the Fate's next gesture is to unsheathe her nails (138). But there is no precedent for *leuare manus* implying hostile intent (*TLL* VII 2.1232.27–44; SB on *Theb.* 6.779–80 n.84). 2.5.21 *attollitque manum* offers a possible parallel, but the action is defensive. Or are we to imagine that the Fate suddenly raised her hands off the loom-wheel and stopped spinning? This however would be a unique variation of the more common cutting short the thread of life (Lattimore 1962: 160–1). *subitas* is a transferred epithet that focuses on the hands as the signifiers of life and death. Sing. *Parca* is rare (McKeown on Ov. *Am.* 2.6.45–6).

138 quo, diua, feros grauis exseris ungues? 'for what purpose, goddess, do you harshly unsheathe your savage nails?'; a dramatic apostrophe and a rare characterisation of the Fate as a physically menacing figure; cf. 2.6.78–9 (Nemesis) *carpsitque immitis adunca | ora uerenda manu*; *Theb.* 2.513 (the Sphinx) *acuens exsertos . . . ungues. exserere* 'to disclose', often of arms or hands (*TLL* v2. 1855.16–35), can connote menace (cf. Virg. *A.* 1.492) and is a metaphor for 'unsheathing a sword' (*OLD* 2b; 2.7.53n.). *ungues*, generally accepted for M's *angues*, continues the ominous focus on 'hands'.

140 hunc: i.e. Glaucias; cf. *ab hoc* (143), *hunc* (144). Here he is compared to young children who met an untimely death at the hands of avenging adults, popular tragic themes: Itys (140), the sons of Jason and Medea (141–2), Learchus (142) and Astyanax (144–5). As at 112–13 the parallels are presented as unreal conditions: if Glaucias had been in their place, his beauty and youth would have saved him.   **nec:** the postposition of *nec* is frequent in the *Siluae*; cf. 2.1.184, 2.2.56, 2.3.60, 2.4.36, 2.6.30, 2.6.91.   **saeua uiro . . . Procne:** after her husband's rape and mutilation of her sister Philomela, Procne murdered her son Itys and served him to Tereus as a cannibalistic feast (Ov. *Met.* 6.424–674); see 2.4.21n. *saeua* has concessive force 'though fierce' (i.e. to her husband).   **carpere:** a grim conflation of its two meanings 'to pluck away in death' (*OLD* 5b; cf. 2.6.78–9 cited above; 5.1.150 *carpitur eximium Fato Priscilla decorem*) and 'to chop into pieces' (*OLD* 6), Procne's method of killing her son.

141 fera . . . Colchis: i.e. Medea, named from her native Colchis; Ov. *Met.* 7.394 uses the epithet to dehumanise Medea and stress her barbarian origins at the moment that she carries out her revenge on Jason by killing their sons; *fera* is thus virtually pleonastic.   **nec . . . crudeles . . . durasset in iras** 'nor would [she] have steeled herself to ruthless wrath' (SB); for this sense of *duro* with *in* see *OLD* 4a.

142 Aeolia . . . Creusa: 'Aeolian' means 'Corinthian'; Creusa, Jason's new wife, was descended from Aeolus, father of Sisyphus, founder of Corinth (Hine on Sen. *Med.* 105 *Aeoliam . . . uirginem*). Even if Glaucias had been the son of Creusa, her hated rival Medea could not have murdered him.

143 toruus . . . Athamas: king of Thebes (and husband of Ino; see 98n.), who killed his infant son Learchus in a fit of madness inspired by vengeful Juno (Ov. *Met.* 4.464–542; *Fast.* 6.489–90). *toruus* describes unbridled, savage emotion (Dewar on *Theb.* 9.381).   **ab hoc . . . insanos flecteret arcus:** there were several versions of the Athamas/Learchus myth in antiquity; see Bömer on Ov. *Met.* 4.512–19. St. departs from Ovid, who has Athamas smash his baby's head with a rock (Ov. *Met.* 4.515–20; at *Fast.* 6.490 the infant dies vaguely 'by the father's hand'). As at *Theb.* 1.12–13 St. follows another tradition, in which Athamas killed the child with arrows (Apollod. 1.9.2; Hyg. *Fab.* 5). *arcus* is a common poetic plural, here with *insanos* as a transferred epithet. On the interchangeability of imperf. subj. and pluperf. subj. in unreal conditions see 115–16n.

144–5 The most famous of tragic children, Astyanax, son of Hector and Andromache, forms the climax with two lines; on such *amplificatio* see 88n.; Cancik 1965: 31.

144 Hectoreos 'of Hector', a stately, epic adjective with Homeric resonance (Ἑκτόρεος) in place of the possessive gen. *Hectoris*; see N–R on Hor. *Carm.* 3.3.26–8; Bömer on Ov. *Met.* 1.779. On the high stylistic register of adjectives denoting possession or attribution ending in *-eus* see McKeown on Ov. *Am.* 1.1.29–30. St. perhaps recalls Virg. *A.* 3.304, the pathos-filled scene with Andromache at Hector's tomb (*Hectoreum ad tumulum*), where she laments Astyanax.

145 turribus e Phrygiis flesset missurus Vlixes: an ironic climax. According to post-Homeric tradition, Odysseus hurled Astyanax from the towers of Troy; cf. Ov. *Met.* 13.415 *mittitur Astyanax illis de turribus*, with Bömer; Virg. *A.* 2.6–8 *quis . . . | duri miles Vlixi | temperet a lacrimis?* Spondaic *flesset* occupies the line's centre, drawing attention to the validity of grief and tears in epic contexts. Yet *missurus*, very possibly predicative in use (106n.), also suggests that this most calculating of epic heroes, though shedding tears, would have thrown the boy.

146–57 The scene at the deathbed is vividly reimagined. Priscilla's deathbed scene has similar details (5.1.170–96), for literary deathbed scenes employ conventional topoi (McKeown on Ov. *Am.* 2.6.45–8). But the pres. tense here lends pathos and immediacy.

146 septima lux: often the critical, final day of an illness (McKeown on Ov. *Am.* 2.6.47). Ellipsis suggests the brevity of the boy's illness.   **frigentia lumina:**

coldness is a sign of death (*OLD frigeo* 1b; Virg. *A.* 3.483 *frigida mors*), as heat is a sign of life; see Pease on Virg. *A.* 4.705 *dilapsus calor.*   **torpent** 'grow dim', a switch to the vivid pres. tense. Cf. Plin. *Nat.* 7.168 (on the signs of approaching death) *hebescunt sensus, membra torpent, praemoritur uisus, auditus, incessus*; the most obvious signs appear in the eyes and nose (*Nat.* 7.171). On the failure of the eyes to focus at the end see Gibson on 5.1.170.

147 iam complexa manu crinem tenet infera Iuno: 'Underworld Juno' is Proserpina (Austin on Virg. *A.* 6.138 *inferna Iuno*). The cutting of a lock of hair to symbolise the release of the soul and the dedication of the deceased to the Underworld first appears at E. *Alc.* 74 (Austin on Virg. *A.* 4.693–705; N–H on Hor. *Carm.* 1.28.20). Glaucias' death is given a distinguished literary pedigree. *complexa* recalls the sinister embrace of *Inuidia* and her inversion of the affectionate foster relationship; see 121–2n.

148 Parcis fragiles urguentibus annos: a rare temporal use of *fragilis* (*OLD* 3c); cf. Ov. *Tr.* 4.8.3 (of old age) *subeunt anni fragiles et inertior aetas.*

149 te uultu moriente uidet: cf. Ov. *Met.* 10.194 *sic uultus moriens iacet* (of Hyacinthus; 112–13n.). By literary convention the dying looks at and addresses the beloved alone, a tragic modification of the erotic trope that lovers have eyes only for one another; cf. 5.1.174–5 *nec sole supremo | lumina sed dulci mauult satiare marito*, with Gibson; *Theb.* 8.649–50 *illam unam . . . | aspicit.* Polyptoton – *te* (149), (*in*) *te* (150), *tibique, tibi* (152) – emphasises the child's love for Melior.

149–50 linguaque cadente | murmurat: 'murmuring', once pleasing babble (62n., 104–5n.), now describes the indistinct speech of the dying; cf. Ov. *Met.* 11.52–3 (of Orpheus) *lingua | murmurat*; *Theb.* 10.440 *supremaque murmura uoluens*, with Williams.

150–1 in te omnes uacui iam pectoris efflat | reliquias 'upon you he breathes his very last from his now empty chest'. The capturing of the dying's last breaths, believed to be the departing soul, was a convention of the deathbed scene; cf. 3.3.19–20; Dewar on *Theb.* 9.898–9. Unusually, St. focuses on the giving rather than the capturing of the last breath; thus Glaucias serves Melior to the end; cf. 5.1.194–5 (of Priscilla) *haerentemque animam non tristis in ora maritis | transtulit*, with Gibson.

150 uacui . . . pectoris: cf. Lucr. 2.46 *uacuum pectus*, with Fowler 2002. Glaucias' chest is empty of breath but also, in the Lucretian sense, now free from mortal cares.

150–1 efflat | reliquias: a variant with Lucretian resonance of the more common *animam efflare* (*OLD efflo* 1b); cf. Lucr. 6.825 *reliquiae uitae.*   **reliquias:** avoided by previous poets apart from Plautus and Lucretius; the dactylic scansion

of the first three syllables is Lucretian. See Kenney on Lucr. 3.648; L–H–S
136.

151–2 solum . . . solumque . . . | . . . tibique . . . tibi: repetition stresses
Glaucias' fidelity to his foster father to the very end.   **uocantem | exaudit:**
cf. 5.1.171–2 *obtunsaeque aures, nisi cum uox sola mariti | noscitur*, with Gibson.

152 relinquit: a response at line end to *reliquias* at line start (151) as *figura
etymologica* (Malby s.v. *reliquiae*), a strong contrast with *Theb.* 11.566–7 (Eteocles'
treacherous death), which uses exactly the same device. Double line-framing is
characteristic of the elegiac couplet in Ovid and Martial (Wills 430–50) and gives
an 'elegiac' effect here at this climactic scene of high pathos.

153 et prohibet gemitus consolaturque dolentem: a conventional prohibition by the dying person against grieving (Vollmer on 2.6.93; Gibson on
5.1.180); cf. 5.1.179–80 *parce precor lacrimis, saeuo ne concute planctu | pectora, nec crucia
fugientem coniugis umbram.* The beloved's last words were also a standard topos
(McKeown on Ov. *Am.* 2.6.47–8). Priscilla speaks at length (5.1.177–93), but this
cannot be expected of a child. St. uses *consolari* only here; it is rare in poetry,
compared to *solari*, which St. uses frequently in the *Siluae* (*TLL* iv 479.25–31).

154 gratum est, Fata: cf. (with similar irony) *Theb.* 12.338–9 *gratum est, Fortuna*;
peracta | spes longinqua uiae: totos inuenimus artus.

154–5 quod non mors lenta iacentis | exedit puerile decus: a grim
alimentary metaphor of death 'eating away' youthful beauty; the three monosyllables sound a death knell. But unlike Priscilla, who lost her beauty to illness
(5.1.150–3), Glaucias could depart as lovely in death as he was in life. *mors lenta* is 'a
lingering death'; cf. Sen. *Her. F.* 420 *et longa fame | mors protrahatur lenta.*   **iacen-
tis** 'as he lay ill' (*OLD iaceo* 2c); cf. *Theb.* 8.646 (the dying Atys).

156 integer et nullo temeratus corpora damno: *integer* = 'unimpaired',
an idea expanded in the rest of the line (N–H on Hor. *Carm.* 1.31.18 *integra cum
mente*); cf. *Ach.* 1.302 *nullo temeratus pectora motu.*

157 qualis erat: an epic formula = *sicut erat* 'just as he was'; cf. Virg. *A.* 2.274,
with Austin; unlike Hector, who appeared as a ghost to Aeneas, Glaucias suffered
no diminution of his beauty (Hardie 1993: 112–13). The striking enjambment (cf.
Theb. 4.314, with Micozzi; *Theb.* 10. 204) draws attention to the shift to the past
tense and brings closure to the emotional deathbed scene; Glaucias is no more,
but beautiful in memory.

157–82 The scene at the pyre, a return to the events described at 19–25. Glaucias' cremation is described in two stages, first the adding of unguents to the
flames, then Melior's violent grief before as well as during the cremation. The
abruptly shifting temporal and spatial perspectives that characterise this poem are
esp. evident here, giving the scene a restless energy that conveys deep emotional
distress.

157–8 quid ego . . . loquar? a transitional opening; see 96n.   **prodiga flammis | dona** 'lavish gifts for the flames', understanding *flammis* as dat. after *dona*, not as abl. with *prodiga* = 'wasteful of' (Van Dam), which would mean the gifts needed a lot of fire for burning, a sense that normally takes the gen. (and the child's pyre is small, 164–5). The lavish funeral is a standard part of the 'consolations' in the *Siluae*; see 2.4.33–7, 2.6.85–93, 3.3.31–42, 5.1.208–21. Glaucias is cremated like a prince. But implicit here is the idea that the poem, as a gift (2 *pr.* 11), is far more durable than funerary offerings; cf. 2.7.103n.; Nauta 2008: 159.

158 maestoque . . . luxu: a striking oxymoron that transfers the mourner's grief to his gifts; cf. 159 *tristis rogus*; 177 *flammis . . . tristibus*; *Theb.* 6.54 (Opheltes' pyre) *tristibus . . . ramis*. Melior's funeral gifts reveal the magnitude of his grief; cf. 21 *turis aceruos.* But their size, appearance and content were also essential to determining the status of the deceased and the donor (Noy 2000: 44–5).   **funera** 'corpse' (22n.).

159 quod is loosely dependent on *loquar* (158) in the sense of 'the fact that'. Its repetition at the start of each line (159–61) and within 160 suggests the piling up of gifts.   **tibi:** a momentary return full of pathos to second-person address of Glaucias.   **purpureo . . . aggere:** two senses of *agger* are conflated here: 'a funeral mound' (*OLD* 5) and 'a heap of things' (*OLD* 6; Luc. 2.230), hence 'a pile of funeral gifts'; cf. *Theb.* 6.58. The use of purple in funerary contexts was prestigious (Zeiner 2005: 97–9); here St. probably refers to expensive purple cloths (including perhaps Glaucias' clothing; 133–4n.) thrown on the pyre, as at Misenus' funeral; cf. Virg. *A.* 6.221 *purpureasque . . . uestes*, with Norden; Opheltes' funeral pyre was crowned with a purple cloth, a sign of royalty (*Theb.* 6.62–3; cf. *Theb.* 5.315). To place goods, often of personal significance to the deceased, on the pyre along with the body was standard Roman practice (Noy 2000: 41–3). Plin. *Ep.* 4.2.3 attacks Regulus for his extravagant funeral gifts to his son – ponies, dogs, song-birds, and parrots – which reflect, however, a child's love of animals and pets.

160 Cilicum flores 'saffron' from Cilicia (2.6.87; Plin. *Nat.* 21.31). Foreign, costly perfumes were a status symbol (Noy 2000: 38; Zeiner 2005: 102–6), though their purpose was to anoint the body and disguise the smell of death (Courtney on Juv. 4.109).   **munera graminis Indi:** India produced a range of spices. As Gibson cautions on 5.1.212 *Indorumque . . . seges*, precise identification is not always possible or necessary. *munera* are 'gifts' or 'products' (*OLD* 5, 7 respectively) with the added nuance of 'funeral offerings' (*OLD* 1d; cf. Cat. 101.3, 8; Hor. *Carm.* 1.28.4).

161 Arabes Phariique Palaestinique liquores: a resonant line, the geographical names conjuring up a sense of opulence rather than specific unguents. Like India, the Middle East produced a variety of spices and perfumes (Gibson on 5.1.211). *Arabs* is a unique adjective; the noun *Arabs, -is* 'an Arabian' is more usual with reference to exported perfumes and spices; e.g. 2.4.35 *Arabum . . . gramine*; *Theb.* 6.59–60 *tertius adsurgens Arabum strue tollitur ordo | Eoas conplexus opes*. *Pharius* is frequent for 'Egyptian' (73n.), but *Palaestini* is rare; cf. 5.1.212–13 *praereptaque templis | tura Palaestinis*, with Gibson. *liquores* 'unguents' occurs in elevated poetry (*OLD* 1a).

162 arsuram lauere comam: the fut. participle (106n.) stresses the transience of the wealth showered on Glaucias, a point reinforced by its antithetical juxta-position with *lauere*; cf. 5.1.212 *Indorumque arsura seges*, with Gibson. The corpse was washed with unguents before the funeral (Virg. *A.* 6.219 *corpusque lauant frigentis et unguunt*; Toynbee 1971: 43–4).

162–4 cupit . . . | . . . non capit ignis: etymological play upon these related verbs (*cupidus a capiendo*; Maltby s.v. *cupidus*) underscores a central paradox of the cremation: Melior wishes to give too much, whereas the pyre (built for a child) cannot take all the gifts.

163 prodigus 'prodigal' (*OLD* 1a); cf. 158–9, here with more negative valence in that Melior seeks to squander his entire fortune on the pyre. A rare crit-icism of the expense; see Gibson on 5.1.210–14. Opheltes' father also brings gifts too weighty for a young child; cf. *Theb.* 6.73 *muneraque in cineres annis grauiora feruntur*. But such conspicuous consumption augments the child's hon-our; cf. *Theb.* 6.70–1 *sed cassa tamen sterilisque dolentes | fama iuuat, paruique auges-cunt funere manes*. **totos . . . succendere census:** Melior's desire to burn his entire 'estate' (*OLD census* 3; Zeiner 2005: 122–8) is underscored by assonance and (false) etymological play between *census* and *succendere* (Vollmer; Maltby s.v. *census*).

164–5 sed non capit ignis | inuidus: *inuidus* contrasts with *prodigus* (163), both in the same metrical position. Usually the funeral pyre is insatiable (182n.), but this fire is 'grudging' (*OLD inuidus* 2) in that it does not take all the gifts and is 'malevolent' (*OLD* 1; 121–2n.) in destroying Glaucias. A monosyllable in the fifth foot followed by two concluding disyllables is unusual metrical practice in St. (Van Dam); with the preceding *sed* it harshly emphasises the contrast with Melior's wild generosity; cf. Mart. 7.27.9 (of a boar too large for roasting) *te non capit ignis*.

165 artae desunt in munera flammae 'the small flames are unequal to the funeral gifts', a symbol of the failure of gifts to alleviate grief. *artae* 'small in size' (*OLD* 7) is unusual of flames, more usual of a funerary urn (cf. Ov. *Ep.* 11.124; Mart. 14.45.2). *deesse* with *in* instead of the simple dat. is rare and emphatically prosaic.

166 horror habet sensus 'a shudder seizes my senses' (SB). The poet's emotional reaction is explained in the next sentence: St. feared for his friend's sanity.

166–8 qualem te . . . | extimui 'how I feared the state you were in', an intensely emotional expression; cf. 5.1.108–9 *qualem te superi . . . | aspexere*, with Gibson.

166 funere summo 'at the end of the funeral rites' (*OLD summus* 5b).

167 Melior placidissime quondam: cf. 2.3.15 *placidi Melioris*; 2.3.64 *placido . . . in pectore*. *placidus* describes those friends of St. who have retired from public life (cf. 1.3.22 *placidi . . . Vopisci*; 2.2.9 *placidi . . . Polli*; 3.1.179 *placidae . . . Pollae*) and suggests their Epicurean calm, now abandoned by Melior in his grief, hence the shock of spondaic *quondam* ('formerly'). The tragic contrast between 'then' and 'now', often marked by *quondam* (ποτέ), is a standard theme of funerary poetry, but more often applied to the deceased than the bereaved (Lattimore 1962: 172–7).

168 tune ille hilaris comisque uideri? 'are you that man who was cheerful and friendly to look at?'; cf. 56–7n. Ellipsis conveys St.'s distress. The agreement of *tu* with *ille* emphasises the contrast between Melior's past and present state; *uideri* in place of the supine *uisu* is esp. poetic usage.

169 unde animi saeuaeque manus et barbarus horror: St. represents Melior's emotions on a tragic scale: 'passion' (*OLD animus* 9), hands 'cruel' in tearing clothes and beating the breast (cf. 171), and convulsive shuddering (cf. 166). *barbarus* 'fierce' (*OLD* 3) also retains its sense of 'un-Roman' (*OLD* 1). A funeral involves inversion on the part of the mourner as well as the deceased (27–8n.). Melior behaves in ways antithetical both to Epicurean values and to the self-contained *mores* of a Roman male. On similar physical signs of grief see Gibson on 5.1.20–2, 23. Violent emotion can be cathartic but here for the first time St. lightly criticises his friend for grief that destroys his true self.

170 fusus humi 'prostrate on the ground'; cf. 3.3.177 *prono fusum . . . uultu*.

171 toruus: cf. 143n. An implied warning perhaps that Melior should not emulate a figure like Athamas by pursuing grief to madness?   **pariter uestes et pectora rumpis:** *rumpis*, unique in the context of mourning, suggests the violence of Melior's actions; elsewhere *pectora rumpere* means 'to kill' (Van Dam).

172–3 dilectosque premis uisus et frigida lambis | oscula? 'do you press closed the beloved eyes and kiss the cold mouth?'; *osculum* has its primary meaning of 'mouth' (*OLD* 2). St. shifts back in time to just before the cremation, with dramatic use of the pres. tense (157–82n.). Commentators have condemned *lambis* ('you lick') on the grounds of taste (*TLL* VII 2.899.15–46). SB follows Van Dam in adopting Peerlkamp's emendation *labris* ('lips' *OLD* 2) for *lambis*, with *premis* as the main verb ('you press with your lips the beloved eyes and the cold mouth'). But *premere uisus* commonly refers to the traditional closing of the dead person's eyes (Toynbee 1971: 44; Hardie on Virg. *A.* 9.487); thus two verbs seem to be needed. Bentley emended *lambis* to *libas*, though when used of kissing *libare* suggests a pleasant experience (not cold lips); cf. Virg. *A.* 1.256 *oscula libauit natae*, with Austin; *OLD* 4. For a Roman reader *lambis* perhaps would not have seemed odd; taste is often culturally specific. Internal rhyme and end rhyme (171–3) accentuate the futility of such loving gestures.

173–4 genitor materque iacentis | maesta: Glaucias' birth parents; *maesta* is ἀπὸ κοινοῦ with both parents. *genitor* is an elevated word for 'father' (though he was a freed slave). Although technically illegal, marriage between slaves was common in the Roman family and indeed encouraged (Bradley 1984: 47–80). *iacentis* means 'of the dead boy'; cf. 154–5n. *iacere* appears often in epitaphs and funerary poetry in the sense 'to lie dead' (*OLD* 6; McKeown on Ov. *Am.* 2.6.20); cf. Ov. *Am.* 3.9.39 *iacet ecce Tibullus.*

174 sed attoniti te spectauere parentes: on competitiveness in grief see 23n. Melior, the real focus of the poem, is the spectacle, not the child and his pyre; cf. 5.1.216–17.

175 plebs cuncta nefas . . . flerunt: *nefas* indicates the violation of sacred order (Ganiban 2007: 34–5), thus here 'premature death'; cf. *Theb.* 5.992, 628, 6.161 (of Opheltes); *Theb.* 9.887 (of Parthenopaeus). The collective sing. noun referring to a large number regularly governs a pl. verb (L–H–S 436–7); cf. *Theb.* 1.561 *plebs . . . litant.*

175–6 et praeuia . . . | agmina: commentators have taken this phrase as the subject of *flerunt*, along with *plebs*, assuming that St. refers to 'the crowds who led the way' to the site of cremation. But at 20 the people watch out of deference as the procession goes past. Thus *praeuia . . . agmina* could mean the funeral train, the object (with *nefas*) of *flerunt*.

176–7 Flaminio quae limite Muluius agger | transuehit: cf. Mart. 6.28.4–5 *hoc sub marmore Glaucias humatus | iuncto Flaminiae iacet sepulchro.* The Flaminian Way was the main artery north from Rome, crossing the Tiber on the Mulvian bridge. Since Roman law forbade cremations and burials within the city, tombs lined the roads outside the walls, providing a record of the deceased's life for passersby (Courtney on Juv. 1.170–1); cf. Prop. 4.7.4 *murmur ad extremae nuper humata uiae.* Tombs housing cinerary urns were often quite elaborate (Toynbee 1971: 48–50, 101–32).

176 agger 'mound', a unique metaphor for 'bridge' (*OLD* 4b) that evokes its arched shape. Bridges served as symbolic liminal points between life and death (Hallett 1970).

177–8 immeritus . . . | . . . meretur: verbal and grammatical play brings out the paradox of Glaucias' death: because he was so young and beautiful Glaucias did not deserve to die, but he deserves lamentation because of his beauty and youth. On this Ovidian 'resumptive' style of syntax see Wills 311–28, esp. 325–6. That the young did not 'deserve' to die is a common theme of epitaphs (Lattimore 1962: 183–4).

177 infans: a term full of pathos for the twelve-year-old Glaucias, 'infancy' traditionally extending to age seven (125n.). It anticipates a final set of mythological comparisons to two very young children important to Hellenistic legend and to St., Palaemon and Opheltes (179–82). Call. fr. 384.25–6 Pf. (cf. *Aet.* 3 fr. 59.5–9 Pf.) mentions the two together in connection with their respective foundations of the Isthmian and Nemean games, a theme which appealed to the learned poet and provided a paradigm for consolation; cf. *Theb.* 6.1–4, 10–14; Smolenaars on *Theb.* 7.97; Newlands 1991: 442. Their extreme youth and connections with foster parenting – Palaemon's mother Ino was Bacchus' nurse, Opheltes was the foster child of Hypsipyle – make them apt points of comparison here.

179–80 talis . . . Palaemon: according to Ovid, after her husband's murder of Learchus (143n.), Ino leapt with her infant son (then known as Melicertes) from a cliff into the sea; but the gods took pity and by divine aid they were conveyed to Corinth where they became divinities with changed names, Palaemon and Leucothea (*Met.* 4.519–42; *Fast.* 6.485–502). According to another tradition that St. seems partly to follow here, the child died en route and the Isthmian games were founded in his honour upon arrival of mother and son in Corinth (*Theb.* 6.10–14). On the popularity of this myth in Hellenistic poetry see Dewar on *Theb.* 9.328–3; *RE* xv 1.514–20. No Roman poet refers to the myth of Palaemon and Ino more than St. At 3.2.39–40 he invokes the favour of Palaemon and his mother for his *Thebaid* (cf. their invocation by Philodemus at *AP* vi 349); he refers to them at the start of the *Thebaid* (1.12–14) and frequently thereafter (Williams on *Theb.* 10.425). St. refers to the myth three times in 2.1: Ino appears as Bacchus' nurse (97–8), her husband as the murderer of their son Learchus (143–4); here St. refers to the end of the story, emphasising the pathos of premature death; Hellenistic poets tended rather to explore the aetiology of the games and the custom of child sacrifice; cf. Call. *Aet.* 4 fr. 91–2 Pf.; Lyc. 229.   **in Isthmiacos prolatus . . . portus | naufragus:** cf. *Theb.* 9.401–2 *qualiter Isthmiaco nondum Nereida portu | Leucothean planxisse ferunt.* The rare adjective *Isthmiacus* occurs only in St. and Silius, a transliteration of the equally rare Greek Ἰσθμιακός (Dewar on *Theb.* 9.401); St. refers to Lechaeum, the Corinthian harbour (2.2.34–5n.), with a hint at the founding of the Isthmian games. *prolatus* is perhaps deliberately vague, for traditions vary about how Palaemon and Ino were conveyed to Corinth from Thebes; at Ov. *Fast.* 6.499–500 the nymphs bear them smoothly ashore; other versions cite a dolphin (*Theb.* 1.121–2, 9.331) or a boat (Bömer on Ov. *Met.* 4.519–42). *naufragus* 'shipwrecked' suggests that Palaemon and his mother set out by boat but had to abandon it for another form of transport. Shipwreck does not occur in any of the other known versions of this myth, but it perhaps explains why

Palaemon drowned, according to St.; cf. *Theb.* 9.403 *frigidus in matrem saeuum mare respuit infans. naufragus*, first in poetry at Cat. 68.3, may evoke another paradigm of tragic loss, Catullus' brother.

180 imposita iacuit sub matre 'and lay with his mother covering his body' (SB). *iacuit* suggests the boy was dead (*OLD* 6; cf. 173–4n.) before he reached Corinth. The mother's protective gesture is thus full of pathos; perhaps she too is dead; cf. *Theb.* 9.401–2.

181 anguiferae . . . Lernae: a marshy region famous for Hercules' slaying of the Hydra (Fitch on Sen. *Her. F.* 241–2), Lerna was near Nemea where Opheltes was killed by another gigantic snake; cf. *Theb.* 5.579 *cognatae stagna indignantia Lernae. anguifer* was coined for the Gorgon by Propertius (2.2.8); see Bömer on Ov. *Met.* 4.741. St. uniquely applies the adjective to a dangerous place; cf. 3.2.119 (of Cleopatra's palace) *anguiferamque domum*. Opheltes is the central child victim of the *Thebaid*, founder of the Nemean games (*Theb.* 5.534–40; *RE* xviii 1.635–40). St. is fond of epicising adjectival compounds ending in *-fer* or *-ger* (Williams on *Theb.* 10.28). **in . . . ludentem gramine:** cf. *Theb.* 4.793–5 *at puer in gremio uernae telluris et alto | gramine nunc faciles sternit procursibus herbas | in uultum nitens.*

182 rescissum squamis: alliteration and assonance grimly reproduce the sound of skin being flayed; Opheltes' body was 'torn open' (*OLD rescindo* 2b) by the accidental flick of the serpent's tail (*Theb.* 5.538–9); cf. *Theb.* 5.598 *totumque in uulnere corpus. squamis* 'scales' is synecdoche for the serpent's tail; cf. *Theb.* 6.247 *squameus* (sc. *serpens*). **auidus bibit ignis:** the unusual *bibit* refers to the quantities of unguents poured on Opheltes' pyre as well, perhaps, to the child's blood-covered body (*Theb.* 5.596–604). The notion of the funeral pyre as greedy is commonplace; cf. Prop. 2.28.56 *ignis auarus*; Ov. *Am.* 3.9.28 *auidos . . . rogos.* Thus Brelich 1937: 21: 'la vita produce, la morte consuma'. Opheltes had a grand funeral (*Theb.* 6.1–248); cf. 163n. **Ophelten:** metrically parallel at line end with *Palaemon*, thus linking the two tragic infants. Glaucias becomes the third 'infant' honoured in St.'s poetry.

183–226 Formal consolation now begins and falls into two parts. The first is devoted to Glaucias' kindly reception in the Underworld (183–207), a conventional motif of literary consolation but given here a personalised slant (McKeown on Ov. *Am.* 2.6.48–59; Setaioli 2005: 254–6); the second part runs through conventional consolatory topoi (208–26). In Roman thought there was no orthodox position about the existence of an afterlife (Lattimore 1962: 21–65). The end of Lucr. 3 (830–1094) urging that death is not to be feared (a major tenet of Epicureanism; see Kenney on Lucr. 3.38–40; Thomas on Virg. *G.* 2.491–2) provides an important model for St. here.

183 pone metus letique minas desiste uereri: a Lucretian injunction that St. proceeds to illustrate in a non-Lucretian way; the Underworld monsters

Cerberus, Charon and the Furies will not harm Glaucias. By contrast Lucr. 3.978–1023 condemns such traditional terrors of the Underworld as irrational products of the imagination (Kenney ad loc.).

184 illum nec terno latrabit Cerberus ore: the three-headed dog Cerberus guarded entrance to the Underworld, threatening to kill all trespassers (Virg. *A.* 6.417–25, with Austin; *Theb.* 2.26–31), and attacking any shades who tried to leave (Hes. *Th.* 769–73). *ternus* 'triple' often characterises the monstrous (e.g. Virg. *A.* 5.120 of the gigantic ship Chimaera; Sil. 1.279 of Geryon); Ovid first uses it of Cerberus (*Met.* 10.22), then Seneca; cf. Sen. *Her. F.* 62 *terna monstri colla*, with Fitch, 784 *terna capita*, 796 *ora . . . terna*. Here St. wittily echoes 1.3.5 (Vopiscus' escape from the Dogstar heat) *illum nec calido latrauit Sirius astro*; Glaucias too will be protected from a fatal 'dog' because of his good character and also, probably, his youth; cf. 5.1.249–50 *nempe times ne Cerbereos Priscilla tremescat | latratus? tacet ille piis.* The theme of the beloved's special protection in the Underworld is elegiac, introduced at Prop. 4.11.25–6 (Cornelia's apotropaic wish) *Cerberus et nullas hodie petat improbus umbras | et iaceat tacita laxa catena sera*; cf. Prop. 4.5.3–4. St. often makes such intercessions for the newly dead; cf. 3.3.26–7 *longe | tergeminus custos*, with Laguna; 5.3.277–87; *Theb.* 4.486–7.

185–6 nulla soror flammis, nulla assurgentibus hydris | terrebit: torches and snakes were conventional attributes of the three Furies, traditionally sisters; cf. *Culex* 218–19 *obuia Tisiphone, serpentibus undique compta | et flammas et saeua quatit mihi uerbera*; Ov. *Met.* 6.662 *uipereasque . . . sorores*, with Bömer. Repetition of *nulla* with asyndeton emphasises that the boy has nothing to fear. Polysyllabic *assurgentibus* in the fifth foot adds horror to the depiction of the Furies; cf. Sil. 6.186 *serpens extulit assurgens caput*.

186 quin ipse auidae trux nauita cumbae: *nauita* is elevated and poetic (Fedeli on Prop. 2.1.43), a rather comic noun for Charon, who ferries the dead over the river Styx in a small boat; *cumba* is used esp. of Charon's (Virg. *A.* 6.385; Norden on Virg. *A.* 6. 413). He is a post-Homeric figure (Austin on Virg. *A.* 6.298–301); his boat is 'greedy' since it tries to take as many souls as possible, a symbol of death's insatiability; cf. 182; *Epic. Drusi* 357–8 *omnes expectat auarus | portitor et turbae uix satis una ratis.* The asseverative use of adverbial *quin* confirms that Glaucias also need not fear Charon.

187 interius . . . subibit: a touching detail that brings to life a conventional scene. Charon, untypically kind, will push the boat closer to shore to help Glaucias embark.

187–8 adusta . . . | litora: *adusta* plays upon φλέγω to suggest the Phlegethon, the river of fire surrounding Tartarus; cf. Hom. *Od.* 10.513; Virg. *A.* 6.550–1 *rapidus flammis ambit torrentibus amnis, | Tartareus Phlegethon*, with Austin. St. also transfers funerary imagery to the Underworld, its shores burned and barren as if by the pyre; cf. Prop. 4.7.8 (the singed dress of Cynthia's ghost) *adusta uestis*; *Theb.* 8.17 *ustaeque paludes*.

188 ne puero dura ascendisse facultas, (sc. *sit*) 'so that the child might not find climbing into the boat difficult', a play on *dura* and *facultas* (a doublet of *facilitas*). St. always uses *facultas* with an infinitive instead of the gerundive required in prose (L–H–S 351).

189–90 quid mihi . . . | nuntiat? a surprising shift to the epiphany of Mercury, messenger of the gods (*nuntiat*; cf. Hor. *Carm.* 1.10.6).

189 gaudenti . . . uirga: as opposed to the *caduceus*, Mercury's herald's staff, *uirga* was generally associated with his role of *psychopompos*, escort of the souls of the dead to the Underworld (N–H on *Carm.* 1.10.17, 18); cf. Hor. *Carm.* 1.24.16 *uirga . . . horrida*. *gaudenti* by contrast suggests the god's care not to frighten the child and marks the poem's shift to overtly consolatory themes – Mercury has come to announce the joyful news of Glaucias' welcome in Elysium. The belief that the righteous after death go to a special place of beauty and delight originates with Homer's Islands of the Blessed (Hom. *Od.* 4.561–9). Virgil popularised the notion of Elysium as a beautiful part of the Underworld set aside for the 'blessed', great warriors, statesmen and poets; cf. *A.* 6.637–78, with Austin. St. opens up Elysium to children too.   **proles Cyllenia:** a grand epic patronymic for Mercury, born on mount Cyllene in Arcadia (first at Hom. *Od.* 24.1 Κυλλήνιος; cf. Virg. *A.* 4.258, with Pease; Ov. *Ars* 3.725, with Gibson). The elevated style and divine intervention suggest the 'epic' solemnity of the descent to the Underworld and the urgent need for a change of heart in Melior. As god of lyric poetry (Hor. *Carm.* 1.10.6 *curuaeque lyrae parentem*) as well as *psychopompos*, Mercury is a fitting interlocutor for the poet. And as Olympus' most precocious infant – he had invented the lyre by noon on the day he was born (*h. Merc.* 17–18; N–H on Hor. *Carm.* 1.10.6) – he aptly intervenes for Glaucias, a child prodigy.

191–2 nouerat effigies generosique ardua Blaesi | ora puer: Glaucias knew Melior's deceased friend Blaesus from his commemorative statues (*effigies*) and busts (*ora*); since *effigies* also means 'shade of the dead', it is thus easy for Glaucias to identify Blaesus in the Underworld (Vessey 1986: 2777). According to Mart. 8.38, Melior had set up an annuity fund for a *collegium* of scribes to honour Blaesus every year on his birthday (12 *ad natalicium diem colendum*); on such commemorative foundations see Hopkins 1983: 247–55. Melior also, it seems, maintained a private cult of Blaesus within his house, like Polla for her husband Lucan (2.7.124–31n.). By making Glaucias meet Blaesus, St. personalises the conventional hope that the deceased continued a blessed existence in the Underworld; as in life his low social status will be overcome by aristocratic protection.

191 Blaesi: he cannot be certainly identified but is possibly Iunius Blaesus, an anti-Flavian aristocrat legate who served under Vitellius in the civil wars of 68–9 (Tac. *Hist.* 1.59, 2.59, 3.39.2); despite his impeccable loyalty he was murdered on the orders of his jealous leader (Tac. *Hist.* 3.38–9; Hardie 1983: 66–7; Nauta 2002: 314–15). His characterisation here as *generosus* 'nobly born' and 'noble-spirited' (*OLD* 1, 2) accords with Tacitus' portraits of the Vitellian Blaesus at *Hist.* 2.59 *genere illustri, largus animo et par opibus*, and *Hist.* 3.39.2 *Blaeso super claritatem natalium et elegantiam morum fidei obstinatio fuit.*   **ardua:** a touch of humour – from the child's foreshortened view (see also 197, 202) Blaesus seems tall; he is also 'high-minded'; cf. 2.3.77 *ardua . . . gloria Blaesi*; *Theb.* 4.129 *pulchraeque docet uirtutis amorem | arduus Hippomedon*, with Micozzi.

192–3 domi noua serta ligantem | te uidet: the binding of garlands suggests perhaps a play on βλαισός 'twisted', an epithet used of ivy garlands at *AP* VII 21.4 (Gow-Page ad loc.) – fit garlands therefore for Blaesus. Fresh wreaths were common sepulchral ornaments for tomb, portrait bust and worshipper (Brelich 1937: 66). Dido decks the image of Sychaeus in a private shrine with fillets and garlands; cf. Virg. *A.* 4.459–60; Ov. *Ep.* 99–100, with Knox; *CE* 1988 (cited by Lattimore 1962: 136) *effigiem pro te teneo solacia nostri, | quam colimus sancte sertaque multa datur. noua* suggests that Melior kept the garlands fresh through constant renewal (2.7.9n.).

193 similes . . . ceras: *ceras* is a strictly poetic term for *imagines* (*OLD cera* 5), portrait busts kept in the atrium to inspire emulation of virtue and often wreathed; thus encaustic painting (Van Dam; 2.2.63n.) is not meant here; cf. Ov. *Fast.* 1.591 *perlege dispositas generosa per atria ceras*, with Bömer; Flower 1996: 33; Courtney on Juv. 8.1–9. *similes* indicates a close likeness (*OLD* 8); cf. 5.1.1 *similes . . . ceras*, with Gibson.   **tergentem pectore:** this puzzling phrase is commonly understood to refer to Melior's embracing Blaesus' statue; see Vollmer ad loc.; Gibson on 5.1.163–4 *pectore terget | limina*. The most common meaning of *tergere* however is 'to clean' (*OLD* 1); *imagines* became sooty from the smoke of the atrium (Juv. 8.8 *fumosos*); cf. *CIL* VIII 2.9052.13 (a testamentary disposition) *ut statuam meam et uxoris meae tergeat et unguat et coronet*; see also Lattimore 1962: 137. Cleaning as well as their adornment with fresh wreaths was part of the regular maintenance of commemorative statues (192–3). *pectore* however is very difficult; the sense we might expect here, 'with all his heart', requires *toto pectore* (*OLD pectus* 4b; cf. 2.2.70). Worship of Blaesus in place of an ancestor highlights a major theme of 2.1, the strong value given to friendship and affective ties rather than kinship; see 84–6n, 86–7n.

194 hunc . . . lustrantem . . . oras: the scene of strolling by a river and a similar metrical pattern evoke Virg. *Ecl.* 6.64 *errantem Permessi ad flumina Gallum*. Gallus and Blaesus died young; was Blaesus also, like Gallus, politically disgraced? See 191n.   **Lethaei . . . gurgitis:** cf. Cat. 65.5 *Lethaeo . . . gurgite*, the first use of *Lethaeus* (Λήθαιος) in Roman poetry (Norden on Virg. *A.* 6.714). *gurges* means 'a sheet of water' or 'river'; cf. 2.6.45 *Ledaeo gurgite* ('by the river Eurotas'). Drinking from the river Lethe meant forgetting one's former life; cf. Virg. *A.* 6.715 *securos latices et longa obliuia*, with Austin; Sil. 13.555 *Lethaeos . . . latices, obliuia mentis.*

195 Ausonios inter proceres seriemque Quirini: a stately line offering a Virgilian view of Elysium as crowded with distinguished Romans (*A.* 6.756–859). *proceres* were leading statesmen; *seriemque Quirini* 'the line of Quirinus [the deified Romulus]' is a grand periphrasis for Roman ancestors (85n.). But St. departs from Virgil by eschewing political themes; Blaesus welcomes a young child.

196 agnouit: enjambment stresses the irony of recognition by the Lethe. The reception of the newly dead in the Underworld by famous figures goes back to the encounter of the suitors' shades with Achilles and Agamemnon (Hom. *Od.* 24.1–204); the topos was variously adapted by Roman elegiac poets; e.g. Drusus is welcomed by his famous forebears (*Epic. Drusi* 329–42); Tibullus imagines his welcome by lovers in Elysium (Tib. 1.3.57–66); Ovid imagines Tibullus' reception by famous poets (Ov. *Am.* 3.59–66); see Gibson on 5.1.254–7. Here St. intertwines the two themes of family and friendship.

196–7 timide primum uestigia iungit | accessu tacito: *timide* and *tacito* touchingly suggest the child's shyness, awe and light step. *tacito* also evokes the conventional silence of the Underworld (cf. Virg. *A.* 6.264–5 *umbraeque silentes | . . . loca nocte tacentia late*; *Theb.* 8.35 *tenebras uitaeque silentis*; Sen. *Her. F.* 794 *loca muta*), with possible ironic play upon the Latin meaning of Blaesus's name, 'stammering' (McKeown on Ov. *Am.* 2.6.24). Vessey 1986: 2774–82 argues that Glaucias' recognition of Blaesus alludes to the scene in Virgil's Underworld where Anchises points out to Aeneas the young Marcellus walking beside his famous ancestor (Virg. *A.* 6.860–86). If so, St. makes a sharp contrast between Virgil's claims of blood in his grand roll-call of Roman heroes, and his poem's promotion of social and emotional ties over ancestral bonds.

197 summosque lacessit amictus: in the silence, Glaucias has to tug Blaesus' cloak to capture his attention. The gesture of tugging at the hem (*summosque . . . amictus*) is characteristic of children, as shown on the Ara Pacis (Rawson 1997: 213–14, 217). As a literary motif it derives from Homer's picture of the young fatherless child tugging at the cloak of one of his father's companions at *Il.* 22. 492–3 δευόμενος δέ τ' ἄνεισι πάϊς ἐς πατρὸς ἑταίρους, | ἄλλον μὲν χλαίνης ἐρύων, ἄλλον δὲ χιτῶνος; cf. *Il.* 16.7–10.

198–9 inde †magis† sequitur; neque enim magis ille trahentem | spernit: *magis* 'to a greater degree' does not make good sense with *sequitur*. Courtney 1968: 54 suspects a scribal error; an adverb meaning 'more boldly' is needed. SB takes the first *magis* in the adversative sense of 'rather', meaning that Glaucias drops behind after having walked with Blaesus (196), but goes on plucking the cloak. This idea is a little awkward but can perhaps be explained by Virg. *A.* 2.723–4 *dextrae se paruus Iulus | implicuit sequiturque patrem non passibus aequis*, where Iulus, leaving Troy, clasped Aeneas' hand but then, unable to match his strides, lagged behind while still holding on. Repetition of *magis* and the predominantly dissyllabic dactylic line convey the child's urgency.

199 ignota . . . de stirpe nepotum 'from an unknown branch of his descendants', 'unknown' to Blaesus because they were born, like Glaucias, after Blaesus' death. The chronology suits his possible identification with the Vitellian Blaesus (191n.).

200 delicias: 71n. **rari . . . amici:** i.e. Melior, a compliment to him as a special friend (*OLD rarus* 6); cf. *2 pr.* 24 (Lucan's wife Polla Argentaria) *rarissima uxorum.* **pignus** 'child' and also a 'pledge' between the two men, with Blaesus now assuming Melior's role of foster father; see 86–7n.

201 sensit: enjambment emphasises recognition; cf. 196 *agnouit* (of Glaucias). **amissi puerum solacia Blaesi:** Glaucias became Melior's foster son to console him for the loss of his friend Blaesus. Finding a 'replacement friend' was a well-worn consolatory topos (2.6.103n.). Vollmer sees an ironic play here on Blaesus' name ('stammering'); Melior found a substitute for Blaesus in a child who was (initially at least) *blaesus*, of indistinct speech; see 104n., 196–7n.

202 tollit humo: Blaesus' gesture replicates Melior's (79), confirming Blaesus' consolatory assumption of the mantle of foster parent in the Underworld. **magnaque ligat ceruice** 'he winds him round his great neck', a vivid, unusual expression for 'embracing' (*OLD ligo* 2b); cf. *Ach.* 1.576 *et ligat amplexus*; for a similar use of the ablative cf. 3.2.132 *me magna ceruice ligatum*. Blaesus further duplicates Melior's role; see 51n. *ligat*, echoing 192 *ligantem*, also acknowledges the emotional ties that 'bind' Melior and Blaesus. *magnaque* evokes the physical and social contrast between the noble adult and the child and hints at Blaesus' 'greatness' of character; see Vessey 1986: 2781.

202–3 diuque | ipse manu . . . uehit: having embraced Glaucias, Blaesus then carries him for a long time. *manu* is odd for the required sense 'in his arms', but Van Dam's and SB's 'on his arm' is unacceptable, esp. with the preceding image of the boy wound round Blaesus' neck. *manu* is thus best taken here as synecdoche for 'arms'; see 66n. **gaudens:** cf. 189 *gaudenti.*

203–4 quae munera mollis | Elysii: sc. *sunt.* The products of the Underworld, offered here as 'gifts' of affection, are also 'funerary offerings' (160n.). Lovers expect gifts (cf. Virg. *Ecl.* 2.45–57; Ov. *Met.* 13.831–2) as do children; cf. Virg. *Ecl.* 4.18 *at tibi prima, puer, nullo munuscula cultu*; Hor. *Ep.* 1.7.17 *non inuisa feres pueris munuscula paruis. mollis* cannot mean 'lush' as at 107, for this Elysium is a barren place (204n.); rather it suggests that the terrain is not harsh (*OLD* 6) and thus not threatening to children.

204 steriles ramos: Virgil's Elysium is pleasingly lush (*A.* 6.639 *locos laetos et amoena uirecta*), with a grove of evergreen laurel (*A.* 6.658), and Augustan elegists described it as a sensuous paradise; cf. Tib. 1.3.61–2 *fert casiam non culta seges totosque per agros | floret odoratis terra benigna rosis*; Prop 4.7.60; Ov. *Am.* 2.6.49–50, with McKeown. But St. seems to have been influenced by Seneca's description of the Underworld as a place of absence and inversion (*Her. F.* 662–829); cf. Sen. *Her. F.* 700–1 *non ulla ramos silua pomiferos habet: | sterilis profundi uastitas squalet soli*, with Fitch on Sen. *Her. F.* 697–705. Thus St.'s Underworld is barren (187 *steriles ripas*; *Theb.* 2.12 *steriles luci*; *Theb.* 8.89), and even his Elysium offers only products that symbolise the negation of life. Fertility in nature is commonly associated with the growth of a child (cf. Virg. *Ecl.* 4.18–30), the tree being a symbol of human life (101–2n.). Blaesus can offer only branches without promise of fruition, symbol of a life cut short. Fruit was a common lover's gift (Virg. *Ecl.* 3.70–1; Ov. *Met.* 13.812–20).   **mutasque uolucres**: almost an oxymoron, for birds are identified with song; assonance mutes this line. Virgil's Elysium, characterised by choral song and Orpheus' lyre (*A.* 6.640–7), is an exception to the general rule of silence in the Underworld (196–7n.); birds too sing in Tibullus' amatory Elysium (1.3.59–60; cf. Ov. *Am.* 2.6.49–58). Birds were also common lover's gifts (cf. Virg. *Ecl.* 3.68–9; Ov. *Met.* 13.832) and children's pets (159n.).

205 porgit: syncopated form of *porrigit*.   **obtunso pallentes germine flores** 'pale flowers nipped in the bud'. *obtunso* is an unusual metaphor from *obtundere* 'to make blunt' (*OLD* 3a), producing a stark visual image of the bud that fails to open and grow; cf. Virg. *G.* 1.433 (of the moon's horns when rain is forecast) *obtunsis . . . cornibus*. The inhabitants and plants of the Underworld are 'pale' from lack of light; cf. 3.3.24 *pallentes . . . lucos*; *Theb.* 2.48 *pallentes . . . umbras*; *Theb.* 4.486–7 *lucis egentis | . . . umbras*. Paleness too is a physical sign of death; cf. Hor. *Carm.* 1.4.13 *pallida Mors*. Flowers were proper gifts for children (Virg. *Ecl.* 4.18–20) and for lovers (Virg. *Ecl.* 2.45–50).

206 nec prohibet meminisse tui: cf. 153 *et prohibet gemitus consolaturque dolentem*. On remembering as an important aspect of consolation see 55n.

206–7 pectora blandus | miscet 'fondly he mingles hearts', fig. for the mutual love among Glaucias and his foster fathers, an emotional triangle; cf. 5.1.43–4 *uos collato pectore mixtos | iunxit . . . Concordia. blandus* links Blaesus with Chiron, the exemplary foster father of a brilliant child (88n.).

207 alternum pueri partitur amorem 'sharing the boy's affection for you and yours for him' (SB), the previous sentiment rephrased. *pueri* is both subjective and objective gen. (*NLS* 72–5; Van Dam).

208–26 The second part of the formal consolation. An emotional style enlivens standard arguments on the transience of all created matter, the harshness of human life, and the inexorability of fate. Adrastus' consolation of Lycurgus,

Opheltes' father, summarises the major ideas; cf. *Theb.* 6.46–8 *solatur Adrastus |
alloquiis genitorem ultro, nunc fata recensens | resque hominum duras et inexorabile pensum.*

208 hic finis rapto, (sc. *datus est*) 'the end has come for him, snatched away';
solemn spondees and verbal ellipsis emphasise the finality and swiftness of death.
finis marks a decided change in direction, here towards closure (Austin on Virg.
A. 1.223).   **quin tu iam uulnera sedas** 'why do you not now soothe your
wounds?'; compare *iam* at line 5, where an attempt at healing words was mistimed.
Melior is now ready for a renewed plea to cease mourning; cf. 2.6.93–5. As Gibson
comments on 5.1.247, the temporal adverb in this type of plea points to the time
of the poem's composition, when St. and Melior stood at the pyre, and also to
the 'time' of the poem, which has now reached the right point for consolation
and conclusion. The repetition of *uulnera* (cf. 4) also connects the poem's start
and finish, charting its progress from raw, stubborn grief towards its conciliatory
close; see also 221n. Interrogative *quin* implies a subsequent denial that there can
be any objection to seeking consolation (*NLS* 185).

209 mersum luctu caput: cf. Cat. 68.13 *quis merser fortunae fluctibus ipse*; 179–
8on.

209–19 The inevitability of death for all living matter is a consolatory common-
place; cf. Hor. *Carm.* 1.28.15–16 *sed omnis una manet nox | et calcanda semel uia leti*,
with N–H; Sen. *Dial.* 6.26.5–6. This section is characterised by the concentrated
variety of words for death: 209 *functa*, 210 *moritura*, *obeunt*, 213 *interitus*, 214 *exitio*,
216 *letalis*, 218 *finem*.

209 omnia functa: emphatic after a strong fourth-foot sense pause. *fungor* is
often used with *uita, fato, officio* in the sense of 'to complete life' and thus 'to die'
(*OLD* 2); cf. *Theb.* 2.15 *functis* = 'the dead'.

210 moritura 'destined to die' (106n.).   **noctesque diesque:** the double
-*que* in the fifth and sixth foot (Homeric τε . . . τε) gives a solemn, elegant effect
(L–H–S 515). St. favours this Graecising feature of epic style, with more than
a hundred examples in the *Thebaid* (Williams on *Theb.* 10.558). The final -*que*
is hypermetric, being elided before *astra* in the following line, an esp. Virgilian
metrical feature (Harrison on Virg. *A.* 10.895; Wills 376–7); see also 220n.

211 nec solidis prodest sua machina terris 'and her structure does not
avail the solid earth' (SB), i.e. even the physical world is subject to decay; cf. Lucr.
5.95–6 *multosque per annos | sustentata ruet moles et machina mundi* (cf. Luer. 2.1150–74).

212 nam populus mortale genus: sc. *est*. Compression conveys the grimness
of thought. The disparagement of *human* life was a consolatory topos designed
to ameliorate grief by stressing the pain of mortal existence; see Setaioli 2005:
257–8.   **plebisque caducae:** *caducae* here means 'about to fall' and thus
'destined to die' (*OLD* 7a); cf. Virg. *A.* 10.622–3 *iuueni . . . | caduco*, with Harrison.

213 hos bella, hos aequora poscunt: warfare and seafaring head a list of
the various causes of death (213–18); traditionally they are the greatest threats to
human existence, a theme deriving from Semon. 1.12.12–15 (N–H on Hor. *Carm.*
1.28.17). Asyndeton and polpytoton (*hos, hos, his, his, hos, illos, hos*) structure the list
(213–17), repetition conveying a sense of inevitability – nobody can escape death.

214 his amor exitio, furor his et saeua cupido: immoderate passions
are 'deadly' for some; cf. Hor. *Carm.* 1.28.18 *exitio est auidum mare nautis*, with
predicative dat. as here. All three of these passions can have an erotic sense but
appear here as separate emotions, 'love', 'madness' and 'fierce greed' (SB). Hor.
Carm. 2.14.13–16 gives warfare, seafaring and disease as the major causes of death;
St. interpolates moral failings.

215 ut sileam morbos 'to say nothing of diseases'; cf. Ov. *Pont.* 1.2.145 *ut de me
sileam*, a conversational turn towards the poem's close. Allusion to other poetic
endings emphasises the poem's movement towards closure; see also 224–6n., 226–
31n.   **ora rigentia brumae** 'the stiffening face of winter' (with snow and
ice); cf. Luc. 1.17 *bruma rigens*. The seasons are vividly personified as frightening
figures of death. Their description begins grimly with winter; by contrast Ov.
Met. 2.27–30 begins with spring and ends with winter; tellingly St. omits spring
with its associations of youth and beauty.

216 implacido letalis Sirius igni: summer is characterised negatively by
the Dogstar, which blazed at the hottest time of year and was widely regarded
as bringing plague (A. R. 2.516; *Theb.* 1.627–35), hence *letalis* 'causing death'; cf.
Germ. fr. 4.41 *letifer . . . Sirius. implacidus* 'restless' is rare and poetic; cf. 167 *Melior
placidissime quondam.*

217 imbrifero pallens autumnus hiatu: autumn is sometimes pictured
lavishly stained with crushed grapes (cf. Ov. *Met.* 2.29; N–H on Hor. *Carm.* 2.5.11),
but its pallor here is deathly (205n.). On the unhealthiness of autumn cf. Juv.
4.56–7 *iam letifero cedente pruinis Autumno*; N–H on Hor. *Carm.* 2.14.15. *imbrifer* first
appears at Virg. *G.* 1.313 of spring, but autumn of course brings rain too. *hiatus*
evokes the personification of winds with gaping mouths (*TLL* VI 3.2683.74–6), an
idea conflated with that of death's maw (*TLL* VI 3.2683.74–2684.7); cf. Sen. *Oed.*
164–5 *mors atra auidos oris hiatus | pandit.*

218 quicquid init ortus, finem timet: the juxtaposition of antithetical
nouns, and the sentence break at the end of the fourth foot, stress the brevity of
life. *init = iniit*; the long second syllable creates a solemn spondaic rhythm across
the strong caesura.

218–19 ibimus omnes, | ibimus: cf. Hor. *Carm.* 2.17.10–12 *ibimus, ibimus
| . . . supremum | . . . carpere iter*, with N–H. This rare verbal gemination imparts an
intensely emotional tone (Wills 73, 105–6).

219 immensis urnam quatit Aeacus umbris: with the exception of Virgil, who has Minos shake the urn containing the lots that determined souls' fates (*A.* 6.432), in Roman literature Aeacus generally plays this role; cf. 3.3.16 *inferna rigidum . . . Aeacon urna*; Prop. 4.11.19 *aut si quis posita iudex sedet Aeacus urna*; Hor. *Carm.* 2.13.22 *et iudicantem uidimus Aeacum*, with N–H; Eden on Sen. *Apoc.* 14.1. *immensis* means 'countless in number' (*OLD* 2c), further implying that no one can escape death.

220–6 The final argument: Glaucias is 'fortunate' in having escaped life's troubles. That death is a release from care and that the dead enjoy a better life were commonplaces of literary consolations and funerary epigrams, esp. apt for the bereaved parent; cf. Lucr. 3.1076–94; Sen. *Ep.* 99.10–13; Strubbe 1998: 58; Griessmair 1966: 98–101.

220 ast: an archaic, strongly adversative alternative for *at*, generally followed by a pronoun as here (Harrison on Virg. *A.* 10.173).   **felix:** a surprising adjective, oxymoronic with *gemimus*; *infelix* is regularly associated with death (Hardie on Virg. *A.* 9.390). St. here draws attention to the basic paradox that the prematurely dead is 'fortunate' in missing life's ills; cf. 5.1.220–1 *illam tranquillo fine solutam | felicemque uocant. felix* also carries the suggestion of 'blessed' (= μάκαρ), an epithet that can connote immortality; cf. Virg. *A.* 6.663 *felices animae*; Sen. *Dial.* 6.26.7. On the theme of the soul's immortality in ancient consolations see Setaioli 2005.   **hominesque deosque:** cf. Virg. *A.* 2.745 *hominumque deorumque*. On the epic rhythm and hypermetric -*que* see 210n.

221 caecae lubrica uitae: a metaphor for the 'pitfalls' (*lubrica*) of life recalling the figure of grief as a 'slippery wound' (4); cf. Sen. *Ep.* 99.9 *nihil non lubricum et fallax et omni tempestate mobilius*; Williams on *Theb.* 10.503–5. Life is 'blind' for one cannot predict the blows of fate; and many are morally 'blind' (N–H on Hor. *Carm.* 1.18.14).

222 immunis fatis 'exempt from fate' (*OLD immunis* 4).

222–3 non ille rogauit, | non timuit meruitue mori: an elegant tricolon with repetition, asyndeton, alliteration and assonance; cf. Sen. *Nat.* 6.32.6 *nec rogaueris nec timueris nec te uelut in aliquod malum exitura[m] tuleris retro. mori* is understood with *rogauit*; Glaucias was neither suicidal nor cowardly. Courtney follows Heinsius' conjecture *renuit* 'he did (not) refuse' (to die) in place of *meruit* on the grounds that *meruit* is out of place in a consolation. But that the young did not deserve death is a consolatory commonplace, stressing the deceased's virtue and beauty; see 177–8n.

223–4 nos anxia plebes, | nos miseri: *nos* contrasts with preceding *ille* (222); those alive are plagued with uncertainty about how and when their end will come. See 2.2.127–8n.

224–6 quibus unde dies suprema, quis aeui | exitus incertum, quibus instet fulmen ab astris, | quae nubes fatale sonet 'for whom it is uncertain whence our final day will come, what manner of death awaits, from what stars the thunderbolt is poised for attack, or what cloud rumbles our doom'. Two pairs of clauses are dependent upon *incertum* (*est*), the first concerned with the unpredictability of death (224–5), the second with astral influences (225–6); the first *quibus* (224) is a relative pronoun modifying *nos miseri*, the second *quibus* (225), along with *quis* and *quae*, are relative adjectives. For the language and sentiment cf. Lucr. 3.1085–6 (a concluding sentiment) *posteraque in dubiost fortunam quam uehat aetas, | quidue ferat nobis casus quiue exitus instet*; Sen. *Nat.* 6.31.2 *fulminibus et terris et magnis naturae partibus petimur*.

224–5 aeui | exitus 'the end of life'; cf. Virg. *A.* 10.630 *nunc manet insontem grauis exitus*, with Harrison; *Theb.* 2.17 *grauis exitus aeui*, with Mulder.

225 fulmen: lit. 'thunderbolt', metaphorically 'catastrophe' (30n.).

226 fatale: adverbial 'in a way causing death and destruction' (*OLD* 4); see 133–4n.

226–31 As final consolation St. invokes Glaucias in hymnic style to return to Melior in a dream; Quint. *Inst.* 4.1.28 recommends pulling out all the stops in a peroration, including 'raising the dead', a topos that originates with Patroclus' appearance to Achilles in a dream (Hom. *Il.* 23.62–108). It has a long history in Roman literature, generally with didactic or prophetic features (Zetzel on Cic. *Rep.* 6.10.3). Prop. 4.7 (the appearance of Cynthia's ghost) provides an amatory precedent; cf. Prop. 4.7.87–8 *nec tu sperne piis uenientia somnia portis: | cum pia uenerunt, somnia pondus habent*, with Hutchinson; Dufallo 2003. Such appearances by the dead often occur towards the start or end of a literary work, the boundaries of literature and life thus being interwoven. Cf. 5.3.288–93 with Gibson; Hutchinson on Prop. 4.7, p. 170.

226–7 nil flecteris istis? | sed flectere libens 'are you not swayed by these arguments? But you will be, gladly'. Polyptoton emphasises the shift from question to assertion.

227 ades huc: a hymnic invocation (*OLD adsum* 13); cf. Virg. *Ecl.* 2.45 *huc ades, o formose puer*, with Clausen; St. validitates his poem for Glaucias by invoking the precedent of *Ecl.* 2; see 2.6.103–4n. St. follows Virgilian practice in using indic. *ades* with imperative force for human beings in place of subj. *adsis* for deities (Thomas on Virg. *G.* 1.18). **emissus:** another closural echo (215n.): cf. Virg. *A.* 6.897–8 *tum natum Anchises unaque Sibyllam | prosequitur dictis portaque emittit eburna*; *Epic. Drusi* 445–6 *ipse tibi emissus nebulosum litus Auerni, | si liceat, forti uerba tot ore sonet*, with Schoonhoven.

227–8 ab atro | limine: cf. Prop. 4.11.2 *ianua nigra* with Hutchinson. 'Threshold' is less usual than 'door' as an image for the entrance to the Underworld and probably derives from Sen. *Her. F.* 47 *limen inferni Iouis*; see Fitch ad loc. *limen* is symbolically associated with the start and end of life (38–9n.). 'Black', whether *ater* or *niger*, is an attribute of death; see 19n.; Maltby on Tib. 1.3.4–5 *Mors nigra . . . | Mors atra.*

228 cui soli cuncta impetrare facultas 'who alone has the facility of getting everything he asks for'. Glaucias is so charming that nobody, in this life or the next, can refuse his requests. *impetrare* is poetic usage for *impetrandi (facultas)*; see 188n.

229 Glaucia: vocative, in initial line position, highlights this first appearance of the boy's name in the poem; at 2.6.81 the boy's name likewise occurs for the first time towards the poem's end. Glaucias is an otherwise metrically impossible name in hexameters. The delay also maximises the pathos when the name finally occurs. Glaucias was a common Greek name for a slave, well attested in sepulchral inscriptions from Rome (Grewing on Mart. 6.28.4). On Glaucias' ambiguous social status see 77–8n.   **nil sontes:** *nil* 'not at all' (*OLD nihil* 11) corrects the metrical dilemma caused by M's *Glaucia insontes*. Courtney 1968: 55 follows earlier editors in suspecting corruption: the slave's name can appear in two forms in Latin, *Glaucias* (Mart. 6.28.4) or *Glaucia* (Mart. 6.29.4); if St. uses the vocative of the former, then the long final *a* will be shortened by correption, which is alien however to St.'s metrical practice; if St. uses the form *Glaucia*, then the short *a* of the vocative creates 'an impossible hiatus'. But St. perhaps wished a fine neoteric ending by echoing Virgil's rare use of hiatus at *G.* 1.437 *Glauco et Panopeae et Inoo Melicertae* (see Mynors); not only does *Glauco* resemble *Glaucia*, but Melicertes is another name for Palaemon (179–80n.; on the rare *Inoo* see 98n.). Hiatus without correption of the unelided vowel is a Graecism (Coleman on Virg. *Ecl.* 3.6) that, if *insontes* is retained, would distinguish the only appearance of Glaucias' name with a neoteric flourish.   **portitor:** i.e. Charon. Properly someone who collects tolls, or a 'harbour master', *portitor* came to mean 'ferryman' through association with *portare* as well as *portus* (Austin on Virg. *A.* 6.298; cf. Luc. 3.16–17 *Acherontis adusti | portitor*); it sounds a lightly prosaic note in an emotional climax.

230 durae comes ille serae: Cerberus, chained to a bar on the gate of the Underworld (Håkanson 1969: 53–5). He was sometimes imagined as unchained at night; cf. Prop. 4.7.90 *errat et abiecta Cerberus ipse sera.* The chained dog is a more comforting image, though *durae* suggests material strength and fate's inexorability; cf. Prop. 4.11.25–6 (cited at 184n.).

230–1 tu pectora mulce, | tu prohibe manare genas: anaphora in prayer style. Freed slaves were expected to continue in their master's service (Hopkins 1978: 129–31). St. asks Glaucias to console Melior as he cheered him in life (56–7n.). *mulce* here = 'soothe' and thus 'console'; cf. 12 *mulceat insanos gemitus. mulcere* is used programmatically in this sense at 5.5.39 *qui uiduos potui mulcere dolores.*

231 noctesque beatas: cf. Luc. 7.28 *noctemque beatam* (in the same metrical position) of Pompey's last night of peaceful sleep before Pharsalia – but Melior will have many such nights, and *beatas* here has participial sense; his nights will be made happy by Glaucias' visits to him in a dream. St. brings the poem to its close by contradicting Lucretius, who attacks the deceptive nature of dreams (Lucr. 1.133–5, 4.37–41).

232 uiuis uultibus 'with lifelike expression'; cf. Virg. *A.* 6.848 (of sculpture) *uiuos uultus* (*OLD uiuus* 3). Dreams, like memorial statues (191–2n.), can console.

233 desolatamque sororem: cf. 67 *desolatique penates*, a quiet reminder of Melior's obligations as head of household: Glaucias' kin, Melior's former slaves, need care also.

234 qui potes 'since you can' = *namque potes*, a prayer formula.   **insinuare:** the verb occurs only here in the *Siluae* and twice in the *Thebaid* (5.448, 7.110). Its basic sense here is 'to recommend' (i.e. to Melior), a rare sense in the classical period (*TLL* VII 1.1915.18–20); cf. Plin. *Pan.* 62.2 *quod penitus illos animo Caesaris insinuauit.* The verb's emotional overtones are important, the play upon *in sinu* providing closure, the boy enfolded in his family, and the poem, which had flowed from the poet's lap (1 *pr.* 4 *de sinu*), now concluded with this inward movement. There may be also final acknowledgment of the importance of Lucretius to this poem, *insinuare* being a favourite word of Lucretius (Bailey on Lucr. 1.113).   **parentes:** mention of the boy's parents (and sister) reveal Glaucias' piety, while serving as a further reminder of Melior's larger obligations to his household. The poem ends with its most contested term, the definition of parenthood.

Siluae 2.2

A description of the villa of Pollius Felix and his wife Polla, situated outside Sorrento on the southern peninsula of the Bay of Naples, an area of prime real estate with many maritime villas. Like Melior, Pollius Felix was a retired man of means and a connoisseur of literature; *Siluae* 3 is dedicated to him. His wife complements him as an exemplar of matronly virtues of prudence and thrift but also learning (10, 147–54).

St. is the originator of the 'villa' poem (cf. 1.3), a full-scale development of epigrammatic descriptions of buildings and works of art. He also reflects a new cultural interest in landscape, prefigured in the development in the Augustan age of a new type of wall painting, seaside scenes and maritime villas (Plin. *Nat.* 35.116; Vitr. 7.5.2). For the Romans, moreover, landscape was an integral part of a villa's design (Purcell 1987: 197–8). Ecphrasis is now generally understood as descriptions of works of art; but in ancient times it had broader application and included buildings and landscapes (*OCD* s.v. *ekphrasis*). The literary description of a wonderful house goes back to Homer, with the home of Hephaestus (*Il.* 18.369–79) and the palace of Alcinous (*Od.* 7.81–132), which provide the programmatic elements of the viewer's wonder and the building's great size, height and radiance (cf. Mart. 4.64.29, 12.31.9–10; Lucian *Dom.* 1). Unlike with the description of a statue or painting, an architectural ecphrasis involves movement; thus 2.2 is characterised by dramatic shifts in spatial and temporal perspective and sudden shifts in address. 2.2 is not a systematic guide to a Roman villa; rather ecphrasis typically provides a perceptual response to a site (Webb and James 1991; Bartsch and Elsner 2007). The villa is largely viewed through a mythological and literary-historical lens, and the description is selective. St. advertises the originality of his poem with that of the villa.

In an era of limited opportunities for self-promotion, the country villa developed as an important symbol of visual self-display and commemoration (Bodel 1997) and also of 'productive leisure' (Myers 2005). Pollius' Greek-style villa, built on harsh terrain, is a showcase for his cultural sophistication and mastery of nature, and thus a metaphor too for philosophical self-control; the poem is constructed on a strong antithesis between *ars* and *natura*. In a sense St. updates Virgil's *Georgics* for the imperial age. The conqueror of nature is no longer a farmer but a villa owner, and though the task is presented as no less heroic, it is acomplished with swiftness and ease. Pollius' domination of nature benefits both the owners and the land and provides in the private sphere a paradigm for moral and civic discourse. St. challenges the strong moralising tradition that derided luxurious private building (e.g. Sen. *Con.* 2.1.11–13; Sen. *Dial.* 10–11; *Ep.* 55 and 86; N–H on Hor. *Carm.* 2.15, 241–4, 2.18, 287–92; Newlands 2002:124–42); in the second part of the poem the villa emerges as an overt symbol of Pollius' Epicurean way of life and values (121–42) that also provides a provocative counterpart to imperial splendour and autocratic rule. The poem is dense with Virgilian allusions. But also, as in 2.1, allusions to Lucretius are important to the poem's conceptual structure.

The date of the poem's composition is probably 90 CE, just eleven years after the devastating eruption of Vesuvius (the poem's assertion of human triumph over nature may have particular point; cf. Tac. *Ann.* 4.67.2). St. visited the villa after competing at the Augustalia, which was held every four years, during Domitian's reign in 82, 86, 90 and 94 CE (Beloch 1879: 270). Attempts to identify Pollius' villa from the various archaeological remains scattered along the Surrentine coast are inconclusive. See Beloch 1879: 269–74; D'Arms 1970: 220–2; Bergmann 1991: 49 n. 3 and 52. D'Arms 1970: 171–232 gives a inventory of the villas on the Bay of Naples owned by prominent Romans between 75 BCE and 400 CE.

Further reading: Cancik 1968; Bergmann 1991; Krüger 1998; Hinds 2000; Newlands 2002: 154–98; Zeiner 2005: 178–90. On the influence of St.'s 'villa' poems on the late antique poets Sidonius Apollinaris and Venantius Fortunatus see Dewar 1996.

1–12 St. describes the location of Pollius' villa and explains the occasion for his visit.

1–3 est . . . uilla: an elevated opening, with a variation on *est locus*, the conventional epic formula for introducing a description of place since Enn. *Ann.* 20; see Hinds 2002: 126; Austin on Virg. *A.* 1.12; Bömer on Ov. *Met.* 15.332.

1 inter notos Sirenum nomine muros: a periphrasis for Surrentum (modern Sorrento), based on the false etymology of the town's name from the Sirens; cf. Plin. *Nat.* 3.62 *Surrentum cum promunturio Mineruae, Sirenum quondam sede.* The location of the Sirens' islands was controversial in antiquity; they were either off Sicily (2.1.10) or offshore from Sorrento (Str. 1.2.12, 5.4.8; Bömer on Ov. *Met.* 14.88). Mention of the Sirens conveys the allure of Pollius' villa where poetry is central (39–40, 112–20), while subtly suggesting its dangers for an ambitious poet who cannot afford, perhaps, to linger too long away from Rome; cf. 3.1.64–5 *notas Sirenum nomine rupes | facundique larem Polli.*   **notos . . . nomine:** *nomen* and *notus* are etymologically linked (Maltby s.v. *nomen*).

2 Tyrrhenae templis . . . Mineruae: the temple of Minerva was founded by Surrentum's early Greek colonists (traditionally by Odysseus), and was situated high on the tip of the promontory that forms the southern end of the Bay of Naples (Capo Ateneo), *not* on the peninsula of Misenum at its north (SB); it was an important landmark for sailors (3.2.23–4; Str. 5.4.8; Beloch 1879: 276–7). Minerva is 'Tyrrhenian', i.e. 'Etruscan', because she overlooks the so-called 'Tyrrhenian' sea between the west coast of Italy, Sardinia and Sicily (Plin. *Nat.* 3.75, 80), and because, perhaps, of Etruscan influence upon Campania (Frederiksen 1984: 117–33; Gibson on 5.3.165–6). The epithet also distinguishes her from the imperial Minerva, Domitian's patron deity. *templis*, a common poetic pl. since Virgil, possibly to indicate grandeur (Austin on Virg. *A.* 6.19), or simply a temple complex, foreshadows the explicit association developed at the poem's end between the villa's topography and Lucretius' *templa* of the wise (Lucr. 2.8).

3 celsa Dicarchei speculatrix uilla profundi 'the villa watching over the Dicarchean deep from on high'; cf. 5.3.166 *Tyrrheni speculatrix uirgo profundi.* The Bay of Naples is named after the reputed founder of Puteoli, Dicaearchus (Plin. *Nat.* 3.61). *Dicarcheus*, with the first dipthong (-*ae*-) dropped, is the standard adjectival form among Roman poets; see Coleman on 4.8.7–8. At this time Puteoli, just to the north of Naples, was the most important commercial centre on the bay, a bustling port (Str. 5.4.6; D'Arms 1974).   **celsa** is largely poetic; cf. Mart. 4.64.10 (of a villa on the Janiculum) *celsae . . . uillae.* Villas were preferably situated by or near the sea (Pliny's Laurentine villa), or on elevated ground for the healthy air and fine views (Pliny's Tusculan villa); Pollius' villa has all these advantages, like Tiberius' Villa Iouis on nearby Capri, which overlooked the Bay of Naples from a height of 334 metres.   **speculatrix**, a rare word in poetry (*OLD* 1a), connotes 'looking out for danger'; cf. Val. Max. 9.8 ext. 1 (of a helmsman's statue) *igitur angusti atque aestuosi maris alto e tumulo speculatrix statua.* The word evokes the military character of the early Roman villa; cf. Sen. *Ep.* 51.11 *uidebatur hoc magis militare, ex edito speculari late longeque subiecta . . . scies non uillas sed castra* (Henderson 2004: 105–6).

4 qua Bromio dilectus ager: sc. *est*; cf. 3.5.102 *caraque non molli iuga Surrentina Lyaeo*; Hor. *Carm.* 2.6.18 *amicus Aulon fertili Baccho*, with N–H; *dilectus* and *amicus* mean 'dear to' and thus 'under the protection of'. *Bromius*, a Greek name for Bacchus, is relatively rare and emphasises the area's Hellenic character. Campania was famous for its wines (and heavy drinking); see N–H on Hor. *Carm.* 2.6.19. On the famous fresco displaying Bacchus with Vesuvius see Watson and Watson on Mart. 4.44.3 (= 80).

5 uritur et prelis non inuidet uua Falernis: cf. Hor. *Carm.* 2.6.19–20 *minimum Falernis | inuidet uuis*. In Augustan times wine from the area around Surrentum began to rival the more established Campanian vintages such as Falernian (Str. 5.4.3; Leary on Mart. 13.110 and 111), Horace's favourite wine (N–H on *Carm.* 1.20.9). *uritur* here has the unusual meaning of 'ripen'; its fig. sense 'smart with resentment' (*OLD* 7) plays upon *inuidet*: though the personified grape 'burns' it does not 'envy' the traditionally superior vintage. The evocation of *Carm.* 2.6 (also 4n.), an ode on Horace's desire for retirement to the moderate climate of south Italy, validates Pollius' choice of residence – and St.'s development of Horatian themes.

6 huc: a form of *hic* or similar word traditionally concludes the *est locus* formula, marking the start of the narrative proper (Austin on Virg. *A.*1.12).   **post patrii . . . quinquennia lustri** 'after the quinquennial games of my native festival', i.e. the Augustalia (or Sebasta), held in Naples every four years (not five, owing to the Romans' inclusive method of counting: *OLD quinquennium*). *lustrum* 'a festival held every fourth or fifth year' (*OLD* 4), glosses *quinquennium*; cf. 3.5.92 *Capitolinis quinquennia proxima lustris.* Instituted by Augustus (Tac. *Ann.* 1.15.2; Dio 55.10), the Augustalia were modelled on the Olympian games but included literary contests; they offered a version of Hellenism adapted to Roman interests and furthered Naples' reputation as a major cultural centre (Caldelli 1993: 28–37; Leiwo 1994: 45–8). *patrii* expresses St.'s pride in his native city (Coleman on 4.7.17–20) and identifies him as Neapolitan; he is putting his signature on this new poem while emphasising the areas's regeneration after the eruption of Vesuvius in 79 CE.   **me . . . laetum:** St.'s suggests his delight in returning 'home' and the possibility that he earned some success at this festival. As a major poet with deep knowledge of the area, he is well qualified to describe Pollius' villa; cf. Lucian, *Dom.* 2–3, 6; Morales 2004: 21.

7–8 cum stadio iam pigra quies canusque sederet | puluis, ad Ambracias conuersa gymnade frondes 'when a lazy lull and pale dust were settling on the stadium after the competitors turned to Ambracian laurels'. A striking syllepsis emphasises that the games had finished; the abstract *quies* and the concrete *puluis* are subjects of *sederet* (*OLD sedeo* 9 'settle'). The negative overtones of *pigra* suggest the unnatural quiet that falls on a site designed for crowds and action; cf. *Ach.* 1.438 *pigram . . . quietem.*

8 Ambracias . . . frondes: synecdoche for the Actian games, instituted by Augustus at Nicopolis in Greece in 27 BCE in honour of Apollo and the victory over Antony and Cleopatra at Actium; cf. Serv. *A.* 3.274; Williams on Virg. *A.* 3.280. 'Leaves' refers to the victory crowns of Apolline laurel (Caldelli 1993: 24–8). *Ambracius* for *Actius* is rare (elswhere in poetry only at Ov. *Ib.* 304); Ambracia was a Greek city north of Nicopolis.   **conuersa gymnade:** St. introduces *gymnas* (γυμνάς) to classical Latin literature, usually with the sense of 'athletic contest'; here by metonymy it has the rare sense of 'group of competitors' (*TLL* VI 2.2378.58–60; Laguna on 3.1.43).

9 trans gentile fretum 'across my native strait'; further local patriotism (6n.). He travels to the villa by sea, south across the bay from Naples.   **placidi facundia Polli:** St. defines his host through his main pursuits, poetry and Epicurean philosophy. *facundia* strengthens the bond between patron and poet, drawing St. frequently to Pollius' villa (3 *pr.* 5). *placidus* is a favourite term for St.'s friends, associating them with Epicurean calm, ἀταραξία; see 2.1.167n.

10 detulit: the main verb of the principal clause governing *me . . . laetum* (6), *cupidum* (11). *defero* is standard for bringing ships or sailors to land (*TLL* V 1.315.29–65).   **nitidae iuuenilis gratia Pollae**: an elegant chiasmus complimenting Polla for 'youthful grace' though she was a grandmother (3.1.175–9, 4.8.13–14). *nitidae* suggests youthful glow and elegance (*OLD* 3 and 6). Usually in the *Siluae* it describes brilliant objects such as stars (1.2.147) or marbles (3.1.5); Polla is thus radiant like her house (cf. 63–72, 85–94). Radiance is a key aesthetic concept of the *Siluae* (Cancik 1965: 43–8), often with moral nuance; cf. Sen. *Ep.* 41.6 (*animus) nullo bono nisi suo nitet*. The metrical pairing of husband and wife at consecutive line ends suggests marital harmony (Wills 282).

11 flectere iam cupidum gressus '[although] I was eager to direct my steps', an epic expression implying change of direction (*TLL* VI 1.894.39–41).   **limite noto** 'with familiar course' (abl. of description), i.e. esp. familiar to St., poet of Rome and Naples.

12 Appia longarum teritur regina uiarum: 'queen' marks the preeminence of the Appian Way as the first major Roman road. This type of topographical compliment begins with Call. *Aet.* 1 fr. 7.34 Pf. καὶ Φᾶσις [ποταμῶν ἡμε]τέρων βασιλεύς; Virgil introduced it to Roman poetry (Mynors on Virg. *G.* 1.482 *fluuiorum rex Eridanus*). Built by Appius Claudius Caecus in 312 BCE, the Via Appia was Rome's major link with the south (Chevallier 1976: 132–3). **teritur:** the Via Appia is 'well travelled' (*OLD* 5b), unlike the quiet Campanian villa; cf. 124. St. hints at the Callimachean metaphor of the broad, well-travelled highway for a lengthy poem on epic themes (Call. *Aet* 1 fr. 1.25–8 Pf.); his visit to the villa means turning to epideictic poetry and new themes.

13–29 The description of Pollius' estate begins systematically with the poet's view of the shore as he approaches from sea (9n.), a perspective favoured by Roman paintings of 'villascapes' (Bergmann 1991). St. also evokes the arrival of Odysseus and Aeneas at the 'safe' shores of Phaeacia and Carthage, esp. Virgil's description of the Carthaginian bay with its nymphs' grotto (*A.* 1.159–68, with Austin on harbour descriptions). But though St., like Aeneas, is bound for Rome, Pollius' villa offers a safe refuge, unlike Carthage.

13 sed iuuere morae 'but delays delighted [me]'; Aeneas' delay in Carthage was pleasant also (but wrong); cf. Virg. *A.* 4.51 *causasque innecte morandi*, with Pease.

13–14 placido lunata recessu | hinc atque hinc curuae perrumpunt aequora rupes 'rocks curving on either side break through the water, shaped into a crescent with a calm bay'; cf. Virg. *A.* 1.162–3 *hinc atque hinc uastae rupes geminique minantur | in caelum scopuli*, with Austin. Like the Carthaginian bay, Pollius' bay is defined by two opposing headlands; *hinc atque hinc* goes better with *curuae*, not with *perrumpunt*, which would suggest a rugged, not a crescent-shaped, shore. *curuae* (*rupes*) is SB's conjecture (Appendix p. 389) for M's *curuas* (Courtney), for rocks breaking the force of the sea and thus creating a calm bay (*OLD perrumpo* 2) make better sense than vice versa; cf. Claudian, *Carmina minora* 5.3–4 (of rocky promontories) *fractasque per undas | ardua tranquillo curuantur bracchia portu. placido* and *perrumpunt* sound a keynote of the poem, the tension between nature's domestication and its violence. *placido* suggests that the bay mirrors Pollius' character (9n.). On this prominent theme in 2.2 see also 22, 26, 29, 107, 151.

15 dat natura locum: nature provides the site, but, as we shall see, human beings shape this rugged landscape to their own needs. On the personification of nature as a way of representing her autonomous power see Kenney on Lucr. 3.931–77.

15–16 montique interuenit unum | litus 'a continuous beach interrupts the cliff wall'. *unum* is difficult and the text may be corrupt. Courtney understands it to mean that the beach forms a 'continuous' (*OLD* 5b) break between the two headlands, yet this sense of *unum* is rare. *unum* has been emended to *imum* (Gronovius), or *udum* (Heinsius, followed by SB), both epithets that are essentially redundant for a beach. The topography is basically clear: St. adopts the perspective of a sailor looking for a safe landing place – a break in the line of steep cliffs running along the peninsula with a substantial beach.

16 in terras scopulis pendentibus exit 'it extends inland (*OLD exire* 10a) between overhanging crags'; cf. Virg. *A.* 1.166–7 *fronte sub aduersa scopulis pendentibus | antrum.*

17–18 gratia prima loci . . . | balnea: cf. Fort. *Carm.* 1.20.21–2; Dewar 1996; 301. St. rejects the moderate Epicurean landscape of shade and running water (Lucr. 2.29–33): the bath-house is the first 'attraction' of Pollius' estate (for this sense of *gratia* cf. Plin. *Ep.* 2.17.1 *desines mirari, cum cognoueris gratiam uillae*); by contrast Aeneas found the Carthaginian coast *inculta* (Virg. *A.* 1.308). *balnea* are private baths in contrast to the public *balneae* (though there was some confusion in terminology); see Var. *L.* 9. 68; Newlands 2002: 206 n.23.

17 gemina testudine: cf. 3.1.100–1 *curui tu litoris ora | clausisti calidas gemina testudine nymphas*, with Laguna. *testudo* is an architectural term for a curved ceiling or roof (*OLD* 4; Austin on Virg. *A.* 1.505); *geminus* in the sense of 'two closely linked' is frequent in St. (e.g. 2.2.24; *Theb.* 3.466 *gemini uates* (Melampus and Amphiaraus)); hence a bath-house with twin roofs or cupolas covering, perhaps, the sea and freshwater room may be meant. But we have no architectural proof of such a design. Private baths were usually small, one-roomed structures; the doubling implied by *gemina* suggests Pollius' great wealth. St. perhaps too plays with the idea of doubling: the villa has two owners; two gods guard the estate (21–9); is it a coincidence that this poem is 2.2? **fumant:** cf. 1.3.43–4 (Vopiscus' baths) *an quae graminea suscepta crepidine fumant | balnea et impositum ripis algentibus ignem*, with verb and subject in the same metrical position as here. Vopiscus' baths were likewise detached from the main house and close to a natural source of water, a river. St. describes the hypocaustic system of underground heat which controlled the temperature; cf. 1.5.57–9.

18–19 e terris occurrit dulcis amaro | nympha mari: *dulcis* means 'fresh water'; cf. Virg. *A.* 1.167 *intus aquae dulces*. The juxtaposition of 'sweet' and 'bitter' (i.e. 'salt water') suggests their harmonious intermingling in the calm villa landscape. The hint of personification in *nympha* 'water' (*OLD* 1b) anticipates the Virgilian nymphs (19–20) and the veering away from 'realistic' description.

19 leuis hic Phorci chorus: cf. Virg. *A.* 5.240 *Phorcique chorus*; *A.* 5.824; Plin. *Nat.* 36.4.26. Phorcus is a sea god, son of Nereus (Hes. *Th.* 237) and father of sea nymphs (V. Fl. 3.726). *chorus* means 'a group', often of nymphs (*OLD* 4a). *leuis* means 'light in weight' and thus 'nimble' (*OLD* 1 and 2 respectively); cf. Hor. *Carm.* 1.1.31 *nympharumque leues cum Satyris chori*. Since the Romans decorated their properties with mythological sculptures and friezes, St. simply goes one step further in making nymphs active participants here; see 98–106n., introd. 5.

19–20 udaque crines Cymodoce: Cymodoce and Galatea were two of the fifty daughters of Nereus and Doris (Hes. *Th.* 240–64; cf. Hom. *Il.* 18.7–50). Cymodoce is part of Neptune's train (Virg. *A.* 5. 826); a Cymodocea, perhaps a different nymph, is gifted in speech (Virg. *A.* 10.225 *fandi doctissima*), appropriate for an owner with literary tastes (9); so too is her Hesiodic role as tamer of the waves (Hes. *Th.* 252–3). *udaque crines* (acc. of respect) may pun on her Greek name Κυμοδόκη 'wave-receiver' (Vollmer).

20 uiridisque . . . Galatea: the sea nymph famous for Polyphemus' hopeless passion for her (Theoc. 11; Ov. *Met.*13.738–899). 'Green' often describes water nymphs (1.5.15, 3.1.144; *Ach.* 1.293; *OLD uiridis* 2b; cf. 21 *caerulus*), but Galatea is usually associated with 'whiteness', given her name's etymological link with γάλα ('milk'); cf. Theocr. 11.19 Ὦ λευκὰ Γαλάτεια; Ov. *Met.* 13.789 *candidior folio niuei, Galatea, ligustri*, with Hopkinson; Michalopoulos 83–4. Here St. refuses the obvious etymological pun.   **cupit . . . lauari:** the sea deities wish to bathe in the bath-house rather than in the open sea, a paradox that stresses the superiority of *ars* to *natura*. On this topos in St.'s 'bath' poetry see 1.3.76–80, 1.5.54–6: Venus would rather have been born from Claudius Etruscus' baths than from the sea (1.5.54)!

21–9 Temples of Neptune and Hercules guard the point of entry. Topographical and ethical language correlate physical with moral control of the sea, a correspondence developed towards the poem's end with Pollius himself (120–42). In 2.2 the sea is an unruly element that can be calmed but, unlike the villa's rocky terrain, not transformed.

21–2 ante domum . . . | excubat 'before his temple the god keeps watch'. As SB suggests, *domum* here must mean Neptune's temple with the god's statue in front, not the villa (e.g. Håkanson 1969: 55 n. 73) since that was situated on the clifftop. Van Dam is surely wrong to suggest that there was only one temple on the shore, the temple of Hercules (23–4), and that the statue of Neptune stood in front of this shrine; it would be highly unusual to place before the temple of one deity the statue of another deity associated with a different sphere of action.

21 tumidae moderator caerulus undae: a periphrasis for Neptune with ethical import. *moderator* 'ruler' (*OLD* 2) has political overtones; *tumidae*, pointedly juxtaposed, suggests the swelling of anger (*OLD* 4). Neptune is here based on Virgil's god (*A.* 1.124–56, 5.779–826), who controls the sea's opposing forces and is a model for moral and civic discourse; cf. Virg. *A.* 1.142 *tumida aequora placat*; *A.* 5.820–1 *undae subsidunt tumidumque sub axe tonanti | sternitur aequor aquis*; Sil. 7.254–9.

22 innocui custos laris: *lar* most likely refers to Pollius' 'home' (*OLD* 2), which Neptune guards from the shore, not to Hercules' temple (or his own) as Van Dam argues (21–2n.); cf. 3.1.65 *facundique larem Polli*; Hor. *Carm.* 1.12.44 *cum lare fundus*, with N–H. Despite its wealth, the villa's 'innocence' is a sign of its owner's moral worth; cf. 2.3.15–16 *placidi Melioris aperti | stant sine fraude lares*.

22–3 amico | . . . salo: the oxymoron suggests Neptune's control of opposing forces; *salum* means 'the sea in motion' or 'the deep' (*OLD* 1 and 2; Krüger 1998: 179).

23 templa: 2n.   **felicia rura:** a pun on Pollius' *cognomen* 'Felix' set off by strong caesura. The pun suggests the symbiotic relationship between Pollius and his land; nature reflects the character of its owner who makes it *felix* 'fertile' (*OLD* 1) by being 'wealthy' (*OLD* 6) and thus 'fortunate' (*OLD* 3); see Pease on Virg. *A.* 4.68. 'nomen est omen!' (Krüger 1998: 84); Nisbet 1995b: 41–2. See also 107, 122, 151, 2 *pr.* 1n.

23–4 tuetur | Alcides: a bilingual pun on Hercules' patronymic and its etymological association with ἀλκή ('defensive strength'). Alcides is frequent in Roman hexameter owing to the metrical intractability of nom. or acc. Hercules. Here he guards the countryside (on his temple see 3.1); as a tamer of nature, he is a fitting companion to Neptune, tamer of the sea.

24 gemino sub numine: Neptune and Hercules; see 17n.

25 hic seruat terras, hic saeuis fluctibus obstat: Håkanson 1969: 56–7 regards this line as spurious because it seems to contradict the sea's calm of 25; SB prints it without translation. But the line explains *why* Pollius' bay is calm: Neptune blocks the savage waves (as do the rocks at 14).

26 mira quies pelagi: ellipsis expresses wonder, a leitmotiv of the 'villa' poem; cf. Luc. 5.442 *saeua quies pelagi*. The calm sea that thwarts Caesar's plans for war has positive associations in 2.2: *quies* is also a common term for Epicurean ἀταραξία; see 140n.

26–7 ponunt hic lassa furorem | aequora et insani spirant clementius austri 'wearied the seas set aside their wrath and the mad winds blow more mildly'; cf. *Theb.* 5.468–9 *detumuere animi maris, et clementior Auster | uela uocat. Austri* are southern, storm-bearing winds (e.g. Hor. *Carm.* 3.3 4 *turbidus Auster*, Tib. 1.1.47 *hibernus Auster*); cf. 2.1.106. *clemens*, used here of 'mild' weather (*OLD* 4), is normally an ethical term, like our 'clement' (*OLD* 1). *lassus* is less frequent in poetry than *fessus* and occurs esp. in non-epic genres (2.1.16n.; Austin on Virg. *A.* 2.739; N–H on *Carm.* 2.6.7, and the statistical survey of Axelson 29–30 (who, however, omits St.). Assonance suggests the soft sound of the winds rustling over Pollius' bay.

28 praeceps minus audet hiems: *hiems* is a frequent poetic term for 'storm'; cf. Virg. *A.* 1.125 *emissamque hiemem sensit Neptunus*. The hint of personification in *minus audet* sustains the moral symbolism; *praeceps* connotes 'headstrong' (*OLD* 3; 2.1.112n.; *Theb.* 12.765 *quae bellum praeceps amentia suasit?*) as well as 'rushing' (*OLD* 2c).

29 stagna modesta iacent: cf. Luc. 5.442–3 *ignaua profundo | stagna iacentis aquae. stagnum* was etymologically derived from *stare* (N–H on *Carm.*

2.15.4; Serv. *A.* 1.126) and in its sense of 'sea' (*OLD* 2a) often connotes calm. *modesta* ('mild') creates a striking personification; elsewhere it always refers to mild-mannered people (*OLD* 1). **dominique imitantia mores:** an overt moral correlation between the landscape and Pollius. *domini* means 'owner' and 'slave-master' (45, 81, 107), emphasising Pollius' benevolent influence upon even the sea, the most unruly of natural elements.

30–3 A description of the portico, a covered walkway supported by columns offering a sheltered means of ascent up the cliff to the villa. The Greek *porticus* became an important feature of Roman villas, creating an elegant front to the house; e.g. Cic. *De orat.* 2.20; Zanker 1998: 136–8, plate 16; *uillae et porticus* were among the topics of a new style of landscape painting introduced in the Augustan age (Plin. *Nat.* 35.116–17). Moralists condemned the portico as a symbol of decadence, a feature of public architecture wrongly appropriated for private display and leisure (N–H on Hor. *Carm.* 2.15.14–16). But Pollius' portico is not part of the house per se but has a practical function: it demonstrates his technological skill as well as his wealth and Hellenism; cf. 3.1.99–100 *nunc tibi distinctis stat porticus alta columnis | ne sorderet iter.*

30 inde: a temporal and spatial marker for the shift in point of view from shore to cliff.   **per obliquas . . . arces:** in the sense of 'crags' or 'cliff' (*OLD* 5a), *arces* suggests the great height of the villa's location and the technological challenge of constructing access to it. *obliquas* is a transferred epithet; the portico is slanted across the cliffs.   **erepit porticus:** a bold personification for gradual ascent, and the first use of *erepo* for a static object (*OLD* 2); cf. Hor. *S.* 1.5.79 *montis . . . quos numquam erepsemus.*

31 urbis opus: this phrase occurs only twice earlier in Latin poetry, at Virg. *A.* 5.119, of the gigantic ship Chimaera, doomed to failure in the ship race, and at Ov. *Fast.* 6.643, of the luxurious mansion of Vedius Pollio. It indicates enormous size (Williams on Virg. *A.* 5.119; cf. *Theb.* 6.86 *montis opus . . . cumulare pyram*) and also moral excess; cf. Sen. *Ep.* 90.43 (on the architectural restraint of an earlier age) *non habebant domos instar urbium*; Hardie 1987: 167. St. removes the phrase's negative associations. The portico is lit. 'a work of a city' in engineering skill as well as size. With this phrase St. wittily alludes to the fate of Vedius Pollio's villa, razed by Augustus and replaced with the *Porticus Liuiae* (*Fast.* 6.639–48); morally upright Pollius keeps both portico and villa!   **longoque . . . dorso** 'with its lengthy spine' (SB). The porticus is further personified, as if seen by a viewer from above. St. perhaps echoes V. Fl. 2. 63 *longo . . . dorso* (of a mountain ridge); unlike the Argonauts, the travellers in Pollius' porticus are journeying in peace. On the poem's shifts in physical perspective see 30n., 48–9 n., 81–2n.   **domat saxa aspera:** *domare* is a key term of 2.2 for both technological and philosophical mastery, with military connotations also (*OLD* 2); see 56n., 124–5n.; Laguna

on 3.1.14; Thomas on Virg. *G.* 2.169–70. The portico is personified as conqueror of rough, harsh terrain; *asper* frequently describes difficult rocky ground
(*OLD* 4a).

32–3 qua prius . . . | nunc: the contrasting of former times with the more
cultured present was a favourite topos of Augustan poets (e.g. Virg. *A.* 8.306–69;
Laguna on 3.1.12–15). Unlike his models, St. attaches no moral ambiguity to the
present but suggests a straightforward narrative of progress; cf. 3.1.97–100.

32 obscuro permixti puluere soles 'sunlight was mixed with dark dust';
the porticus by contrast offers shade and clear air. Pl. *soles* is poetic for 'the heat
of the sun'; cf. 4.4.19.

33 et feritas inamoena uiae, nunc ire uoluptas: the opposing concepts of
'wildness' and 'pleasure' frame the line, representing the transformation Pollius
has wrought upon the land. The short final colon (with active verb) following the
longer preceding *qua* clause emphasises the new ease of travel. *uoluptas* implies
also Epicurean 'pleasure', a condition achieved through a moderate life that is
free from pain (Bailey on Lucr.1.1). *inamoenus* occurs elsewhere in classical Roman
poetry only at Ov. *Met.* 10.15 *inamoenaque regna*, and *Theb.* 1.89–90 *inamoenum . . . |
Cocyton*, both describing infernal gloom and barrenness. Pollius has by contrast
created a *locus amoenus*; cf. Serv. *A.* 5.734 *'amoena' sunt loca solius uoluptatis plena*.

**34–5 qualis, si subeas Ephyres Baccheidos altum | culmen, ab Inoo
fert semita tecta Lechaeo** 'like the covered way that runs from Ino's [harbour
of] Lechaeum, if you should climb to the lofty heights of ancient Corinth, once
ruled by the Bacchiadae'.   **Ephyres Baccheidos:** *Ephyre* is an old name for
Corinth (Hom. *Il.* 6.152), used in learned style; e.g. Virg. *G.* 2.464; Ov. *Met.* 2.240;
Theb. 2.379. *Baccheis* is a unique epithet meaning 'belonging to the Bacchiadae',
the first ruling family at Corinth before the age of the tyrants (Ov. *Met.* 5.407;
Plin. *Nat.* 35.152).   **altum | culmen:** an etymological gloss on Acro-corinth,
'high Corinth'.

35 semita tecta 'covered way', a periphrasis for the portico.   **Inoo:** a rare
poetic adjective (here abl.) with neoteric resonance (2.1.98n.).   **Lechaeo:**
Baehrens' conjecture for M's *lyceo*, followed by SB; Courtney (also Van Dam) reads
Lyaeo. Both readings are problematic. There is no evidence for a famous temple
to Dionysus (Lyaeus) at Corinth; the temple of Aphrodite on the Acrocorinth
was the city's most notable shrine (Paus. 2.5.1; *OCD* s.v. 'Corinthian cults and
myths'). But a portico ascending from Lechaeum, the Corinthian harbour, to the
Acrocorinth would have been impossibly long; archaeologists have found only a
road from the port to the city centre (Fowler and Stillwell 1941: 148–58). Yet in
favour of *Inoo . . . Lechaeo* is a similar phrase at *Theb.* 2.381 *Palaemonio . . . Lechaeo*.
St.'s topography is often evocative rather than exact; mention of the port where
Theban Ino and her son Palaemon arrived touches on an important myth of the

Siluae and *Thebaid* (2.1.179–80n.); mention of the Acrocorinth, site of the spring Pirene (37–8n.), suggests that the portico leads upwards to a new fount of poetry.

36–44 None of the traditional fountains of poetic inspiration can do justice to the villa; for a similar sentiment cf. 1.4.25–30. St. reformulates the 'hundred mouths' topos (cf. Hom. *Il.* 2.489) for expressing poetic inadequacy in the face of marvels, the very point in a poem where excessiveness is called for (P. R. Hardie 1997: 154–5; Pollmann on *Theb.* 12.797–9). The claim of poetic insufficiency also draws attention to the poet's achievements (Hinds 1998: 35–47), esp. in a new literary form where he must strive to match his style to the splendour of what he sees; Lucian *Dom.* offers relevant reflections on this theme.

36 non, mihi si cunctos Helicon indulgeat amnes: the first of four unreal conditions. Helicon, the site of Hesiod's encounter with the Muses (Hes. *Th.* 23) boasted two poetic springs, the most famous, the Hippocrene, near the summit, and Aganippe further down; at the mountain's foot were the rivers Permessus and Olmeius. On the topography of Helicon see Wallace 1974; Clausen on Virg. *Ecl.* 6.64; on poetic mountains and springs in general see Bömer on Ov. *Met.* 2.282–5.

37 Piplea: 'the Pimplean spring' was in Pieria, Macedonia, near Mount Olympus (Call. *Del.* 7); it was the Muses' traditional home (Hes. *Th.* 53) before their move to Helicon. The form without *m* was regular in Latin poetry (N–H on Hor. *Carm.* 1.26.9).   **superet . . . sitim:** etymological play on the spring's name *Pi(m)plea* and its derivation from the Greek verb 'fill' (πίμπλημι; Vollmer on 1.4.25–6).

37–8 largeque uolantis | ungula sedet equi: probably not the Hippocrene (Greek 'horse fountain'), the most famous of the springs created by the blow of Pegasus' hoof (Arat. *Phaen.* 216–23; Ov. *Met.* 5.256–64; *Fast.* 5. 449–58; Hinds 1985: 21–4), for Helicon was mentioned at 36, but rather the Corinthian Pirene, where Bellerophon first tamed Pegasus as he was drinking (Pi. *Ol.* 13.60–92; Paus. 2.3.2–3; D–S 1 684–5; *LIMC* VII 1.214–5 s.v. 'Pegasus'); St. is unique in Roman poetry in attributing this spring's origins also to Pegasus; cf. *Theb.* 4.60–1 *uatum qua conscius amnis | Gorgoneo percussus equo*; here *percussus* definitely suggests a hoof-blow; 2.7.4n. M reads *sedet* ('slakes' (*sc.* his thirst) *OLD* 2a), synonymous with *superet*. Gronovius' *se det* ('(generously) offers itself'), adopted by Courtney and SB on the grounds that a 'hoof' cannot slake thirst, is unnecessary; *ungula* is synecdoche for the spring.

38 reseretque 'should unbar' (*OLD* 1), but used for poetic revelation and originality (*OLD* 4b) since Enn. *Ann.* fr. 210 *nos ausi reserare*, with Skutsch; 2.7.57n.

38–9 arcana pudicos | Phemonoe fontes: two bilingual puns: *pudicus* (synonymous with *castus*), refers to the Castalian springs (Κασταλια) at Delphi where Phemonoe was the first priestess (Luc. 5.120–224); cf. *Theb.* 1.697–8 *rore* *pudico* | *Castaliae*; McKeown on Ov. *Am.* 1.15.35–6. *arcana*, a rare epithet for a deity and unprecedented for a prophetess (*TLL* II. 434.55–67, 435.82–3; McKeown on Ov. *Am.* 1.7.9–10) puns on her name's association with prophetic speech (φήμη). On the Castalian springs as sources of poetic inspiration see Fedeli on Prop. 3.2.13–14.

39 uel quos 'or even those which' (sc. *fontes*).

39–40 meus . . . | . . . Pollius: cf. 2 *pr.* 12 *Polli mei.*

40 altius immersa . . . urna 'by dipping quite deeply his urn', instrumental abl., the participle with contemporaneous aspect. Generally poets drink directly from the source; but cf. Prop. 4.6.4 (on Callimachean inspiration) *Cyrenaeas urna ministret aquas. altius* has epic resonance, suggesting grand-scale composition; cf. Lucr. 1.412 *largos haustus e fontibu' magnis.* Pollius has his own poetic spring – the villa crowns a new Helicon.   **turbauit:** used of stirring up or muddying calm water (*OLD* 3a), *turbauit* suggests the Callimachean metaphor of the 'great but muddied river' of grand-scale poetry (Call. *Ap.* 108–9). Pollius approaches poetry as he does landscape, in heroic style (cf. 52–62). For the matching of descriptive verb to poetic theme and style see 2.7.53n.

41 innumeras . . . species cultusque locorum 'the countless sights and ornaments of the area' (SB). *species* suggests the outward appearance of things or places (*OLD* 5), *cultus* their adornment (*OLD* 6); cf. 4.2.30 *longa supra species.*

42 Pieriis . . . modis: cf. Hor. *Ars* 405 (on encomiastic lyric) *Pieriis . . . modis,* with Brink. 'Pierian' is a conventional epithet for the Muses (*OLD Pierius* 1), but the specific allusion to Horace aptly concludes a passage on the challenge of writing praise poetry.

42–3 uix ordine longo | suffecere oculi 'because of the long array [causal abl.] my eyes scarcely held out'; *ordine longo* suggests St.'s movement through the villa. Hinds 2000: 252 notes that St. refers to the procession of famous Romans who reveal the history of Rome to Aeneas in the Underworld, the entrance to which was near Naples at Lake Avernus; cf. Virg. *A.* 6.754–5 *unde omnis longo ordine posset* | *aduersos legere.* The witty play with Aeneas' experience in the Underworld (see also 43–4n.) acknowledges the prestige derived from the region's Virgilian history while emphasising that the villa, filled with light and beautiful works of art, by contrast exalts the value of private life detached from an ambitious or a nationalistic agenda. On Pollius' inspirational models in life see 69n.

43–4 uix, dum per singula ducor, | suffecere gradus: cf. Virg. *A.* 6.888 *quae postquam Anchises natum per singula duxit.* Repeated *uix* and the metrical parallelism of line-initial *suffecere* stress the theme of poetic inability in the face of marvels (36–44n.); cf. 3.1.102 *uix opera enumerem*; 4.2.30 *fessis uix culmina prendas* |

uisibus. The spondaic rhythm dramatises St.'s slow movement as he is led (*ducor*) through the villa; the three monosyllables after the strong caesura suggest a halting pace as he perhaps stops to admire. Viewing is a physical and emotional as well as aesthetic experience. St. does not specify his guide; unlike Aeneas, his experience seems unmediated.

44–51 St. describes the ideal orientation of the villa, its rooms situated so as to control the intake of light and shade, heat and cold as desired.

44–5 locine | ingenium an domini mirer prius?: *mirer* is deliberative subj.; on the encomiastic strategy of the 'difficulty of knowing where to begin' see 2.1.36–8n. St. blurs two senses of *ingenium*, the inherent character of the place (*OLD* 2) and the creative abilities (*OLD* 4) of Pollius, probably with further play on literary abilities (*OLD* 5) since Pollius is a poet; see 2.3.59n.

45–7 haec domus ortus | aspicit . . . illa cadentem | detinet: precise exposure to different seasons and times of day was an important feature of the Roman villa; cf. Vitr. 6.1.2; Plin. *Nat.* 18.33; Plin. *Ep.* 2.17.6; Sen. *Con.* 5.5; Lucian, *Dom.* 6. Pollius' villa is made up of several buildings (*haec domus* 'this part'; *illa* 'that part'; cf. 50 *tecta*; Purcell 1987: 197), oriented differently so as to capture the early morning sun (*ortus*), or retain it in the evening beyond its natural duration. Personification animates the scene; see 30n.

46 Phoebi tenerum iubar 'young' (or 'early') light of day (*OLD tener* 2c).

47 exactamque negat dimittere lucem 'and refuses to dismiss the light now spent' (SB). The relationship between technology and nature is described in the hierarchical terms of the master–slave relationship. The personified house treats the sunlight as a weary slave who has been detained beyond his conventional term of duty. The 'villa' poem typically does not acknowledge the slave labour crucial to running the estate (Williams 1973); Plin. *Ep.* 2.17.9 mentions slave quarters only briefly. Slavery instead is a metaphor for human mastery of the environment; see 29n.

48–9 in aequora montis opaci | umbra cadit uitreoque natant praetoria ponto: a shift in perspective: at dusk, looking down from the house, the reflection (*umbra*) of the darkening mountain on the sea joins that of the mansions, briefly rendering harmony between art and nature; *uitreo* 'glassy' suggests that the sea has been transformed into a precious artefact, a striking example of nature imitating art rather than vice versa; see 2.3.5n. On reflection in St. see 2.3.4n., 2.3.59n.; Cancik 1965: 48–56. St.'s interest in reflection on water influenced later poets such as Ausonius (e.g. *Mos.* 189–99).

49 praetoria: a common word for military headquarters (*OLD* 1), first used of villas in the Flavian period (*OLD* 3 and used by St. only in this new sense; cf. 1.3.25, 2.2.82). The villa's military associations (3n.) complement Pollius' role as 'conqueror' of nature (see 52–62), yet here the building 'floats' (*natant*), simply weightless and beautiful to look at.

50–1 haec . . . fremunt, haec . . . | . . . silentia malunt: sound (or its absence) as well as view was important in the villa's orientation; cf. 1.3.39–42.

52–62 A praise of technological progress, Pollius' alteration of the land to build his villa. For moralists, tampering with nature was perverse, the mark of the tyrant (e.g. Sen. *Con.* 2.1.12–13; Purcell 1987: 190–5), but Pollius' conquest of nature comes not from a desire for luxury but for improvement of himself and his land; he brings civilisation to a wilderness; cf. 3.1.166–70. St. adapts to the villa the Hesiodic metaphor of farming as a type of noble warfare, developed in Virgil's *Georgics* (Bradley 1969; Hardie on Virg. *A.* 9.607–8); Gale 2000: 252–9 notes Virgil's double use of the military metaphor, with nature as ally or stubborn enemy. Pollius belongs to the tradition of the enlightened farmer/general/ruler. As in panegyrics of military commanders, his 'victory' over the land is enhanced by the tremendous difficulty of the terrain (Woodman on Vell. 2.96.3). But the transference of agricultural and martial imagery to the villa also provocatively charts the gap between public and private life, between the Republican past and the imperial present; estate management provides a blueprint for self-governance rather than for civic administration.

52–3 his fauit natura locis, hic uicta colenti | cessit 'Nature has favoured some places, in others she has been conquered and yielded to the developer'. The first of a series of antithetical cola (52–6); asyndeton and polyptoton (adjectival *his*, adverbial *hic*) emphasise a Lucretian contrast between two aspects of nature, either amenable to human needs and thus productive through loving care (Lucr. 5.1361–78) or obdurate and thus forcibly subjugated (Lucr. 5.206–34; cf. Virg. *G.* 1.197–203).

53 ignotos docilis mansueuit in usus: Nature is personified as 'teachable', like a captured animal which has 'become tame' (*OLD mansuesco* 1a) and learned new skills; see 2.5.1n.; N–R on Hor. *Carm.* 3.11.1–2. The land's compliance hints at the gendered dynamics within the Graeco-Roman language of land domination (Keith 2000: 36–64).

54 mons erat hic ubi plana uides: on the excavation or destruction of mountains to create flat surfaces or terraces for villas see Purcell 1987: 193–4. The shifts in tense from past to pres. and in person from third to second invite the reader to join in the poet's wonder; see also 54–5, 55–6. Such temporal and perspectival shifts are a feature of Virg. *A.* 8.306–69, where Evander points out to Aeneas the sites of Rome's future greatness, an important model here. On St.'s adaptation of the 'then and now' contrast see 32–3n.

54–5 et lustra fuerunt | quae nunc tecta subis 'the buildings which you now approach were [once] wilderness'; cf. 3.1.168–9 *uertis in usum | lustra habitata feris.* Places previously impenetrable are now easily approached; the reader 'walks' with the poet.

55–6 ubi nunc nemora ardua cernis | hic nec terra fuit: with the third and final contrast St. reverses the temporal order, with the present now preceding the past; cf. Virg. *A.* 8.348 *aurea nunc, olim siluestribus horrida dumis.* Pollius has created magnificent groves where there was previously 'not even' (*nec*) decent soil (*OLD terra* 4a); or perhaps he has boldly reclaimed the land from the sea, an act often derided by moralists (e.g. Sen. *Con.* 2.1.13 *ex hoc litoribus quoque moles iniungunt congestisque in alto terris exaggerant sinus*; N–H on Hor. *Carm.* 2.18.21), though it could be beneficial; cf. Suet. *Claud.* 20; Purcell 1987: 191–2. Today woods are cleared to make room for buildings, but in Roman times the carefully landscaped grove enhanced a villa owner's property and added to its financial value; cf. 1.3.17–18 *nemora alta citatis | incubuere uadis*; Plin. *Nat.* 17.1–6; Sen. *Con.* 5.5 (invective against artificial groves) *in summis culminibus mentita nemora.*

56 domuit possessor: cf. 3.1.165–7 *qui rigidas rupes infecundaeque pudenda | naturae deserta domas*; 31n. *possessor* is a quasi-legal term for the owner of property, with the notion of strong control; cf. 4.6.102; Coleman on Virg. *Ecl.* 9.3 *possessor agelli.*

57 formantem rupes expugnantemque: the participles link the two aspects of Pollius' relationship to nature, his benevolence in treating the land like a sculptor shaping harsh stone into pleasing forms (*OLD formo* 1a), and his heroic prowess in taking a fortified position by storm (*OLD expugno* 1). Slow spondees emphasise the effort involved.

57–8 secuta | gaudet humus: since nature willingly complies and takes pleasure in its change, its improvement is validated; cf. 3.1.78–9 *innumerae gaudentia rura superne | insedere domus*, with Laguna. As he points out, *gaudet . . . humus* is a calque on Hom. *Il.* 19.362 γέλασσε δὲ πᾶσα περὶ χθών, the military context of the Greek passage (the earth shining with pleasure from the flashing armour) being appropriate here: the land, conquered, shines with new buildings. See Cancik 1968: 68–70; Myers 2000: 114–5; Newlands 2002: 178–84.

58 nunc cerne: a vivid direct imperative (cf. 55 *cernis*) to the reader to 'view'.   **iugum discentia saxa** 'rocks learning the yoke'. St. combines a pun on the common meaning of *iugum* as 'mountain ridge' and thus 'rocks' (Van Dam) with a metaphor that suggests the ideas of taming animals (by yoking them together) and of military conquest: a conquered army submitted to authority by passing under a 'yoke-shaped' configuration of spears (*OLD* 5).

59 intrantesque domos iussumque recedere montem 'the houses entering [the rocks] and the mountain ordered to retreat'. Courtney reads Rothstein's emendation *intrantemque* (*domos*); *montem* then modifies both participles with the idea that first the mountain encroaches on the house and is then 'ordered' to retreat as the building progresses. But that Pollius started building before excavating the mountain seems odd. As Van Dam points out, the idea of houses 'entering' the rocky landscape follows naturally upon *iugum discentia saxa* (58); the villa is like a victorious army that takes over the rough terrain, a vivid metaphor for the mountain's excavation (on the military use of *intrare* see *TLL* VII 2.57.11-13); cf. 3.1.21–2 (Hercules' building of his new temple) *et magno pectore montem | reppulit.* Post 79 CE, 'the mountain ordered to retreat' has a topical ring.

60–2 The theme of dominating nature concludes with a new set of comparisons for Pollius, who surpasses the legendary poets famous for miraculously taming nature, Arion, Amphion, Orpheus. St. follows Ovid in mentioning all three, two being more usual (Gibson on Ov. *Ars* 3. 321–6), though he reverses Ovid's order in beginning with Arion.

60 Methymnaei uatis manus: St. uses *Methymnaeus*, a grand spondaic epithet, only here. Arion was reputedly born in the town of Methymna on the island of Lesbos; he is esp. associated with the sea, his most famous exploit being his charming of a dolphin that rescued him after pirates threw him overboard (Ov. *Fast.* 2.79–118). Arion's appearance here in a relatively clichéd topos anticipates the metaphor of the sea as a symbol of troubled human life, made calm by philosophy (129–31, 139–42; cf. 119–20).

60–1 chelys una | Thebais 'along with the Theban lyre'. Like Pollius, Amphion was poet and builder; his lyre charmed the stones and built the walls of Thebes; cf. *Theb.* 1.9–10 *quo carmine muris | iusserit Amphion Tyrios accedere montes*; Hor. *Carm.* 3.11.2 *mouit Amphion lapides canendo*; Hinds 2000: 243 n.53. *una* is adverbial, not adjectival in the sense of 'unique' or 'sole' as Van Dam takes it, for others can claim the 'Theban lyre' – Pindar, born in Thebes and an important model for St. (4.7.7–8), and St. himself, who slips in here a reference to his *Thebaid*. *Thebais*, emphasised here by enjambment, occurs nowhere else in Roman poetry as an adjective; as a noun it is the name of St.'s epic; cf. *Theb.* 12.812. *chelys* is an esp. Statian word (2.1.7n.).

61 Getici . . . gloria plectri: St. favours the poetic *Geticus* for Orpheus' country of origin, Thrace (Hor. *Carm.* 1.24.13 *Threicio . . . Orpheo*); see Laguna on 3.117.   **cedat:** *manus, chelys, gloria* are the subjects. St. is fond of statements of 'outdoing' in encomia; when formulated with *cedere* 'to yield', the context is generally literary; cf. 146, 2.4.9–10, 2.6.36, 2.7.75; Curtius 1953: 162–5.

62 et tu saxa moues et te nemora alta sequuntur: cf. Ov. *Ars* 3.321 *saxa feraque lyra mouit . . . Orpheus.* Pollius forms the climax of the mythological sequence with sudden direct address, emphasised by polyptoton (*tu . . . te*).

63–72 The villa was the ideal place for displaying art (Neudecker 1998); at Rome, Pliny claims, people are too busy to appreciate art (*Nat.* 36.27). The nature of Pollius' collection, like that of Novius Vindex (4.6.25–30), is conservative and suggests the high premium put upon ancient Greek art, whether originals or copies, as signs of social status and artistic discrimination. Pollius probably owned mostly copies of old Greek masters, for by this period most originals were in imperial, not private, hands. This does not mean that St. exaggerates the value of Pollius' art collection (thus Cancik 1968: 74; Van Dam ad loc.), for copies, often made in Italian workshops, were highly valued and highly priced too (Bartman 1991: 76–9; Perry 2005; Coleman on 4.6.24). St. does not say where Pollius' art collection was displayed, but the atrium or peristyle were likely places; the Villa of the Papyri at Herculaneum displayed a large sculpture collection in a long peristyle, where visitors could stroll and admire at leisure (Neudecker 1988: 105–14; Beard and Henderson 2001: 93–6).

63 quid referam: not 'why should I tell of?' (thus SB) but 'what can I tell of?', a transitional question that emphasises wonder and the poetic challenge of finding adequate words to do justice to Pollius' art collection; see 2.1.96n.   **ueteres ceraeque aerisque figuras:** sculptures in bronze and possibly also wax, used for busts and ancestral masks (2.1.193n.) and also for 'high end' works of art; Novius Vindex owned sculptures of bronze, ivory and wax (Coleman on 4.6.21). But *cerae* could also refer to encaustic painting which used pigments mixed with heated wax (*OLD cera* 3e; Plin. *Nat.* 35.122–3; *OCD* s.v. 'painting, Greek'), an art practised by Apelles, the painter celebrated in the next line (cf. 1.1.100 *Apelleae . . . cerae*). *figuras* in the sense of 'artistic image' (*OLD* 8a) can apply to either medium.

64 si quid Apellei gaudent animasse colores 'whatever the colours of Apelles have happily brought to life', in apposition to *figuras*; the indefinite *si quid* is modelled after Greek εἴ τις, an appropriate opening to a list of Greek artists. Apelles (latter half of the fourth century BCE) is the only painter whom St. mentions (Coleman on 4.6.29). Regarded by antiquity as its greatest painter, he was admired for his use of brilliant colours and of an intensifying, subtle glaze; Alexander the Great allowed only Apelles to paint his portrait (Plin. *Nat.* 35.79–97; Gibson on 5.1.5). The adjective *Apelleus* is attested for the first time at Prop. 1.2.22, then only here and at 5.1.5; it can mean either 'of Apelles' or 'such as Apelles would have used'; the latter meaning is better suited to fine copies of this 'old master'; see 63–72n. *animare* in the sense of 'to give life to a painting or sculpture' (*OLD* 3a; Gibson on 5.1.2) expresses the mimetic realism valued by the ancients in art; cf. Plin. *Nat.* 35.65–6. *gaudent* suggests by transference the pleasure of viewing fine art; cf. 58.

65–6 si quid . . . tamen admirabile . . . | Phidiacae rasere manus: cf. 4.6.27 *ebur Pisaeo pollice rasum*; 5.1.6 *Phidiaca uel rasa manu*, with Gibson. The fifth-century BCE sculptor Phidias was famous for his colossal statues, esp. the ivory statue of Zeus at Olympia (Plin. *Nat.* 34.49, 54), considered his masterpiece (Quint.

Inst. 12.10.9; Fedeli on Prop. 3.9.15), and the ivory and gold statue of Athena in the Parthenon (Plin. *Nat.* 34.54, 36.18); he also excelled in bronzes (Plin. *Nat.* 34.49, 36.18–19). *Phidiacus* means 'of Phidias' or 'worthy of Phidias'. *tamen admirabile* agrees with *quid*; though not the most famous (i.e. colossal) sculptures, the works Pollius owns (perhaps miniatures or copies) are 'nonetheless wonderful'; line-initial anaphora expresses admiration (43–4n.). Only St. applies *radere* ('to rub smooth') to sculpture. Metaphorically it can describe a 'polished' literary work; cf. Ov. *Pont.* 2. 4.17 *meus lima rasus liber*; Mart. 4.10.1. Pollius has the same refined tastes in the visual arts as he does in literature; see 2.7.105–6n.

65 adhuc uacua . . . Pisa 'when Olympia was still empty', abl. abs. with temporal force; i.e. before Phidias' colossus of Zeus at Olympia was built; cf. Juv. 3.2 *uacuis . . . Cumis*, with Courtney. Pisa is synonymous with nearby Olympia (Coleman on 4.6.27).

66–7 quod ab arte Myronis | aut Polycliteo iussum est quod uiuere caelo 'whatever has been ordered to come alive by the art of Myron or the chisel of Polyclitus', again an emphasis on mimetic realism as carrying particular value (64n.). Myron and Polyclitus were contemporaries. Myron was esp. famous for his realistic statue of a heifer, the theme of many ecphrastic epigrams (*AP* IX 713–42; Posidipp. 66); cf. Prop. 2.31.7–8 *armenta Myronis | . . . uiuida signa*; Ov. *Pont.* 4.1.34 *similis uerae uacca Myronis opus*; Plin. *Nat.* 34.57). A late source (Procop. *Goth.* 4.21) claims the famous cow was transferred from Athens to Vespasian's *Templum Pacis* in Rome. Polyclitus was regarded as having brought to perfection Phidias' art (Plin. *Nat.* 34.55–6; Coleman on 4.6.28). The rare *Polycliteus* can mean 'belonging to Polyclitus' or 'modelled after his style'. In 4.6 St. adds Praxiteles between Myron and Polyclitus; otherwise the list of sculptors is identical.

68 aeraque ab Isthmiacis auro potiora fauillis 'bronzes from the ashes of Corinth more valuable than gold', a syntactic switch with *aera* (and *ora* 69) the direct objects of *referam* (63). The most renowned of ancient bronzes, Corinthian was reputedly produced by chance when the city was burned by Roman forces in 146 BCE (Plin. *Nat.* 34.6–8; cf. Petr. 50, with Smith). It had an addictive allure: Verres was proscribed for refusing to give Mark Antony some pieces of Corinthian ware (Plin. *Nat.* 34.6); cf. Sen. *Dial.* 10.12.2 *Corinthia, paucorum furore pretiosa*; Plin. *Ep.* 3.1.9. On *Isthmiacus* see 2.1.179–80n.

69 ora ducum ac uatum sapientumque ora priorum: a stately line, with homoeoteleuton, assonance of -*or*-, and close repetition. 'Portrait busts' (*ora*) of famous men of antiquity often formed part of a villa's sculptural programme (Neudecker 1988: 67); cf. Plin. *Ep.* 3.7.8 (of Silius Italicus) *multum ubique librorum, multum statuarum, multum imaginum, quas non habebat modo, uerum etiam uenerabatur*, with Henderson 2002: 115. Plin. *Nat.* 35.4–8 attacks the custom of substituting for ancestral portraits statues whose only value (he claims) lay in their price; cf. *Nat.* 35.5 *imagines pecuniae, non suas, relinquunt*. But Pollius' *imagines* serve an exemplary purpose and reflect contemporary Roman discourse on the nature of true nobility, acquired through great achievements rather than descent; cf. Cic. *Arch.* 14 (playing on the sculptural metaphor) *quam multas nobis imagines non solum ad intuendum uerum etiam ad imitandum fortissimorum uirorum expressas scriptores et Graeci et Latini reliquerunt!*; Sen. *Ep.* 44.3 (on Socrates and Cleanthes) *omnes hi maiores*; Bernstein 2008: 119. The three professions of generals, poets and philosophers match Pollius' representation in this poem as conqueror, poet and Epicurean; cf. *Ach.* 1.15–16 (of Domitian, omitting the *sapientes*) *cui geminae florent uatumque ducumque | certatim laurus.*

70 quos tibi cura sequi: St. again addresses Pollius (62n.) with ellipsis of *est*. *quos* refers to all three professions which Pollius takes as his model; cf. 57 *secuta*, 62 *sequuntur*, where nature follows his lead.

71 expers curarum: polyptoton (*cura, curarum*) marks the paradox that 'effort' (*OLD cura* 3) is needed to be carefree, i.e. in a state of Epicurean ἀταραξία (*OLD* 1).

72–85 A description of the views from the windows, their number and variety proof of Pollius' wealth and social prestige; cf. 3.1.147–53 for a similar catalogue of views. St. is now in the interior, looking out. In the architectural and social design of the Roman house the view was very important; paintings of seaside villas show porticoes, terraces and piers prominently oriented to look out and also be seen; e.g. Vitr. 6.4; Plin. *Ep.* 5.6.7–16; Purcell 1987: 196–200; Elsner 1995: 49–87. The views from Pollius' villa are esp. rich in literary associations; history forms an important part of the spatial description; see Hinds 2000: 247–51.

72 compositus 'untroubled by passions, calm' (*OLD* 7), here with *animum* (71), acc. of respect. Pollius is calm like his environment; *compositus* is first used of the sea in Augustan poetry (Gibson on Ov. *Ars* 3.259–60).   **semperque tuus** 'and always your own person', i.e. in control of yourself (*OLD tuus* 3b); cf. Cic. *Fin.* 4.4.10 (*poterit*) *semperque esse in disputando suus*. St. may have in mind Horace's notion of *sibi uiuere*; see Cancik 1968: 72 n.36.   **quid . . . reuoluam:** another transitional question to introduce a new topic (63n.). *reuoluam* 'recall to memory' (*OLD* 2c), also suggests 'roll back a scroll' (*OLD* 2b; Austin on Virg. *A.* 2.101). Remembering the visit to Pollius' villa resembles rereading, and reproducing, a written text. St. draws attention to his poem's 'literariness' despite its overall impression of immediacy.

72–3 mille . . . | culmina 'countless vantage points' (for viewing, thus Van Dam), *culmen* being a high point of a building or a natural feature such as a mountain as at 35. The hyperbolic *mille* in the sense of 'countless' expresses the challenge to the poet's descriptive powers; cf. 3.5.105 *mille tibi nostrae referam telluris amores?*

73 uisendique uices 'opportunities for viewing' (*OLD uicis* 1a).

73-4 sua cuique uoluptas atque omni proprium thalamo mare 'each room has its own delight, each its own sea', i.e. its own different view over the bay; cf. Plin. *Ep.* 2.17.20. St. alludes humorously to Virg. *Ecl.* 2.65 *trahit sua quemque uoluptas*, the clumsy philosophising of the shepherd Corydon (Clausen), here applied to the villa's rooms in anticipation of the Virgilian nature of the view (76n.). Windows frame the sea as if it were a wall painting, thus blurring the boundaries between art and nature.

74-5 transque iacentem | Nerea: the sea god Nereus is a common epic metonymy for the sea (*OLD* 3b). *iacentem* suggests the sea is still (*OLD iaceo* 8), thus like a work of art; it also suggests subjugation (*OLD* 3, 5), for it serves human needs for visual pleasure.

75 diuersis seruit sua terra fenestris 'each separate window commands its own landscape' (SB); a rephrasing of 73-4. *seruit* continues the idea of subjugation.

76 haec uidet Inarimen: sc. *haec* [*fenestra*]. *Inarime* (modern Ischia) first occurs in Latin literature at Virg. *A.* 9.715. The legend that Typhoeus was imprisoned under this island after his defeat in the Gigantomachy explained its volcanic character (Hardie on Virg. *A.* 9.715-16). **illinc Prochyta aspera:** St. follows Virg. *A.* 9.715-16 and Ov. *Met.* 14.89 in pairing Ischia and the island of Prochyta (modern Procida), seen 'from another window', thus adverbial *illinc*. Like Pliny in his villa descriptions St. offers few spatial markers and typically notes adjacency rather than direction or route; see Riggsby 2003: 169-70. Virgil's mention of the two islands concludes a simile referring to the laying of foundations for piers or villas in the seabed off Naples (*A.* 9.710-16, with Hardie); St. perhaps indirectly alludes to Virgil's admiration for Roman engineering, a precedent for his own praise of technology; see 98-9n. *aspera* means 'rugged' (31n.), a reference to Procida's volcanic nature (Plin. *Nat.* 2.87) and a possible correction of Virgil's puzzling *alta* (*A.* 9.715) for this low-lying island; see *EV* IV 289-91. **paret:** St. plays on the two senses 'comes into view' (*OLD* 5) and, in keeping with the idea of subjugation, 'obeys' (*OLD* 1); cf. Virg. *A.* 9. 715 *Prochyta . . . tremit.*

77 armiger . . . magni . . . Hectoris: a periphrasis for the Cape of Misenum (Capo Miseno), forming the northern arm of the Bay of Naples. It was named after Misenus, Hector's 'armour bearer' at Troy and later Aeneas' trumpeter, who was buried on the Cape shortly after the Trojans' arrival in Italy (Virg. *A.* 6.156-235). The Plautine *armiger* was introduced to high poetry by Virgil (Austin on Virg. *A.* 2.477; *TLL* I 613.77-614.19). This view was esp. prestigious; the Cape was associated with Roman wealth and power as well as with the state's heroic origins: Marius built a villa there, later owned by Lucullus before it became imperial property (Plut. *Mar.* 34.3-4). Although St. emphasises the wildness of the terrain that Pollius' villa looks out upon (Krüger 1998: 107-8), much of the bay was imperial, inhabited property. Through its view, Pollius' villa appropriates the major real estate of the Bay of Naples. **hac**

[sc. *fenestra*] . . . **inde:** alternation of adjective and adverb as spatial markers as at 76.

77–8 malignum | aera respirat: only St. and Lucan claim that Nesis is volcanic, with sulphurous fumes vented from underground cavities; cf. Luc. 6.90–1 *tali spiramine Nesis | emittit Stygium nebulosis aera saxis*; yet cf. 3.1.148 *siluaque quae fixam pelago Nesida coronat*, which perhaps suggests it was habitable (Krüger 1998: 198); Brutus had a villa there (Cic. *Att.* 16.2.3; Jolivet 1987: 885), and the island subsequently became imperial property. But it may have ceased to be habitable by the mid first century CE, a period of intense volcanic and seismic activity around the Bay of Naples (Jolivet 1987: 891).

78 pelago circumflua Nesis: lit. 'Nesis flowed round by the sea', or 'seagirt Nesis' (SB), an etymological gloss on νησίς ('small island').

79 uagis omen felix Euploca carinis: another etymological gloss, εὔπλοια meaning 'propitious sailing'; cf. 3.1.149 *omenque Euploea carinis*, with Laguna. The temple of Aphrodite Euploea in Naples protected sailors (Frederiksen 1984: 91).

80 quaeque ferit curuos exserta Megalia fluctus 'and Megalia which jutting out [into the sea] strikes the curving waves'; the antecedent *Megalia* is attracted into the relative clause; cf. 2.4.20, 2.4.21. Megalia, or Megaris (Plin. *Nat.* 3.82), was a small island near Naples where Lucullus had an estate, now imperial property (Beloch 1879: 81–3). *exserere* commonly refers to parts of the body (2.1.138n.); St. first applies it topographically, a rare personification (*TLL* v 2.1856.64–9). *ferit* boldly suggests that the land reaches out to attack the sea instead of the more usual idea of rocks breaking the waves' force; cf. 13–14n.; Sen. *Dial.* 2.3.5 *proiecti quidam in altum scopuli mare frangunt*.

81–2 angitur et domino contra recubante proculque | Surrentina tuus spectat praetoria Limon: a shift to a dual perspective: Pollius' Surrentine villa exchanges looks with another of his villas, Limon (< λειμών = 'meadow'; cf. 3.1.149 *placidus Limon*), situated across the bay at Misenum (hence *procul*, 'at a distance', from Surrentum), and perhaps better serving Pollius' business interests in Puteoli. An inscription from 65 CE found at Posilypon (Dessau, *ILS* 5798 *Villa Polli Felicis quae est epilimones*) perhaps refers to St.'s friend or to his father (Vollmer). Roman villa owners were fond of architectural vistas (Kuttner 1998) and also tried to secure the best vantage points from which their villa could be seen (Purcell 1987: 196). *angitur* 'feels vexed' (*OLD* 4), a largely prosaic word, personifies Limon as a rival, annoyed at Pollius' preference for his Surrentine property. St. enhances the description of Pollius' villa through the theme of rivalry with other properties; see also 107–11n. Elite Romans generally had several villas outside Rome, but to possess two villas in the area of Italy's prime real estate suggests exceptional wealth and Pollius' widespread influence in the region. *tuus* emphasises ownership; cf. 84 *tibi*.

83 una tamen cunctis, procul eminet una diaetis 'one room however, one room stands out by far from all the others'. Repetition of the initial word in the fifth foot is a neoteric device (Vollmer; cf. 69); the contrast of *una* with *cunctis* singles out this room as the most special in the villa, decorated with marbles and commanding the grandest view, that of Naples. *eminet* has a dual sense: it is the highest room and the most important (Van Dam). *procul* (cf. 81–2n.) has here a comparative, metaphorical, sense = *longe* 'by far' (2.6.6–8n.). The Greek term *diaeta* first appears in the Latin architectural vocabulary in the early Empire, but with uncertain meaning: in Pliny it suggests a private suite of rooms either detached from the main house (*Ep.* 2.17.12, with Sherwin-White) or in the main house itself (*Ep.* 5.6.20); see Leach 2004: 49–50. *una* suggests that *diaeta* can also refer to a single room. Common to both forms of *diaeta* is the idea of privacy and exclusivity; Augustus had a room high up in the *Domus Augusta* for his personal retreat (Suet. *Aug.* 72.2). St.'s entry to the *diaeta* suggests his privileged relationship with his hosts.

84–5 tibi Parthenopen . . . | ingerit: a paradox, one private room essentially contains all the cultural wealth of Naples. Traditionally the city was first named after the Siren Parthenope, washed up and buried on the Campanian shore (Lyc. 717–21; cf. 4.4.52–3; Plin. *Nat.* 3. 62; Sil. 12.33–6; Gibson on 5.3.104). As a name for Naples Parthenope enters Latin poetry at Virg. *G.* 4.563–4 to signify a place of poetic inspiration; the Greek name thus carries considerable cultural prestige. The room 'forcibly brings [Parthenope] to notice' (*OLD ingero* 3b), suggesting her subservience to Pollius; cf. 116–17 where another Siren flies to his songs.

84 derecto limite ponti: Naples is sighted 'in a straight line over the sea' from the window of the *diaeta*; cf. Luc. 3.218–19 *has ad bella rates non flexo limite ponti | . . . duxit Cynosura.* This is the only reference to a straight line in the poem. Naples is thus linked to the villa as if by a Roman road, becoming a key part of the design. The tour of the villa is otherwise singularly lacking in spatial directions, a reflection of the poet's state of amazement.

85–94 A list of foreign marbles that decorate the *diaeta*. St. is the first Roman poet to introduce the theme of coloured marbles to literary encomium, though their negative description at Luc.10.111–26 offered a probable model (Gnoli 1988: 5–6, 35); see Vollmer on 1.2.148–51 (Violentilla's house) and 1.5.34–40 (the baths of Claudius Etruscus); Gnoli 1988: 35–8. Marble was the luxury material *par excellence*, a sign of both high social status and vast material wealth (Zeiner 2005: 84–90); coloured marbles were esp. prized and thus subject to moral disapproval (Plin. *Nat.* 36.1–3; Gnoli 1988: 8–12; Carey 2003: 91–2). The marbles of the *diaeta* were probably displayed as flooring and as veneer on the walls, the latter a practice that typically used coloured marbles and that began to supplant wall painting in the middle of the first century CE, at least in the most important rooms of the wealthiest houses, e.g. in Nero's *Domus aurea* (Tybout 2001: 45–8). Pollius is thus *au courant* with contemporary decorative fashion. Sumptuous language conveys the marbles' beauty and their rich geographic and mythological assocations; though secluded, the *diaeta* incorporates the vast resources of empire, suggesting that the villa is a microcosm of the imperial palace. Described as a vibrant substance, marbles also resolve the tension between art and nature. On marbles common to both St. and Martial see Henriksén on Mart. 9.75.7–8.

85 hic follows a word break after the first foot to introduce the new 'catalogue'.   **metallis** 'quarries'; cf. 1.5.36.

86 quod Eoae respergit uena Syenes: *quod* is the relative pronoun after the antecedent *saxa* ('marbles'), divided into individual types. First, red granite from Syene, a town on the upper Nile (modern Aswan). It was often used for monumental, regal purposes, e.g. for Egyptian obelisks (Plin. *Nat.* 36.63–4), and for Domitian's palace; cf. 4.2.27 *multa Syene*, with Coleman; Gnoli 1988: 145–7. *respergit* 'splashes', animates the stone, suggesting that its mottled colour comes from a cut vein. See 87–8n.

87–8 Synnade quod maesta Phrygiae fodere secures | per Cybeles lugentis agros: second, an expensive Phrygian marble, white flecked with purple spots ('pavonazetto'), from quarries near the town of Synnas (Gnoli 1988: 169–71; Henriksén on Mart. 9.75.8). It was the mythical site of the self-castration of Attis, devotee of the Phrygian goddess Cybele (Cat. 63; Ov. *Fast.* 4.223–44), hence *Synnade . . . maesta*; cf. 1.5.37–8 *sola cauo Phrygiae quam Synnados antro | ipse cruentauit maculis lucentibus Attis*, where the marble is said to preserve flecks of Attis' blood. Myth's sufferings are transcended through art. The marble was used to stunning effect in columns for the Basilica Aemilia in the Roman forum (Plin. *Nat.* 36.102). Postponed *quod* is rare in the *Siluae*, occurring in book 2 only here and at 2.5.27 and 2.6.90 (Van Dam).

88 marmore picto 'coloured marble', stressing its illusionary nature; its flecks make it look *as if* it has been painted. There was a contemporary fashion for painted imitation marble walls, but Pollius could afford the real thing, marble veneer (85–94n.).

89 candida purpureo distinguitur area gyro 'the white surface is marked out by purple circles', a Golden Line acknowledging the splendour of Phrygian marble. The juxtaposition of purple and white suggest Attis' beauty as well as his pain; art aestheticises tragedy. On these colours as standard features of beauty see 2.1.41n.

90–1 hic et Amyclaei caesum de monte Lycurgi | quod uiret: third, vivid green serpentine from the Spartan mountain Taygetus, extremely popular throughout the Empire (Plin. *Nat.* 36.55; Gnoli 1988: 141–4; Henriksén on Mart. 9.75.9). *uiret*, normally used of flourishing plants, again animates the hard stone; cf. 4.2.148–9 *dura Laconum | saxa uirent*. Lycurgus, traditionally the founder of Sparta's constitution, is called 'Amyclaean', i.e. 'Spartan' (2.1.111n.), to distinguish him from the mythological Lycurgus (persecutor of Bacchus) and also from the Athenian orator.

91 et molles imitatur rupibus herbas: whereas Phrygian marble looked painted, Spartan marble imitates 'soft grass'; mimesis collapses the boundaries between hard rock and pliant herb, harsh and cooperative nature, exterior and interior.

92 hic Nomadum . . . flauentia saxa: fourth, yellowish-red Numidian marble (*giallo antico*), North Africa's main export along with wild beasts for the amphitheatre (Plin. *Nat.* 5.23); the Greek form *Nomadum* (< νομάς) rather than *Numidarum* is *metri causa*. Numidian was among the first coloured marbles introduced to Rome; the late Republican M. Lepidus caused a scandal by using it for the thresholds of his house (Plin. *Nat.* 36.49), but in the Empire it was imported on a vast scale; Domitian used Numidian in his palace (4.2.27), the first emperor after Augustus to use this marble publicly for an extensive project (Gnoli 1988: 166–8; Henriksén on Mart. 9.75.8).   **lucent** highlights the special reflective qualities of ancient marble, creating light within the interior; cf. 1.5.36 *sola nitet flauis Nomadum decisa metallis*; 4.2.27 *mons Libys . . . nitet*. On the moral associations of 'shine' see 10n.; Cancik 1965: 77–8.

92–3 Thasosque | . . . Chios . . . Carystos: last, by metonymy of the source for the product, three famous marbles from Aegean islands. Marble from Thasos was the most widespread and important of fine white marbles after the Parian and was widely used in Rome in imperial residences (Plin. *Nat.* 36.44; Gnoli 1988: 262–3). Sen. *Ep.* 86.6 complains of its lavish use in baths instead of in temples: *Thasius lapis, quondam rarum in aliquot spectaculum templo, piscinas nostras circumdedit*. Marble from Chios was subtly coloured, probably a grey-pink (4.2.28; Plin. *Nat.* 36.46; Gnoli 1988: 172–3). Carystian marble from the Aegean island of Euboea was a blueish-green colour with an undulating pattern ('cipollino'; Gnoli 1988: 181–3; Henriksén on Mart. 9.75.7). Julius Caesar's chief engineer Mamurra used this marble for columns in his Caelian house (Plin. *Nat.* 36.48).

93 gaudens fluctus aequare Carystos: *aequare* 'to rival' (*OLD* 11; cf. 42) is Salmasius' emendation for M's weak *spectare* (Håkanson 1969: 58–9); cf. (in the same verse-position) Virg. *A.* 3.671 *Ionios fluctus aequare sequendo*. Like *imitatur* (91), *aequare* stresses the illusionary nature of Roman wall decoration; St. consistently associates this marble with the sea; cf. 1.2.149–50 *et concolor alto | uena mari*; 1.5.34; 4.2.28. The poem's tension between art and nature also supports *aequare*. On this metaphor of rivalry, a modification of the topos of 'pre-eminence' in Hellenistic panegyric, see 61n.; also 81–2n.; 107–11n.; Coleman on 4.2.26–7 *aemulus illic | mons Libys Iliacusque nitet. gaudens* (see 57–8n.) suggests the marble's delight in rivalling the sea, an unstable element.

94 Chalcidicas turres: i.e. Cumae, founded by colonists from Chalcis, a town in Euboea; cf. 1.2.263 *tellus Eubois*; Gibson on 5.3.168. Its acropolis was a high point on the northern peninsula of the Bay of Naples. *Chalcidicus* is Virgilian (Virg. *Ecl.* 10.50; *A.* 6.17 *Chalcidicaque… arce*), then first here (cf. also 4.3.118, 4.4.78, 5.3.182, 5.3.226). It is not simply a rare elevated epithet for 'Neapolitan' (SB, Van Dam); rather it also alludes to Virgil's ecphrasis of the temple of Apollo at Cumae (Virg. *A.* 6.14–41), an important model for descriptions of works of art and buildings. But St. goes beyond the Sibyl's injunction at *A.* 6.37 *non hoc ista sibi tempus spectacula poscit*; he summons Virgilian topography for new ends and makes a complete poem out of *spectacula*.   **omnia… salutant:** a conclusion to the catalogue of marbles. Acknowledgment (*salutant*) of Virgilian Cumae incorporates Pollius' villa into Roman literary tradition.

95–7 A coda to the description of the works of art praising Pollius' philhellenic tastes.

95–6 macte animo, quod Graia probas, quod Graia frequentas | arua: cf. 3.1.166 *macte animis*, also in conclusion. Anaphora and asyndeton give this statement particular emphasis. *macte* can confer both hope for future blessings and congratulations for present achievements (Gibson on 5.2.97). *Graia*, a more elevated term than *Graecus* (Axelson 51–2), is a generally accepted emendation of M's *grata* (but cf. Krüger 1998: 43–5). Van Dam takes the first *Graia*, which is substantive, as referring to the marble *diaeta*, but there is no need to be so specific; Pollius loves all things Greek and inhabits the Greek territory (*arua*) of Campania; cf. 3.5.111 *Graia Parthenope*; Sil. 8.533–4.

96–7 Dicarchi | moenia: Puteoli, Pollius' birthplace (3n.).

97 nos docto melius potiemur alumno: *alumnus* 'foster son' means Pollius is an honorary citizen of Naples, St.'s native city (thus *nos*; see 136n.). *alumnus* may also be an honorific title given a benefactor (Corbier 1989); Pollius was generous to both Naples and Puteoli (3.1.91–3). *melius* 'more fitly' (SB), for Naples with its literary and artistic culture had more appropriate claims upon 'the learned' Pollius than the mercantile Puteoli; cf. Mart. 5.78.15 *docta Neapolis*.

98–106 The description of Pollius' villa concludes outdoors among his vineyards. The other 'villa' poems (1.3, 2.3, 3.1) do not refer to the agricultural part of the estate needed to sustain a villa economy. Viticulture was a prestigious, lucrative activity, but St. transforms Pollius' vineyards into an idyllic playground for nymphs and satyrs. Harvesting grapes was hard work, but like many wall paintings from Pompeii which show erotes happily performing the tasks of slaves (e.g. House of M. Lucretius), the 'villa' poem occludes real labour. St.'s use of myth reflects Roman attitudes to landscape as a site of interaction between the human and the divine – realised through the sculptural programmes of gardens, which were popularly decorated with statues of nymphs and deities such as Pan and Bacchus and his entourage (Grimal 1943: 337–53, 359–65; Cancik 1965: 52; Szelest 1972). St. evokes an Ovidian world but without the violence.

98 quid nunc . . . dicam?: a transitional question expressing wonder; see 63n.; 72n.

98–9 pontoque noualia . . . | iniecta: cf. Virg. *A*. 9.712 (of a pile of mortar for a pier or villa foundation) *ponto iaciunt*, with Hardie; 76n. Building out over the sea for private gain was a common moral topos; see 55–6n. But Pollius extends fertile fields out over the sea to support viticulture.

99 madidas Baccheo nectare rupes: light personification with the pun on *madidus* 'wet' (*OLD* 1) and 'inebriated' (*OLD* 6); cf. Mart. 1.70.9 *madidi Lyaei*; Mart. 9.61.11. Adjectival *Baccheus* is a rare Greek coinage (Βακχεῖος) found previously only in Ov. *Met*. 3.691 and 11.17. The rocks are now wet not with the sea but with the juice from the grapes.

100 pubescente Lyaeo 'when Lyaeus is maturing', i.e. when the grapes are ripening; *Lyaeus*, a frequent cult-title of Bacchus, is often used by metonymy for grapes. But the sexual overtones of *pubescente* also suggest the nymph has an assignation with the attractive young god who presides over this land; see 4n.

101–3 conscendit . . . | Nereis: cf. 19–20, where a Nereid admires the bathhouse from the sea; now a Nereid climbs ashore to enjoy the fruits of human progress and cultivation – the grapes. The second syllable of *Nereis* is here short; on its metrical variation see Hopkinson on Ov. *Met*. 13.749.

102 palmite maturo rorantia lumina tersit: the Nereid uses 'a ripened vine branch' (*OLD palmes* 1; Coleman on Virg. *Ecl*. 7.48) to dry her eyes. Håkanson 1969: 60–1 objected that a sea nymph should not be bothered by water in her eyes and advocated emending *rorantia lumina tersit* to *rorantia munera carpsit* ('she plucked the dew-wet grapes'). But this makes redundant the following line, where the Nereid 'snatched' (*rapuit*) the grapes. The manuscript reading can stand; somewhat similar is Thetis' gesture of shaking off seawater when she surfaces at *Ach*. 1.30 (*discusso . . . ponto*); cf. *Ach*. 2.4. Håkanson also finds a vine ripe with grapes a curious instrument for drying the eyes; but twice elsewhere in the *Siluae* St. refers to an unusual instrument for this purpose; cf. 1.2.92–3 *blandisque madentia plumis | lumina detersi*; 2.7.105–6 *leuiterque decidentes | abrasit lacrimas nitente plectro* – Cupid's feathers and Calliope's plectrum may be unorthodox but they are contextually appropriate, like the vine branch.

103 rapuit: on the sexual overtones of this passage see 100n.

104–5 saepe et uicino sparsa est uindemia fluctu | et Satyri cecidere uadis: *uindemia* means the 'vintage' (*OLD* 1). Critics have argued that St. elliptically refers to the Nereid's return to the water when she catches sight of the Satyrs; see Håkanson 1969: 61–2. But repeated *saepe* (cf. 100) suggests that St. starts a new anecdote here. The second *et* (105) is epexegetical, explaining that the grapes were sprinkled *by* the nearby spray from the sea because the Satyrs fell into the water, either because they were drunk, or were in pursuit of Doris, the sea nymph of the following line (106). In a typical Statian paradox the Satyrs plunge into the water, just as the Nereid in the previous anecdote had climbed out of water onto land; cf. Auson. *Mos* 183 *et Satyros uadis*. The use of *cado* with the abl. rather than the more usual *in* + acc. for movement is unusual; for St.'s freedom with the local ablative see Dilke on *Ach.* 1.43–4 *cum primum gurgite nostro | Rhoeteae cecidere trabes*; Williams 1951.

105–6 nudamque per undas | Dorida: Doris was either the mother of the Nereids or one of her daughters of the same name (West on Hes. *Th.* 241; Hopkinson on Ov. *Met.* 13.742). Her nudity comically contrasts with the shaggy Pans and Satyrs who typically lust after her; cf. Ov. *Fast.* 1.397 *Panes et in Venerem Satyrorum prona iuuentus*. There is no need to assume that Doris is the Nereid of 101–3; see 104–5n.

106 montani cupierunt prendere Panes: cf. Ov. *Ep.* 4.171 *montanaque numina Panes*; *Met.* 1.705 *Panaque, cum prensam sibi iam Syringa putaret*, where *prendere*, as here, appears in the rare sense of 'abduct' (*OLD* 4a); but desire remains unfulfilled, for water is an alien element to mountain deities; see 2.3.35–7n. *montanus* also implies rusticity (Courtney on Juv. 6.5). On pl. *Panes* see 2.3.7n.; Bömer on Ov. *Fast.* 1.397.

107–11 The villa's description ends with wishes for its long prosperity, an unusual twist on the conventional wish for the patron's longevity (cf. 2.3.72–4), combined here with the idea of rivalry among properties; see 81–2n.

107 sis felix, tellus: a pun upon Pollius' *cognomen* (23n.).   **dominis ambobus** 'for both owners', i.e. Pollius and Polla. *domini* = 'man and woman' (McKeown on Ov. *Am.* 2.8.24). St. suggests the economic importance of Polla in her own right, a theme developed at the poem's end (147–55).   **in annos** 'up to the years [of]'.

108 Mygdonii Pyliique senis: cf. 3.4.103–4 *eat, oro, per annos | Iliacos Pyliosque simul*, with Laguna; the estate's longevity is measured by the amalgamated years of proverbial *senes*. 'Mygdonian', a learned epithet for 'Phrygian' or 'Trojan', suggests either Tithonus, the husband of Aurora, who possessed immortality but not eternal youth, or king Priam (N–H on Hor. *Carm.* 2.12.22 and 2.16.30); St. mentions both at 2.3.73 (*Iliacos . . . senes*; cf. 5.3.255–6) and perhaps means both here. Nestor was king of Pylos, who reached the third generation of men (Hom. *Il.* 1.247); see N–H on Hor. *Carm.* 2.9.13.

108–9 nobile ... | seruitium 'noble servitude'; cf. 2.6.15–16 *dulce... | seruitium*, oxymora that describe the master–slave relationship as mutually beneficial, not degrading.

109–10 nec te cultu Tirynthia uincat | aula: an oblique reference to one of Pollius' properties which was associated with a temple of Hercules, probably at Tibur where this god had a famous temple (1.3.79, 3.1.184, with Laguna). The allusion in the next line to Hor. *Carm.* 2.6, which claims Tibur (5–8) and Tarentum (9–20) as ideal places of retirement, supports this identification; cf. 5n. Property near Herculaneum must be ruled out, since the town had been buried by Vesuvius' ash. *aula* in the sense of 'temple' is found only in the poetry of St. and Martial (Laguna on 3.1.10). On the competitive context see 93n.

110 Dicarcheique sinus: the northern part of the Bay of Naples by Puteoli (3n.), and thus probably a reference to Limon (81–2n.).

110–11 nec saepius istis | blanda Therapnaei placeant uineta Galaesi: a learned allusion to a property at Tarentum, a Spartan colony located by the river Galaesus in southern Italy, granted here a Golden Line; cf. Hor. *Carm.* 2.6.10–11 *dulce... Galaesi | flumen. Therapnaeus* is a Hellenistic coinage (A. R. 2.163) for 'Spartan' (*OLD* 1b), derived from Therapne, Helen's birthplace and site of her cult with Menelaus (N–H on Hor. *Carm.* 2.6.11; Howell on Mart. 5.37.2); Ovid introduced *Therapnaeus* to Latin poetry (Gibson on Ov. *Ars* 3.49). Van Dam follows M in reading *isti... placent* 'may they [*sc.* Polla and Pollius] not placate' (more often the vineyards), with possible play on Pollius' attribute *placidus* (9). But the meaning is strained; *placare* moreover is generally used of angry people or objects (Håkanson 1969: 63). The alternative reading *placeant*, with dat. *istis*, is generally accepted and better suits the context of rivalry among places for Pollius and Polla's favour; cf. 1.2.265 *nec Pompeiani placeant magis otia Sarni.* (SB tentatively reads dat. sing. *isti* with *placeant*; but St. implicitly addresses both owners; see 107n.). Horace chose Tarentum for retirement (*Carm.* 2.6.9–20); Virgil placed his Corycian gardener there (*G.* 4.116–48); but the villa at Surrentum stands out as a new, superior, site for cultured withdrawal; see 4n., 5n.

112–20 St. praises Pollius' talents as a poet, referred to briefly at 39–40 and 60–2. Nauta 2002: 318–21 argues that Pollius departs from Epicurean tenets by writing poetry. But Lucretius, so important for this poem, provided an important precedent in reconciling Epicurus' educational goals with poetry (Asmis 1996). In general writing poetry in retirement was seen as a respectable activity; e.g. Plin. *Ep.* 3.1.7 praises the retired triple consular Vestricius Spurinna for his regular writing of lyric poetry.

112 hic: i.e. here in the Surrentine villa, as opposed to the other properties.   **exercet** 'practises' (*OLD* 7), rarely used of poetry; cf. Virg. *G.*1.403 (of an owl's song); Sil. 7.129–30. St. exploits the military and agricultural connotations of *exercere*, suggesting that the discipline of poetic composition is a counterpart to putting the land in order; cf. Virg. *G.* 2.3.356, 370, with Gale 2000: 255.

113 seu uoluit monitus quos dat Gargettius auctor: Pollius follows the didactic teachings (*monitus*) of Epicurus, who was born in the Attic deme of Gargettus; cf. 1.3.94 *senior Gargettius*. But does he do so in poetry or in prose? Vollmer argues that *uoluit*, which suggests the unrolling of a book scroll for serious scrutiny (*OLD* 9), refers solely to Pollius' preliminary study of Epicurean philosophy; Van Dam proposes that Pollius wrote a prose treatise or translation of Epicurus' writings. But St. uses the compound *reuoluam* (72) to mean poetic composition; *Pierias ... artes* (112; cf. 42n.) also suggests that St. refers solely to poetry. Pollius, inspired by his studies of Epicurus and following Lucretius' example, writes didactic, philosophical poetry (Nisbet 1995b: 29–30).

114 seu nostram quatit ille chelyn: *chelys* can symbolise epic as well as lyric poetry (Harrison 1995b: 120–1) and is emblematic of St.'s dactylic verse, hence *nostram*; see 2.1.7n. *quatit* indicates epic vigour; cf. *Ach.* 2.156–8 *nec maior in istis | sudor, Apollineo quam fila sonantia plectro | cum quaterem priscosque uirum mirarer honores.* See 40n.

114–15 seu dissona nectit | carmina: elegiac poetry, identified by the unevenness of its couplet; cf. Hor. *Ars* 75 *uersibus impariter iunctis querimonia. nectit* suggests the poet's skill in smoothly weaving together the elegiac distich.

115 ultorem ... iambon: invective poetry, described by its traditional metre and aggressive style. *ultorem* 'avenging' plays on the popular etymology of *iambus* (ἴαμβος) from ἰάπτω ('hurl' (a weapon)); traditionally the seventh-century BCE Greek poet Archilochus invented iambic poetry to lambast his enemy Lycambes (Brink on Hor. *Ars* 79 *Archilochum proprio rabies armauit iambo*; Mayer on Hor. *Ep.* 1.19.25).   **stringit:** cf. Ov. *Rem.* 377 *liber in aduersos hostes stringatur iambos.* The metaphor of 'unsheathing' a poem like a sword suggests iambic aggressiveness; see 2.7.53n.

116–17 hinc ... | ... hinc: St. mentions two local landmarks, the Sirens' rocks offshore (1n.), and the temple of Tyrrhenian Minerva overlooking the bay (2n.).

116 leuis ... Siren: the Siren is 'nimble' (19n.) because she can fly and is eager to hear Pollius's songs. St. ignores here the tradition that the Sirens killed themselves after Odysseus successfully passed them by (Lyc. 712–37; Williams on Virg. *A.* 5.864).   **meliora ad carmina** 'to better songs' than the Siren's. A compliment to Pollius with the suggestion that his verse is not deceptive but gives genuine pleasure and instruction.

117 Tritonia: a recondite title for Minerva, coined by Cat. 64.395 from rare Hellenistic usage (A. R. 1.109; see Pfeiffer on Call. *Aet.* 1 fr. 37.1; Austin on Virg. *A.* 2.171, 226).   **motis . . . cristis:** Minerva amusingly moves her helmeted head to the music. A feather-crested (*cristis*) helmet was Italian-style (Harrison on Virg. *A.* 10.187).

118 rapidi ponunt flatus: *ponunt* is intransitive (cf. 26–7n.), meaning *se ponunt* 'calm themselves', 'subside' (SB); cf. Virg. *A.* 10.103 *tum Zephyri posuere*, with Harrison. *rapidus* 'swift' and thus carrying away everything in its path (*OLD* 1) is a common epithet for winds (e.g. Virg. *A.* 6.75 *rapidis . . . uentis*); *rabidi* (Van Dam) is unnecessary.

118–19 maria ipsa uetantur | obstrepere: Pollius, like Arion (6on.), calms the sea with his poetry. A calm sea commonly symbolised Epicurean tranquillity (Fowler 2002: 31–2), rough (as often with the Bay of Naples) human waywardness; cf. Sen. *Dial.* 11.9.7.

119–20 doctamque . . . | ad chelyn: cf. 97. Pollius' poetry is 'learned', like that of St.; cf. 1.2.259 (St. and Stella) *et sociam doctis haurimus ab amnibus undam.*

120 blandi . . . delphines: dolphins were traditionally believed to be friendly to humans and to be soothed by music (Plin. *Nat.* 9.24–32); see 6on.   **aderrant** 'stray towards', a neologism with dat. *scopulis*; cf. *Theb.* 9.178, with Dewar. St. wittily suggests that Pollius is a better 'Siren'; it is safe to be lured to *his* rocks; Lovatt 2007: 151–2.

121–42 Praise of Pollius for his *moral* standing; the estate assumes philosophical meaning as a symbol of Epicurean virtue. Particular influences here are Virg. *G.* 2. 495–540, Lucr. 2.1–39, Sen. *Thy.* 339–403, passages that define exemplary virtue by contrast with misguided human ambition; see esp. 123–4n., 129–32n.

121 uiue: i.e. 'may you live long', a shift to direct address of Pollius; cf. 107n.   **Midae gazis et Lydo ditior auro:** *gaza*, a Persian borrowing meaning 'treasure', retains its oriental resonance in Latin literature (Austin on Virg. *A.* 2.763). 'Lydian gold' refers by metonymy to king Croesus, the epitome of Eastern wealth, lost however in a coup (Hdt. 1.85–91); Midas too was known for his fabulous wealth and its foolish use (Ov. *Met.* 11.85–145). As Epicurean Pollius is morally 'richer' than the Eastern kings in knowing how to use (and retain) his wealth wisely; cf. 1.3.105–6 *digne Midae Croesique bonis et Perside gaza, | macte bonis animi*; wealth enables virtue, while virtue makes wise use of wealth. Pl. *gazae* was less common than the sing. (N–H on Hor. *Carm.* 1.29.1–2); St. may have in mind Lucr. 2.37–8 (a renunciation of material wealth) *nil nostro in corpore gazae | proficient neque nobilitas nec gloria regni.* But Philodemus, who was roughly contemporary with Lucretius, revised Epicurean strictures against wealth to suit the needs of the Roman elite (Asmis 2004).

122 Troica et Euphratae supra diademata felix 'superior in fortune to the diadems of Troy and of the Euphrates', an elegant variation of descriptive adjective followed by gen. noun; genitive *Euphratae* is attested also at *Theb.* 8.290. The diadem, an ornamental headband of white cloth worn by Persian rulers, by metonymy symbolises foreign kings (cf. 'the crown'); cf. 3.3.51 *premit felix regum diademata Roma*; N–H on Hor. *Carm.* 2.2.21. King Priam of Troy and the kings of Babylon, a city on the river Euphrates, were renowned for their wealth; but such wealth was ultimately transient and invited rapacity; cf. Virg. *A.* 2.763–6. Troy and the Euphrates, the latter a military frontier, also connote the anxiety of war from which Pollius is free. *felix* puns again on Pollius' *cognomen*, thus linking material with moral wealth; see 23n., 107n.

123–24 quem non ambigui fasces . . . | . . . terent: *quem* (with reference to Pollius) is the first of three relative clauses praising Pollius in hymnic style with asyndeton and repetition (*quem non* (123), *qui* (124), *quem non* (127)). The virtues of the fortunate man, as at Virg. *G.* 2.495–512, are expressed through negative contrast with those who pursue a public career with its attendant anxieties, hence the repetition of *non* (123, 124, 127); cf. *G.* 2.495–6 *illum non populi fasces, non purpura regum* | *flexit*, with Thomas. *fasces* were a mark of high political office, carried by a lictor before consuls and praetors; *ambigui* suggests the possibility of moral corruption and the uncertainty of power, esp. of elective offices; see Austin on Virg. *A.* 1.661 *domum . . . ambiguam.*

123 non mobile uulgus 'not the fickle populace'; cf. Hor. *Carm.* 1.1.7 *mobilium turba Quiritium*, with N–H; Sen. *Thy.* 350–2 *quem non ambitio impotens* | *et numquam stabilis fauor* | *uulgi praecipitis mouet.*

124 non leges, non castra 'not legal duties, not military duties'; cf. Sen. *Thy.* 363–4 *quem non lancea militis* | *non strictus domuit chalybs.*

124–5 qui pectore magno | spemque metumque domas: the opposites *spes, metus* are commonly linked; they occur in initial-line position first at Virg. *A.* 1.218 *spemque metumque inter dubii* (cf. Luc. 6.419, 7.211; V. Fl. 7.192); the correlatives *-que . . . -que*, like Greek τε . . . τε, lend epic weight (Norden on Virg. *A.* 6.336). Pollius conquers the disabling emotions of hope (connoting ambition) and fear as he conquered his land (cf. 31, 56). On the chest as the seat of reason see Kenney on Lucr. 3.138.

125 uoto sublimior omni 'loftier than any desire' (SB), i.e. Pollius has achieved the Epicurean condition of ἀταραξία. St. plays on the villa's clifftop location.

126–7 exemptus Fatis indignantemque refellens | Fortunam 'immune from what Fate holds in store and rebuffing indignant Fortune'. *fata* has the sense of future events (*OLD* 2c), while Fortune directs the present and thus is indignant that Pollius will not serve her.

127–8 dubio quem non in turbine rerum | deprendet suprema dies 'whom the final day will not take by surprise in the uncertain whirlpool of human affairs'; enjambment emphasises the surprise connoted by *depr⟨eh⟩endet* (*OLD* 5a). The image of the 'whirlpool' expresses the chaos of ordinary human affairs by drawing on the notorious roughness of the Bay of Naples (118–19n.).

128–9 sed abire paratum | ac plenum uita: cf. Lucr. 3.938 *cur non ut plenus uitae conuiua recedes?*, with Kenney: the dying man should resemble a guest 'satisfied' (*OLD plenus* 8a) with life; cf. Hor. *S.* 1.1.118. St. normally uses the abl. rather than the gen. after *plenus*.

129–32 St. models these lines after Lucr. 2.1–13, where the Epicurean sage looks down from a citadel upon people storm-tossed by the sea; e.g. Lucr. 2.1–2 *suaue, mari magno turbantibus aequora uentis, | e terra magnum alterius spectare laborem.* The image is apt for the owner of the clifftop villa. See Fowler 2002 on Lucr. 2.7–13.

129 nos, uilis turba 'we, a mob of little account'; cf. Virg. *A.* 11.372–3 *nos animae uiles, inhumata infletaque turba | sternamur campis*, with Horsfall on the polemical use of *uilis* and *turba*. The strong caesura after *uita* and before *nos* separates Pollius from the unenlightened majority, among whom St. includes himself.

129–30 caducis | deseruire bonis: whereas Lucr. 2.12–13 attacks wealth (⟨*alios*⟩ *noctes atque dies niti praestante labore | ad summas emergere opes rerumque potiri*), St. targets the more general *bonis* 'goods', since wealth in 2.2 is the enabler of virtue (121n.). *caducus* means 'transitory' (*OLD* 8) with the suggestion of 'futile' (*OLD* 9); cf. Ov. *Ib.* 88 *ut sit pars uoti nulla caduci mei! deseruire* occurs only here in St.; the verb generally carries a scornful undertone (*TLL* v 1.692.36–48).

130 semperque optare parati: cf. 128 *abire paratum*. The absolute use of *optare* suggests the addiction of humanity to any kind of desire and thus their liability to disappointment.

131 spargimur in casus 'we are scattered in all directions to chance' (*OLD spargo* 5a), an image of shipwreck evoking epic casualties; cf. Virg. *A.* 1.602 *gentis Dardaniae, magnum quae sparsa per orbem.* For *spargor* with *in* cf. *Theb.* 6.444, 9.33.   **celsa tu mentis ab arce:** the image of 'the lofty citadel of the mind' makes explicit the metaphorical meaning of the villa as a symbol of the tranquillity enjoyed by Lucretius' *sapiens* (129–32 n.); cf. Lucr. 2.7–8 *sed nil dulcius est, | bene quam munita tenere | edita doctrina sapientum templa serena*; Cancik 1968: 71–5. *celsa* recalls the villa's opening description *celsa Dicarchei speculatrix uilla profundi* (3):

physical height is now transformed into moral superiority (*OLD celsus* 2 and 5 respectively). *arx*, used often of Pollius' villa (3.1.19, 3.1.115, 3.1.136; cf. 2.2.30), connotes a moral and spiritual refuge (*OLD* 4) as well as a hill-top; see N–H on Hor. *Carm.* 2.6.21.

132 despicis errantes: cf. Lucr. 2.9–10 *despicere unde queas alios passimque uidere | errare atque uiam palantis quaerere uitae*. 'Wandering in error' conflates the ideas of random travel and moral confusion; those who do not study philosophy err in having no plan for life. See Fowler 2002 on Lucr. 2.9 and 2.10.   **humanaque gaudia rides:** St. adjusts Lucretius' model of the *sapiens* for whom it is 'sweet' (Lucr. 2.1, 4, 5, 7) to look down upon the troubles of others, for many an ethically disturbing position (Konstan 1973: 3–12). Pollius laughs not at people but at the material pleasures that disturb the soul with longing; like Lucan's Pompey (Luc. 9.13–14), he mocks the falsity of human hopes and ambitions.

133 tempus erat: an epic formula (e.g. Virg. *A.* 2.268; *Theb.* 11.157), introducing two temporal clauses describing Pollius' youthful pursuit of worldly ambition.

133–4 cum te geminae suffragia terrae | diriperent: a circumstantial *cum* clause (*NLS* 235) meaning that Pollius had dual citizenship in his hometown of Puteoli and in Naples. St.'s father likewise had a dual heritage, born in Velia but long a citizen of Naples (5.3.124–32). Honorary citizenship, then as now, was awarded to those who had made special contributions to society; Cicero claims in defence of the Greek poet Archias that he had been made a citizen of Tarentum, Rhegium and Naples (*Arch.* 3). Pollius' dual citizenship was probably awarded because of his public benefactions (97n., 136n.). *diriperent* 'were competing' is post-Augustan usage (*OLD* 2b; Vioque on Mart. 7.76.1): both cities wished to receive Pollius' favours. The verb hints at the aggressiveness of public life (cf. 5.3.130–1 *aliaeque aliis natalibus urbes | diripiunt*, with Gibson), though competition over one's birthplace was an exceptional honour.

134 celsusque duas ueherere per urbes 'you were carried aloft through two cities', i.e. through Naples and Puteoli by litter, a mark of distinction reserved for the rich and famous; Domitian withdrew from disgraced women the right to be carried by litter (Suet. *Dom.* 8); on Roman litters see D-S III 1004–6. *celsus* suggests Pollius' physical elevation in a litter and his distinguished rank but also pride (*TLL* III 774.16–21); cf. Lucr. 2.12–13 on false elevation, cited at 129–30n. Repeated *celsus* forms an ethical strand throughout the poem, suggesting that Pollius has now achieved morally secure heights; see 131n.

135 inde Dicarcheis . . . colonis: the citizens of Puteoli (3n.); *inde* 'on the one side/there', corresponding to *hinc* (134), is enumerative rather than temporal.

136 hinc ascite meis 'here enrolled among my people', i.e. the Neapolitans. *ascite* has the technical sense of acquiring formal citizenship (*OLD ascisco* 1b) and thus the right to vote and stand for office in both cities;

cf. 5.3.126.   **pariterque his largus et illis:** cf. 3.1.91–3 *tune | . . . largitor opum, qui mente profusa | tecta Dicaearchi pariter iuuenisque replesti | Parthenopen.* On the important role of the local elite as public benefactors see Lomas 2003.

137 ac iuuenile calens 'fired up with youthful enthusiasm'; Pollius' ambition was legitimate as he was young. Nauta 2002: 318 suggests that there may be a veiled reference to Pollius' possible involvement in the brawls between the citizens of Puteoli and their local magistrates (Tac. *Ann.* 13.48), which led to an early retirement. But it would then be strange that he was honoured with dual citizenship (134n.).   **rectique errore superbus** 'proud in error as regards what is right', or 'proud in your mistaken values' (SB). M reads *plectri errore*, explained by Hardie 1983: 67 n.76. to imply that the youthful Pollius had been a successful professional poet who 'travelled'('wandered') through the Mediterranean; he now still practised poetry but only in his villa (*plectri* is synedoche for poetry; cf. 61). But a reference to poetry comes oddly in the midst of reference to Pollius' civic activities (thus Håkanson 1969: 63–6); besides, if Pollius still practises poetry (112–20), it cannot be an 'error' (besides, poetry was acceptable to Roman Epicureanism, 112–20n.). Courtney's (1971: 95) emendation of *plectri* to *recti* (objective gen.) has some support from 5.3.248 *quantus amor recti* (an easier gen.), and *Theb.* 2.360; the succeeding lines imply that the 'error' was philosophical (SB 133 n.37). *errore* recalls the moral inflection of 132 *despicis errantes.*

138–9 discussa rerum caligine uerum | aspicis: philosophical enlightenment resembles the clearing of a mental fog; cf. Lucr. 1.146–8 (= 2.59–61) *hunc igitur terrorem animi tenebrasque necessest | non radii solis neque lucida tela diei | discutiant, sed naturae species ratioque*; see Fowler 2002 on Lucr. 2.14 and 2.61. *discutio* describes the scattering of clouds or darkness (*OLD* 3a). The spondees convey the gradual dawning of the truth.

139 illo alii rursus iactantur in alto: see 131n. *illo* modifies *alto*, the 'sea' syntactically engulfing benighted humans; cf. Sen. *Dial.* 11.9.7 *assidueque iactans, numquam stabili consistimus loco, pendemus et fluctuamur et alter in alterum illidimur et aliquando naufragium facimus, semper timemus. rursus* 'in their turn' (*OLD* 4) enforces the separation between Pollius and those who do not follow the path of philosophy.

140 securos portus placidamque quietem: cf. 13 *placido . . . recessu.* The image of a ship reaching safe harbour is a figure both of the calm soul and of the completed task (4.4.88–9). Pollius has reached his life-time goal, the haven of Epicurean philosophy. The language is Lucretian; *securos* means 'safe' in the sense of 'care-free' (*se-curus*); cf. Lucr. 3.211 *secura quies* (also Lucr. 3.939), an expression for Epicurean ἀταραξία and the first blessing enjoyed by Virgil's ideal farmer; cf. Virg. *G.* 2.467, with Thomas. *placidam* likewise suggests ἀταραξία; cf. Lucr. 1.40 *placidam pacem*, with Bailey; cf. 9 *placidi . . . Polli.* On the philosophical use of *placidus* and *quies* in St. see Pitcher 1990: 91–4.

141 intrauit non quassa ratis: *ratis*, a poetic word for 'ship', is used metaphorically here for a human life; cf. Ov. *Pont.* 3.2.6 *tu lacerae remanes ancora sola rati.* Unlike Ovid, Pollius has passed through the storms of public life apparently unshaken.   **sic perge:** characteristically St. concludes his encomium with personal directives, but here the didactic tone is esp. appropriate to the Epicurean character of the poem's close. He evokes the metaphor of the philosopher's life as a direct journey through life that only he follows; see Fowler 2002 on Lucr. 2.10 *uiam . . . uitae*; cf. Lucr. 1.1115–17.

142 emeritam . . . puppem 'your ship which has earned an honourable discharge', a continuation of the nautical metaphor for life. *emerere* is a military term for serving out one's term of office and thus earning a reward (*OLD* 1 and 2); cf. 3.5.7–8 (on the completion of the *Thebaid*) *quattuor emeritis per bella, per aequora lustris | errarem.*   **in nostras . . . procellas:** like *nos* (129), *nostras* provides a different angle upon the imagery of the storm-tossed sea. As an ambitious poet (cf. 11 *cupidum*) St. chooses the uncertainties of competitive literary life over the pursuit of Epicurean calm; cf. Tac. *Dial.* 41.5 *nemo eodem tempore adsequi potest magnam famam et magnam quietem.* On St. as a figure of Aeneas (or Odysseus) see 13–29n., 42–3n., 43–4n.; Hinds 2000: 254.

147–55 These lines, in praise of Polla, are transposed by most editors to follow directly after praise of Pollius (contra Krüger 1998: 188). Transposition avoids the surprising shift to plural *discite* (143) after the singular address to Pollius; the poem then concludes with the couple's joint praise (143–6). Polla provides a worthy counterpart to Pollius, exemplifying moderation in the domestic sphere. For a different model of the estate owner's wife cf. Col. 12 *pr.* 10, a criticism of the contemporary *matrona* who devotes herself to luxury, allowing the bailiff's wife to do all the work of managing the estate.

147 tuque: i.e. Polla.   **nurus inter longe** 'among the young married women, by far . . . ' A lacuna of at least one line is generally supposed to follow in the text. *longe* is a probable emendation for the transmitted *longae*; a descriptive epithet can be assumed to have followed, but otherwise we are completely in the realm of conjecture. SB prints Hardie's (1904) *praedocta Latinas | parque uiro mentem, cui non* 'most distinguished among Latian ladies with mind to match your man, for whom no [*sc.* cares] etc.' *nurus* in the sense of 'young married women' (*OLD* 2) compliments Polla; see 10n., 2.6.24–5n.

148–9 praecordia curae, | non frontem uertere minae 'cares have not altered her heart, nor threats her brow'; an initial *non* before *praecordia* must be assumed. Nisbet 1995b: 43, arguing that Polla is Lucan's widow (introd. 21–2), suggests that St. tactfully alludes to her diplomacy in fending off threats in the aftermath of the Pisonian conspiracy.

149–50 candida semper | gaudia: sc. *tibi sunt*; cf. 3.5.17–18 (of St.'s wife) *et sordida numquam | gaudia. candidus* metaphorically suggests Polla's cheerful disposition and her moral purity (*OLD* 7 and 8 respectively), with the sense also of transparency, for she has nothing to hide; see 2.7.85n. (of Polla, Lucan's widow).

150 et in uultu curarum ignara uoluptas: *in uultu* is ἀπὸ κοινοῦ with *gaudia* and *uoluptas*. *curarum ignara* = *securus* (140n.).

151–2 non tibi sepositas infelix strangulat arca | diuitias: *strangulat*, generally a prose word, is a hapax here meaning 'suffocates' (*OLD* 2). St. personifies wealth, suggesting both that the miser's chest is stuffed full of money with little room to spare, and that the hoarding of money prevents its proper use. *infelix* puns on Pollius' *cognomen* (23n., 107n., 122n.) to dissociate Pollius and his wife from the vice of avarice.

152–3 auidique animum dispendia torquent | fenoris 'and the loss from greedy payment of interest does not torture your mind,' i.e. Polla does not borrow and go into debt; she is the model of a thrifty Roman wife who uses wealth wisely. *dispendium* (*OLD* 2a) and *fenus* (*OLD* 2) are prosaic monetary terms; *auidique* is a striking transferred epithet (the unnamed lender is the greedy one), borrowed from Luc. 1.181 *auidumque...fenus*. These banking terms may support the identification of this Polla with Lucan's widow, Polla Argentaria, whose *cognomen* connotes money (Nisbet 1995b: 40–2).

153 expositi census 'the value of your fortune is open to all'. St. approves of his patrons' openness with their wealth, which represents a right relation to it (2.3.70–1n.; Hardie 1983: 76). St. refutes Lucretius' dismissal of riches (121n.). On the distinction between *census*, the 'family fortune' (*OLD* 3), and *diuitiae*, riches that contribute to the *census*, see Zeiner 2005: 123–4.

153–4 et docta fruendi | temperies 'and you show educated restraint in your enjoyment of it'. Polla avoids the vices of prodigality and avarice, excesses on both sides of the mean. *temperies* is used of a moderate climate (*OLD* 2); Polla morally reflects her harmonious physical environment. *docta* also links her with her husband (97, 119–20).

154 deo meliore 'in the presence of a more auspicious deity', abl. abs.   **cohaerent** 'unite', only here in St.'s works.

155 non alias docuit Concordia mentes: a final adumbration of an important imperial concept; *Concordia* was closely associated with the marital harmony of the imperial family (*LIMC* v 1.479–98, esp. 495); Polla and Pollius provide an alternate ideal in the private sphere; cf. 1.2.240, 5.1.43–4. *docuit* requires a following phrase or infinitive, hence the lacuna here; see 147–55n.

143–6 A concluding exhortation for the couple's continuing prosperity.

143 discite securi: cf. 140 *securos*; St. emphasises their shared Epicurean values.

143–4　quorum de pectore mixtae | in longum coiere faces 'from whose hearts the flames of love, intermingled, have united for a long time to come', i.e. erotic desire has been regularised by marriage, *mixtae* suggesting *dextrarum iunctio*. For this adverbial temporal sense of *longus* see *OLD* 9b. Flaming brands were carried at a Roman wedding and were part of the standard iconography of Hymen, god of marriage (*LIMC* v 1.583–5); torches were also symbols of erotic passion (*OLD fax* 7). *coire* occurs in poetry and post-Augustan prose of the joining of a couple in marriage, often with sexual overtones (*TLL* III 1418.7–50); cf. Ov. *Met.* 4.60–1 *taedae quoque iure coissent | sed uetuere patres.*

144–5　sanctusque pudicae | seruat amicitiae leges amor: the solemn moral and religious language echoes Cat. 109.6 *aeternum hoc sanctae foedus amicitiae.* His description of love as 'friendship' (in the Roman sense of mutual, obligatory relations) was not repeated by the Augustan elegiac poets; St. provides the only parallel (Ross 1969: 80–4). But St. also revises his predecessor's view of love as a form of 'friendship' in that *amicitia* is happily rooted in marriage. *leges* and *pudicae* probably acknowledge the vigorous promotion of Domitianic legislation, including revival of the Augustan *lex Iulia*, to encourage and stabilise marriage. See D'Ambra 1993: 36–9.

145–6　ite per annos | saeculaque: the wish for his friends' continuing fame is also a concluding envoi to the poem that can guarantee that fame.

146　et priscae titulos praecedite famae 'and exceed the titles of former fame'. *tituli* were the inscriptions carved on tombs or statue bases providing a resumé of the deceased's career (*Theb.* 6.127–8 *titulisque pios testantur honores | gentis quisque suae*; Flower 1996: 159–60). But Pollius and Polla will earn their own noble *tituli* (and portrait statues) because of their virtue, not their ancestry (a major theme of book 2; introd. to 2.1). Villa owners were often buried on their estates; St. alludes here to the close connection between the villa, which displayed the virtues of the owner, and commemoration of the dead (Bodel 1997). *titulus* also means a chapter or book heading (*OLD* 3); St. suggests that through his poetry also the couple will be commemorated as *documenta uirtutis*.

Siluae 2.3

2.3 is a novel development of a popular Augustan genre, the birthday poem (Feeney 2007: 148–60); but it does not reveal the occasion for which it was written, Melior's birthday, until towards the poem's end (62). The bulk of the poem is an Ovidian-style aetiological myth, set in Melior's Caelian estate in Rome, which explains his curiously shaped plane tree, an appropriate symbol however of growth and longevity. As 'the best example of Ovidian narrative in the *Siluae*' (Dewar 2002: 398), 2.3 is linked to 2.4 on Melior's parrot, and also to 2.7, another unusual example of the *genethliacon* (introd. to 2.7). St. playfully conflates here two types of Ovidian narrative – the violent sexual pursuit typical of the *Metamorphoses* (esp. the myths of Apollo and Daphne (*Met.* 1.452–567), Pan and Syrinx (*Met.* 1.689–712), and Arethusa (*Met.* 5.572–641)), and the farcical, *foiled* attack on a sleeping nymph or goddess typical of the *Fasti* (the myths of Priapus and Lotis (*Fast.* 1.391–440), Priapus and Vesta (*Fast.* 6.319–48), and Faunus, Hercules and Omphale (*Fast.* 2.303–58); see Green 391–440). The physical setting of tree and lake replicates on Roman ground the key elements of the Ovidian *locus amoenus* of the *Metamorphoses*, routinely violated however by sexual violence (Hinds 2002: 131–6); in 2.3 violence is averted, and change occurs only in the landscape which, from wilderness, becomes the peaceful haven of Melior's garden. The poem's final surprise is its 'metamorphosis' from aetion to birthday poem. 2.3 humorously deploys and dismantles Ovidian tropes; it is a gift intended to delight Melior with the poet's ingenuity. Set in Rome, however, the poem has a serious subtext (introd. 13–15).

With their elaborate sculptural programmes of deities, including Bacchus and his entourage, Roman gardens were 'landscapes of allusion' (Bergmann 2001); typically they evoked famous myths, inviting a visitor's aesthetic and intellectual participation and linking past and present. With his new myth St. makes the basic elements of tree and water into a garden in the Roman sense, thus giving this part of the Caelian, a hill of little cultic significance (*LTUR* I 209), a cultural history. The art of narrative here brings order to a wilderness. The tree, perhaps, is also a figure of St.'s *Siluae* (introd. 15). Mart. 9.61, a poem on a plane tree planted by Julius Caesar, seems to be a politicising response to this poem; see Henriksén on Mart. 9 54–6; Hardie 2005: 215–17; introd. 14 n.97.

Further reading: Cancik 1965: 48–56 sees 2.3 as a prime example of the 'mannerist aesthetic'; Vessey 1981 reads the poem as political allegory. See also Pederzani; Dewar 2002: 398–403; Nauta 2002: 312–15; Hardie 2005; Rühl 2006: 290–3.

1–5 An opening description of the tree; elaborate hyperbaton emphasises its curious shape. St. combines here the idea of the *locus amoenus*, the idyllic landscape whose basic features were tree, shade and clear water, with that of the poetic grove, a common metaphor of inspiration for poets and a symbol of exclusive poetry; see Curtius 1953: 70–1, 79–83; N–H on Hor. *Carm.* 1.30.

1–2 stat... | arbor 'there stands... a tree'; cf. Ov. *Am.* 3.1.1 *stat uetus et multos incaedua silua per annos*; the allusion hints that, like Ovid's grove, Melior's tree will have poetic significance. St. follows Virgil's general practice in placing *stat* at the start of a line (and clause); see Pease on Virg. *A.* 4.135; Van Dam on 2.5.11; cf. Mart. 9.61.5–6 *aedibus in mediis totos amplexa penates | stat platanus*. More than the common *est* (2.2.1–3n.), *stat* suggests fixity and durability (N–H on Hor. *Carm.* 1.9.1); it also recalls 1.1.2, the opening lines on Domitian's equestrian statue; see 2n.   **quae... opacet:** rel. clause of characteristic; the verb offers a clue to the kind of tree, though it is not named till 39. Planes were popular in gardens for their shade (Mosch. 4.11 ὑπὸ πλατάνωι βαθυφύλλωι; Cic. *Poet.* 22.10 *sub platano umbrifero*; Virg. *G.* 4.146 *iamque ministrantem platanum potantibus umbras*; N–H on Hor. *Carm.* 2.11.13). It had considerable cultural prestige; cf. Hdt. 7.27 on Darius' golden plane tree.   **nitidi Melioris** 'of elegant Melior'; 2.2.10n.; cf. Mart. 4.54.8 *nitido Meliore*. Ovid is the first to use *nitidus* 'glittering' of water; cf. Ov. *Met.* 3.407 (Narcissus' pool) *nitidis argenteus undis*, with Bömer; [Ov.] *Ep. Sapph.* 157–8 *est nitidus uitroque magis perlucidus omni | fons sacer*. The juxtaposition of *nitidi* with *perspicuas* suggests the shading of the physical into the metaphorical; Melior's virtues, esp. of openness and calmness as well as general excellence, are here reflected in his garden. See 2.2.23n.   **perspicuas ... | aquas:** *perspicuus* is Ovidian for exceptionally clear water (with erotic undertones); cf. Ov. *Met.* 4.300 (the pool of Salmacis) *perspicuus liquor est*; *Met.* 5. 587–8 (Arethusa's swimming pool) *aquas ... perspicuas ad humum*; then in the Flavian poets (*TLL* x 1.1748.10–25); cf. *Anth. Lat.* 1 265.3–4 (of Narcissus) *perspicuoque lacu se puer ipse uidet*. Trees were planted by clear water for their attractive reflections; cf. Plin. *Ep.* 8.8.4 *ripae fraxino multa, multa populo uestiuntur, quas perspicuus amnis uelut mersas uiridi imagine adnumerat.*

2 complexa lacus: cf. 1.1.2 (Domitian's equestrian statue) *stat Latium complexa forum*; St. introduces in 2.3 an alternative Rome based on the contrasts art/nature, statue/tree, politics/leisure, public/private. *lacus* is a common poetic pl. The idea of 'embrace' suggests the tree's ample shade and foreshadows the erotic tenor of the upcoming myth.   **quae:** this second *quae* governs indic. *redit* (3) = *ea* 'this tree'. The first clause suggests the kind of tree (a shade tree); the second describes its shape.   **robore ab imo** 'from the base of its trunk'.

3 <in>curuata uadis 'curved over the waters', an old emendation for M's *curuata*, which metrically leaves a syllable missing in the text; *uadis* = dat. of direction (*TLL* VII 1.1095.32, 1096.10–11; *NLS* 58). Courtney, following Havet, reads *cur curuata* on the grounds that a question is appropriate to an aetiological poem (for similar initial reduplication see 2.1.99 *se secura*). Palaeographically this is the easiest solution, yet a question seems out of place in the set ecphrasis. Questioning otherwise begins at 6.

3–4 redit inde cacumine recto | ardua 'from there it shoots back up tall with straight top'. The tree is in the shape of a 'V': firmly rooted poolside, its trunk bends down to the lake, then rises straight up into the air. *ardua* is common of trees to indicate height, esp. in poetic description. Since planes need frequent irrigation (Hor. *Carm.* 2.15.4), and wine was sometimes used to nourish their roots (Ov. *Rem.* 141–2; Plin. *Nat.* 12.8), St. perhaps plays off the aural connection of *ardua* with ἀρδόμενος ('watered'); cf. *Theb.* 9.418–9 *stetit arduus alto | amne*; Hardie 2008: 102.

4 ceu mediis iterum nascatur ab undis 'as if it were born anew from the centre of the lake', unreal condition, for St. describes the *illusion* created by the tree's reflection in the water. *ceu* is frequent in Roman epic from Ennius, but not in prose before Seneca (Harrison on Virg. *A.* 10.97). St. uses *ceu* twelve times in the *Siluae* (twice in book 2; cf. 2.5.26), sixty-seven times in the *Thebaid* (Van Dam ad loc.). Its archaic resonance foreshadows the setting of the aetiological myth in early Rome. St. begins in a grand manner, despite his prefatory claim that this poem is like an epigram (2 *pr.* 14–16). *nascatur* subtly alludes to the poem's occasion, Melior's *birth*day.

5 habitet: further personification of the tree (cf. 4 *nascatur*), developed at 43–61.   **uitreum . . . amnem**: cf. Hor. *Carm.* 3.13.1 *o fons Bandusiae, splendidior uitro*, with N–R. *uitreus* is an elevated poetic term for the sheen of water (*OLD uitreus* 3); cf. 2.2.49; Barchiesi and Rosati on Ov. *Met.* 3.407. St. varies the vocabulary for 'water' and 'lake'; *amnis* in the general sense of 'water' is likewise elevated; see Horsfall on Virg. *A.* 7.465 *spumis exuberat amnis*; N–H on Hor. *Carm.* 3.29.40–1.   **tacitis radicibus**: abl. of description 'with hidden roots' (*OLD tacitus* 8). St. perhaps anticipates the concluding emphasis on Melior's seclusion, e.g. 69.

6–7 St. seeks inspiration for a poem explaining the origins of the tree.

6 quid Phoebum tam parua rogem?: double acc. with verb of asking. St. sometimes opens a poem with a *praeteritio*, modestly dismissing deities too grand for his light, festive theme and refusing the grand themes of epic and tragedy (cf. 1.5.1–5, 1.6.1–3); cf. Ov. *Fast.* 6.320 *est mihi fabula parua ioci* (the tale of Vesta and Priapus); on such 'safety formulae' for a poet embarking on an erotic tale see Barchiesi 1997: 241. Rejecting Apollo means also rejecting the politics of Ovid's Apollo/Daphne myth (62–77n.). *parua* is also a neoteric term indicating minute care and polish; cf. Prop. 3.3.18 *mollia sunt paruis prata terenda rotis*; Bömer on Ov. *Fast.* 2.3–4. On poetic 'modesty' in St. see 2 *pr.* 3n.   **causas** signals an aetiological poem; cf. Ov. *Fast.* 1.1–2 *tempora cum causis . . . | canam*.

7 Naides: a fitting invocation, for the heroine is a Naiad, a water nymph (of land or sea); see 30n.; cf. 1.5.6 *Naidas, undarum dominas* (inspirers of poetry on baths).   **faciles . . . Fauni:** Faunus, properly speaking, was an Italian rustic deity (N–H on Hor. *Carm.* 1.17.2). Pluralisation, as with the Greek god Pan (with whom he was often identified; Bömer on Ov. *Fast.* 2.271), was not uncommon (e.g. 2.2.106; Lucr. 4.580; Ov. *Met.* 1.193). Faunus' name was popularly derived from either *fauere* (cf. Serv. *G.* 1.10 *quidam Faunos putant dictos ab eo quod frugibus faueant . . . quidam Faunum appellatum uolunt eum quem nos propitium dicimus*), or from *fari*, through his association with prophetic speech (Var. *L.* 7.36); see Fantham on Ov. *Fast.* 4.650; Maltby s.v. Faunus. *faciles*, which can mean 'propitious' (*OLD* 9b) and 'fluent of speech' (*OLD* 11d; cf. Cic. *Brut.* 253, 333), puns on both these etymologies, with a hint also of its sense 'lascivious'; cf. Virg. *Ecl.* 3.9 *faciles . . . nymphae*.

In invoking the Fauns for inspiration St. humorously contradicts the Ennian tradition associating them with unsophisticated if oracular poetry; cf. *Ann.* 206 Sk. *uorsibus quos olim Faunei uatesque canebant*, with Skutsch; Cic. *Brut.* 75; Var. *L.* 7.36. Fauns and nymphs were among the first inhabitants of early Italy (Virg. *A.* 8.314 *haec nemora indigenae Fauni nymphaeque tenebant*); the origins of St.'s aetiological tale thus lie far back before Rome's foundation.   **satis:** a programmatic word, setting limits to a theme and its style; cf. *Theb.* 1.33–4 *nunc tendo chelyn satis arma referre* | *Aonia*; 1.5.6–8 *Naidas . . .* | *elicuisse satis. satis* here marks the rejection of epic sources of inspiration.

8–61 The aetiological myth. Lucr. 4.580–94 scorns belief in satyrs, nymphs, fauns and Pan; but such figures regularly populated the Roman garden as part of its sculptural programme; see 2.2.98–106n.

8 nympharum tenerae fugiebant Pana cateruae: an elegant line where the physical delicacy of the nymphs (*OLD tener* 1, here a transferred epithet) contrasts sharply with the hairy roughness of the pursuing Pan (2.2.105–6n.); cf. Ov. *Met.* 11.153 *Pan . . . teneris iactat sua carmina nymphis.* The imperf. tense sets up the narrative while suggesting that the situation (of nymphs fleeing Pan) is stereotypical; cf. Mart. 9.61.13–14.   **Pana:** Greek form of the acc. Pan was a fast runner; cf. Ov. *Fast.* 2.285–6 *deus uelox discurrere gaudet in altis* | *montibus, et subitas concipit ipse fugas*, with Bömer; and was notoriously lascivious; cf. Ov. *Fast.* 1.397 *Panes et in Venerem Satyrorum prona iuuentus*; N–R on Hor. *Carm.* 3.18.1 (Faunus) *fugientium nympharum amator.*

9 ille quidem it cunctas tamquam uelit, it tamen unam: a line composed entirely of monosyllables and disyllables. Homoeoteleuton and the repetition of *it*, including the beginning of a new word with the same syllable as the preceding one (*uelit, it*), creates the impression of rustic simplicity. The shift to the historic pres. creates immediacy.   **cunctas:** a likely pun on πᾶν ('all'); cf. Serv. *Ecl.* 2.31 *nam Pan deus est rusticus in naturae similitudinem formatus, unde et Pan dictus est, id est omne.*   **tamquam:** avoided by poets apart from Ovid (Van Dam).

9–10 unam | in Pholoen 'after Pholoe alone'. In Horace, Pholoe is the name of a girl reluctant to be pursued (cf. Hor. *Carm.* 2.5.17 *fugax Pholoe*), and in Tib. 1.8 and 1.9 of a hard-hearted girl (Maltby on Tib. 1.8.69). Pholoe is also the name of a mountain in Thessaly (*Theb.* 3.604, 10.288; *Ach.* 1.168); the nymph's name may suggest her stubborn character, hard like the mountain (N–H on Hor. *Carm.* 1.33.7).

10 siluis . . . fluminibusque 'by woods and rivers', a poetic use of the abl. (L–H–S 146).

10–11 sequentis | . . . hirtos gressus 'her pursuer's hairy legs', a comic touch. Pan was part goat (Ov. *Met.* 14.515 *semicaper Pan*; *Theb.* 4.696

cornipedum . . . Faunorum; Sil. 13.327–42), with cloven feet, shaggy legs and a human face crowned by horns (D–S IV 299–302; *LIMC* suppl. VIII 1.923–40, esp. 927–31). *gressus* usually means 'feet' (*OLD* 1c); since Pan has hooves, *gressus* by extension means 'legs' (Williams on *Theb.* 10.877).

11 improba cornua: a transferred epithet suggesting the nymph's terrified point of view. Pan's horns are 'lewd' (*OLD improbus* 7) because he is attempting rape (cf. Ov. *Fast.* 2.331 (of Faunus' *amor improbus*); St. also puns on *cornu* 'penis' (Adams 1982: 22).

12–13 iamque . . . atraque . . . | . . . Quirinalesque: threefold repetition emphasises the swiftness of the chase over the hills of future Rome. St. historicises his Ovidian models.

12 belligerum Iani nemus: Janus, the double-visaged god, was the first king of early Italy and founder of a settlement on the Janiculum (Green on Ov. *Fast.* 1.245–6). No 'grove of Janus' is known. Vollmer suggests it was 'at the foot of the Argiletum' (Livy 1.19.2) where Numa's temple of Janus stood; if so, it is perhaps to be identified with the *sacri . . . nemus Argileti* (Virg. *A.* 8.345) shown Aeneas on his tour of early Rome. But the presiding deity of this Virgilian grove is not known (Gransden on Virg. *A.* 8.346), and the location of the Argiletum is controversial (*LTUR* I 125–6). *belligerum*, an Ovidian coinage, is also problematic. The Janiculum, a sacred hill, was not associated with war (*LTUR* III 89–90) and under Janus' rule was a site for simple pasture (Ov. *Fast.* 1.243–4). Taken as a transferred epithet, *belligerum* is an unusual attribute of Janus (elsewhere only at Luc. 1.62; of deities see *TLL* II 1814.7–24); Janus balanced peace and war and in Ovid's *Fasti* was esp. associated with peace (Green on Ov. *Fast.* 1.253–4; Coleman on 4.1.13). Hardie 2005: 215 n.24. suggests that the 'warlike grove' may be the Porta Ianualis, where the nymphs (or Janus, according to Ovid's *Fasti*) saved the day for the Romans by sending hot springs against the enemy (Ov. *Met.* 14.775–804; *Fast.* 1.259–76); though Ovid does not mention a grove, perhaps one existed before the Porta Ianualis was built.

12–13 atraque Caci | rura: the Aventine, home of the monstrous Cacus (Virg. *A.* 8.231; Ov. *Fast.* 1.551) until conquered by Hercules (Virg. *A.* 8.184–279; Ov. *Fast.* 1.543–82). *atra* suggests that the area at this time (pre-Hercules) was blackened from Cacus' fire-breathing; cf. Virg. *A.* 8.198–9 *illius atros | ore uomens ignis*. In poetry *ater* often has emotional overtones such as 'sinister' (*OLD*). St.'s early Italy is wild and dangerous.

13 Quirinalesque . . . per agros: postponed *per* governs *nemus, rura* and *agros*, a unique case of triple ἀπὸ κοινοῦ (Van Dam). *agros* is synonymous here with *rura* 'territory' (*OLD ager* 1); we are not to imagine that the Quirinal hill was cultivated at this time; cf. Ov. *Met.* 14.422 (the early Italy of Canens) *Latios . . . per agros*. Domitian celebrated the Quirinal as his birthplace and he built there the *Templum gentis Flauiae* to commemorate the deified members of the Flavian dynasty; see Mart. 9.20. What the Palatine was to Augustus the Quirinal was to Domitian.   **fuga suspensa:** *not* 'on tiptoe' (SB), for the nymph is running, but 'skimming in flight' (*OLD suspendo* 5a): her feet scarcely touch the ground; cf. Virg. *A.* 7.810–1 *uel mare per medium fluctu suspensa tumenti | ferret iter celeris nec tingeret aequore plantas.*

14 Caelica 'Caelian', only here in Latin literature. Its initial position in the line, and the jingle *ca* with the following *tesca*, draw attention to the Caelian, then a primitive site but by Melior's time chiefly residential (*LTUR* 1 208–11; Colini 1944).   **tesca** 'wilds'; cf. Hor. *Ep.* 1.14.19–20 *nam quae deserta et inhospita tesqua | credis, amoena uocat mecum qui sentit,* with Mayer. *tesca* (or *tesqua*), a rare archaic word of uncertain origin, means rough, uncultivated terrain sacred to the gods (Paul. Fest. p. 538 Lindsay *loca augurio designata*; Var. *L.* 7.10 *loca quaedam agrestia, quae alicuius dei sunt, dicuntur tesca*); cf. Luc. 6.41 *saltus nemorosaque tesqua.* M reads *tecta*, but the archaic resonance of *tesca* sharpens the contrast with imperial Rome; no beautiful gardens were created yet on the Caelian. *tesca* also suggests that Melior's garden is sacred space.   **subit:** contracted perfect with long -*it* at the strong caesura, concluding Pholoe's flight.

14–15 uicta labore, | fessa metu: cf. Ov. *Met.* 1.544 (of Daphne) *uicta labore fugae*; *Met.* 14.426–7 (of Canens) *luctuque uiaque | fessa.* Pholoe's physical and mental exhaustion anticipates (and partly explains) her collapse into a stupor; see 29–30n.

15 qua 'where' introduces a parenthetical clause that abruptly interrupts the narrative by fastforwarding to the present and the calm and safety of Melior's estate.   **nunc** marks the contrast between past and present typical of an aetiological narrative; cf. Virg. *A.* 8.347–8 *Capitolia . . . | aurea nunc, olim siluestribus horrida dumis.* Virgil contrasts early Rome with its present *public* grandeur; here a *private* estate on the Caelian is the foil, and the contrast with the past is chiefly moral, for virtue, not material wealth, is emphasised. As in 2.2, the opposition between wildness and order is centred on the estate; in 2.3, however, the wildness belongs firmly to a distant past.   **placidi Melioris:** he is calm like his lake (5n.); cf. 64, 2.1.167n., 2.2.13–14n.

15–16 aperti | stant sine fraude lares: *aperti* agrees with *lares* (16), yet, with *placidi*, it frames Melior's name, thus emphasising his generosity (*OLD apertus* 10). An open-doored house suggests hospitality and bounty (*OLD apertus* 2b) as well as transparency (*OLD* 9). Vessey 1981 explains the reference to 'lack of deceit' as a hint that Melior had fallen foul of imperial politics; the myth of a nymph seeking refuge is a political allegory defending Melior from the suspicion of plotting against Domitian at the time of the mutiny of Saturninus in 88/9 CE. See also White 1975: 272; Nauta 2002: 312–15 is rightly sceptical (introd. 20). The point may simply be the contrast between the region's dangers in pre-Roman times and the present: Melior's house, though open, is safe. The *lares* were deities fundamental to the Roman house and were associated with traditional domestic virtues. Initial *stant* emphasises the stability of his home, in contrast to the restless world of nymphs and Pans; see 1n.

16–17 fluxos collegit amictus | artius: a return to the main narrative; Pholoe gathers her clothing tightly around her. M reads *flauos*, which is normally used of hair (4.3.67; Gel. 2.26.12–13); or of silt-bearing rivers (1.3.107), esp. the Tiber (4.4.5; N–H on Hor. *Carm.* 1.2.13); cf. Virg. *G.* 4.339 (of a Naiad) *flaua Lycorias*; thus Vollmer suggests that the colour of Pholoe's clothes would assimilate her to her natural element. However, *flauus* is never used of lakes (and would be odd here, given the water's clarity); and St. never uses *flauus* elsewhere of clothing. *fluxos*, accepted by most editors, suggests the flowing form of her clothing; cf. *Ach.* 1.533 (of Achilles' female dress) *fluxae . . . uestes*; Luc. 2.362 (of a bride's dress) *fluxos . . . amictus*. See Håkanson 1969: 66–7.

17 †niueae† . . . ripae: another 'colour' word that seems not to fit with its noun. 'White as snow' generally applies to the body, not to riverbanks in Rome; cf. Ov. *Fast.* 1.427 (of Lotis) *niueae . . . nymphae*, with Green. A possible parallel at 1.5.51 *niueo . . . margine* describes a bank lined with marble, not a feature of a primitive landscape. No plausible emendation has been proposed. Håkanson 1969: 67–9 and Pederzani propose that *niueae* means 'icy cold' (*OLD* 3), a quality more usually associated with water than with river banks; they thus argue that *ripa* can occasionally refer to water itself, but the evidence is slight. A variant reading at Ov. *Met.* 14.427 *in gelida . . . ripa* could support our text: Pholoe, like Canens, lay down 'on the cool bank' (see below).   **posuit se margine ripae:** an unusual twist on the sexual chase: Daphne and Syrinx pray to change form (Ov. *Met.* 1.546–7, 703–4), but here the exhausted nymph (14–15) collapses on the river bank; cf. 1.2.242–3 *sic uicta sopore doloso | Martia fluminea posuit latus Ilia ripa*; Ov. *Met.* 14.427 (of Canens) *et iam longa [gelida?] ponentem corpora ripa*. In Ovid's *Fasti* Lotis (1.423–4), Hercules in drag (2.332–4) and Vesta (6.331–2) are all sleeping, worn out from festivities when attacked.

18 uelox pecorum deus: a conflation of Ov. *Fast.* 2.271 *Pana deum pecoris* and *Fast.* 2.285 *deus uelox*.

18–19 et sua credit | conubia (sc. *esse*) 'and he believes that marriage is his'; cf. Ov. *Met.* 1.490 *Phoebus . . . uisaeque cupit conubia Daphnes*, with Anderson. Enjambment emphasises the irony of *conubia*, which can be accommodated metrically to the line only with altered scansion, the shortening of *u*. The switch to the pres. tense and the compressed syntax suggest Pan's speed and haste.

19–20 ardenti . . . suspiria librat | pectore 'with burning heart he checks his excited breathing'. The pursuer's audible, tangible breathing is a standard feature of the chase from Hom. *Il.* 23.765–6; e.g. Daphne fleeing feels Apollo's breath on her neck (Ov. *Met.* 1.542). But checking one's breath and movement is characteristic of rape narratives in Ovid's *Fasti*: Priapus holds his breath and balances on his toes over the sleeping Lotis (*Fast.* 1.428–9); Priapus tiptoes with thumping heart towards the sleeping Vesta (*Fast.* 6.338). The unusual metaphor *suspiria librat* for checking breath perhaps alludes to the Lotis and Priapus myth, where *librare* occurs in the commoner sense of balancing on one's toes; cf. Ov. *Fast.* 1.429 *corpus librabat*, with Green. *ardenti* suggests Pan's sexual longing (*OLD ardeo* 3); *suspiria* also has erotic connotations (*OLD* 1). **iamiam . . . | . . . iam:** St. is fond of the emphatic duplicated adverb *iamiam* (*Theb.* fifteen times; *Siluae* twice), a feature of epic diction (Wills 106–7) that here adds to the mock-heroic timbre of the chase and, with anaphora, creates suspense, for it commonly indicates the aggressor's proximity to his prey; cf. *Theb.* 5.168 (of a doe chased by wolves) *praecipitat suspensa fugam, iamiamque teneri | credit et elusos audit concurrere morsus*; on the simile's Virgilian and Ovidian antecedents see Williams on Virg. *A.* 12.754–5. St. here creates sympathy for the nymph and assimilates Pan to a predatory animal.

20 iam praedae leuis imminet: with the pause at the fourth-foot diaeresis the verb slows the action, holding the outcome in suspense. *imminet* suggests desire as well as physical stance: Pan 'leans over' (*OLD* 2a) and 'threatens' (*OLD* 5) the nymph; cf. *Theb.* 4.194–5 *spoliisque . . . | imminet Argiae*, with Micozzi; Ov. *Met.* 1.541–2 (Apollo and Daphne) *tergoque fugacis imminet*; Cat. 61.164–6. *immineo* is also used of trees which overhang natural features such as caves or lakes (e.g. Virg. *Ecl.* 9.41–2 *candida populus antro | imminet*), and thus anticipates the story's conclusion. *praedae* (dat. with *imminet*) continues the 'hunting' metaphor and is more blunt than *conubia* (19).

20–37 Diana comes to the nymph's rescue.

20 ecce . . . | Diana: a dramatic change of scene, with Diana's sudden, unsolicited arrival, a *dea ex machina*. There was perhaps an early cult to Diana on the Caelian; Cicero (*Har. resp.* 32) refers to a shrine (*maximum et sanctissimum Dianae sacellum in Caeliculo*) that was destroyed in 58 BCE by L. Calpurnius Piso. She comes as helper, unlike in Ovid's *Metamorphoses*, where she punishes Callisto (*Met.* 2.453–65) and Actaeon (*Met.* 3.138–255). Dewar 2002: 399–400 suggests as another model Ov. *Met.* 2.453–65 (Diana's sudden appearance to Callisto (but after her rape)) *ecce suo comitata choro Dictynna | . . . et caede superba ferarum*: St.'s Diana 'knows her Ovid'; she seeks to avoid for Pholoe the fate suffered by Callisto – pregnancy, and banishment from Diana's band. *ecce* regularly occurs in the fifth foot in the poetry of St. (Pederzani); cf. Ov. *Fast.* 1.434 *ecce rudens rauco uector asellus | intempestiuos edidit ore sonos*. **citatos | aduertit Diana gradus** 'Diana turns her hurried steps towards them'.

21 iuga septem: the seven hills of Rome; cf. 2.7.45.

22 Auentinaeque . . . ceruae: the Aventine, *collis Dianae* (Mart. 7.73.1 and 12.8.3), was the site of Diana's first and most important temple in Rome, traditionally founded by Servius Tullius as the common sanctuary of the league of Latin and Roman peoples (Var. *L.* 5.43; Livy 1.45.2–6; *LTUR* II 11–13). Her cult was celebrated on 13 August (3.1.55–60; Mart. 12.67.2). *ceruae* refers to the pre-foundation days.   **legit uestigia ceruae** 'follows the tracks of a doe' (*OLD lego* 7a). The expression *uestigia legere* is Virgilian; cf. Virg. *A.* 9.392–3; *Theb.* 9.171, 12.272–3; Bömer on Ov. *Met.* 3.17. St. also echoes Cat. 64.341 *uestigia ceruae.*

23 paenituit uidisse deam 'the goddess was irked by what she saw' (for she is a virgin deity and nymphs are her special care). For this sense of *paenitet* see *OLD* 1b.

24–25 numquamne auidis arcebo rapinae | hoc petulans foedumque pecus: cf. *Theb.* 4.696 (Bacchus' promise to the Nemean nymphs) *cupidas Faunorum arcebo rapinas. rapinae* generally means 'spoils of war'; Diana views the assaults on her nymphs as a direct attack on her power and possessions. Her speech starts abruptly without the usual introductory formulae (e.g. *ait*); alliteration and angry plosives further express her rage.

25 petulans 'wanton' (*OLD* 1c), etymologically associated with *petere* (Maltby s.v. *petulans, petulantia*).   **pecus:** collective sing. for Pan and his followers, his 'brood' (SB), a metaphor for sheer stupidity (*TLL* X 1.956.7–25). Diana insults 'the god of flocks' (18n.) by reducing him to the animals he normally protects.

25–6 semperque pudici | decrescet mihi turba chori?: *mihi* is dat. of disadvantage. Diana's complaint that she keeps losing her nymphs functions as a kind of learned footnote to the Callisto myth (Ov. *Met.* 2.401–65); see 20n. *pudici* at line end draws attention to the often suspect chastity of Diana's followers (cf. Ov. *Met.* 2.451–2).

26 turba chori 'the number of my band', epexegetical gen. *chorus* is a quasi-technical term for Diana's following; e.g. Virg. *A.* 1.499 *exercet Diana choros*; Ov. *Met.* 2.441.   **sic deinde locuta:** this Virgilian epic phrase occurs always at line end; St. grandly marks the conclusion of Diana's speech; cf. 24–5n.

27 depromit: a Virgilian word for taking arrows out of a quiver, used only here in St.; cf. Virg. *A.* 11.590 *ultricem pharetra deprome sagittam*, Diana's command to the nymph Opis to avenge Camilla's death; *A.* 11.859. St. maintains the high stylistic level. The shift back to the pres. tense conveys the immediacy of the tense situation.   **telum breue:** *telum* commonly means 'arrow' (*OLD* 2b; Virg. *A.* 5.501 *depromunt tela pharetris*); *breue* suggests the arrow will lack purchase.

27–8 quod neque flexis | cornibus aut solito torquet stridore: assonance and alliteration replicate an arrow's sound; cf. Virg. *A.* 5.502 *neruo stridente* *sagitta. cornibus* refers to the bow's two tips or 'horns' (*OLD* 7c). *torquet* is commonly used of hurling weapons with force; cf. *Theb.* 4.325; Virg. *Ecl.* 10.59–60, with Clausen.

28–9 sed una | emisit contenta manu 'but satisfied she sent forth (the arrow) with one hand'. Abl. *una . . . manu* is ἀπὸ κοινοῦ with *emisit* and *contenta* (lit. 'she sent with one hand, content with one hand'). St. puns on *contenta*, past participle of *contendo* 'draw a bow' (*OLD* 1a; Virg. *A.* 12.815). The initial spondees of 29 slow the action, suggesting the throw's lack of force. Normal narrative expectations are here reversed; Diana aims not at Pan but at his intended victim and without using her bow, which would give the arrow force and sound. She wishes only to rouse Pholoe, not harm her.

29–30 laeuumque soporem | . . . fertur tetigisse: critics have scorned St. for making his nymph fall asleep in the heat of the chase (14–15n.; Van Dam). But Plin. *Nat.* 21.119 distinguishes *sopor* from *somnus*, the former being more sinister and akin to a coma; the nymph has fainted from fear and exhaustion and is not in a natural sleep (at V. Fl. 2. 221 the Argonauts are *soporos* ('torpid'), with food and wine). *laeuumque*, an alternative reading for M's *leuamque*, aptly suggests that this 'sleep' is harmful (*OLD laeuus* 5); see Håkanson 1969: 69. But commentators have argued that the metaphor is too bold, esp. since *tangere* usually has a concrete object; cf. however 3.3.123 (Lucina) *grauidos tetigit . . . labores*. SB follows Krohn's conjecture *laeuamque soporae* ('the left hand of the sleepy nymph'). But why would Diana aim for Pholoe's left hand in particular?

30 Naidos (fresh) 'water nymph' may anticipate Pholoe's future residence in the lake; see 60n. But the distinction between land and water nymphs was fluid; cf. Ov. *Met.* 1.690–1 (of Syrinx) *inter Hamadryadas celeberrima Nonacrinas | Naias*, with Bömer.   **auersa . . . sagitta** 'with the arrow reversed', i.e. with the feathered end foremost (*OLD auersus* 2a).   **fertur:** an Alexandrian footnote (Ross 1975: 78) ironically deployed, for the tale is new.

31–2 illa diem pariter surgens hostemque proteruum | uidit: an ironic recall of the adoring gaze of Pygmalion's statue at Ov. *Met.* 10.294 *pariter cum caelo uidit amantem. proteruum* is a virtual synonym with *petulans* (25); cf. Hor. *Ars* 233 *Satyris . . . proteruis*.

32–3 et in fontem, niueos ne panderet artus, | sic tota cum ueste ruit: St. has fun with the Ovidian template. Ovid's victims arouse their assailant's lust by bathing naked in clear water (Hermaphroditus (*Met.* 4.339–455), Arethusa (*Met.* 5.593–8)), but St.'s nymph prudently keeps her clothes on; this unique instance of *pandere* in the sense of 'disclose' with the body as object (*OLD* 5) draws attention to what Pholoe does *not* do; cf. Ov. *Met.* 5.601 (Arethusa) *sicut eram, fugio sine uestibus*, a line that inspired Markland's emendation *sicut erat* (for *sic tota*; cf. Ov. *Met.* 5.601 above) on the grounds that with *sic* there is no point of comparison for *how* the nymph rushes into the lake, and *tota* seems redundant, for why would the nymph even partially disrobe if she is in a hurry? But Håkanson 1969: 69–71 argues that *sic* can in rare instances, where it accompanies movement into water, be equivalent to *sicut erat. tota* then is hyperbolic, emphasising St.'s humorous inversion of the Arethusa paradigm.

33 stagnisque sub altis: collective pl. of water; see Harrison on Virg. *A.* 10.764–5.

34 ima latus implicat alga: Pholoe's concealment of her body with pondweed is a variation of the end of the myth of Pan and Syrinx, where Syrinx is metamorphosed into the pond's reeds (Ov. *Met.* 1.705–8). *alga* normally refers to seaweed; but Isid. *Orig.* 17.9.99 claims there are two related types of *alga*, pondweed and seaweed.

35 quid faceret?: the third-person deliberative subj. occurs only here in book 2 (Van Dam) and is a distinctive feature of epyllia, conveying despair and pathos (Thomas on Virg. *G.* 4.504–5).   **praedo** 'a predator' (often sexual), a pejorative recall of *praeda* (20n.), with which it is etymologically linked (Maltby s.v. *praedo*). Aeneas' enemies call him *praedo* for 'robbing' them of Lavinia (Virg. *A.* 7.362, 11.484; cf. *A.* 10.774); cf. Ov. *Fast.* 4.591 (Pluto, abductor of Persephone) *praedone marito.* See *TLL* x 2.584.13–34.

35–7 nec altis | credere corpus aquis hirtae sibi conscius audet | pellis 'nor does he dare entrust his body to the deep water, conscious of his shaggy hide', a touch of comic realism; as a mountain god with a thick hide (10–11n.), Pan cannot swim; see 2.2.106n. *conscius* often takes the dat. reflexive pronoun to indicate personal awareness (*OLD* 3).

37 a tenero 'from a young age' (*OLD tener* 2c), implying that Pan was now rough and old. Ov. *Fast.* 2.271–2 traces the cult of Pan back to the early Arcadians.   **nandi rudis** 'untrained in swimming' (*OLD rudis* 6a); cf. *Theb.* 2.391 (Tydeus) *rudis fandi.* Pan never had swimming lessons when young, a comic excuse.

38 immitem Brimo: a witty intrusion into this Roman myth of the recondite Greek name for Diana/Hecate, found elsewhere in Latin poetry only at Prop. 2.2.12; Pan speaks poshly. Scaliger's emendation for M's *Bromium* (Bacchus) must be right. Nothing has prepared us for the appearance of Bacchus in this myth of woodland deities, whereas Diana is a key figure in the narrative. Βριμώ occurs in Apollonius Rhodius (3.861, 862, 1211) to evoke the goddess' dreadful aspect; *immitem* 'harsh, merciless' (*OLD* 2) puns on the Greek etymological meaning 'roarer', thus 'terrible one' (see Hunter on A. R. 3.860–1). Roman poets generally avoid the Greek acc. sing. ending in long *o*; e.g. Virgil avoids the acc. with 'Dido'; see Smyth 279; Mynors on Virg. *G.* 1.332.   **stagna inuida et inuida tela:** a striking example of homoeoteleuton with chiasmus and double elision that

mocks Pan's anger and frustration. The tricolon of Pan's complaints that begins
grandly with *immitem Brimo* ends in bathos as Pan can only repeat himself. On
St.'s restraint in the use of homoeoteleuton see Håkanson 1982: 93. St. follows
Ovid in using *inuidus* 'hostile' (*OLD* 1) to indicate divine hostility to lovers; see
McKeown on Ov. *Am.* 1.13.31–2. *tela* is poetic pl., as is *stagna* (33n.).

39–62 A surprising denouement. St. deviates from the paradigm of the *Fasti*
where the frustrated lover is mocked. Instead Pan assumes a dignified role,
planting a young tree by the lake as a memorial of his love. St. was perhaps
influenced by an ancient Roman tradition that identified Pan with Silvanus,
god of trees (Bömer on Ov. *Fast.* 2.271). Daphne is changed into a laurel, which
symbolises Apollo's love (Ov. *Met.* 1.548–67); here the plane provides a similar
memorial of Pan's love while the Naiad, however, remains safely hidden in her
lake. There is no bodily metamorphosis; instead the landscape loses its wildness
and becomes a garden. The shift takes place in the exact centre of the poem.

39 primaeuam . . . platanum: the only reference to the tree as a plane.
primaeuus means it was a sapling; elsewhere this adjective describes people, not
trees, but St., like Virgil, personifies trees (Thomas on Virg. *G.* 2.19), here with a
view to the identification between tree and lover, tree and Melior, in the poem's
second half; see 5n., 40n.   **nisu** 'with an effort', a common emendation of
M's *uisu* which, taken with *primaeuam*, must mean 'young to look at', pleonastic,
for saplings *are* young. But *nisu* is also odd, for as a mountain god Pan is strong
(but perhaps weary from the run); the effort required to uproot and replant the
tree may suggest its special properties.   **longa propago:** 2.1.86n. With the
metrically short initial 'o' in *propago* St. follows normal scansion (Virgil has long
o at *G.* 2.26 and 63); see Mankin on Hor. *Epod.* 2.9.9.

40 innumeraeque manus et iturus in aethera uertex: *uertex* 'head' is
a common metaphor for a tree top (*OLD* 3b) but 'hands' is a rare, possibly
unique, metaphor for 'branches', 'arms' being more common (e.g. Ov. *Met.* 1.550
in frondem crines, in ramos bracchia crescunt); as a shade tree the plane has many
branches. Personification serves as a reminder of the metamorphosis into a tree
that did *not* happen. On Roman anthropomorphic terminology for trees see
Nisbet 1995a: 203.

41 deposuit 'planted firmly'; cf. Virg. *G.* 2. 23–4 *hic plantas . . . | deposuit sul-
cis*. On *ponere* as a technical term for planting trees see N–H on Hor. *Carm.*
2.13.1; cf. Mart. 9.61.7 (of a plane tree) *posuit . . . dextra felix*.   **iuxta** 'close by'
(adverb).   **uiuamque . . . harenam:** the epithet 'living' is unusual for sand.
When applied to natural substances, esp. rock, *uiuus* means 'natural' or 'not man-
made' (*OLD* 4), but with a hint of life within; see Austin on Virg. *A.* 1.167 (of the
nymphs' cave) *uiuoque . . . saxo*; Ov. *Met.* 14.713 *saxo quod adhuc uiuum radice tenetur*.
OLD 2c suggests the meaning 'containing the essence of life'; thus perhaps St.
suggests the sand has special properties that can help the tree grow; cf. *Theb.*

4.444 (an oxymoronic use) *uiuoque . . . sola pinguia tabo*. Despite the lack of metamorphosis, this landscape is 'alive'. Sand is often found by and in rivers as well as at the sea; Ovid's Pan chases Syrinx to the 'sandy waters of the peaceful river Ladon' (*Met.* 1.702 *harenosi placidum Ladonis ad amnem*).

42 optatisque aspergit aquis: water is 'desired' because it is necessary to irrigate a new planting and because a plane craves water (see 1–2n.); but water is desired too because it is a virtual metonymy for Pholoe who hides within it.

42–52 As in Ovid's myth of Apollo and Daphne, the erotic, failed hunt ends with a speech, here in prayer form (46 *precor*), emphasising the endurance of love (*Met.* 1.557–65); note the specific reference to Apollo's laurel at 51. As Apollo prays to his new tree, so Pan addresses the sapling; on the parallels see Dewar 2002: 402–3. Though not the product of metamorphosis, Pan's tree is ordered to assume a form symbolising both erotic desire and loving protection; Pan too changes by taking on a georgic role, the tree planter being traditionally regarded as a benefactor of posterity; see N–H on Hor. *Carm.* 2.13.3. Pan's prayer is divided into two parts, first the order to the tree to love and protect the nymph and her pool (43–8), then the promise of lasting fame for the tree (49–52).

42 talia mandat: a grand expression for introducing a speech, esp. in epic (Pease on Virg. *A.* 4.30), e.g. Jupiter's command to Mercury to urge Aeneas to leave Dido and return to higher purposes (Virg. *A.* 4.222; cf. *Theb.* 7.76). St. wittily inverts the thrust of Jupiter's speech: as Aeneas is to be extricated from a disastrous passion, Pan's tree is ordered to fall in love – but in a 'platonic' way. The phrase here indicates the change in narrative direction from sex to ethics, wilderness to garden.

43 uiue diu: see 2.2.121n. The imperative (to the tree) combines the basic sense of 'live' (41n.) with the idea 'live on' in memory; *diu* emphasises the desire for prolonged fame. *uiuere* also connotes immortality through poetry (N–H on Hor. *Carm.* 2.2.5); St. may allude here to *Theb.* 12.816 *uiue, precor*, his envoi to his epic (with allusion to Ov. *Met.* 15.879 *uiuam* and Luc. 9.985–6 *Pharsalia nostra | uiuet*). If so, then he wittily alludes to his wish for the immortality of the *Siluae* through a tree; see 63n.   **nostri pignus memorabile uoti** 'proof of my love worthy of remembrance'. A solemn phrase emphasising the idea of enduring fame (through memory). *memorabile* often modifies *nomen* (cf. 1.1.67; Austin on Virg. *A.* 2.583); but cf. Luc. 9.994 *Pallas . . . pignus memorabile*; Caesar's address to the Palladium as a pledge of eternal security of empire follows directly upon Lucan's proud assertion that poetry alone can infer immortality (9.980–6). The tree is metonymy for the poem about the tree.   **uoti** 'desire' (*OLD* 3b).

44 et haec durae latebrosa cubilia nymphae: cf. Ov. *Fast.* 1.427 (of Lotis) *niueae secreta cubilia nymphae*, with similar chiasmus; *cubilia*, poetic pl., has an erotic sense (*OLD* 2). *latebrosa*, a rare adjective, occurs only here in

St. *durus* 'hard-hearted' is a common poetic term for the pitiless beloved (*OLD* 5b).

45   tu saltem declinis ama: with this emphatic pronominal address Pan turns the tree into a surrogate lover, a symbol of desire. *declinis* 'drooping' is an unusual epithet here, otherwise used of the setting sun or stars or in an astronomical context (*OLD*). St. inverts the situation in Ovid's myth of Apollo and Daphne where the tree resists the god's sexual advances; cf. Ov. *Met.* 1.556 *refugit tamen oscula lignum.*   **preme frondibus undam** 'press the water with your fronds', i.e. 'overshadow it' (*OLD premo* 17); *premere* also has erotic connotations ranging from kisses (*Theb.* 3.154) to copulation (Mart. 3.58.17); see *TLL* x 2.1170.26–39; Cancik 1965: 55; the water becomes a substitute for the hidden nymph. St. offers a witty aetion for the plane's noted properties of shade. Asyndeton, juxtaposing *ama* and *preme*, emphasises the sensual context; *frondibus* suggests only gentle contact.

46–47   illa quidem meruit, sed ne, precor, igne superno | aestuet: 'admittedly [being hard-hearted] she deserved to suffer, but may she not, I pray, swelter in the heat from above'. The negative hortatory clause clarifies the initially ambiguous *illa* (the nymph, not the water). Concessive *quidem* is usually followed by *sed* (*OLD quidem* 4). *precor* is often parenthetical, stressing solemn intent; cf. 2.6.103. St. plays with metaphors of sexual heat: *aestuet* (*OLD* 3); *igne superno*, a unique periphrasis for the sun, puns on 'fire' as a common symbol of sexual desire (Barchiesi and Rosati on Ov. *Met.* 4.194–5). The nymph is to be protected from lust including, perhaps, her own! St. reverses here the pattern of Ovid's myth of Narcissus: the chaste shaded pool (Ov. *Met.* 3.412 *siluaque sole locum passura tepescere nullo*) is here created *after* the erotic event, not before; see 1n.

47   dura . . . grandine: though the nymph is *dura* (44), Pan magnanimously prays she will be spared the violent effects of 'hard' hail. On close repetition of the same word, here with a different nuance, see 75n.; also 70–1n. (*facilis*). Pan's words 'metamorphose' this wilderness (cf. 12 *belligerum Iani nemus)* into a peaceful, temperate refuge.

47–8   tantum | spargere tu laticem et foliis turbare memento 'only you be mindful to scatter and ruffle the water with leaves', a solemn, final injunction to the tree. The archaic imperative *memento* always occurs at line end in hexameter poetry (*TLL* VIII 653.64–5); *foliis* is ἀπὸ κοινοῦ with *spargere* and *turbare*. Van Dam sees a reference to the *paraclausithyron* here, the excluded lover leaving his crown of leaves or flowers at the beloved's threshold; see 61n.; McKeown's introd. to Ov. *Am.* 1.6.

48   laticem: an elevated poetic word, etymologically linked with *latere* 'to hide' (Serv. *A.* 1.686 (*aqua*) *quod inter terrae uenas lateat*; Maltby s.v. *latex*).   **turbare:** cf. Ov. *Met.* 3.410 (of Narcissus' pool) *nec fera turbarat nec lapsus ab arbore ramus.* St. again reverses the narrative pattern of Ovid's myth; Narcissus' pool was

untouched until it was churned by his tears of frustrated passion; cf. Ov. *Met.*
3.475 *et lacrimis turbauit aquas. turbare* can have erotic connotations (e.g. Ov. *Ars 2.*
563 *Mars pater, insano Veneris turbatus amore*).

49 teque diu recolam: the idea of agricultural cultivation (*OLD recolo* 2)
is combined with the idea of worship (*OLD* 3) in both a religious and erotic
sense, with an emphasis on the idea of regular renewal of ritual (*Theb.* 1.667,
4.723).   **dominamque:** both 'mistress of the property' and elegiac 'mistress'
or 'beloved'.

49–50 benignae | sedis: *benignus* usually refers to human generosity (Cole-
man on 4.6.3–4 *benigni* | *Vindicis*); St. personifies the garden complex of tree and
pool (rather than the Naiad's quarters specifically; cf. SB), anticipating Melior's
beneficence; cf. 70–1; 3.1.151–2 (of Pollius' Naples) *benigna* | *Parthenope.*

50 illaesa tutabor utramque senecta: cf. 3.1.174 (of Pollius Felix) *teque nihil*
laesum uiridi renouabo senecta. Myth explains the notable longevity of the plane tree
(Plin. *Nat.* 16.238, 240); under Pan's protection the tree and nymph (*utramque*) will
grow old but will not show signs of age. St. often concludes a poem by wishing for
long life for his addressees, though sometimes with variations (the villa at 2.2.107–
11, the tree here). *illaesus* means physically unharmed or unimpaired (*OLD* 1);
Melior's garden is thus both inviting *and* safe, unlike Ovid's ideal landscapes that
are inviting and treacherous.

51–2 ut Iouis, ut Phoebi frondes, ut discolor umbra | populus: a
grand conclusion to Pan's speech with a *tricolon crescens*, linked by asyndeton
and unusual multiple anaphora (Wills 369–71), and set within a purpose clause
(*ut . . . stupeant*). The trees of Jove and Phoebus are the oak and the laurel, both
long-lived (Plin. *Nat.* 16. 239); they stood outside Augustus' house on the Palatine in
honour of his civic and military achievements; cf. Ov. *Fast.* 4.953–4 *state Palatinae*
laurus, praetextaque quercu | *stet domus.* The laurel also evokes Ovid's Daphne,
metamorphosed into a symbol of frustrated desire and successful politics (Ov.
Met. 1.560–3, with Barchiesi). The poplar, sacred to Hercules, was a favourite
garden tree (3.1.185; N–H on Hor. *Carm.* 2.3.9) which provided ample shade
(Virg. *Ecl.* 9.41–2), though not as thick as the plane's; the white poplar, which has
leaves that are white on one side, green below (Plin. *Nat.* 16.85–6; N–H on Hor.
Carm. 2.3.9), must be meant; St. uses *discolor* 'of diverse colours' sometimes of two
colours (e.g. *Theb.* 9.685 *discolor . . . tigris* 'the striped tiger').

52 stupeant: pres. subj. in a purpose clause. On wonder as a feature of St.'s
encomia see 2.1.119n. On the topos of 'outdoing' in St.'s poetry see 2.2.6n.   **et**
nostrae . . . pinus: a surprising addition to the tricolon; even Pan's sacred tree
(Prop. 1.18.20 *Arcadio pinus amica deo*) will be surpassed by Melior's plane. The
pine was a mountain tree (Virg. *Ecl.* 10.14–15 *pinifer . . .* | *Maenalus*), also popular
in gardens for its height and shade (Virg. *Ecl.* 7.65 *pinus in hortis*; N–H on Hor.

Carm. 2.3.9 *pinus ingens*, paired, as here, with the poplar). Pine garlands were Pan's attribute (Lucr. 4.586–7 *Pan | pinea semiferi capitis uelamina quassans*; Ov. *Met.* 1.699 *Pan . . . pinuque caput praecinctus acuta*; Sil. 13.331 *cingit acuta comas et opacal tempora pinus*). The trees' personification and the agonistic context perhaps hint at the debate between the olive and the laurel over their respective merits (Call. *Iamb.* 4). **tua germina** 'your budding branches' (*TLL* VI 2.1922.42–54), referring to the plane.

53–61 St. approximates the idea of metamorphosis with the change of the tree's shape into the symbolic figure of a protective lover; he thus reverses the usual downward direction of Ovidian metamorphosis from human to plant.

53 illa: the plane tree is grammatically feminine in gender, and thus, in this erotic allegory, relatively safe, posing no threat of actual penetration!   **ueteres . . . calores** 'long-standing passion' (*OLD uetus* 3); cf. Virg. *A.* 4.23 *ueteris uestigia flammae*; Ov. *Met.* 5.576 *fluminis Elei ueteres narrauit amores. calor* suggests sexual desire (*OLD* 6; 46–7n.); cf. 1.2.89–90 *minor ille calor quo saeua tepebant | aequora.*   **imitata:** M reads *animata* 'alive', that is, with the god's ancient flame of desire; but the verb is rare and St. uses it elsewhere with *in* (*Theb.* 6.269) or the abl. (*Theb.* 3.224). Markland's conjecture *imitata* marks the process of change whereby the sapling becomes like a lover; *imitari* is a favourite word of St. in the *Siluae*; as in Ovid's *Metamorphoses* it conveys a fascination with the blurring between appearance and reality and also suggests literary imitation (Burrow 1999). St. possibly alludes to Ov. *Met.* 9.340 (of Lotis/the lotos flower) *haud procul a stagno Tyrios imitata colores.* If so, St. refers to another Ovidian 'rape narrative' with Lotis (*Met.* 9.340–8; cf. *Fast.* 1.391–44) and also another tree metamorphosis, that of Dryope, punished by Lotis for attempting to pluck her flower (*Met.* 9.324–93), signs of his rich literary heritage.

54 uberibus stagnis: dat. with *incubat* (55). *uber* appears only here in St.; it means 'copious' of water with a hint of fecundity (*OLD* 1b), ironical for protecting Pholoe's chastity; cf. Ov. *Met.* 3.31 (*specus*) *uberibus fecundus aquis.*   **obliquo pendula trunco** 'drooping down with slanting trunk'; cf. 2 *<in>curuata uadis. pendula* has the sense of 'precariously poised' (Coleman on 4.3.28).

55 incubat 'leans over'; cf. Prop. 4.7.81 *ramosis Anio qua pomifer incubat aruis*, where *incubat* suggests that the river god watches over (and thus fertilises) the fields. In the *Siluae incubare* likewise expresses benign protection by a powerful being; Lucan's portrait watches over his widow's sleep (2.7.130–1n.), Aesculapius guards his healing serpent (3.4.25). By contrast in St.'s epic *incubo* can have ominous connotations, used of death-bringing Sleep (*Theb.* 10.108, 303), and of Oedipus (*Theb.* 11.698).   **umbris scrutatur amantibus undas:** *scrutari* always conveys the sense of searching for something hidden (*OLD* 1). The search for union with the beloved happens through reflection (*umbra*), without the tree penetrating the water's surface (Cancik 1965: 55).

56 sperat et amplexus: cf. 2 *complexa. et* here means 'even'.   **aquarum spiritus:** the natural 'breeze' (*OLD spiritus* 8) that often ruffles the water of a lake suggests the Naiad's 'breath' (*OLD* 3); the water too is personified. Pederzani suggests that St. alludes to scientific reasons for the origin of wind from water; see Sen. *Nat.* 5.3–14; Williams 2005: 423–6.   **arcet:** cf. 24 *arcebo*; Diana's wish has now been fulfilled with an echo perhaps of Daphne's final rejection of Apollo (Pederzani); cf. Ov. *Met.* 1.556 *refugit tamen oscula lignum*. The line, framed neatly between *sperat* and *arcet*, reinforces the split between desire and rejection, with division in sense at the strong caesura after *amplexus*.

57 nec patitur tactus: *tactus* too has erotic connotations (Cancik 1965: 56).

57–60 The description of the tree's strange shape is difficult in sense, though straightforward in syntax; some of the difficulty is removed if we accept that St. describes the tree as a paradoxical symbol of both love and frustrated desire; and also that he describes the *reflection* of the tree as well as the tree itself. The tree grows in the shape of a V (see 3–4n.). Having bent down towards the pool (53–7), its reflection suggests an underwater tree reaching for the air (57); finally it soars upwards again to its top (58–9), a movement made possible by its firm embedding by the lake; reflection gives the appearance of another tree growing *down* to the bottom of the pool (59–60). See the discussion of these lines in Hardie 2005: 209–11.

57 eluctata sub auras 'having struggled up [from the surface] to the air' (*NLS* 5); cf. *Theb.* 6.854–7 (of a bent cypress) *Alpini ueluti regina cupressus... | uix sese radice tenens terraeque propinquat, | iamdudum aetherias eadem reditura sub auras.*

58 libratur fundo 'it is balanced on its firm base'. The sense of *fundo* is difficult. Van Dam suggests 'the bottom of the pool' (also SB), but the previous lines have emphasised that the tree cannot touch the water (55–7). Pederzani suggests 'tree roots'. Although this meaning is attested only in late Latin and with reference mostly to smaller plants (*TLL* v 1.1575.24–34; *fundamentum* more clearly refers to tree roots (*TLL* v 1.1552.11–15)), the use of *fundus* in the *Thebaid* lends some support; there it refers to the bottom of a body of water (*Theb.* 1.57, 9.271, 468; cf. *Silv.* 1.5.52), the hold of ship (*Theb.* 5.82), the foundation of the earth (*Theb.* 3.208, 436), the foundation of a city (*Theb.* 3.248) and the sea bed of an anchor (*Theb.* 4.25); common to all these uses is the idea of a firm base. Thus *fundo* probably means the roots but also the earth in which the trunk is grounded and that allows it to be balanced over the water; cf. 2 *robore ab imo. libratur* refers to the tree's bipartite form, the trunk sloping down towards the water, and the trunk soaring aloft (cf. Plin. *Nat.* 16.5 *libratae stantes nauigant*, of uprooted oaks balanced by islands of earth to keep them upright; *TLL* VII 2.1350.29–43, esp. 33–6), and also to the split image of the tree achieved by reflection. *libratur* recalls *librat* of Pan (19) and marks the tree's role as surrogate lover.   **enode cacumen:** *cacumen* usually means a tree's 'crown' but here refers to the upper part of the trunk, which is quite smooth, without 'knots' in its bark (*OLD nodus* 8a).

59 ingeniosa: a favourite word of Ovid's, though not used by other Augustan poets and only here in St. (McKeown on Ov. *Am.* 1.8.62). It means 'fertile' of plants (Ov. *Fast.* 4.684 *ad segetes ingeniosus ager*; *TLL* VII 1.1521.39–42) and thus suggests the tree's natural vigour. More commonly it refers to natural human talent, often in the literary sphere (Hardie 2005: 211; *OLD* 3; SB translates 'cunningly'). *ingeniosa* thus continues the personification of the tree, symbol now of poetic creativity as well as of love and subtly linked to St.'s 'ingenious' *Siluae*. See 2.2.44 – 5n.; Wray 2007: 142–3.   **leuat, ueluti descendat:** the antithetical verbs mirror reflection; the upwardly soaring tree seems (*ueluti*) to grow downwards, the subjunctive with *ueluti* suggesting only appearance (*OLD* 5). In reflection, the tree achieves consummation of its desire, an aesthetically pleasing result. See Hardie 2005: 210.

59–60 in imos | . . . lacus: 2n.

60 stirpe . . . alia: this 'other root' is illusory, generated by reflection; see 4n.   **Phoebeia Nais** 'Diana's Naiad'. *Phoebeia* in this sense is a hapax; *Phoebe(i)us* normally refers to Apollo. A final reminder perhaps of Daphne and her different fate?

61 exclusos inuitat gurgite ramos: the paradoxical juxtaposition of *exclusus* and *inuitat* emphasises frustrated desire and the nymph's simultaneous rejection of penetration and acceptance of protection. The ambiguity of *gurgite*, abl. of separation with *exclusos* or instrumental abl. with *inuitat*, reinforces this paradoxical play with prefixes; see Cancik 1965: 56; Hardie 2005: 211. *exclusos* suggests again the idea of the *paraclausithyron* (e.g. Tib. 2.4.39 *at tibi, quae pretio uictos excludis amantes*); see 47–8n. The lake perpetually enacts an elegiac topos. Spondees bring the action to a stately close.

62–77 A surprising shift in conclusion to the themes of a birthday poem. As with Pollius and Polla (2.2.121–55), formal praise of the addressee occurs at the end; Melior is addressed directly (62 *tibi*) for the first time. St. develops the analogy between Melior and the garden adumbrated at 1–5; see Hardie 2005: 211–12. Ovid praised Augustus through the laurel at the end of the Apollo and Daphne myth (*Met.* 1.553–67); praise of Melior by contrast emphasises the apolitical turn of 2.3; see Dewar 2002: 402–3.

62–3 haec tibi parua quidem genitali luce paramus | dona: the brisk dactyls of 62 after the previous spondees signal the change to present, festive time: the poem is a birthday gift, *paramus* suggesting attention to its special presentation. *parua dona* is poetic pl., echoing *tam parua* (6). *quidem*, followed by *sed* (61) is concessive ('though small'; see 6n.); typical poetic modesty is followed by the tentative assertion of poetic immortality in the next line. On birthday gift-giving see Ov. *Ars* 1.429–30. *genitali* 'connected with one's birthday' (*OLD* 3), a rather rare sense occurring first in poetry at Ov. *Tr.* 3.13.17 (*genitale . . . tempus*), then here; see 2.7.132n.

63 sed ingenti forsan uictura sub aeuo: a claim for the poem's immortality normally reserved for the grandeur of epic or lyric, *forsan* suggesting the risk involved in pursuing the short, occasional poem; see Henderson 1998: 114; cf. Mart. 9.61.21 *perpetuos sperare licet tibi frondis honores*. Temporal *sub* 'during' (*OLD* 12) becomes frequent with Augustan writers (L–H–S 279) but the temporal use of *ingens* is very rare (*TLL* VII 1.1538.24–6); it emphasises the contrast between *luce*, one day and occasion, and *aeuo*, a vast tract of time, thus between the birthday and the poem's reception. St. always places the adjective before *aeuo* (2.7.73 and 4.6.93). *uictura* draws an explicit analogy between the poem and the tree inspired by Virg. *Ecl.* 10.53–4, 72–4; cf. 43 *uiue diu*; Hardie 2005: 212–13.

64 tu: the pronoun (cf. 62 *tibi*), boldly separated from its predicate, the imperative *persta* (73), introduces a long, encomiastic period constructed from a series of descriptive relative clauses (64 *cuius*, 66 *cui*) and phrases (66–74), all connected by simple coordinates. Like the tree, the portrait of Melior here is basically oxymoronic; he is a man of moderation equally poised between public and private virtues, a follower of the Horatian model of *aurea mediocritas* (Pederzani 196; Hardie 2005: 218–19).   **placido . . . in pectore:** *placidus* describes water (e.g. *Theb.* 3.527, 11.214; *Ach.* 1.57, 230, 696) as well as temperament and links Melior closely with his landscape; see 15n. St. may allude to *Culex* 96–7 *aemulus Ascraeo pastor sibi quisque poetae | securam placido traducit pectore uitam*; if so, he locates himself in a distinguished tradition of bucolic/rural poetry with a neoteric focus on mock-heroic play.   **posuere . . . sedem:** cf. 41 *deposuit* (*platanum*); 50 *sedis*. Virtues have planted themselves in Melior's heart as firmly as the tree was planted in his garden.

65 blandus honos 'charming dignity'. *blandus* is a favourite word of St., occurring in various contexts in book 2 (2.1.45, 2.1.88, 2.1.206, 2.2.111, 2.2.120, 2.6.41, 2.7.38, 2.7.84), but is an unusual epithet for a Roman virtue (Hardie 2005: 214). The same oxymoronic quality endows Vopiscus' villa (1.3.11 *blandumque . . . honorem*), a gift from Venus; St. accommodates traditional Roman virtues to private life.   **hilarisque tamen cum pondere uirtus:** another striking oxymoron. *uirtus* connotes 'manliness', a state of physical containment (Gleason 1995 *passim*); *hilaris* 'light-hearted' suggests its opposite, physical relaxation. Melior is *hilaris* at 2.1.168, but its use of qualities rather than people is rare, occurring first in poetry at Ov. *Pont.* 2.1.9 *hilari pietate*. St. develops this oxymoronic use; cf. 5.1.65 (*fides*), 5.2.73 (*probitas*), *TLL* VI 3.2788.30–9. *cum pondere* 'with gravity' (*OLD pondus* 7) bridges epithet and weightier noun. *uirtus* assumes new meaning as an inner form of manly 'containment', the moral tranquillity of villa owners; cf. 1.3.91, 2.2.71.

66–7 cui nec pigra quies nec iniqua potentia nec spes | improba: an elegant tricolon of paired opposites linked by *nec . . . nec . . . nec* (66–7), with the order of adjective and | noun reversed in the final pair; St. emphasises that Melior avoids the extremes of sloth, tyrannical power and ambition, vices of public life contrasted with Melior's private virtues. Here St. articulates the value of a social order based on friendship rather than on political careerism. *cui* is dat. of possession (cf. 64 *cuius*), with *sunt* understood.   **nec pigra quies** 'peace that is not indolent'; cf. 1.6.91 (of the Colosseum) *fugit pigra Quies*; 2.2.7 (of the stadium for the Neapolitan games) *stadio iam pigra quies*; *nec* thus emphasiscs that Melior, though away from the bustle of public space, makes good use of his tranquillity. *quies* is a favourite ethical noun of St.; see 2.2.140n.   **iniqua potentia:** *potentia* occurs only here in St., *potestas* being more common; *iniqua* brings out its negative connotations.   **nec spes | improba** 'nor immoderate hope', i.e. 'nor vaulting ambition' (SB; *OLD improbus* 6). The two monosyllables make a rare conclusion to the line; see 2.1.123–4n. Enjambment highlights *improba*; cf. Pan's *improba cornua* (11).

67 sed medius per honesta et dulcia limes 'but [you take] a middle path through the honourable and pleasurable things of life'. It is not a question of a choice *between* duty and pleasure (thus Mozley), for *per* does not mean *inter*, but of finding a path that balances between them; cf. Hor. *Ars* 343 *qui miscuit utile dulci*, with Rudd. Melior follows the 'golden mean'. *limes* conveys the idea of a path in life's journey (*OLD* 4c); see 2.2.140n. *dulcis* has positive value in St.; cf. 3 *pr.* 1 *Polli dulcissime*.

68 incorrupte fidem 'of stainless trustworthiness' (*not* 'faith' SB); *fidem* is acc. of respect; cf. Hor. *Carm.* 1.24.7 *incorrupta Fides*. On *fides* as a cardinal virtue of Roman relationships see Ross 1969: 85–6. The syntax changes from relative clauses to vocatives in a second *tricolon crescens*; see 69n.   **nullosque experte tumultus:** Melior enjoys the perfect calm of the Epicurean *sapiens*; for the storm imagery cf. 2.2.139–41.

69 et secrete palam quod digeris ordine uitam 'and living in private [but] openly because you plant your life in order', a typical Statian paradox though there may be some corruption in the text: *quod* 'because' is semantically strained, but so are the alternatives *quo* (Baehrens) and *quom* (Vollmer). *secrete*, paradoxically juxtaposed with *palam*, is ambiguous, and can be understood either as an adverb or as a vocative; it is probably best taken as the latter, the final vocative in a descriptive tricolon (68–9, *incorrupte . . . experte . . . | et secrete*), modified by the adverbial *palam*. Some editors (e.g. SB) take *palam* to modify *ordine digeris*, punctuating with a comma after *secrete*, but this undercuts a striking and characteristic Statian oxymoron. As Pederzani ad loc. notes, Melior lives in seclusion in the heart of Rome without closing his house to his friends; he thus follows two key Epicurean tenets, the cultivation of friendship and of seclusion from public life.   **digeris:** an agricultural metaphor (*OLD* 4a) appropriate to the garden that assimilates Melior in character to his environment and to traditional Roman virtue. St. perhaps here echoes Virg. *Ecl.* 1.73 *pone ordine uitem*, a metaphorical directive for the organisation of one's life through the orderly planting of the vineyard; on possible aural play see 53n.

70–1 idem auri facilis contemptor et optimus idem | promere diuitias: framing of the line with *idem* emphasises the pun on Melior's name. The syntax now shifts to descriptive nom. nouns and adjectives. St. gives a positive nuance to the often negative *contemptor*, occurring in the *Siluae* only here; cf. *Theb.* 3.602 and 9.550 *superum contemptor*, echoing Virg. *A.* 7.648 *contemptor diuum Mezentius* and Ov. *Met.* 3.514 *contemptor superum Pentheus*. Melior is 'a ready despiser' of wealth (*OLD facilis* 9) who, like Pollius and Polla (2.2.151–4), makes moderate use of his riches: he does not hoard and he gives easily; *promere*, the generally accepted emendation for M's *comere*, suggests his generosity. Contempt of wealth is a prominent Horatian theme; see Hardie 2005: 218 on Hor. *Carm.* 3.3.49–52. *facilis* lightens the moral tone with recall of *faciles Fauni* (7), a hint that Melior too has provided inspiration for this poem.

71 opibusque immittere lucem: cf. 2.2.153 *expositi census*. The metaphor of 'letting in light to wealth' suggests Melior displays and shares his riches without fear of the charge of corruption or meanness. The phrase gives full meaning to the epithet *nitidus* (1n.); Melior is not only 'elegant', he is also ethically enlightened.

72 hac longum florens animi morumque iuuenta: *florens* connects Melior metaphorically with his tree (64n.); both 'flourish' with long life; *longum* = *diu*; cf. 43 (Pan's command to the tree) *uiue diu*. Melior is elderly (cf. 2.1.70), but St. typically compliments him for his youthful mind and behaviour. See 2.2.10n.

73–4 Iliacos aequare senes et uincere persta | quos pater Elysio, genetrix quos detulit annos 'steadfastly persist in equalling and surpassing the years which your father and mother took down to Elysium'. The Trojans Priam and Tithonus were proverbial for longevity; see 2.2.108n. St. characteristically expresses the wish for his addressee's long life in mythological terms; cf. 1.3.109–10, 1.4.125–7, 2.2.107–8, 3.4.103–4, 4.3.150–2. The hope for a friend's very long life also guarantees the longevity of his own work (Habinek 1998: 112–13). Roman poets preferred circumlocutory expressions for death (Axelson 65–8). For the poetic expression *Elysio deferre* with dat. cf. *Theb.* 7.784–5 *laurus | quas Erebo deferre nefas. genetrix* is an elevated term for 'mother' (cf. 2.6.83). Melior's parents introduce a personal note after the mythological allusions; cf. 2.1.234. St. compliments Melior by placing his parents in Elysium; cf. 2.6.98–100.

73 persta (with epexegetical infinitives; *OLD* 3) echoes the poem's opening *stat*, thus linking the tree's longevity with Melior's.

75 hoc illi duras exorauere sorores 'they obtained this by entreaty from the harsh sisters', a steady spondaic line with double acc. with *exoro* (*OLD* 2b). The 'sisters' are the *Parcae* (2.1.120n.). *duras* recalls 44 *durae nymphae* with the sharper nuance of 'inexorable' rather than 'hard-hearted'.

76–7 hoc, quae te sub teste situm fugitura tacentem | ardua magnanimi reuirescet gloria Blaesi 'this the lofty renown of magnanimous Blaesus [obtained], which will escape silent decay by your witness and grow green again'. A grand conclusion ending in a Golden Line. On Melior's friend Blaesus see 2.1.191–2n. Blaesus' memory, like the tree, will flourish, thanks to Melior's devotion and St.'s poem.

76 te sub teste: cf. 5.3.227.   **situm tacentem:** cf. 5 *tacitis radicibus*; 2.3 ends, like 2.1 and 2.2, with repetition as a sign of closure. *situm* alludes not only to senile decay (cf. 1.4.127) but also to literary oblivion (hence *tacentem*), which poets and patrons alone can forestall; cf. 1 *pr.* 24–5 (*Vopiscus*)... *qui praecipue uindicat a situ | litteras iam paene fugientes. tacentem* perhaps lightly plays on Blaesus' name, lit. 'stammering'; see 2.1.201n.; Nisbet 1995b: 41.

77 ardua... gloria Blaesi: cf. 2.1.191–2 *ardua Blaesi | ora. ardua* metaphorically links Blaesus' glorious memory, cultivated by Melior, and the tree (4 *ardua*).   **reuirescet:** cf. 4 *iterum nascatur.* Associated with vegetation, growth and trees (e.g. Virg. *G.* 2. 313), *reuirescet* weaves together the themes of tree, Melior and poetry. St. rephrases the concluding sentiment of Virg. *Ecl.* 10.73–4 *Gallo, cuius amor tantum mihi crescit in horas | quantum uere nouo uiridis se subicit alnus;* see 63n.   **magnanimi:** a grand Homeric epithet (μεγάθυμος) for Melior's friend, giving him a heroic cast; cf. *Ach.* 1.1 *magnanimum Aeaciden;* Austin on Virg. *A.* 6.307.   **Blaesi:** the poem's last word wittily links 2.3 with 2.4 on Melior's parrot. *blaesus* first occurs in Latin at Ov. *Am.* 2.6.24 to describe Corinna's parrot (McKeown ad loc.; Hardie 2005: 207–8). St. ends as well as begins 2.3 with an Ovidian allusion that acknowledges his debt to his predecessor while demonstrating his creative use of Ovidian paradigms.

Siluae 2.4

A poem consoling Melior on the death of his pet parrot, a further display of the poet's Ovidian ingenuity and a play on the book's consolatory and architectural themes; it was perhaps written to amuse in a symposiastic context (4–7). The death of a beloved animal or bird is a familiar topic of epigram (e.g. *AP* VII 191, 199, 202–3; McKeown introd. to Ov. *Am.* 2.6). But the chief models for 2.4 are Ov. *Am.* 2.6, a lament for the death of Corinna's parrot, and, to a lesser extent, Cat. 3, the lament for Lesbia's sparrow, though unlike Ovid and Catullus St.

makes no mention of the owner's grief (cf. Cat. 3.17–18; Ov. *Am.* 2.6.43–8) and introduces new features with the description of the birdcage (11–15) and the inset song of lament (24–37). St. takes a playful approach to consolatory conventions with his consistent anthropomorphism and hyperbolic style; he also humorously parodies his own style in 2.2 with the description of the birdcage (11–15n.). 2.4 is also intimately concerned with imitation, the parrot's mimicry of human speech and St.'s relationship to his models. St. follows Ovid in using the 'parrot poem' to demonstrate his literary-critical ideals (Myers 1990, 2002). Just as Ovid's parrot is a more substantial bird than Catullus' sparrow, so St.'s parrot is more flamboyant than Ovid's and the poem's tone more grandiose, interweaving the bathetic and the mock-heroic. But St. 'is no parrot-poet' (Myers 2002: 197). The poem has possibly a political dimension. Unlike his models, St. esp. emphasises the parrot's speech, suggesting a concern with constraints on speech imposed by the patronage system and autocratic rule (Dietrich 2002; Newlands 2005). In early modern and recent times the parrot as human mimic has inspired a rich artistic tradition, from Skelton's satirical 'Speke parrot' (sixteenth century) to Monty Python's 'Dead parrot' sketch (Courtney and James 2006).

Talking birds were popular pets in antiquity, esp. given by lovers; cf. Plin. *Nat.* 10.117–25, esp. 117 on parrots; Plut. *Mor.* 12.973A–974B; Leary on Mart. 14.73–6. Man. 5.378–87 decries the fashion for talking birds and the high price they command. Mart. 7.87 mocks the fashion of giving pet birds funerals; see 17n.

Further reading: on epitaphs preserved on animal tombs see Herrlinger 1930: 14–51. On pet birds see Jennison 1937: 116–21; Toynbee 1973: 247–9; Arnott 2007: 201–3. On the parodic relation of 2.4 to Ov. *Am.* 2.6 see Herrlinger 1930: 87–90; Van Dam 336–41. On 2.4 in particular see Colton 1967; Cawsey 1983; Myers 2002; Dietrich 2002; Newlands 2005; James 2006.

1–10 A humorously grandiloquent opening praising the parrot's talent in speech. St. plays on the tension between his heightened style and his subject, a pretentious 'pet'.

1 Psittace: consolation is normally addressed to the living, and the dead are generally referred to in the third person past tense; St. makes a surprising empathetic shift to the vocative; cf. Ov. *Am.* 2.6.1–2 *psittacus... occidit*; Cat. 3.3 *passer mortuus est*. Appeal to the dead person (or creature) usually comes later in the lament; cf. 2.1.35–8, 2.6.34–47, 2.6.81; Ov. *Am.* 2.6.17–20. St. opens by acknowledging his Ovidian model and his challenge to it.   **dux uolucrum:** another surprise, for traditionally the eagle was king of the birds (Plin. *Nat.* 10.6); but St. gives here primacy to the parrot for its supremacy in speech; cf. Plin. *Nat.* 10.117 *super omnia humanas uoces reddunt, psittaci quidem etiam sermocinantes*. Such appositional phrases were a regular feature of encomiastic epicedia (McKeown on Ov. *Am.* 2.6.37–8; Coleman on Mart. *Sp.* 21.2), but here it starts a grand *tricolon crescens* praising the parrot's eloquence.   **domini facunda uoluptas:** a humorous play on Lucr. 1.1 (of Venus) *hominum diuumque uoluptas* (1.1), repeated at Lucr. 6.94

of Calliope – a joking reference perhaps to the 'eloquent' parrot as the inspiration for St.'s poem! *domini* contrasts with *dux*, suggesting the bird's servile status as one of Melior's prized possessions; cf. 2.1.76. *domini* also teasingly alludes to the eroticism of Catullus' and Ovid's poems; Lesbia and Corinna were *dominae* in the double sense of pet owners and mistresses (Cat. 3.10; Ov. *Am.* 2.6.19, 61), whereas Melior, who is not named until 32, is simply 'owner'.   **facunda:** St.'s parrot is 'eloquent', Ovid's *garrulus* 'prattling' (*Am.* 2.6.26); see Mynors on Virg. *G.* 4.307. Eloquence is a special virtue in St.'s friends (2.2.9n.). *facunda* humorously challenges the long association between the parrot and bad poetry; cf. Pers. *prol.* 8 on the parrot as a type of unoriginal poet driven to flattery by his appetites, an image drawn from Hellenistic poetry (cf. Call. *Iamb.* 2.11 fr. 192 Pf.; Bing 1981). On the negative association between poets and talking birds see Myers 2002: 193–5.

2 humanae . . . linguae: these key words, stressing the parrot's particular talent for linguistic mimicry, are artfully placed at the start and end points of the line, bringing the tricolon to an emphatic climax; cf. Ov. *Am.* 2.6.37 *loquax humanae uocis imago.*   **sollers** 'skilled' (in speech); Ovid's parrot stammered its words (*Am.* 2.6.24 *blaeso . . . sono,* with McKeown), while Lesbia's sparrow could only 'cheep' (Cat. 3.10 *pipiabat*).   **imitator:** only here in St., and the metrical centre of the line; the parrot is both a natural mimic (Mart. 14.73.1 *psittacus a uobis aliorum nomina discam*) and literary 'imitator' of Catullus' and Ovid's birds; cf. Ov. *Am.* 2.6.1 *imitatrix ales,* with Hinds 1987: 5.   **psittace:** the repeated vocative acknowledges Catullus as model; cf. Cat. 3.3–4 *passer mortuus est meae puellae,* | *passer, deliciae meae puellae*; see Wills 60 n.27.

3 quis . . . ?: as in 2.5.1, St. opens his poem with a motif normally reserved for later in a lament, a question directed against fate for allowing the good or the talented to die prematurely. Alliteration and assonance of *t* in this line reinforce the poet's indignation.   **subito . . . fato?:** premature death is often blamed on a malignant fate; cf. 2.1.137–8; McKeown on Ov. *Am.* 2.6.39. *fatum* is traditionally derived from *fari* 'to speak' (Maltby s.v. *fatum*); the 'utterance' of fate ironically ends the parrot's own utterances; see 7n.   **praeclusit:** metaphorically 'stifled' (*OLD* 3b), but with a hint at the literal sense 'barred' or 'closed off' (*OLD* 1 and 2) appropriate to a caged bird; cf. 32 *recluso.* The stifling of the parrot's voice may allude to a prominent theme of Ovid's *Metamorphoses*: the deprivation of speech is often a punishment for those who rely on the voice, esp. women and poets; cf. Ov. *Met.* 2.658 (of the prophetess Ocyroe) *uocisque meae praecluditur usus.* See Myers 2002: 198; Dietrich 2002: 101–3.   **murmura:** often of birds and animals (*OLD* 1b) as well as children; see 2.1.62n.

4 hesternas . . . dapes: Corinna's parrot died after seven days, the seventh day of an illness being critical (2.1.146); but Melior's parrot was alive and well at dinner the evening before its sudden death; Nauta 2002: 258 gives *hesternas* the adverbial, tragic force 'only yesterday'. St. stresses the immediacy of his poem. **moriturus:** for the pathetic force of the predicative fut. participle see 2.1.106n. Parrots are long-lived birds (Pond 2006: 193–4), unlike the sparrow, so its sudden death is surprising. Feasting and the theme of *memento mori* were traditionally linked; Roman dinner utensils were sometimes decorated with skeletons (Edwards 2007: 165–7). **miserande:** usually of people, often those who have died (*TLL* VIII 1134.63–71), here playfully anthropomorphic (Cawsey 1983: 75–6); cf. Ov. *Am.* 2.6.20 *infelix*. **inisti:** syncopated perfect; cf. 2.5.18. *inire* is a formal expression for 'partaking' in a social function such as a banquet (*OLD* 2); cf. 1.6.48 (of Domitian) *sacras dapes inisti*. The parrot was not a private plaything, like Corinna's bird, but a prized possession that was displayed to Melior's friends.

5 nobiscum: enjambment increases the pathos while emphasising that St. is on intimate terms with Melior as his dinner guest of the previous night. **carpentem:** understand *te*; the parrot is now the object of *uidimus* (7). *carpentem* and *errantemque* (6) suggest the daintiness of the bird's dining habits as it pecks for crumbs and roams over the couches; cf. Ov. *Ars* 3.755 *carpe cibos digitis*, with Gibson. The parrot represents discrimination, not gluttony (Cawsey 1983: 70–1). **gratae . . . munera mensae:** a compliment to Melior, suggesting he was a generous and genial host; cf. Mart. 2.69.7 on coveted invitations to Melior's dinner parties. *mensa*, like our word 'table', can be both the physical object and 'a symbol of hospitable entertainment' (*OLD* 5); *munera* means both 'gifts' and 'last rites' (*OLD* 1d; 2.1.160n.), for this was the parrot's last meal on earth. Myers 1990: 370 associates Corinna's parrot's simple diet of nuts, poppy seeds and water (Ov. *Am.* 2.6.29–32) with Callimachean ideals of refined poetry; in keeping with his mock-epic style, St. suggests that the food the parrot ate was more ample (and perhaps fatal to it (Jennison 1937: 121)). On the long tradition whereby birds articulate stylistic and generic concepts see Steiner 2007.

6 errantemque: cf. Cat. 3.9 *circumsiliens modo huc modo illuc*. Roaming marks the bird's subordinate status; while Roman diners reclined, their slaves were on the move serving dinner or providing entertainment; cf. Petr. 31.23–7; Roller 2006: 19–22. **mediae plus tempore noctis** 'beyond midnight' (lit. 'more than the time of the middle of the night'); *plus* is acc. of extent of time (*OLD* 4b). The parrot's late-night activity suggests that Melior's dinner parties were successfully prolonged but not debauched; the dinner of Vindex lasted till dawn and offered fine conversation rather than gourmet food (4.6.5–19). Melior's parrot provided harmless entertainment, untrue perhaps to type; cf. Plin. *Nat.* 10.117 (on the parrot) *in uino praecipue lasciua*.

7 uidimus: the poet has first-hand experience as part of a community of friends. **affatus** 'utterances', a grand word generally applied to solemn or prophetic speech, here ironically echoing *fatum* (3n.); cf. *Theb.* 3.638 (of augural birds) *uolucrum affatus*. **meditataque uerba** 'practised words'; cf. 2.1.74, there with the negative sense of falsely flattering speech but here appropriate to a bird trained in mimicry. The parrot is so clever that it can 'parrot' St.'s first poem for Melior! On the passive sense of deponent *meditari* see 2.1.74n. The pet starling and nightingales of the young Nero and Britannicus practised (*meditantes*) speaking Greek and Latin constantly (Plin. *Nat.* 10.120).

8 reddideras: *reddere* means 'to reproduce another sound or speech' (*OLD* 5); cf. 31; Ov. *Am.* 2.6.24 *reddebas blaeso tam bene uerba sono*, with McKeown; Plin. *Nat.* 10.117 (quoted in 1n.). The pluperf. tense may be for metrical reasons, *reddidisti* being impossible in hexameters, but along with the return to second-person address it emotionally emphasises the finality of death, the end of the parrot's quixotic activities; cf. 7 *uidimus*, likewise at sentence end and emphasised by enjambment.   **aeterna silentia:** poetic pl. (2.1.68n.). 'Never-ending [*OLD aeternus* 1b] silence' is a cruel fate for a talkative bird; cf. *AP* VII 199.3–4. The theme of the tiny creature's grandiose descent to the Underworld derives from Cat. 3.11–15; cf. *Culex* 210–384.   **Lethes:** gen. sing. as at 2.6.100 *per amoena silentia Lethes*. Corinna's parrot goes to Elysium, peopled by 'pious' birds (Ov. *Am.* 2.6.49–58). But ironically St.'s parrot, whose chief skill is memorisation, descends to the site of forgetfulness (2.1.194n.).

9 ille canorus '[though] that famous songster', an encomiastic use of the pronominal adjective (McKeown on Ov. *Am.* 2.6.37). *canorus* is typically applied not to squawking birds like parrots but to tuneful creatures (*OLD* 2; 5.3.80, a swan) or musical people and places; e.g. 1.2.3 (Helicon), 1.2.225 (Apollo), 5.3.52 (his poet father).

9–10 cedat Phaethontia uulgi | fabula 'let the common people's story about Phaethon give way', i.e. to the parrot's song and by implication to St.'s poem; on *cedere* in encomia see 2.2.61n. The juxtaposition of the grand adjective and *uulgi* humorously dismisses Ovid's Phaethon myth; on the negative literary valence of *uulgi* cf. 1.2.29 *consumpta est fabula uulgi*; N–H on Hor. *Carm.* 1.1.32. *Phaethontius* 'connected with/about Phaethon' is used only by St. here and Silius Italicus (Sil. 7.149, 10.110, 540, 17.496); the more usual form is *Phaethontis*, though the similar *Phaethonteus* occurs once in Ovid; cf. *Met.* 4.246 *post Phaethonteos . . . ignes*, with Bömer. St. refers to the aftermath of Phaethon's death (Ov. *Met.* 2.367–80; cf. Virg. *A.* 10.187–93, with Harrison): Cycnus, Phaethon's kin and lover, was so grief-stricken that he was transformed into the first swan.

10 non soli celebrant sua funera cycni: a humorous comparison between the swan and the parrot, with perhaps a play, given the connection with Phaethon, on the common etymological association between *solus* and *sol* (Maltby s.v. *sol*). On the belief that swans sing most sweetly as death approaches cf. 5.3.80–1; Cic. *Tusc.* 1.30.73; Plin. *Nat.* 10.63; further references in Bömer on Ov. *Fast.* 2.110; Thompson 1936: 180–3. Arnott 1977 claims this is true of the rarer whooper swan, not the mute.   **celebrant:** cf. *Met.* 2.252–3 *et quae Maeonias celebrabant carmine* *ripas | flumineae uolucres*, Ovid's first (anachronistic) mention of swans and an allusion to Lucr. 2.252–3; see Keith 1992: 137–40 for a metaliterary interpretation of Ovid's lines. St. plays here on the dual meaning of this verb as 'celebrate' (*OLD* 3) and 'make famous' (*OLD* 7) with an eye perhaps on the fame of his own 'bird' poem.

11–15 A lavish description of the parrot's cage which imitates the décor of a grand villa; even the parrot's home is mimicry. St. also self-imitates (7n.): the attention to rich materials and to the beauty of the cage (in place of the physical beauty that characterises Corinna's parrot (Ov. *Am.* 2.6.17–22)), and the correlation between the birdcage and its occupant, are familiar themes of St.'s architectural descriptions (e.g. 2.2). The birdcage has 'musical' qualities also; see 11n., 13n., 14n.; Myers 2002: 195–6.

11 at tibi quanta domus 'but what a great house you had' (dat. of possession); the cage is like a mansion, far exceeding the small bird's proportions. *at* is not contrastive with the preceding verses but introduces a new theme with emotional heightening (Håkanson 1969: 72). *domus* is commonly used for birds' nests (*TLL* v 1.1972.18–31); St. uniquely and ironically extends its use to the 'cage' (*TLL* v 1.1972.47–8). Plin. *Nat.* 10.141 complains that the caging of songbirds is a decadent practice contrary to nature.   **rutila testudine fulgens:** typically a parrot's cage was made of wicker (*AP* ix 562.1 λυγοτευχέα); tortoiseshell inlay was a domestic luxury (Mynors on Virg. *G.* 2.463 *uarios . . . pulchra testudine postis*); *rutila* 'glowing golden red' describes its gleam when polished. There is no need to assume that *testudo* here means 'dome' (thus SB, following Van Dam and Vollmer; cf. 2.2.17). Radiance is a typical feature of architectural ecphrasis (introd. to 2.2), a sign of an owner's wealth, taste, and moral and social status; cf. 1.3.53–6, 2.2.85–94, 4.2.26–31; *Theb.* 1.526; 2.3.1n. As a common metonym for the 'lyre' (cf. 5.3.93, with Gibson), *testudo* punningly suggests that this is a musical house for a musical bird. Parrots can sing (after a fashion) as well as talk; see Pond 2006: 200.

12 conexusque ebori uirgarum argenteus ordo 'a silver row of rods connected to ivory', a vividly descriptive line woven together with two elisions; cf. Ov. *Met.* 2.108 (of the Sun's chariot (about to be driven by Phaethon)) *radiorum argenteus ordo*. *uirga*, commonly a 'twig' or 'tree branch' (*OLD* 1), is a metaphor for the delicate 'rods' of a birdcage (cf. Ov. *Ars* 2.209 on a parasol; *OLD* 4) that ironically recalls a bird's natural habitat (Cawsey 1983: 76). *argenteus*, used by St. only here, describes the rods by enallage. Like tortoiseshell, ivory was a luxury material; cf. Ov. *Met.* 2.737 (on royal bedchambers) *ebore et testudine cultos*; N–H on Hor. *Carm.* 2.18.1. Ivory alone, being brittle, would not withstand a parrot's hard beak (Plin. *Nat.* 10.117). An ivory cage would have suited Catullus' sparrow (Mart. 14.77, with Leary), but rods or bars of silver, a hard metal, are necessary for the parrot (Thompson 1936: 337).

13 argutumque 'shrilly', adverbial acc. modifying *stridentia*. On *argutus* as a literary term see Myers 2002: 195.   **stridentia limina:** St. here may mean simply 'threshold' (thus SB), but cf. Virg. *A*. 7.613 (of the doors of the temple of Janus) *stridentia limina*, with Horsfall. *stridere* describes the sound made by grand doors as they open (cf. also Virg. *A*. 1.449; *A*. 6.573); the parrot's hard beak 'grates' on the cage door.   **cornu:** an Ovidian metonym for 'beak' (in place of the usual *rostrum*); cf. Ov. *Met*. 14.503-4 *oraque cornu | indurata rigent*, with Bömer. St. may play upon the more usual meaning of *cornu* as a musical instrument; the gates of Janus open to the sound of bronze horns (Virg. *A*. 7.615 *cornua*), while here the parrot's 'horn' provides the raucous 'music' for its grand cage.

14 et querulae iam sponte fores! 'and the doors now spontaneously making lament!', a hyperbolic exclamation with personification; cf. Ov. *Fast*. 3.642 *querulas . . . fores*. *querulus* is a literary-critical term associated with poetic lament and the origins of elegy (Hinds 1985: 103-4; McKeown on Ov. *Am*. 2.4.27-8; N–H on Hor. *Carm*. 1.33.2). *iam* marks the sudden shift to the mournful present. The sharp contrast between past and present time is frequent in laments; cf. Cat. 3.11 *qui nunc it per iter tenebricosum*.

14-15 uacat ille beatus | carcer: a harsh oxymoron: *beatus* means 'rich' (1.6.49) and also 'fortunate' (*OLD* 1) as the home of such a clever, pampered parrot. But *carcer* 'prison' is surprising; *cauea* is the common word for 'birdcage' (*OLD* 1a; cf. Petr. 28.9 *cauea . . . aurea*). Luc. 4.237 uses *carcer* of a wild animal's cage, Plin. *Nat*. 10.141 pejoratively of an aviary. The parrot's cage paradoxically represents both privilege and enslavement. *uacat* then hints at the bird's release from 'imprisonment', albeit through death, a theme developed at the poem's end. On *ille* see 9n.

15 augusti . . . tecti: cf. 4.2.18 *tectum augustum* (of Domitian's palace, with a playful spin upon the emperor's title 'Augustus'; cf. 4.1.32; Virg. *A*. 7.170 *tectum augustum* (of Latinus' palace). But Courtney and SB read *angusti* for M's *augusti*, following Håkanson 1969: 72, who argues that St. would not have described Domitian's palace in the same way as a parrot's cage. Yet *augusti* reflects the mock-epic character of 2.4 and its play with architectural as well as consolatory themes; part of its humour is the parrot's palatial housing. Myers 2002: 195-6 n. 43 argues that *angustus* is another literary term for the cage associated with elegiac lament; but *augustus* can refer also to a heightened style (*OLD* 3b).   **nusquam conuicia:** *conuicium* can describe usually rather raucous animal or bird sound (*TLL* iv 873.82-874.18); cf. 5.5.67 (an Egyptian slave boy's repartee) *sui conuicia Nili*; Ov. *Met*. 5.676 (magpies) *nemorum conuicia, picae*; *Culex* 209 (the accusatory gnat) *conuicia mortis*; St. ends the description with a bathetic contrast between the grand home and its occupant's 'chatter'. On the theme of the silent house after death cf. 2.1.67-8.

16–23 A summons to other talking birds to attend the parrot's funeral and learn a new song, a dirge for the parrot. Like Ovid, St. parodies the traditional invitation to mourners (5.3.80–99). But Ovid's invitation to the parrot's funeral occurs at the poem's start (*Am.* 2.6.1–12); here it begins the poem's second half. The nightingale is the only bird from St.'s list that also appears in *Am.* 2.6 (7–10). Instead, with the exception of the starling, St.'s birds are drawn from Ovid's *Metamorphoses*, all punished for misuse of speech or art (Dietrich 2002: 101–3).

16 huc doctae stipentur aues 'let learned birds come here in great numbers', a virtual paraphrase of Ov. *Am.* 2.6.2–3 *exsequias ite frequenter, aues*; | *ite, piae uolucres*, except that the birds are *doctae*, an epithet with literary-critical overtones ('scholar birds' SB); cf. 2.5.7 (of the tamed lion) *uastator docte*; McKeown on Ov. *Am.* 2.6.61–2. *doctae* humorously associates birds trained to talk with Callimachean values of learned poetry.   **quis** = *quibus.*

16–17 nobile fandi | ius natura dedit: a grand compliment to the birds. But this *captatio beneuolentiae* hints too at the paradox of the talking bird whose speech may be a natural 'right' but can be exercised only on prompt; cf. Man. 5.380 (on the bird trainer) *uerba praecipiet naturae lege negata.*

17 Phoebeius ales: first in the catalogue of mourners is the raven, probably because it is sacred to Apollo, god of poetry; perhaps too because its dark plumage is the colour of mourning (thus Van Dam). *Phoebeius* is Ovidian and strictly poetic, first appearing at *Met.* 2.544–5 *ales* | . . . *Phoebeius* of the raven who was punished for tattling. Pliny includes it among talking birds; a raven famous for greeting Tiberius, Germanicus and Drusus Caesar each morning from the rostrum was given a grand public funeral (*Nat.* 10.121–3). See Thompson 1936: 159–64; Arnott 2007: 109–12.   **plangat:** beating the breast was a sign of mourning (2.1.169n.); cf. Ov. *Am.* 2.6.3 *et plangite pectora pinnis.*

18–19 auditasque memor penitus demittere uoces | sturnus 'the starling whose memory can absorb by heart the words it has heard'. The starling is the only non-Ovidian bird of the catalogue. On starlings trained to talk see 7n.; Thompson 1936: 334–5; Arnott 2007: 199–200. *memor* occurs only here with the infinitive in the sense of 'having a memory able to' (*OLD* 3b). The strong caesura after *memor* suggests that *penitus* modifies not *memor* 'deeply [mindful]' but *demittere*, in the sense of 'by heart' or 'faithfully' (SB). See the discussion in Van Dam ad loc.

19 Aonio uersae certamine picae 'magpies changed in the Aonian contest', a reference to Ov. *Met.* 5.294–678, the metamorphosis of the Pierides into magpies (or possibly jays; Thompson 1936: 146–8), after their defeat in a poetic competition with the Muses; *uerto* is a key word of Ovidian metamorphosis (*OLD* 23b), used thus ninety-two times in the *Metamorphoses* (Anderson 1963: 2–3). 'Aonian' is a favourite poetic epithet of St. for 'Boeotian', i.e. from Mount Helicon, the chief home of the Muses (2.7.13n.). Plin. *Nat.* 10.118 puts the magpie second to the parrot in imitative skills; cf. Ov. *Met.* 5.299 *imitantes omnia picae*; *Met.* 5.678 *raucaque garrulitas studiumque immane loquendi*; Mart. 14.76 *pica loquax*; Petr. 28.9 (on a magpie that greeted Trimalchio's guests from its golden cage).

20 quique refert iungens iterata uocabula perdix 'and the partridge which echoes words, putting them when repeated into sequence'; i.e. in sentences. Here and at 21 the subject is attracted into the relative clause; cf. 2.2.80. *uocabula* is ἀπὸ κοινοῦ with *refert* and *iungens*. SB objects that the partridge is not a talking bird; also Thompson 1936: 234–8. But St. refers not to the modern species but to Ovid's partridge, known for its garrulity (Ov. *Met.* 8.238 *garrula . . . perdix*); see Bömer on Ov. *Met.* 8.236–59 p. 84. Perdix, Daedalus' talented nephew, was murdered by his jealous uncle; Athena saved his life by changing him to a bird. *iungens* may refer to Perdix's talent in 'joining' as inventor of the compass (Ov. *Met.* 8.247–9) and now as a bird able to 'join' words in sentences.

21 et quae Bistonio queritur soror orba cubili: an allusion to the myth of Procne, Philomela and Tereus, who were changed into birds (2.1.140n.); cf. Ov. *Am.* 2.6.7 *quod scelus Ismarii quereris, Philomela, tyranni*. St. draws attention to the close imitation: second foot *Bistonio* echoes Ovid's *Ismarii* (*Am.* 2.6.7), both poetic epithets for 'Thracian' (Tereus' nationality) in the same metrical position and followed respectively by *queritur/quereris*, which neatly conflates the natural sound of birds (*OLD* 4) and lamentation (Colton 1967: 75). But Ovid does not specify which bird is meant by 'Philomela'. Tradition varies as to whether she is the swallow or the nightingale (Bömer on Ov. *Met.* 6.677; McKeown on Ov. *Am.* 2.6.7–10), though the nightingale is a likely candidate in *Am.* 2.6, given its fame since Hesiod as songster, often with metapoetic significance (Steiner 2007). St. is also not specific about which *sister* is meant. If *orba* is taken in conjunction with abl. *cubili* to mean 'bereft of her bedroom [i.e. marriage]', then Procne, Tereus' wife, is meant; if taken absolutely in the sense of 'desolate', with *cubili . . . Bistonio* as abl. of place (thus SB), then either sister could be meant. With his ambiguous 'bereft sister' St., like Ovid, slyly comments on the frequent confusion in Latin literature between the sisters and the birds.

22 ferte simul gemitus 'voice your laments together'; cf. 2.1.35 *confer gemitus*. This is an unusual sense of *ferre gemitus* which normally means 'to endure sorrow'; cf. *Theb.* 6.438–9 *prior Hippodamus fert ora sequentum, | fert gemitus. gemitus* here conflates bird sounds (*OLD* 1b; Plin. *Nat.* 18.267) with human groans.

22–3 cognataque . . . | funera 'your relative's corpse' (2.1.22n.), for the parrot is 'kin' with other talking birds.

23 cunctae: i.e. *doctae . . . aues* (16); *auis* is grammatically feminine. *cunctae* is higher in the poetic register than *omnes* and starts the alliterative tenor of the line.   **miserandum . . . carmen** 'lament'; *miserandum* is virtually active in sense here, meaning 'causing tears' or 'worthy of tears'. This wording occurs elswhere only at Man. 5.559 (the halycons' lament for Andromeda) *miserando carmine*; cf. Virg. *G.* 4.514 *miserabile carmen*; *Epic. Drusi* 3 *miserabile . . . carmen*. The allusion to Manilius is pointed, for Andromeda is rescued from death and made immortal; on the parrot's immortality see 37n.   **addiscite** 'learn in addition', i.e. to the songs or sounds you already know. An uncommon word, introduced to poetry by Ovid (*Am.* 2.5.56, with McKeown; *Met.* 3.593), and occurring elsewhere in poetry only here and at 3.1.151. Pliny uses it as a technical term for birds learning to talk (*Nat.* 10.119, 124). Playing upon the birds' ability to imitate, not create, St. commands the birds to learn a song he has himself composed; cf. 5.3.80–5, a complaint that mourning birds make hackneyed laments.

24–37 The poem ends wittily with a song within a song, a frequent Ovidian narrative device but a new approach here to the 'dead bird' poem. As Colton 1967: 75 points out, St. expands into full-fledged song Ov. *Am.* 2.6.6 *resonent carmina uestra*.

24–5 occidit . . . | psittacus: cf. Ov. *Am.* 2.6.1–2 *psittacus . . . | occidit*; 1n. St. reverses the Ovidian word order and begins with the solemn *occidit*; he extends Ovid's opening line and a half into a ten-line period with a series of relative clauses (25–33).

24 aeriae celeberrima gloria gentis, a mock-heroic periphrasis; cf. Ov. *Am.* 2.6.20 *auium gloria*. Melior's parrot is the most famous (*celeberrima*) of all 'poetic' birds.

25 psittacus, ille: 9n.   **plagae uiridis regnator Eoae** 'green sovereign of the Eastern region', a grandiloquent variation of *dux uolucrum* (1), though simple 'green' for Ovid's rather gaudy colours (*Am.* 2.6.21–2) adds some comic bathos. *regnator* is an elevated poetic word for 'ruler' and one who is 'supreme in one's class'; e.g. Alexander the Great (4.6.59–60, 4.6.106), Domitian (4.2.14), Pindar (4.7.5). The Romans seem to have known only green parrots which came from India; cf. Ov. *Am.* 2.6.1 *Eois imitatrix ales ab Indis*; Plin. *Nat.* 10.117 *India hanc auem mittit*; McKeown on Ov. *Am.* 2.6.21–2; Arnott 2007: 201. *Eous*, a poetic epithet, loosely describes regions east from Rome, including India.

26–7 quem non . . . | uinceret inceret aspectu: the parrot is praised through comparison with three birds that were highly prized in Rome, the peacock, the pheasant and the guinea fowl (Plin. *Nat.* 10.132); they are described in periphrastic style without being directly named. The imperf. potential subj. *uinceret* ('would [not] have surpassed', *NLS* 121) governs all three birds and is followed by the abl. of respect. Strictly speaking *aspectu* refers to the peacock, alone prized for its looks; but the two other birds, though not singled out by ancient writers for beauty (the golden pheasant seems to have been unknown), can be said to be striking to look at as exotic birds, marvels of empire. Pheasants, guinea fowls and parrots appeared in the great procession of Ptolemy Philadelphus in Alexandria as exotic breeds (Athen. 10.387d).

26 gemmata uolucris Iunonia cauda 'Juno's bird with her jewelled tail', i.e. the peacock, a beautiful chiastic phrase for a striking bird. Juno created the peacock's tail from the hundred eyes of Argus (Ov. *Met.* 1.668–723); cf. Ov. *Met.* 1.723 *gemmis caudam stellantibus implet. Iunonia* is a relatively rare Virgilian epithet (cf. Virg. *A.* 1.671), first used by Ovid of the peacock; cf. Ov. *Am.* 2.6.55 *ales Iunonia*, with McKeown. Although St. refers to the male, he follows Ovid in retaining the normal feminine gender of birds in Latin (23n.). The peacock was bred for show and for the Roman table, the orator Hortensius being the first to serve peacock as a dish (Plin. *Nat.* 10.43–5). On peacocks see Arnott 2007: 235–8.

27 gelidi . . . Phasidis ales: the pheasant, named from the river Phasis, the wild bird's main breeding ground; it flows into the Black Sea at Colchis, hence 'cold'; cf. 1.6.77 *horridusque Phasis*. The pheasant was domesticated early on and bred as a gourmet item, being a delicacy of Eastern kings (Thompson 1936: 298– 300; Arnott 2007: 186–7). Pheasants and partridges were distributed as special gifts to the people at Domitian's Saturnalian spectacle (1.6.75–80). But at the refined dinner party of Vindex, *Phasidis ales* was rejected as unsuitable fare for the discriminating intellectual (4.6.8).

28 nec quas umenti Numidae rapuere sub austro 'nor those whom the Numidians living beneath the wet south wind have culled', a syntactic shift to a relative clause; *eae* should be understood before *quas*. Guinea fowl were hunted as delicacies in Numidia, North Africa (Var. *R.* 3.9.18 *gallinae Africanae*; Plin. *Nat.* 10.132 *Numidicae*; Thompson 1936: 198–200; Arnott 2007: 138–40). This line is almost identical to 1.6.78 *quas udo Numidae legunt sub austro*; like pheasants, guinea fowl were special prizes at Domitian's Saturnalia. St. humorously undercuts the dignity of the lament by hinting at the birds' current imperial value as culinary delicacies – even parrots were not exempt from the table (Thompson 1936: 337; Plin. *Nat.* 10.141–2 condemns the actor Asopus for eating a dish of talking/songbirds valued at 100,000 sesterces). The guinea fowl is also fittingly cited in a lament; after his death Meleager's grieving sisters were changed to guinea fowl (Bömer on Ov. *Met.* 8.533–46 p. 167; cf. *Epic. Drusi* 109–10).   **umenti . . . sub austro:** *umenti* contrasts with *gelidi* (27); similarly Man. 5.375–6 cites Phasis and Numidia together as representative of the geographical extremes sought by the Romans for luxury foods. Climate change has made North Africa much dryer than it was in St.'s lifetime; on the *Auster* see 2.1.106n.

29 ille: 9n.   **salutator regum:** cf. Mart. 14.74.1 *corue salutator*, the first appearance in poetry of the rare prose *salutator*. As today, talking birds commonly learned to greet people; cf. Mart. 14.76.1 *pica loquax certa dominum te uoce saluto*; Petr. 28.9 *pica uaria intrantes salutabat*; Pers. *prol.* 8 *quis expediuit psittaco suum chaere?*

Melior's parrot is unlikely to have encountered kings! But *regum* is in keeping with the poem's hyperbolic style.

29–30 nomenque locutus | Caesareum: a pompous circumlocution for the commonplace *aue Caesar*, often taught talking birds; cf. Plin. *Nat.* 10.117 *imperatores salutat*; Mart. 14.73.2 (of the raven) *hoc didici per me dicere: 'Caesar haue'*, with Leary; *AP* IX 562.3–4 of an escaped parrot that taught the wild birds 'hail Caesar'. *Caesareus*, of Greek origin (Καισάρειος), is a grand poetic epithet first used in Latin poetry at Ov. *Met.* 1.201 (cf. *Fast.* 1.282); cf. 5.3.229. On adjectives ending in *-eus* see 2.1.144n.

30 queruli quondam uice functus amici 'having now performed the role of mourning friend'; cf. Cat. 2.7 *et solaciolum sui doloris. querulus* conflates the sound of a bird with that of lament (21n.); cf. Ov. *Tr.* 5.1.60 *querulam Procnen. quondam*, correlated with *nunc* in the following line, is unusual (K–S 73). Like *modo . . . modo*, *quondam . . . nunc* suggests not one occasion but repetitive action and contrasting roles; the parrot was 'now' a mourner, 'now' a jester. As a sympathetic friend, it has here a similar role to St., who shared in Melior's grief for Glaucias (2.1) and Blaesus (2.3.76–7).

31 nunc conuiua leuis: a light-hearted play on *leuis* in the sense of 'light in weight' and 'lightweight'; the parrot made an amusing dinner guest. Cf. 4–7.

31–2 monstrataque reddere uerba | tam facilis 'so quick to repeat the words it had been taught', a witty echo of lines 7–8. *monstrare* means 'teach by example' (*OLD* 2).

32–3 quo tu, Melior dilecte, recluso | numquam solus eras 'with whom, when it had been set free from its cage, you, beloved Melior, were never alone'. A sudden shift of address to Melior, named for the first time in the poem; like Lesbia's sparrow (Cat. 3.8–10), the parrot too was a constant companion. *recluso* 'set free' (*OLD recludo* 4) is a bathetic reminder that the 'green sovereign' (25) was a caged bird, entirely subject to its master's wishes. *dilecte* lightly plays on the amatory context of the Catullan/Ovidian parrot poems, here adapted to the social needs of the aspiring poet for a patron's friendship; cf. 1.5.9 *dilecto uolo lasciuire sodali*.

33–4 at non inglorius umbris | mittitur: litotes; the parrot will have a funeral (and a dirge) worthy of a hero; by contrast a tiny inscribed stone (Ov. *Am.* 2.6.60 *lapis exiguus*) marks the grave of Corinna's parrot. The funeral is a unique feature of St.'s parrot poem. Lesbia's sparrow is swallowed up by the Underworld (Cat. 3.11–14); Corinna's parrot goes directly to 'the grove of pious birds' in Elysium (Ov. *Am.* 2.6.49–62). The pres. tense suggests the performative nature of the song that accompanies the funeral procession.

at here is an adversative particle marking the start of consolation proper (Van Dam).

34 Assyrio cineres adolentur amomo: a redolent line with the suggestion of lament in the prominent alliteration of *a*; cf. Virg. *Ecl.* 4.25 *Assyrium . . . amomum*, a feature of the Golden Age connoting rarity and opulence; Tib. 1.3.7 *Assyrios . . . odores*, with Maltby; N–H on Hor. *Carm.* 2.11.16. The parrot has an expensive funeral. *amomum* may be cardamon, a costly, sweet-smelling spice from a Syrian shrub (Coleman on *Ecl.* 3.89; contra Clausen); but identification of Eastern spices and perfumes is often impossible (2.1.160n.); they are appropriate here for a bird that came from India. *adolere* is a solemn ritual verb for 'burn' (Clausen on Virg. *Ecl.* 8.65); *cineres* reverses the chronological order of the cremation. But St. perhaps anticipates the poem's ending, when the parrot becomes a phoenix from the scented ashes; the particular framing of this line recalls Ov. *Met.* 15.393–4 (on the phoenix) *Assyrii Phoenica uocant . . . | suco uiuit amomi*; see 37n.

35 et tenues Arabum respirant gramine plumae 'his slender feathers breathe with herbs from the Arabians', another resonant line; cf. Prop. 2.29.17 *Arabum de gramine odores* (*gramen* = 'herb' *OLD* 2); 2.1.16tn. The abl. with this sense of *respirare* is unprecedented (*OLD* 3d). *tenues* marks the contrast between the grand funeral and the small parrot; it is also a frequent literary-critical term for elegiac or non-epic poetry, the equivalent of Callimachus' λεπτός (*Aet.* 1 fr. 1.11 Pf.; McKeown on Ov. *Am.* 1.1.17–18). The parrot's body is associated with literary theme and style; its slender feathers drenched with exotic perfume are an emblem of the 'pumped up' parrot poem.

36 Sicaniisque crocis 'saffron', a sweet-smelling plant for attracting bees (Virg. *G.* 4.182). *Sicanius* is a poetic adjective for 'Sicilian'. In antiquity Sicilian saffron was highly prized after the most famous Cicilian (Plin. *Nat.* 21.31).

36–7 senio nec fessus inerti | scandet odoratos phoenix felicior ignes 'unwearied by sluggish old age it will ascend the scented pyre, a more fortunate phoenix'. Escaping the evils of old age was a commonplace of consolation for early death. *nec* modifies *fessus*, not *scandet* as Van Dam takes it (translating 'and the phoenix, tired by old age, will not mount his fragrant pyre more happily'), thus missing the parrot's 'metamorphosis'; cf. 5.3.258–9 (of St.'s father) *nec segnis labe senili | exitus*. On *fessus* see 2.1.16n.

37 phoenix: the metamorphosis of the parrot makes final acknowledgment of Ovid, who gave a full account of the phoenix, widely accepted in antiquity as an authentic bird (*Met.* 15.391–407; cf. Hdt. 2.73; Plin. *Nat.* 10.3–5; Tac. *Ann.* 6.28.6). When it grew old, it built a nest which was both funeral pyre and cradle in that a new phoenix was born from the ashes. As an example of extremely long life (500 or 1,000 years; Howell on Mart. 5.7.2) and of regeneration, the phoenix was associated with consolation (2.6.87–8n.). Ov. *Am.* 2.6.61–2 has an epitaphic ending in which the parrot 'speaks' again (Ramsby 2005: 369–73); 2.4 closes with the poet's large claims for the parrot and his 'light' (2 *pr.* 15) poem: they will be unique, as only one phoenix exists at any one time (Ov. *Am.* 2.6.54 *unica semper auis*). The metamorphosis moreover gives the parrot and his poem immortality.   **felicior** 'more fortunate' because, unlike the phoenix, it will not grow old; and because it will now never truly die. The comparative adjective is also a final gesture of one-upmanship over Ovid; Corinna's parrot meets the phoenix in Elysium (Ov. *Am.* 2.6.54), whereas Melior's parrot becomes a phoenix (and thus even more 'fortunate'); cf. 3.4.12 *Pergame, pinifera multum felicior Ida*, a similar expression of literary rivalry with Cat. 63 (Vout 2007: 192–3); Mart. 1.7.4–5 (the superiority of Stella's 'dove' poem to Catullus' *passer*) *tanto Stella meus tuo Catullo | quanto passere maior est columba*. St. may respond also to Mart. 5.37 (published 89/90 CE; Howell on Mart. 5 pp. 2–3), which begins with a string of comparative adjectives (5.37.1–3; cf. 1.109.1–4) and cites *indecens . . . pauo | . . . et frequens phoenix* as commonplace poetic comparisons; see Kenney 1964. Is this St.'s response to Martial as well as to Catullus and Ovid, that he can give conventional symbols new life? Is 'Melior's parrot' a *better* 'bird' poem?

Siluae 2.5

The occasion for this poem is the unscripted death of a tame lion at an animal show in the most famous of Flavian monuments, the Colosseum. The amphitheatre is usually associated with the mass slaughter of wild animals (e.g. Sen. *Ep.* 7.2–5; Futtrell 1997; Kyle 1998); yet a day at the Colosseum was generally varied (Potter 1999: 303–5). Parades of exotic animals (Calp. *Ecl.* 7.57–72) and performances of trained animal catered to the Roman fascination with *mirabilia*; animal trainers at Rome were highly skilled (Sen. *Ep.* 85.41; Plut. *Mor.* 968b–e; Plin. *Nat.* 8.2–3; Beagon 1992: 128–9). The display of lions in Rome had a long history, the earliest recorded show being a hunt with lions and panthers put on by M. Fulvius Nobilior in 186 BCE (Livy 39.22.1–2). A poem on the death of a *tamed* lion is unusual; the closest parallels are Mart. *Sp.*12 on a lion that turned traitor to its trainer; Mart. *Sp.* 21 on a tamed tigress that mauled a wild lion; Mart. 8.53 on the death of a lion in a wild beast hunt lacks St.'s sympathy (Watson and Watson 179–80). St. provides an eyewitness account of the lion's death (2 *pr.* 16–18). A sense of immediacy permeates 2.5, which assumes an audience's familiarity with the events it vividly recreates (11n.).

St. ventures here into the territory of Martial, who had made the 'arena' poem his own with the *Liber spectaculorum*. But 2.5 is longer than a traditional epigram (though the shortest poem in book 2). Since the lion is a more substantial animal than the parrot, a symbol of royalty and the epic animal *par excellence* with a long tradition of admirable human traits such as courage and clemency (Howell on Mart. 1.14.6), 2.5 plays extensively with epic themes and conventions, esp. with the

Thebaid, a reminder of St.'s prowess as an epic poet here wittily displayed on the small scale. It also plays upon an imperial literary subgenre that flourished in this period, *exitus illustrium uirorum* (Plin. *Ep.* 8.12.4; Coleman 2000: 22–3; Marx 1937–8; Martin and Woodman 128; Ash 1999: 87; N–P IV 344–5). The lion's heroic stand against the odds reflects contemporary interest in this new type of 'biography' in which death (ordered or encouraged by the emperor) was often constructed as a performance, with an appreciative audience or readership (Edwards 2007: 144–60).

The success of the games largely depended on the emperor's generosity and behaviour as seen by the crowd (Hopkins 1983: 15–20). Domitian was known for his splendid shows in the amphitheatre (Suet. *Dom.* 4.1 *spectacula assidue magnifica et sumptuosa edidit*). But in contrast to 1.6 on the Saturnalian games, with its focus on the emperor's beneficent presence, in 2.5 Domitian is observer, not stage-manager. And whereas in Martial's epigrams, esp. those on the lion, the arena is the venue for imperial panegyric (Coleman on Mart. *Sp.* pp. lxxi–lxxii), in 2.5 Domitian is absent till the end and his portrayal is enigmatic (30n.). The tone of 2.5 is thus hard to gauge; partly an epicising *jeu d'esprit*, it also conveys sympathy for the lion through its consistent anthropomorphism. The art/nature theme is problematised in the arena; unlike in Pollius' villa, art seems destructive, not beneficial.

2.5 falls into two symmetrical parts, first a lament that the animal was mortally injured (1–15), and then consolation in its heroic manner of death (16–30).

Further reading: on lions in antiquity and in literary tradition see Plin. *Nat.* 8.41–58; Toynbee 1973: 16–19, 61–9; Zaganiaris 1977; on animal shows Jennison 1937: 60–82; on the Colosseum and on imperial spectacle as an instrument of propaganda and a feature of panegyric Coleman on Mart. *Sp.* pp. lxv–lxxv, lxxix–lxxxi. For discussions of 2.5: Herrlinger 1930: 70–1; Cancik 1971; Garvey 1989; Nauta 2002: 402–4; Newlands 2005; Augoustakis 2007.

1–15 Lament for the fallen lion.

1 Quid tibi . . . mansuescere profuit? St. abruptly starts the poem with a series of questions organised in a *tricolon crescens* (1–6) that conveys rising indignation; cf. 5.1.154–5 *quid probitas aut casta fides, quid numina prosunt | culta deum*? The questioning of the value of a life is a feature of laments going back to Homer (*Il.* 6.145–9; N–H on Hor. *Carm.* 1.28.40), but is unusual here in being addressed to the deceased, not the bereaved; *tibi* is the lion, treated from the start in an anthropomorphic manner. St. here introduces the poem's theme of the relationship between nature and culture.   **monstrata . . . ira** 'once your anger had been displayed' (ablative abs.). Courtney argues that M's *monstrata* is an error created by similarity with 2.4.31 *monstrataque . . . uerba*; the humanist reading *constrata* is preferable; i.e. once the lion's anger had been 'calmed', it then became tame. But this sense of *consternere* occurs in classical Latin poetry only at Man.

3.652 of the calming of the sea (*OLD* 3a); *constrata . . . ira* would be a very bold metaphor. *monstrata* is surely an etymological pun: *monstrum*, a term for a lion (cf. Mart. 4.57.5, 5.65.9), was commonly derived from *monstrare* (Maltby s.v. *monstrum*). St. withholds the word 'lion' to the end (30), but hints at its identity by typical initial name play (2 *pr.* 1n.), here with pleasing alliteration. The juxtaposition of *monstrata* with *mansuescere* emphasises the slippage between the lion's true nature and its acquired gentle behaviour.   **ira:** anger is a standard attribute of the lion; cf. Lucr. 3.296–8 *in primis uis est uiolenta leonum, | pectora qui fremitu rumpunt plerumque gementes | nec capere irarum fluctus in pectore possunt*; *Theb.* 12.740 *magnos alit ira leones*; N–H on Hor. *Carm.* 1.16.15.   **mansuescere:** the verb is intransitive = 'to become tame' (*OLD* 1a), an opening reference perhaps to the title accorded this poem at 2 *pr.* 16 *leo mansuetus*.

2 quid: sc. *profuit*; also at 4. Repetition of *quid* (1, 4) punctuates the tricolon.   **scelus humanasque . . . caedes** 'the crime of human slaughter' (hendiadys). In anthropomorphic terms, the lion's natural desire to kill is presented as morally wrong.   **dediscere** 'to unlearn'. The verb first occurs in Roman poetry at Ov. *Rem.* 211 with the specific meaning of forgetting important acquired skills; cf. 5.3.6–7 *quicquid ab Ismariis monstrarat collibus Euhan, | dedidici*; Ov. *Tr.* 3.16.16, 5.5.6, 5.12.57. 'Unlearning' natural rather than tamed behaviour thus hints at the perversity of taming a lion. Cf. Mart. 2.75.3 (a more conventional use) *leo dedidicit pacem subito feritate reuersa*.

3 imperiumque: a grand word with political overtones of 'supreme administrative power' (*OLD* 1), a reminder that the lion, though subject to a trainer, belongs to Domitian.   **pati et . . . parere:** alliterative plosives convey the poet's indignation; the infinitives emphasise the tamed lion's passivity. Seneca criticises the tamed lion (decked out with gilded mane) as docile but lethargic, compared to one of unbroken spirit; cf. *Ep.* 41.6 *leo aurata iuba mittitur, dum contractatur et ad patientiam recipiendi ornamenti cogitur fatigatus, aliter incultus, integri spiritus*; see Augoustakis 2007: 210–13.   **domino . . . minori** 'an inferior manager' (*OLD dominus* 2), i.e. less bold than the lion. The common name for an animal trainer was not *dominus* but *magister* (*OLD* 6a; Coleman on Mart. *Sp.* 12.1). St. makes antonymic play here on the etymology of *magister* from *magis* (Paul. Fest. p. 126 Lindsay *magistri . . . quia omnes hi magis ceteris possunt*; Maltby s.v. *magister*), emphasised by the echo of *minor* in *domino*; paradoxically the trainer can do 'less' than the 'king of the beasts', despite its lowly lot in captivity; cf. 3.3.74–5 on the trainer as tyrant; Sen. *Ep.* 85.41 on the trainer as a model of the *sapiens*.

4–5 quid quod . . . suetus: sc. *eras*. St. shifts from infinitives with *profuit* (here understood) to a following noun clause (*NLS* 210); *quid quod* is a transitional prosaic formula; see N–H on Hor. *Carm.* 2.18.23, where, as here, it introduces a worse alternative (the lion's demeaning series of tricks, 4–6).

4 domo: a unique euphemism for the lion's cage; *domus* generally applies to natural habitat; see 2.4.11n. Animals were forced by blazing straw from their cages along the passages into the arena (Jennison 1937: 159–61).   **claustra:** an ironic word for 'cage' connoting 'a prison' (*TLL* III 1320.81–1321.9); cf. 2.4.14– 15n.; Livy 42.59.2 *Thraces, haud secus quam diu claustris retentae ferae.* St. stresses the marvel that the lion voluntarily returns to captivity.   **reuerti** 'to return', deponent as usual in the pres. system.

5 a capta iam sponte recedere praeda: the lion's most common 'prey' for this trick was the hare; cf. Mart. 1.6, 14, 22, 48, 51, 60, 104. *iam* goes closely with *capta*; the lion refused the easy gift of a hare that 'had already been captured'. In variations of this trick the hare would play around the lion's paws and even in its mouth; cf. Mart. 1.6.4. The lion was well fed beforehand, so the small hare would be of little interest (Howell on Mart. 1.6, p.119). On Martial's 'lion and hare' cycle see Lorenz 2002: 126–34.   **sponte** emphasises the marvel of the lion's restraint; cf. Mart. 1.14.5–6 *unde potest auidus captae leo parcere praedae? | sed tamen esse tuus dicitur: ergo potest,* a piece of flattery that identifies the lion with the emperor in clemency; cf. Mart. 1.6.5–6, 1.104.21–2. By contrast St. does not use the lion as a pivot for imperial adulation.

6 insertasque manus: cf. Mart. 2.75.2 *insertamque pati blandus in ora manum*; Sen. *Ben.* 1.2.5; *Ep.* 85.41 (on common animal tricks) *leonibus magister manum insertat, osculatur tigrim suus custos, elephantum minimus Aethiops iubet subsidere in genua et ambulare per funem.* St. rounds off the tricolon with recall in *manus* of *mansuescere* (1); a tame lion is one 'accustomed to the hand'.   **laxo . . . morsu** 'with relaxed jaw'; cf. Mart. 1.104.16–18 (of hares playing within lions' jaws) *et securior est in ore praeda, | laxos cui dare peruiosque rictus | gaudent.*

7 occidis: a blunt opening verb, heading a heavily spondaic line, conveys the finality of the animal's death; cf. 2.4.24; Ov. *Am.* 2.6.1.   **altarum uasta- tor docte ferarum** 'educated ravager of tall beasts' (SB), a grand oxymoronic periphrasis, with heavy *r* assonance and 'leonine' rhyme. *uastator* is a predom- inantly poetic word first found at Virg. *A.* 9.772 (of a hunter); cf. *Ach.* 2.32 (of Achilles). Ov. *Met.* 9.192 first uses it of a wild animal; cf. *Silv.* 4.6.41 (of the Nemean lion) *uastator Nemees,* perhaps an ironic nod to the phrase here.   **altarum:** a grand, rare Virgilian epithet, used of horses at Virg. *A.* 7.624–5 *pars arduus altis | . . . equis furit,* with emphasis on the horses' elevation of their riders; cf. *Theb.* 7.755–6. Otherwise this is an odd adjective for large animals (*TLL* I 1774.80– 1775.2), the lion itself not being esp. 'tall'. Perhaps it means that the lion naturally preys on animals that are its match or more so in height, rather than on tiny hares; cf. Mart. 1.22.3 *seruantur magnis isti ceruicibus ungues,* with Howell.   **docte:** an ironic recall of *dediscere* (2); cf. 2.4.16 *doctae . . . aues.* The epithet means 'trained in an art' (N–H on Hor. *Carm.* 1.1.29), not of killing in the arena (Van Dam) but of performing tricks; the paradoxical contrast with *uastator* highlights the disjunction between the lion's true nature and its 'civilised' state.

8–10 Three methods of hunting lions: surrounding the animal with nets (8); making a ring of spears over which the cornered animal tries to jump (9); and digging a hidden pit (10). Ironically the lion was not killed when it was hunted or later in a *uenatio* staged in the amphitheatre; Rome, not the North African desert, provides the place and means of its death. On the popular *uenationes* of the amphitheatre see Coleman on Mart. *Sp.* pp. lxxii–lxxiii.

8 non grege Massylo: the Massylians were a North African tribe skilled in hunting (Virg. *A.* 4.132; Plin. *Nat.* 5.3). *Massylus* is often used in connection with the lion; cf. *Theb.* 2.675–81, 5.332; 8.124–6, 11.27–9; Mart. 9.71.1 *Massyli leo fama iugi.* **curuaque indagine clausus:** a ring of nets thrown round a wood to prevent the escape of game; cf. *Theb.* 2.553–4 *clausas indagine | ...feras*; *Ach.* 1.459–60 *sic curua feras indago latente | claudit.* The ring perhaps recalls the oval shape of the amphitheatre (Garvey 1989: 629–30). It often appears on hunting mosaics; see Coleman, on Mart. *Sp.* plate 25.

9 non formidato supra uenabula saltu 'not with dreaded leap over the hunting spears'; cf. Virg. *A.* 9.551–3 *ut fera, quae densa uenantum saepta corona | contra tela furit... | et saltu supra uenabula fertur*, with Hardie. *formidato* expresses the hunters' viewpoint; the lion's leap over the spears is a terrifying but admirable show of prowess.

10 incitus 'rushing headlong' or 'plunging' (over the spears), rare and poetic.   **aut caeco foueae deceptus hiatu** 'or deceived by the pit's hidden cavity'. *fouea* means a 'pit with a concealed mouth used to trap game', the most common method of capturing a lion according to Plin. *Nat.* 8.54 *capere eos ardui erat quondam operis, foueisque maxime. caeco* in the sense of 'concealed' is rather pleonastic but this adjective often implies treachery (*OLD* 9); *hiatus* 'cavity' plays on the common meaning of a 'wide-open mouth' or 'jaws' (*OLD* 3); cf. Lucr. 5.24 *magnus hiatus ille leoni.* Such language hints that human cunning is to be feared more than the bite of animals. *deceptus* plays on *captus*; a wild lion, innocent of human wiles, is captured by deception.

11 uictus fugiente fera: an even greater humiliation than being captured by hunters: in an unscripted accident the lion is mortally wounded by an animal which flees. Alliteration of *f* expresses contempt for its cowardice, a sign that animals in captivity can act in perverse ways (see Coleman on Mart. *Sp.* 21.6, an epigram in which a 'tame' tigress unexpectedly kills a *wild* lion in the arena). Van Dam, following Cancik 1971: 79, suggests that the lion was killed in a real fight. But the lion was trained to perform harmless tricks, not to kill (1–6). Having written this poem on the spot, St. assumes in the first instance a knowledgeable audience and does not specify either the site of the fatal wound (Jennison 1937:

80 suggests the lower backbone as the lion's weak spot), or which animal dealt the mortal blow; a range of animals including a snake, an antelope, an elephant or another lion have been proposed; see Van Dam ad loc; Augoustakis 2007: 214–15.

11–12 stat cardine aperto | infelix cauea 'the luckless cage stands open-doored'. On initial *stat* see 2.3.1–2n. *cardo*, the door's 'hinge' (Austin on Virg. *A.* 1.449), is synecdoche for 'door'; the epithet *infelix* is transferred from lion to cage. On *cauea* see 2.4.14–15n.

12 clausis circum undique portis 'when the gates had been closed all around', an old conjecture adopted by SB for M's *clausas circum undique portas* ('all around the closed gates'), which seems not to describe the lions *within* their cages, the required sense. See the full discussion in Van Dam ad loc. There were various methods of bringing cages into the arena, most commonly raising them on windlasses or placing them in recesses, such as those extant in the podium wall of the Colosseum; see Jennison 1937: 159.

13 licuisse nefas: a sharp antithesis suggesting this unplanned killing represents a perversion of the natural and indeed moral order. *nefas* 'abomination' is a leitmotiv of the fraternal conflict in the *Thebaid* (Ganiban 2007: 33–43). The perfect infinitive occurs in indirect statement after a verb of emotion, here *tumuere* (K–S 691–2).   **placidi tumuere leones:** another paradox; cf. Mart. 1.22 *saeua . . . placidi . . . ora leonis. placidi* means these lions too were tamed, but *tumuere* hints at their true nature, 'swelling' being a sign of anger in animals and humans; cf. Virg. *A.* 2.381 (a snake) *attollentem iras et caerula colla tumentem*, with Austin; *Theb.* 3.599–600 (Capaneus) *longam pridem indignantia pacem | corda tumens*. On 'swelling' as part of the lexicon of anger see Braund and Gilbert 2003: 280–1. M reads *timuere*, which does not make sense with *licuisse* and removes the paradox of the tame lion.

14 cecidere iubae: the lions are 'crestfallen', their shame (*puduitque*) expressed physically by their falling manes. By contrast, the rising of manes was thought to suggest fear or excitement; cf. Virg. *A.* 10.726 (*leo*) *comas arrexit*, with Harrison; Luc. 1.209 *erexitque iubam; Theb.* 4. 678–9 *Hyrcanae ad signa iugales | intumuere iubas.*

14–15 puduitque relatum | aspicere 'they [*sc.* the lions] were ashamed to see him brought back', compressed syntax; cf. Livy 9.44.15 *consulem cum uolnere graui relatum in castra.* In an inversion of the traditional epic comparison of heroes to animals the lion is treated like a fallen warrior whose body is ceremonially carried back to base, a military sense of *referre (OLD* 1a); see 19–23n.

15 totas duxere in lumina frontes 'they drew their entire brows over their eyes', a gesture indicating shame (Ael. *NA* 3.1) that is true to the lion's appearance as carefully depicted by ancient artists – the markings on its forehead resemble a frown; see Toynbee 1973: 65–6, with plates 18, 20. St. may allude ironically to the Homeric simile (*Il.* 17.132–6) in which Ajax, protecting the body of Patroclus, is compared to a powerful lion protecting its young from hunters and drawing down its brow to hide its eyes, a gesture of angry self-protection as missiles are hurled at it.

16–30 Consolation: the lion's glorious death. St. backtracks in time to describe the lion's dying moments, modelled on the heroic idea of a glorious death (Edwards 2007: 19–28); the lion recovers its natural aggression and goes down fighting. The idea that a person's manner of death vindicates his character became an important imperial literary theme; cf. Luc. 8.621 (of Pompey) *seque probat moriens.* Ironically, when the tamed lion here reverts to 'nature', it reveals its true nobility and courage and acts like an epic hero. The lion's 'last stand' evokes several epic deaths: of the weak, elderly Priam attempting to kill Neoptolemus (Virg. *A.* 2.506–58); of the wounded Mezentius attempting to avenge his son (Virg. *A.* 10.762–908); and of Eteocles and Polynices fighting one another in defiance of their wounds (*Theb.* 11.539–73); on allusions to the *Thebaid* see 13n., 18n., 19–23n.; Augoustakis 2007: 215–19. The death of Paulus in battle (Sil. 10.1–308) also provides suggestive parallels: when mortally wounded, Paulus strikes a last fatal blow; epic similes compare him to a wild animal surrounded by hunters and braving death (Sil. 10.1–5); to a fierce lion (Sil. 10.17–24); to a wounded lion in the arena (Sil. 10.241–6); to a dying tigress still however raging (Sil. 10.292–7).

16 at non te: contrastive *at* and the three monosyllables marks the shift to consolation at the exact mid-point of the poem.   **primo fusum . . . ictu:** concessive 'though laid low by the first blow' (*OLD fundo* 13b) – a humiliation that does not however stop the lion from trying to retaliate.   **obruit:** the compulsive force of this verb contrasts with the passivity expressed by *fusum*: the lion was laid low but not crushed by shame.

16–17 nouus . . . | ille pudor: shame is 'new' because the 'king of the beasts' is not used to humiliation. On *pudor* as a key emotion in Roman culture see Kaster 2005: 28–65, esp. 29: since those who value honour highly feel shame intensely, *pudor* can be a goad to virtue; Mezentius is spurred to heroic action by *ingens . . . pudor* (Virg. *A.* 10.870–1).

17 uirtus: the *mot juste* of the heroic warrior (*OLD* 1b), a striking anthropomorphism here; cf. Lucr. 5.863 *genus acre leonum . . . tutatast uirtus, uulpis dolus.*   **cadenti:** the pres. participle vividly dramatises the surprising moment when courage returns to the lion even as it falls to the ground.

18 a media iam morte 'from the midst of death'; cf. Virg. *A.* 2.533 (Priam's death) *in media iam morte*, with Austin; Gibson on 5.1.172. The phrase 'the middle of death' occurs in the *Thebaid* to emphasise the unspeakable horror of a warrior's final moments; cf. *Theb.* 8.729–30 (of Tydeus about to demand his opponent's head) *mediaque in morte negantem | exspirare*; *Theb.* 11.554–5 (of Eteocles' final treachery) *fraudemque supremam | a media iam morte parat*; see Augoustakis 2007: 217. The allusions to St.'s epic contrast human treachery, even among the greatest heroes, with the lion's nobility.   **redit:** contracted form of perfect *rediit* (2.4.4n.), the long vowel at the fourth-foot caesura creating an emphatic pause.

18–19 nec protinus omnes | terga dedere minae: cf. Virg. *A.* 9.794–5 (of a cornered lion) *et neque terga | ira dare aut uirtus patitur*, with Hardie. *terga dare* is a military metaphor for surrendering to the enemy; see Harrison on Virg. *A.* 10.646; cf. 2.6.93–4n. Its abstract subject *minae* ('signs of threat') is unusual and emphasises the lion's bravery.

19–23 sicut . . . miles . . . requirit: a striking inverted epic simile: the lion is compared to a wounded soldier rather than vice versa; see 14–15n. In Homer (and Virgil) the lion is the most frequent symbol of heroic courage (*RE* XIII 1.986; Lonsdale 1990: Appendix D; Harrison on Virg. *A.* 10.723–9). St. uses lion similes frequently in the *Thebaid*, esp. of Polynices, who wears a lion skin (*Theb.* 1.483–7, 4.85–6); in the *Achilleid* Achilles is closely associated with the lion through his diet of raw lion flesh (*Ach.* 2.99–100).

19 sibi conscius: see 2.3.35–7n.

20 moriens has concessive force; 'though dying' the soldier bravely attacks.

21 attollitque manum et ferro labente minatur: the juxtaposition of *labente* and *minatur* (cf. 19 *minae*) suggests heroic, doomed resistance. The framing of the line by two verbs is a feature of Virgilian hexameter narrative (Norden 392–3).

22 sic piger ille gradu 'thus sluggish in step'; *ille* is again the lion.   **solitoque exutus honore** 'though stripped of its usual dignity', a metaphorical use of *exuere* 'strip off clothing/animal skin' (*OLD* 1); cf. *Theb.* 6.30–1 *sedet ipse exutus honoro | uittarum nexu genitor*; Sall. *Hist.* 1.55.11 *populus Romanus exutus imperio gloria iure*.

23 firmat . . . requirit: on the framing of the line see 21n. Antiquity admired the lion for confronting its enemies squarely in fight and not backing down; see Zaganiaris 1977: 41. St. shifts from empathetic personal address of the lion to the third person; in these final moments the lion is on its own. The dactylic line quickens the pace of the action.   **hians** 'open-jawed' (*OLD* 1b), a Homeric image (*Il.* 20.168) indicating the lion's 'last gasp' (cf. *Theb.* 2. 679) and also its ferocity; see Harrison on Virg. *A.*10.726–7.   **oculos:** the lion's fierce gaze in combat derives from Homer's simile comparing Achilles to a wounded lion that musters its strength (*Il.* 20.164–75) and rushes to attack 'fiercely glaring' (*Il.* 20.172 γλαυκιόων); cf. Plin. *Nat.* 21.54 (of the lion) *uidelicet omnis uis constat in oculis*.   **animamque hostemque requirit:** syllepsis, emphasising the brief, intense final effort of the lion to recover its pride and avenge itself on its enemy; cf. Enn. *Ann.* 484 Sk. *micant oculi lucemque requirunt,* with Skutsch; Virg. *A.* 4.692 (of Dido) *quaesiuit caelo lucem.*

24–5 magna . . . subiti . . . solacia leti | . . . feres 'you will carry great consolation for a sudden death'. In a heroic context consolation is derived from death at the hand of a worthy opponent; cf. Ov. *Met.* 5.191 *magna feres tacitas solacia mortis ad umbras.* St. here chooses the grander word *leti* for *mortis.* But *feres* here recalls its etymological relation, the ignoble *fera* (11) that mortally wounded the lion (Maltby s.v. *fera*). For the lion its killer offers no consolation; 'great consolation' will come from catching the attention of 'great Caesar' (27) and from rousing the audience to pity.

25 uicte 'though conquered' (concessive voc.). To enhance the pathos of the lion's death, St. again addresses the beast directly; cf. 24 *tecum.* **maesti populusque patresque:** i.e. SPQR, governed by *maesti.* The *princeps* is reserved for the second *quod* clause (27–30). For the solemn epic rhythm see 2.1.210n.

25–7 quod te . . . ingemuere mori: the first of two causal clauses; the main verb *ingemuere* is divided from its subject (*populusque patresque*) by an epic simile; see 26n.

26 ceu notus caderes tristi gladiator harena 'as though you were a famous gladiator falling on the grim sand'. Archaic *ceu* here introduces a second epic simile embedded in an unreal conditional clause of comparison in historic sequence (*NLS* 254, 255); cf. 2.3.4n. *gladiator* occurs only here in St. and lowers the heroic register, for most gladiators were slaves or condemned criminals, social outcasts from their close contact with death, though the amphitheatre adored the individual star, hence *notus* here; see Hopkins 1983: 20–7; Potter 1999: 324. Though gladiators are not a feature of elevated poetry, gladiatorial *imagery* is frequent in martial epic; see Harrison on Virg. *A.* 10.907 (Mezentius' death); Leigh 1997: 234–91. In writings of the early Empire, esp. in Seneca's works, the gladiator offered a powerful image of how to meet death with courage; see Edwards 2007: 46–77.

27 ingemuere mori 'they groaned deeply that you were dying [i.e. at your death]'; indirect statement after a main verb of emotion; see 13n. *ingemere* is a Virgilian coinage, marking deep emotion; see Harrison on Virg. *A.* 10.789. St. conveys the spectators' empathy by choosing a verb associated with wild animal sounds as well as with human grief; 2.6.10n.; *Theb.* 11.746–7 (*leo*) *uires . . . solutas* | *ingemit Theb.* 12.714.

27–30 magni quod Caesaris ora . . . | tetigit iactura leonis: this final causal clause, linked to the first by asyndeton, makes the climactic point that

imperial recognition provides compensation for the lion's death; the separation of the subject (*iactura*) and main verb (*tetigit*) from the ideologically important object (*magni . . . Caesaris ora*) keeps Caesar's reaction in suspense. On post-
poned *quod* see 2.2.87–8n. The imperial box was situated on the short axis
of the amphitheatre for the best view (Coleman on Mart. *Sp.* p. lxxii). Domitian is both spectator and object of display, not masterminder of the show as
in 1.6.

28–9 inter . . . | feras: a parenthetical phrase indicating the main regions of
supply for animals (Jennison 1937: 80–1). St. indicates the extent of empire on the
four points of the compass, the margins of empire drawn to the imperial centre,
the Roman amphitheatre.

28 tot: vast numbers of animals were brought to Rome for entertainment.
Sources claim that at the opening of the Colosseum 9,000 animals were killed in
100 days, 11,000 in 123 days to celebrate Trajan's Dacian triumphs (Dio 66.25,
68.15; Suet. *Tit.* 7.3), though these were exceptional occasions (Coleman 1998:
20–1).   **Scythicas:** bears were frequently brought to Rome from Scythia,
which lay north of the Black Sea and for the Romans often represented a vague
geographical region 'far north'; cf. [Sen.] *Her. O.* 40 *ursae Scythicae*.   **Libycasque:** 'Libyan' or more generally 'North African' (i.e. the south). Although
they came from Syria and Mesopotamia as well as Asia, 'lions usually came
from Africa in the imagination of poets' (Jennison 1937: 53); cf. *Theb.* 9.16, with
Dewar.   **et litore Rheni:** i.e. *et de litore Rheni*; see 29n. Germany or the west
provided elk and wild oxen. On the gen. of the noun instead of a geographical
epithet see 2.2.122n.

29 et Pharia de gente: the east; see 2.1.73n. The postponement of the prepo-
sition to the second unit is unusual; cf. Ov. *Ars* 3.150 *nec quot apes Hybla nec quot
in Alpe ferae*. For further examples in St. see Vollmer ad loc. Crocodiles and hip-
popotami came from the Nile and were exhibited at Rome for the first time in 58
BCE (Plin. *Nat.* 8. 96).   **uile** 'considered of little account or importance' (*OLD*
4), by comparison with the lion. Was Domitian's reaction prompted by his sense
of economic loss?

30 unius amissi tetigit iactura leonis: an elegant final line with
verb set between two epithets and two nouns, not quite a Golden Line
(2.1.89n.).   **unius:** by contrast with *tot* (28); this one animal stood out for
its bravery.   **amissi** 'lost through death' (*OLD* 9b); cf. 2.1.201 *amissi . . . solacia
Blaesi*.   **iactura** can indicate financial loss (*OLD* 6) but also a real sense of
deprivation (*OLD* 5); cf. Plin. *Ep.* 1.12.1 *iacturam grauissimam feci, si iactura dicenda est
tanti uiri amissio*.   **tetigit** 'affected' (Caesar's face) (*OLD* 8), an enigmatic verb
here. Many critics assume that Domitian wept for the lion; Mozley translates
'drew a tear'. To have caused the emperor's tears meant a great compliment
in certain circumstances; cf. Prop. 4.11.60 *et lacrimas uidimus ire deo*; *Epic. Drusi*

209 *et uoce et lacrimis laudasti, Caesar, alumnum,* with Schoonhoven; Titus wept at
the closing of the public games (Suet. *Tit.* 10.1). But *tetigit* does not necessarily
imply 'wept' or denote a deep sorrow. Domitian was perhaps 'moved' by the
animal's heroism and also by its loss as a valuable performer; perhaps too he was
'moved' by the implicit lesson of the 'king of the beasts' so treacherously brought
low (Newlands 2005). *tetigit* draws attention to the inscrutability of Domitian's
face; on its known ambiguity see Ogilvie and Richmond on Tac. *Agr.* 45.2. Cf.
Mart. 8.78.15–16, an open declaration of the honour of Domitian's presence that
surpasses all the shows' delights.   **leonis:** the last word in the poem and its
first occurrence. St. abandons his anthropomorphic approach. Dead, the lion is
now material for poetry.

Siluae 2.6

2.6 consoles Flavius Ursus for his slave Philetos, who died in his eighteenth year
(70–2). St. again breaks with tradition by writing a full-scale poem on the death of
a slave, instead of epigram; e.g. Mart. 5.34, 5.37 and 10.61 on Erotion. The poem
is less intimate than 2.1 and lacks its individualising details, perhaps because
Ursus was young and had not established such close ties with St.; perhaps too
Philetos' servile status explains the poem's reserve and a certain lightness of tone;
St. observes decorum in the hierarchy of mourning. Philetos is praised largely
through myth, which elevates him in status but also here introduces humour.

   Literary and epigraphic evidence suggest that it was not unusual for an owner
to grieve over the death of a slave, particularly one of special abilities (like
Philetos) (Citroni 306–7); such grief however often carried apologetic overtones;
cf. Cic. *Att.* 1.12.4 *nam puer festiuus anagnostes noster Sositheus decesserat meque plus quam
serui mors debere uidebatur commouerat.* Plin. *Ep.* 8.16 claims that while for many
the death of a slave is merely a financial loss, it is a mark of true humanity to
feel a degree of sorrow. St. shares the same intellectual climate as Seneca, who
championed the slave's moral worth while accepting the institution itself (Bradley
1994: 136–40). Much of 2.6 is concerned with demonstrating the humanity and
high moral character of Philetos, an argument pursued largely through myth.
St. also interweaves another common theme at this time, whether true nobility is
inherited or not; cf. Sen. *Ep.* 44.5 *quis est generosus? ad uirtutem bene a natura compositus*;
Juv. 8, with Courtney pp. 381–4.

   The 'title' describes Philetos as *puer delicatus,* a term suggestive of a sexual relationship between master and slave (*TLL* v 1.444.80–445.14) and rather misleading
(on the *tituli* introd. 7), for Philetos is not called *delicatus* or *deliciae* in the poem.
Certainly sex with slaves was one of the prerogatives of slave ownership (Bradley
1994: 28), and La Penna 1996 argues for a sexual relationship between Ursus and
Philetos. But despite the erotic associations of Philetos' name ('worthy of love') –
a common enough slave name – the poem emphasises Philetos' manliness; he is
presented as an epic hero, a Roman Parthenopaeus, not an effeminate youth.

Further reading: Kenney 1964 (on Martial's ironic, yet humane, approach to the theme of grief for a beloved slave); Cancik 1965: 29 (on the poem's structure); Hardie 1983: 103–9; Fantham 1999: 67–9; Markus 2004: 128–9).

1–20 Slavery is introduced at the start as an important issue. St. emphasises that though Philetos was a slave, he was worthy of being mourned as a free man. Legal slavery is an external, not an internal, condition, though all human beings are prone to ethical slavery.

1–2 Saeue nimis, lacrimis quisquis discrimina ponis | lugendique modos: the phonetic strangeness of these opening lines, with harsh homoeoteleuton and assonance of *s* and *i*, creates an impassioned opening apostrophe against the person – too 'harsh' (*OLD saeuus* 1) – who thinks that distinctions or limits can be placed upon grief, a common philosophical position (e.g. Sen. *Ep.* 63.2 *lacrimandum est, non plorandum*) that poetry tends to query; cf. 5.5.59–61 *o . . . nimium crudelis et expers | imperii, Fortuna, tui qui dicere legem | fletibus aut fines audet censere dolendi*, with Gibson; Hor. *Carm.* 1.24.1–2 *quis desiderio sit pudor aut modus | tam cari capitis?*, with N–H; *Epic. Drusi* 7 *et quisquam leges audet tibi dicere flendi?*, with Schoonhoven. The second-person general address suggests entry into a heated debate; cf. the personal address of 2.1.1.

2–6 St. specifies the causes for grief, all involving close kin: a parent's loss of a child (2–3), a husband's loss of a wife (4–5), and siblings' loss of one another (5–6). Juvenal seems to allude to this passage; cf. 10.240–2 *ducenda tamen sunt | funera natorum, rogus aspiciendus amatae | coniugis et fratris plenaeque sororibus urnae*, with Courtney.

2–3 primaeua . . . | pignora 'children in early youth'; the most tragic loss comes first. From its first appearance at Cat. 64.401 *primaeuus* (Homeric πρωθήβης) was closely associated with premature death (Hardie on Virg. *A.* 9.545).

3 surgentesque . . . accendere natos: a harsh contrast between verbs connoting vital plant growth and cremation; *accendere* with a personal object occurs in Latin poetry only here and at *Theb.* 9.398 *accensure nepotem* (Van Dam).   **(nefas!):** a parenthetical intrusion of outrage that the young should die (2.1.175n.); the following fourth-foot strong caesura dramatises the breaking of the natural order; cf. (with the same metrical pattern) *Theb.* 12.83–4 (Creon's lament for his son) *meque super, cui uita (nefas!) et sanguine nati | partus honos.*

4–5 durum et deserti praerepta coniuge partem | conclamare tori: second, a husband's grief at the empty bedside for his wife who 'has been snatched away before her time' (2.1.11n.); cf. *Epic. Drusi* 328 *quaeris et in uacui parte priore tori?* *durum (est)* = 'it is hard to bear' (*OLD* 8), with *marito* ('for a husband') understood, in parallel to *parenti* (2). The harsh alliteration of line 4 is reinforced by its solemn spondaic rhythm.

5 conclamare expresses formal lamentation (*OLD* 4), the calling of the deceased by name to establish the fact of death by the relatives gathered round the body (Toynbee 1971: 44; Nisbet on Cic. *Dom.* 98.5); cf. Luc. 2. 22–3 *cum corpora nondum | conclamata iacent*. Here the body is already gone, so the verb conveys particular pathos.

5–6 maesta et lamenta . . . | et . . . gemitus: understand *sunt*. The grief of siblings.

6–8 alte tamen aut procul intrat | altius in sensus maioraque uul-nera uincit | plaga minor 'yet a lesser stroke enters the feelings as deep or far deeper, surpassing greater wounds', SB's text and translation for M's corrupt † *ad te tamen at* †, obelised by Courtney. With *alte* for *ad te* SB follows Markland; he himself emends *at* to *aut*. Courtney 1988: 43 objects to the 'unstylish Latinity' of Markland's emendation. But the emended text makes good sense and is a typical Statian paradox: Ursus grieves more for his slave boy ('a lesser stroke' because of his low social status) than others do when a family member dies. St. touches on a major theme of 2.1, the exaltation of affective over kinship ties (cf. 2.1.82–105; Gibson on *Silu.* 5 pp. xlvi–xlvii).

6 procul with the comparative *altius* in the sense of *longe* 'by far' is unusual; but cf. 34–5 *procul . . . | pulchrius* (*OLD* 6b); 2.2.83n.

8 famulum: unlike *seruus, famulus*, etymologically associated with *familia*, generally indicates a household slave (Maltby s.v. *famulus*).

8–9 quia rerum nomina caeca | sic miscet Fortuna manu: blindness is a common attribute of Fortune (*OLD caecus* 1c), understood in the Greek sense of a wilful, indiscriminate deity (N–H ii 386–8). *caeca* most likely modifies *manu*, not *Fortuna*, on analogy with the bold metaphor at Sen. *Phaed.* 980 *res humanas . . . Fortuna regit sparsitque manu munera caeca*; in both cases the transferred epithet emphasises the goddess's indiscriminate actions. St. means that verbal signs are arbitrary; hence the name 'slave' is detached from any meaningful referent, a point developed in this poem to show that Philetos does not have a servile mentality.

9 nec pectora nouit: Fortune cannot 'see' inside a person's heart where his true nature resides; cf. 4.6.89–90 *si mores humanaque pectora curae | nosse deis*.

10 sed famulum . . . pium: *famulum*, emphatically repeated (see 8), is here concessive; though Philetos was a slave, he was loyal. The Romans often stereotyped slaves as lacking in loyalty (Bradley 1984: 28–40). The postponement of *pium* emphasises that Philetos was exceptional and thus fully deserving of his master's sorrow.   **gemis, Vrse:** the first mention of Ursus' name, possibly with a pun on its meaning 'Bear'; *gemere* can denote the sound made by animals and birds (*OLD* 2) as well as lament (*OLD* 4); cf. Hor. *Epod.* 16.51 *nec uespertinus circumgemit ursus ouile*; Virg. *Ecl.* 5.27 *ingemuisse leones*. St. may be playing, not simply in jest, upon Ursus' name: if a 'Bear' is a good man, then names such as 'slave' are poor indicators of character.   **sed amore fideque:** instrumental ablatives with *meritum* (11). The unusual anaphora of *sed* emphasises these unusual qualities in a slave.

11–12 cui maior stemmate cuncto | libertas ex mente fuit 'whose freedom, greater than any lineage, was from the mind'; cf. Sen. *Ep.* 47.17 *'seruus est.' sed fortasse liber animo*; true slavery is immoral subjection to the passions (Fitzgerald 2000: 91–2). *stemmate* is a metaphor for 'pedigree' (cf. 4.4.75 *stemmate materno felix*; 4.6.88) derived from *stemmata* 'family trees'. No family trees have survived but they were probably displayed on painted panels in an aristocratic atrium (Mart. 4.40.1 *atria Pisonum stabant cum stemmate toto*; Flower 1996: 211–12), the names linked by lines (Plin. *Nat.* 35.6 *stemmata uero lineis discurrebant ad imagines pictas*), hence *cuncto* is preferable to M's pleonastic *iuncto* 'joined' (SB). Juv. 8.1–9 claims *stemmata* are no guarantee of true nobility (Courtney ad loc.); St. makes a similar point with the ironic pun of *maior* on *maiores*.

12–13 ne comprime fletus, | ne pudeat 'do not check your tears, do not be ashamed', i.e. 'do not be ashamed to weep'; see 2.1.14n. An elegant variation of negative commands; *ne* with the imperative, common only in poetry, is followed by the more usual *ne* with the third-person pres. subj. (*NLS* 128 (ii), 129).

13 rumpat frenos dolor iste: an equestrian metaphor for grief, likened to a horse breaking free from its controlling reins (*OLD frenum* 2c).

13–14 deisque | si tam dura placent 'and if such harsh pain pleases the gods'. This conditional clause is suspect, for it lacks a meaningful apodosis, hence editors print a following lacuna. *deis* is Calderini's conjecture for M's *dies*, meaningless with *rumpat* since St. talks of Ursus' continuing grief, not that of one day; see Håkanson 1969: 72–4. *dura* = 'things hard to bear' as at line 4 (*durum*), because Philetos died young; cf. Hor. *Carm.* 1.24.19–20 *durum: sed leuius fit patientia | quidquid corrigere est nefas*, with N–H.

14 hominem gemis: cf. 10 *famulum gemis*. Verbal repetition (also 15n.) strengthens the connection of ideas in the comparison between slave and man; see Wills 68 on the 'resumptive syntax' of 8–15; cf. 2.1.177–8. Philetos' character, not his condition in life, is what truly matters; cf. Sen. *Ep.* 47.1 *'serui sunt.' immo homines*.   **ei mihi:** highly emotional (Austin on Virg. *A.* 2.274). The interjection shows that St. shares in Ursus' grief (2.1.17–18n.). M has *heu mihi*; *heu* occurs often in St.'s work, but never + dat., whereas *ei mihi* occurs several times (Håkanson 1969: 73).

14–15 subdo | ipse faces 'I myself apply the torches', a fairly common expression for lighting the funeral pyre; cf. Lucr. 6.1285; Prop. 4.11.9–10. The pres. tense suggests the sense is metaphorical; cf. Lucr. 3.303 *irai fax subdita*; St. stokes the fires of Ursus' grief, suggesting his solidarity with the bereaved and hence his authority to write this poem.

15 hominem, Vrse, tuum: 14n. *tuum* puts Philetos in a special category, technically a slave but not slavish in character, rather worthy of love.

15–16 cui dulce uolenti | seruitium, cui triste nihil '[a man] for whom servitude [i.e. to you] of his own will was sweet, for whom nothing was a hardship'. The oxymoron 'sweet slavery' recalls the elegiac theme of *seruitium amoris* (Fantham 1999: 69 n.25). *uolenti* mitigates the force of *seruitium* with a further paradox – servitude was voluntary.

16–17 qui sponte sibique | imperiosus erat 'who acted of his own accord, fully his own master'; cf. Hor. *S.* 2.7.83–4 *quisnam igitur liber? sapiens sibique imperiosus | quem neque pauperies neque mors neque uincula terrent* – a sentiment appropriate to St.'s Stoicising discourse on slavery; *imperiosus* and *sponte* invert the normally passive condition of the slave. But M's *sibique* causes a difficult ellipsis, hence Courtney obelises *-que*. Heinsius' conjecture *sibi ipse* is attractive: it emphasises the notion of voluntariness (cf. Virg. *Ecl.* 4.43–5), and invites play on *ipse* 'the master' (*OLD* 12). But the apparent imitation of Horace suggests retention of *sibique*. SB assumes that a verb like *faciebat* should be understood after *sponte*, as translated here; *-que* thus links two separate ideas, though such an ellipse is very bold. The syntactic shift from *cui* to nom. *qui* marks the conclusion of the tricolon.

17 quisnam: a further allusion to Hor. *S.* 2.7.83 (see above). St. refers back to the *saeuus* (1) who would set a limit to grief.

17–18 haec in funera missos | . . . luctus 'tears released for such a death'; *mittere luctus* is unusual and perhaps ironically plays on the sense of *mittere* 'to free a slave' (*OLD* 3).

18–20 St. justifies Ursus' sorrow with four examples of human grief for animals – a seeming inconsistency after his insistence on Philetos' humanity. But while literature provides striking similarities between human and animal 'pets', no ancient writer actually *equates* such children with domestic animals (Laes 2003: 316–17). St. moreover chooses here not domestic pets but creatures with heroic and literary associations. As he has just shown (2.4, 2.5), the death of animals is a recognised literary theme: if even animals are mourned, why not a slave, so he implies, who was as good as a free man?

18–19 gemit inter bella peremptum | Parthus equum: the third occurrence of *gemit* in the poem (see 10, 14) introduces the comparisons. The horse was crucial to the Parthian style of warfare, mounted archery (N–H on Hor.

Carm. 1.19.11). In the Graeco-Roman world famous horses had special memorials; Alexander the Great built a tomb for Bucephalus, as did Augustus when his favourite horse died (Plin. *Nat.* 8.154–5).

19 fidosque canes fleuere Molossi: the Molossians, from Epirus, were famous for their powerful hunting dogs and watchdogs (Coleman on Mart. *Sp.* 33.1).

20 et uolucres habuere rogum 'and birds have had a pyre', i.e. they had people who cared enough about them to give them proper cremation. St. shifts to literature, with self-allusion to 2.4.34–7, the cremation of Melior's parrot. The self-reference not only advertises St.'s 'parrot' poem; it also draws the book together as a *collection*.   **ceruusque Maronem:** the tame stag shot by Iulus and thus the catalyst for the war between Trojans and Latins (Virg. *A.* 7.483–502). Virgil, called by his rarely cited *cognomen* Maro, is here linked with St. as poets of lament, both sharing the same line.

21–57 A eulogy that 'proves' Philetos' noble character and appearance. On 'remembering' as an aspect of consolation see 2.1.36–68n.

21 quid si nec famulus? 'what if he were not a slave?', a colloquial gambit that opens up to speculation Philetos' true origins (22–3n., 99n.). Unlike Glaucias, he seems not to have been home-born.   **uidi ipse:** this declaration of autopsy validates his eulogy.   **habitusque** 'the demeanour' (Williams on *Theb.* 10.678).

22 te tantum cupientis erum 'of [the young man] desiring only you as his master'; on *erus* see 2.1.75n. To desire a master suggests servility; thus SB adopts Heinsius' *capientis*, which allows for the paradox that a slave 'captures' a master. But St. plays with the topos of *seruitium amoris* (15–16n.).

22–3 sed maior in ore | spiritus 'but there is a spirit greater [than a slave's] in his face'. *maior* assumes abl. of comparison *seruo*, a typical Statian ellipsis. *sed* strengthens the contrast between Philetos' willing service to Ursus and his noble bearing – he looks freeborn. There is no need to substitute *spe* (Housman, followed by Courtney).

24–5 optarent multum Graiae cuperentque Latinae | sic peperisse nurus 'Greek and Roman young women would fondly wish and long to have produced such a son', a witty variation on the common wish for a sexual or marital partner (cf. Cat. 62.44 *multi illum pueri, multae optauere puellae*; Ov. *Met.* 3.353 *multi illum iuuenes, multae cupiere puellae*), for only with *peperisse* does the reader realise that 'desire' is for a son, not a sexual partner. Virgil adapted the topos to mothers hoping for eligible daughters-in-law; cf. Virg. *A.* 11.581–2 (of Camilla) *multae illam frustra Tyrrhena per oppida matres | optauere nurum*, with

Horsfall; Wills 280–1. St. domesticates and expands this topos by encompass-
ing Greek as well as Roman mothers; the potential subj. adds pathos, stressing
the impossibility of fulfilment. *nurus* strictly speaking means 'daughter-in-law'
but poets, esp. Ovid, often use it coupled with an ethnic adjective, as here, to
refer to young women who are married but not yet child-bearing (Gibson on *Ars*
3.248).

25–37 Philetos is praised through comparison to the mythological heroes Theseus, Paris, Achilles and Troilus (cf. 2.1.88–105n.). Though beauty is the common
denominator, flawed character distinguishes the heroes from Philetos. Negative
mythological comparisons are esp. a feature of Propertius' poetry (Fedeli on Prop.
1.2.15). 2.6 gives little actual description of Philetos, for he represents the *idea* of
innate nobility.

25–8 introd. 24–6.

29 non fallo: a pointed parenthesis separates the two heroic lovers from the two
warriors; cf. 2.1.50 *nil ueris affingo bonis*, a similar protestation of poetic authority
in the context of 'lavish mythological comparison, beyond the reach of autopsy'
(Hutchinson 1993: 38). *fallo* echoes ancient formulae for swearing oaths (Fedeli
on Prop. 2.20.16) and wittily contrasts the 'trustworthy' poet with the deceitful
Theseus and Paris.   **assueta licentia:** the claim that his praise of Philetos
is *not* governed by customary 'poetic licence' (his own and others') humorously
draws attention to St.'s extreme licence in comparing a slave to the heavyweight
royalty of classical myth.

30 uidi et adhuc uideo: sc. *eum*, i.e. Philetos. Polyptoton emphasises St.'s
authority.

30–1 qualem nec bella cauentem | … Thetis occultauit Achillem
'unlike Achilles, whom, wary of war, Thetis hid'; implied *eum* is the antecedent
of *qualem nec*; cf. 25 *nec talem*. Philetos was not like Achilles hiding out in drag on
Scyros, the theme of the extant *Achilleid*, but was more manly. There may be a
sly bit of self-promotion (depending on dating) of St.'s forthcoming second epic.
There is no need to mitigate the slur on Achilles by emending *cauentem* ('avoiding'
OLD caueo 6) to *canentem* (e.g. Vollmer; SB prints *cauentem*, but translates 'singing').
Achilles sings not on Scyros but in Chiron's cave (on Scyros Achilles teaches
Deidamia music, *Ach.* 1.572–6; she sings, he kisses), and his theme is not war but
individual heroic deeds (*Ach.* 1.188–94).

31 litore uirgineo: the seashore of Scyros where Achilles first saw Deidamia
(*Ach.* 1.285–9). *uirgineo*, referring here to a place where young women congregate,
is a rare Ovidian epithet for Helicon, the Muses' mountain (Ov. *Met.* 2.219,
5.254). St. perhaps again refers to his second epic (possibly in progress; cf. 4.4.93–
4; 4.7.21–4), which unusually places a temple of the virginal Pallas on the shore
of Scyros; cf. *Ach.* 1.285 *Palladi litoreae*.

32–3 nec... | Troilon 'and you were unlike Troilus [whom]...'; *qualem* should be understood after *nec*. Troilus, the handsome youngest son of Priam and Hecuba, was killed by Achilles; cf. Virg. *A.* 1.474–5 *Troilus*... | *infelix puer*, with Austin, who cites a tradition that Troy would not fall if Troilus lived to the age of twenty. In age, beauty and early death he provides a close point of comparison for the eighteen-year-old Philetos; on Troilus' death as an exemplum of *mors immatura* see N–H on Hor. *Carm.* 2.9.16.

32 circum saeui... moenia Phoebi: Achilles is more usually described as *saeuus* (e.g. Virg. *A.* 1.459, 2.29); only St. applies *saeuus* to Apollo (Carter); e.g. *Theb.* 3.639, 9.657. Here he is 'harsh' possibly because, having helped build the walls of Troy (Ov. *Ep.* 1.67), he participated in their destruction because of non-payment for the work; possibly too St. refers to the tradition that Troilus was the son not of Priam but of Apollo (Apollod. 3.12.5), hence the god is harsh in abandoning his son to an inglorious death.   **fugientem:** cf. Virg. *A.* 474 *fugiens amissis Troilus armis*. There were various traditions about Troilus' manner of death and its place. According to Virg. *A.* 1.474–8 Troilus met Achilles in combat; he fled in his chariot but, wounded, fell backwards, became entangled in the chariot's traces, and was dragged along the ground (Austin ad loc.). In other versions Troilus was ambushed by Achilles while drawing water at a fountain outside the walls of Troy, fled and was killed at the altar of the temple of Apollo. In an erotic version of the myth, which St. may refer to here, he was ambushed and killed by Achilles because he had spurned his love (Lyc. 307–13; on St.'s knowledge of Lycophron see 5.3.157); *fugiens* typically characterises the erotic chase (e.g. 2.3.8). On the various versions of Troilus' killing by Achilles see *LIMC* VIII 1.91–4.

33 Haemoniae... lancea dextrae: *Haemonius* 'Thessalian' is often used of Achilles, perhaps for its connotations of 'blood' (2.1.89n.).   **deprendit** (= *deprehendit*); St. does not make clear whether Troilus was killed in battle or in ambush (see 33n.); but this verb suggests the latter, as it connotes violent surprise; cf. *Theb.* 9.553–4 *animam sub pectore magno* | *deprendit*, with Dewar; 2.2.127–8n. An elegant line, the main verb framed by two proper names and two nouns, concludes the exempla.

34 qualis eras 'how fair you were!' (SB). An emotional, elevated exclamation; cf. Virg. *A.* 2.274 *ei mihi, qualis eras, quantum mutatus*, with Austin.

34–5 procul en cunctis puerisque uirisque | pulchrior: on the epic, emphatic tone of repeated fifth- and sixth-foot -*que* see 2.1.210n. The reference to 'boys and men' captures the ambiguity of Philetos' adolescent beauty. *procul = longe* 'by far' (6–8n.).

35 et tantum domino minor! 'and inferior (in beauty) only to his master!' The echo of *minor* in *domino* (2.5.3n.) emphasises Philetos' status as slave and anticipates the upcoming simile (36–7).

35–6 illius unus | ante decor 'his beauty [i.e. that of Ursus] alone surpassed yours', an elliptical phrase: Ursus too was still young (2 *pr.* 19 *iuuenem*).

36–7 quantum praecedit clara minores | luna faces: cf. Hor. *Carm.* 1.12.46–8 *micat inter omnes | Iulium sidus uelut inter ignes | luna minores*, with N–H; the 'lesser torches/fires' = the stars; St. translates Horace's Augustan political hierarchy into that of master/slave; *praecedit* implies poetic allusion and rivalry (2.2.61n. on *cedat*). On similar audacity with Horace's simile, but retaining a political context, see Henderson 1998: 55–6 on 1.4.36–7. The comparison of the person praised to the moon, sun and evening/morning star was common in encomia, whether political or erotic.

37 quantumque alios premit Hesperos ignes 'and as Hesperus [the evening star, here Greek nom.] dims other stars' (*OLD premo* 17); cf. *Theb.* 6.580–1 (praise of Parthenopaeus' beauty) *sed clarior omnia supra | Hesperos exercet radios*, with Lovatt 2005: 63–7, 71–2, 75–6. Although complimenting Ursus esp. here, St. anticipates the extended parallel between Philetos and Parthenopaeus (40–5).

38 non tibi femineum uultu decus 'no feminine beauty was in your face', a vigorous denial of any lingering femininity implied by Philetos' youth. *decor* (cf. 36) usually applies to external beauty, *decus* to abstract worth, though the two are sometimes conflated; cf. Virg. *A.* 4.150 *tantum egregio decus enitet ore*, with Pease.

38–9 non . . . oraque supra | mollis honos 'and there was no unmanly charm on your face'. *mollis* connotes effeminacy, a quality shameful in a Roman male (*mulier* was believed to derive from *mollities* (Maltby s.v. *mulier, mollire* = 'castrate' (3.4.68)); see Coleman on 4.3.14; Richlin 1992: 258 n.3 on the derogatory vocabulary of 'softness'. *supra* in the sense of 'on' had archaic resonance since Lucretius and adds a stern note to the refutation of unmanliness (L–H–S 250–1).

39–40 quales dubiae quos crimina formae | de sexu transire iubent 'such as those possess whom reproach of ambiguous beauty makes change sex'; for this sense of *dubius* cf. *Ach.* 1.744 (Achilles in female dress) *dubia facies suspecta figura*; *TLL* v 1.2109.59–62; cf. *Ach.* 1.356–7 *fallitque tuentes | ambiguus tenuique latens discrimine sexus*. The sense here is difficult. *quales* (nom. plur.), is perhaps best taken as = *quales sunt eis*, with reference to 'feminine beauty' and 'unmanly charm' (38–9); *quos* is Baehrens' conjecture for M's impossible *post*. St. seems to refer to the practice of castration of young males; cf. 3.4.70–1 *leniter . . . corpus | de sexu transire iubet*. But there is a chronological problem: Domitian outlawed castration early in his reign (Coleman on 4.3.13–15). Van Dam argues that *iubent* has the weakened sense of 'bids' or 'makes' (*OLD* 7), but this hardly helps if castration was illegal. Possibly St. refers to eunuchs in general, not specifically in a contemporary Roman context. And since manly beauty is the ideal of 2.6, *crimina* means 'reproach', not 'crime'; effeminacy is a physical flaw, a source of shame.

40–1 torua... | gratia: an oxymoron underlining the tension between adolescent beauty and virility. As a complimentary poetic epithet for warriors, *toruus* emphasises their fighting spirit (Harrison on Virg. *A.* 10.170–1). Following Ovid, St. promotes a type of beauty based on aesthetic contradictions; see Sanna 2008: 200–4.

41 nec petulans acies: Philetos had a modest look in his 'eyes' (*OLD acies* 3); cf. Ov. *Met.* 2.776 (of *Inuidia*) *nusquam recta acies. petulans* = 'wanton' (2.3.25n.).

41–2 blandique seuero | igne oculi: another oxymoron, emphasised by chiasmus and enjambment; cf. *Ach.* 1.164 *tranquillaeque faces oculis*, with Dewar 2002: 394–6.

42–7 A second set of mythological comparisons: Philetos is now positively compared to famous heroes and athletes (cf. Glaucias of 2.1, compared to unwarlike youths such as Hyacinth and Hylas (112–13) or the infants Palaemon and Opheltes (179–82)). The beauty of the warrior in his prime was regarded as an important aspect of the Homeric warrior's ἀρετή, a tradition carried on by Virgil and St. (Harrison on Virg. *A.* 10.345–6). The first example, Parthenopaeus, was like Philetos on the ambiguous cusp between boyhood and manhood (Hardie 1993: 48). He is the youngest of the seven Argive warriors against Thebes (*Theb.* 4.246–74, 6.561–645, 9.570–907), a paradigm of the beautiful yet virile young man who cared only for martial prowess, not for his looks (*Theb.* 6.574 *ipse tamen formae laudem aspernatur*; *Theb.* 9.704–6). See Dewar on *Theb.* 9.683–711; La Penna 1996: 165–72; Lovatt 2005: 55–79.

42–3 qualis bellus iam casside uisu | Parthenopaeus erat: *qualis* and *uisu* go together: 'so to look at was Parthenopaeus, now handsome in his helmet'; cf. *Ach.* 1.161 (young Achilles) *dulcis adhuc uisu.* The abl. noun (or supine) with *qualis* is rare (Håkanson 1969: 76–7). *bellus* is Krohn's conjecture for M's *bellis*, supported by SB (Appendix p. 390); but for Courtney it is too vulgar a word; it appears only here in St. He prefers Baehrens' *liber* 'free of' (his helmet), assuming a reference to *Theb.* 9.699–703, where Parthenopaeus' full beauty is strikingly revealed when he removes his helmet (Courtney 2004: 451); Mart. 9.56.8 *casside dum liber Parthenopaeus erat* perhaps alludes to this scene in St.'s epic. But the emendation is very bold. As SB points out, it is the *kind* of beauty that matters here: the image of Parthenopaeus handsome *in his helmet* supports the emphasis on Philetos' manliness; *iam* goes with *bellus*, suggesting that Parthenopaeus, once a young hunter in the Arcadian glades (*Theb.* 4.254–9), is now ready for war and looks good in armour too (*Theb.* 9.685–99). The punning association of *bellus* with *bellum* conveys the oxymoronic quality of these young men's looks; cf. Ov. *Am.* 1.9.6 *bella puella*, with McKeown.

43–4 simplexque horrore decoro | crinis 'your hair was unadorned, its roughness attractive', another typical Statian oxymoron, emphasised by

assonance; cf. *Theb.* 2.716 (Minerva's Gorgon helmet) *cui torua genis horrore decoro |
cassis. horror* of bristling hair is post-Augustan and poetic; cf. V. Fl. 1.229 *non ullo
horrore comarum terribilis.* Rough hair signified virility, as opposed to the sleek locks
of the effeminate; on such hirsute contrasts cf. Mart. 7.58.

44–5 et obsessae nondum primoque micantes | flore genae 'and
cheeks not yet thickly covered with hair but glowing with first down', a
rare metaphorical use of *obsidere* (*OLD* 7a), deployed for its martial resonance.
Parthenopaeus too was known for his glowing beauty; cf. *Theb.* 9.701–2 *tunc dulce
comae radiisque trementes | dulce nitent uisus*, with Dewar; 37n.; La Penna 1996: 167.
Traditionally the young hero's down was just starting to spread (*OLD flos* 4c;
Aesch. *Sept.* 534–5), a sign of the turning from youth to manhood, though at *Theb.*
9.703 Parthenopaeus is oddly still smooth-cheeked (*nondum mutatae rosea lanugine
malae*); Dewar on *Theb.* 9.702–3.

45 talem introduces positive comparisons to athletic youth.

45–6 Ledaeo gurgite pubem | educat Eurotas: the river Eurotas flowed
through Sparta and was associated both with the hardiness of that country's
youth (cf. *Ach.* 1.180–1) and with Jupiter's rape of Leda. *pubem* means Spartan
youths in general, and Castor and Pollux in particular, Leda's male offspring
and Roman divine heroes (*OCD* s.v. 'Castor and Pollux'), thus a Roman as well
as Greek point of reference for standards of masculinity. *gurges* (here local abl.)
means 'river'; see 2.1.194n.; *Theb.* 10.504, with Williams.

46 teneri . . . integer aeui: *integer aeui* is a common expression meaning
'unimpaired by age' and thus 'youthful' (gen. of sphere of application); see 97n.;
Austin on Virg. *A.* 2.638. The unusual addition of the epithet *teneri* is pleonastic
(cf. 49 *teneroque animus maturior aeuo*) but emphasises that the athlete is very young
indeed; see 2.1.40n.

47 Elin: i.e. Olympia, situated in the Greek state of Elis.   **primosque
Ioui puer approbat annos** 'the boy proves to Jupiter the excellence of his
first years' (*OLD approbo* 3). At the Olympic games, founded in honour of Jupiter
(3.1.140–1), competitors were divided into two groups, men and boys, the dividing
line between them probably being around age seventeen, depending on physical development; boys competed from their early teens (Miller 2004: 14). This
final example implies that Philetos as young and athletic is worthy of divine
approval.

48 nam pudor ingenuae mentis: St. now praises character, with 'modesty' the first of Philetos' virtues in a *tricolon crescens* (48–9). *ingenuae* is Heinsius' generally accepted conjecture for M's corrupt *unde notae*; it means 'honourable' as is typical of a freeborn male, or one who acts as such (*OLD* 2
and 3).

49 temperies 'moderation of character', a sense unique to St.; otherwise it refers to physical phenomena (2.2.153–4n.).   **teneroque animus maturior aeuo:** the climax of the tricolon. On the theme of the precocity of the deceased see 2.1.40n.

50 carmine quo patuisse queant? 'with what song could [these qualities of *pudor, temperies, animus* (48–9)] be revealed?' The conjectural *patuisse* is accepted by Courtney and SB (but not Van Dam); *queant* for M's *queam* avoids an anacoluthon. On the textual problems of 48–50 see Håkanson 1969: 77–9. St. often makes claims of poetic insufficiency in eulogistic descriptions (2.2.36–44n.). The perfect inf. after *quire/posse* is conventional and metrically convenient (L–H–S 351–2).

50–1 uolentem | castigabat erum: a striking reversal of the master–slave relationship: Philetos would reprimand his master, who gladly accepted it; enjambment highlights the paradox; cf. 15–16 *cui dulce uolenti | seruitium*.

52 tecum tristisque hilarisque: Philetos accommodated to all Ursus' moods; Glaucias by contrast would often playfully change Melior's mood for the better; cf. 2.1.56–66.

52–3 nec umquam | ille suus 'his mood [was] never his own' (SB), for Philetos was not a free man, *sui iuris*. But St. suggests that Philetos' devotion springs from love and good character, not compulsion.

54–7 A third and final set of mythological comparisons, celebrating loyal but *unequal* friendships between a famous hero and his junior partner or servant. St. thus gracefully compliments Ursus as well as Philetos.

54 Haemonium Pyladen: Pylades, loyal friend of Orestes, was son of the king of Phocis in central Greece (Hyg. *Fab.* 119.2). But 'Haemonian' ('Thessalian', from Northern Greece; 33n.) better suits Patroclus, Achilles' friend; St. thus compactly refers to two of the most famous junior partners in standard paradigms of ideal friendship (Gibson on 5.2.156–7; Dewar on *Theb.* 9.68); for a similar conflation see 2.2.108n.   **praecedere fama:** on the use of *cedo* or its compounds in comparisons see 36–7n. *fama* implies literary fame also.

55 Cecropiamque fidem: an abstract noun now denotes the Athenian hero Theseus and his friend Pirithous; Cecrops was Athens' first king. The strong caesura after *fidem* throws particular emphasis upon Theseus' loyalty; at 25–6 St. hints at his treachery.

55–6 sed laudum terminus esto | quem fortuna sinit 'but let the end to my praises be such as his fortune allows', i.e. praise should be tailored to a person's lot in life; *laudes* = 'eulogy' (*OLD* 1b). St.'s final, surprising, point of comparison is Odysseus' devoted swineherd Eumaeus, a man of royal birth but, after his capture by pirates, sold as a slave to Laertes (Hom. *Od.* 15.403–92). Eumaeus illustrates St.'s opening claim that true slavery is a state of mind. The comparison also hints that Philetos (like Eumaeus) might not be of servile origin (99n.). Though in other respects the aged swineherd is a comic point of comparison for the young and beautiful Philetos, this final example is highly complimentary to Ursus, who is implicitly compared to Odysseus.

55 esto: third-person future imperative, an archaic form that occurs only here in the *Siluae* and lends solemn emphasis to the climax.

56 mente . . . aegra 'though he was sick in his mind with worry' over Ulysses' failure to return home, Eumaeus remained steadfast in hope and loyalty.

57 tardi . . . Vlixis: 2.1.118n.   **Eumaeus:** the only occurrence of this name in Latin literature.

58–70 A lament over the tragedy of premature death.

58–9 quis deus aut quisnam . . . casus | eligit? unde manus . . . ?: an elegantly varied *tricolon crescens*, with an echo of Nisus' speech of selfless love to Euryalus; cf. Virg. *A.* 9.211–12 *si quis in aduersum rapiat casusue deusue,* | *te superesse uelim*. A complaint against gods and fate was conventional in consolatory poems; cf. 2.1.120–24, 2.1.137–45, 5.1.137, where it occurs at a similar transitional point after the eulogy of the deceased.   **casus | eligit:** a paradoxical juxtaposition of *casus* 'chance' with *eligit* 'chooses'.

59 unde manus Fatis tam certa nocendi? 'from where did the Fates come by a hand so certain to harm?' The Fates manually spin and cut the thread of life (2.1.120n.).

60–1 o quam . . . | fortior, Vrse, fores!: St. addresses Ursus by name more than any other person in book 2 (cf. 10, 15, 61, 94), perhaps to create the effect of emotional involvement and compensate for the lack of personal details in this poem.

60 diuitiis censuque exutus opimo 'even if you had been stripped of your wealth and ample inheritance', an economical use of the past participle in lieu of a conditional clause; on metaphorical *exutus* see 2.5.22n. *census* refers specifically to family wealth or 'the family fortune' (2.2.153n.).

61–8 An elaborate period, apparently referring to several of Ursus' properties or sources of revenue, is organised as a series of 'unreal conditions' (61 *si*, 63, 64 *seu*, 66 *siue*); if they had been affected by natural disaster, he would have borne their loss with equanimity. St. compliments Ursus for the extent of his propertied wealth while subtly reminding him of the obligations wealth entails; see 95n. Place names typically cause textual problems, as here.

61–2 si uel fumante ruina | ructassent dites Vesuuina incendia Locroe 'if wealthy Locri had belched Vesuvian fires in smoking avalanche', thus SB with apt play on *ruo/ruina*, the smoking ashes 'falling down'. The commonly accepted nom. *Locroe* for M's *Locros* makes better grammatical sense, though unattested elsewhere; Locri presumably was a source of Ursus' wealth (hence *dites*). *ructassent* however is puzzling. Locri was a Greek colony situated in Bruttium, on the south-east coast at Italy's toe and thus far from Mount Vesuvius on the Bay of Naples; it was not a volcanic region (Williams on Virg. *A.* 3.399). At best its closeness to Sicily and to the volcanic Aeolian islands meant it could have felt ash from an eruption; according to Livy, ashes from Etna fell upon southern Italy as a portent of Julius Caesar's murder (Serv. *G.* 1.472; cf. Luc. 1.545–7). *Vesuuinus* ocurrs elsewhere only at 3.5.72 and Sil. 12.152, there in the sense 'of Vesuvius'; here the sense required is '[fires] like those of Vesuvius'. Mention of the volcano, which erupted in 79 CE, would have made vivid for readers the thought of possible disaster; cf. 3.5.72, 4.4.79–80, 4.8.5.

62 ructassent: a typical physiological metaphor for volcanic eruption, the spondees emphasising volcanic force; cf. Virg. *A.* 3.575–6 (of Etna) . . . *scopulos auulsaque uiscera montis | erigit eructans*; Sil. 17.593 *euomuit pastos per saecula Vesuuius ignes.*

63 seu Pollentinos mersissent flumina saltus: slow spondees and assonance vividly represent the next natural disaster, flooding in the north; the glades of Pollentia at the foot of the Alps made good commercial pasture (Sil. 8.597). *flumina* refers to the river Po, which often flooded, and its tributaries (Plin. *Nat.* 3.117–19; Luc. 2.409–10).

64 seu Lucanus Acir: M reads *Lucanus ager*, which requires an impossible ellipsis such as *mersus esset*. Another river is needed here, and a probable candidate is the *Aciris*, named at Plin. *Nat.* 3.97 as one of the rivers of Lucania, a region of southern Italy. *Acir* may be a variant form, though unattested elsewhere; it thus is the second river in a sequence linked by *seu . . . seu*, with main verb *torsisset* (65).

64–5 seu Thybridis impetus altas | in dextrum torsisset aquas: a stylised reference to the Tiber's flooding of its right (western) bank, where the rich, including perhaps Ursus, had suburban villas (cf. 4.1.7); *torsisset* depicts the river's violent turn from its natural course; cf. Hor. *Carm.* 1.2. 3–14 *Tiberim retortis litore Etrusco uiolenter undis*. The Greek form *Thybris* is almost universal in poetry after Ovid (Austin on Virg. *A.* 1.782). The Tiber was liable to sudden flooding (N–H on Hor. *Carm.* 1.2.13, 14).

65 in dextrum: sc. *latus.*

65–6 paterere serena | fronte deos 'you would now be enduring the gods [i.e. what the gods bring] with serene face'. The imperf. potential subj. in the apodosis of an 'unreal condition' expresses what was bound to happen in the present, should a disaster have occurred (*NLS* 197). For the Epicureans, a calm expression outwardly showed philosophical rise above material concerns; cf. Hor. *Carm.* 1.37.26 *uoltu sereno*, with N–H. *serena*, a term for calm weather (*OLD* 1), is an appropriate metaphor in the context of hypothetical disasters caused by adverse weather conditions.

66 fidem messesque 'promised harvests' (hendiadys); *OLD fides* 5.

67 Cretaque Cyreneque: the pairing reflects an administrative reality: Cyrene in North Africa and Crete were a single Roman province (*CIL* XII 3164). Ursus' wealth extends outside Italy to the southern Mediterranean.

67–8 et qua tibi cumque beato | larga redit Fortuna sinu 'and wherever generous Fortune makes return to you with bountiful lap'; cf. Hor. *Carm.* 1.7.25 *quo nos cumque feret . . . fortuna*. Tmesis of *quicumque* with the personal pronoun, not in itself uncommon, here as a final compliment inserts Ursus into unspecified but bountiful properties. As a *Roman* goddess, *Fortuna* was associated with positive attributes, in particular with the sustenance of the family, individual, or nation (N–H on Hor. *Carm.* 1.35 pp. 386–8); *larga* is a unique epithet for Fortuna (Carter). More commonly in literature she appears as a malevolent force; cf. 8–9n.

69 Inuidia infelix . . . uidit: cf. Virg. *G.* 3.37 *Inuidia infelix*. On the malevolence of the personified Envy towards the young see 2.1.121–2n. Here she targets the owner, not the slave. St. plays upon the semantic and aural associations of *uidere* and *inuidia*, the condition of looking askance at someone (*OLD inuideo* 1); cf. Sen. *Dial.* 12.16.6 *sine inuidia uidebit*; Ov. *Met.* 2.768–70 *uidet . . . Inuidia*, with Barchiesi and Rosati. *Fortuna* and *Inuidia* are paired as hostile deities at 5.1.137–41 (Gibson ad loc.).   **animi uitalia** 'the vital parts of your soul' (*OLD uitalis* 3). The entire line is striking for the sound patterning of *in, ui, d* and *t* that reinforces the ominous presence of *Inuidia*, who seeks where she can inflict the greatest hurt on Ursus.

70 laedendique uias 'the paths to injury'; cf. *Theb.* 2.554 *medendi uia*; *Theb.* 2.558 *uia prona nocendi*, with Mulder.

70–82 A return to Philetos and his fatal illness and death. There is no personalised, moving deathbed scene as at 2.1.146–57; death is grimly personified by the nightmarish Nemesis.

70 uitae modo margine adultae 'just now at the threshold of adult life', thus SB for M's *carmen*, obelised by Courtney. Such a metaphorical use of *margo*, lit. 'margin' or border', is unattested; yet it could be a fig. extension of its meaning of 'a temple's threshold' at 4.4.54 and *Theb.* 10.49. Van Dam proposes *limine* on analogy with 2.1.38 *in limine uitae*, but this is hard to justify palaeographically; *margine* can be explained by metathesis. Cf. 2.1.44–5.

71 nectere 'join in a continuous series' (*OLD* 8), with *unam trieterida* as its object. The verb's strong associations with weaving ominously conjure up the Fates, who alone are responsible for the length of the thread of life.

72 cum tribus Eleis unam trieterida lustris 'one three-year period with three Olympian five-year periods', an elegant periphrasis stating that Philetos was in his eighteenth year; cf. Ov. *Met.* 14.324–5 (of nineteen-year-old Picus) *nec adhuc spectasse per annos | quinquennem poterat Graia quater Elide pugnam*, with Bömer. Simple numerals were avoided in poetry as too difficult metrically (Grewing on Mart. 6.28.8). St. gives Philetos' age through Greek and Roman measurements of time: *trieteris*, a transliteration of τριετηρίς 'a three-year period', first appears in Flavian poetry. *Eleis* (nom. *Eleus*) 'of Elis' refers to a Greek measurement of time known as the 'Olympiad' coined from the celebration of the first Olympic games at Elis (47n.; Feeney 2007: 19, 84–5). Though the games were held every four years, for the Romans the Olympiad generally denoted a period of five years (*OLD Olympias* 2b; cf. Mart. 4.45.4, 10.23.2) and was often seen as interchangeable with the *lustrum*, the Roman censorial five-year period (2.2.6n.; Hinds 2005: 225 n. 145). Epitaphs commonly gave the exact age of a deceased child, thus emphasising the untimely intervention of death (Watson and Watson on Mart. 5.34.5–6 (= 83)).

73 attendit toruo tristis Rhamnusia uultu: *Rhamnusia*, an epithet for Nemesis, is a neoteric coinage found first in Roman poetry at Cat. 66.71 and 68.77; it derives from the site of her earliest temple (sixth century BCE) in the Attic deme of Rhamnus (Paus. 1.32.2–8). Nemesis was the grim goddess of Fate, a child of deadly Night, 'a source of suffering to mortals' (Hes. *Th.* 223–4), and from the Hellenistic period the punisher of unfaithful lovers (Barchiesi and Rosati on Ov. *Met.* 3.406); cf. Ov. *Tr.* 5.8.9 *ultrix Rhamnusia. toruus*, frequently used of warriors (40–1n.), suggests her hostile intent of destroying the bond between Ursus and Philetos. *attendere* in the sense of 'closely observe' can have a sinister resonance; cf. *Theb.* 11.419. Heavy assonance and spondaic rhythm sound a doom-laden note.

74–5 ac primum impleuitque . . . | . . . leuauit: Nemesis filled out Philetos' muscles, added sparkle to his eyes and made him taller than average – a grim version of the epic motif whereby a favouring deity grants the hero superhuman beauty and size (Hom. *Od.* 6.229–31, 23.156–62; Virg. *A.* 1.588–93). Nemesis acts like *Luchesis* and *Inuidia*, who make Glaucias very attractive in order that his early death be all the more tragic (2.1.120–4).

75 solito sublimius ora leuauit 'she raised his head higher than would be usual'; cf. Ov. *Met.* 1.85 *(deus) os homini sublime dedit*.

76 heu misero letale fauens 'favouring the poor boy with deadly intent, alas'; on adverbial *letale* see 2.1.133–4n. Its paradoxical juxtaposition with *fauens* suggests Nemesis' perversity; cf. *Theb.* 12.760 *letale furens* (without the jarring contrast).

76–7 seseque uidendo | torsit et inuidit 'by looking [at him] she tortured herself and envied him'. St. virtually identifies *Rhamnusia* with *Inuidia* (69n.)

through similar play on the etymological association between *uidere* and *inuidere*. Ellis's conjecture *inuidit*, adopted by Courtney (though not SB), addresses the problem of the syntactical harshness of *uidendo torsit et inuidia* (M). *inuidit* has exegetical force: to torture oneself by 'seeing' makes one become envious; cf. Ov. *Met.* 2.780–1 (the personified *Inuidia*) *sed uidet ingratos intabescitque uidendo | successus hominum*.

77–8 mortisque amplexa iacenti | iniecit nexus 'embracing him, she cast upon him the bonds of death as he lay ill'; cf. 2.1.121–2 (Envy's grim embrace of Glaucias) *complexa fouebat | Inuidia*. Håkanson 1969: 80–1 interprets *mortis nexus* as 'the chains of death', a hunting metaphor associated with Hor. *Carm.* 3.24.8 *mortis laqueis* ('the snares of death'; cf. 5.1.155–6 *furuae . . . leti | . . . plagae* 'the dark hunting nets of death'). Rather *mortis nexus inicere* is a unique legal metaphor that combines into one figure the term for the 'bond' between creditor and debtor (*OLD nexus* 3) and the term for the assertion of one's rights by *manus iniectio*; Nemesis makes Philetos her bondsman 'by right' in death; cf. Call. *Epigr.* 2.8 ἁρπακτὴς Ἀΐδης οὐκ ἐπὶ χεῖρα βαλεῖ; Ov. *Am.* 3.9.20 (of Death) *omnibus obscuras inicit illa manus*; McKeown on Ov. *Am.* 2.6.39–40. Baehrens's generally accepted conjecture *mortis* solves the problem of M's *mortem*, impossible with *amplexa*.

78–9 carpsitque immitis adunca | ora uerenda manu: another grim image of Nemesis 'plucking away' the boy's beauty by clawing 'at the face she should have revered'. *carpere*, often used of picking flowers, emphasises the brevity of the youth's life. Unlike with Glaucias (cf. 2.1.155–7), mortal illness seems to have destroyed Philetos' beauty; cf. 5.1.150 *carpitur eximium Fato Priscilla decorum*, with Gibson. The 'hooked hand', i.e. 'talons', is not part of Nemesis' standard iconography (D–S vii 1.52–5), but St. here associates Nemesis with the *Parca* who threatens Glaucias with 'unsheathed nails' (2.1.138); *adunca* more grimly suggests that Nemesis 'gouges' Philetos' face; in epic 'hooked hands' help heroes climb up rocks by digging in deeply; cf. Virg. *A.* 6.360 *uncis manibus*; Mulder on *Theb.* 2.556; Dewar on *Theb.* 9.495–6. Nemesis is *immitis* in showing no pity to Philetos, who deserved to live, or to Ursus, who lost a beloved slave.

79–80 quinto uix Phosphoros ortu | rorantem sternebat equum: a lovely assonant periphrasis for conveying the length of illness and the time of death, contrasting with the harshness of 76–9. The precise time of Philetos' death however is problematic, for M reads *quinta . . . hora* 'at the fifth hour', i.e. late morning according to ancient time reckoning by the twelve-hour day (cf. Mart. 4.8.3 *in quintam uarios extendit Roma labores*; Pers. 3.4). Yet the rest of the sentence seems to describe dawn, though it began at the 'first hour': *Phosphoros* is a Grecism (Φωσφόρος) for the far more common *Lucifer*, the morning star or 'light-bringer' (Cic. *N.D.* 2.53); cf. Sen. *Her. F.* 128 *cogit nitidum Phosphoros agmen*, with Fitch; Mart. 8.21.1 (a gloss) *Phosphore, redde diem*; *equum sternere* probably means 'to saddle' or 'put a cloth upon a horse for riding', as at Livy 37.20.4 and 12 (*OLD sterno* 2b), and thus Phosphoros is setting out on a journey, not returning (on Lucifer as horse-rider see McKeown on Ov. *Am.* 2.11.55–6); the horse is dripping with the dew that will suffuse the earth, not sweating on return, for *rorantem* etymologically alludes to the dawn (Michalopoulos s.v. *Aurora*; cf. *Ach.* 1.242–3 *humilique ex aequore Titan* | *rorantes euoluit equos*); finally *uix* suggests Phosphoros was just about to set out when Philetos died. M's (*h*)*ora* is probably a corruption from attraction with *ora* at line start. Schrader's conjecture (accepted by SB) *quinto . . . ortu* explains that the time of death was just before dawn at the star's fifth rising, i.e. on the fifth day of the illness (though the seventh day was more common; 2.1.146n.). Stars are often referred to in terms of their risings or settings; 'fifth' moreover calls for a temporal noun. Postgate's *Oeta*, accepted by Courtney, refers to the mountain site of Hercules' funeral pyre, which was associated in poetry with the rising of the evening or morning star (Quinn on Cat. 62.7 *Oetaeos . . . ignes*; Clausen on Virg. *Ecl.* 8.30 *deserit Hesperus Oetam*). *quinta . . . Oeta* would mean the fifth rising of the morning star (Courtney 2004: 450). Suggestive is the mention of Phosphoros and Oeta in subsequent lines at Sen. *Her. F.* 182–3. But the modification of Oeta with a temporal epithet would be unparalleled.

80–1 litora duri | saeua . . . senis: Charon, who ferries souls across the Underworld river Styx, described as 'pitiless' (*OLD durus* 5), since he spares nobody (2.1.186n.). *saeue* is the poem's first word, *durum* appears at the start of line 4 (with the different sense 'hard to bear'). Verbal repetition marks the move towards closure (2.1.208n.).

81 Philete: the first mention of the young man's name, φιλητός = 'worthy of love/beloved', interjected at the emotional highpoint of the poem, his descent to the Underworld. On the delayed introduction of the deceased's name see 2.1.229n. His name perhaps echoes that of Philitas of Cos (there were variant spellings of his name, Spanoudakis 2002: 19–23), one of the most famous of the Hellenistic elegists (singled out by St. at 1.2.252; cf. Prop. 3.1.1–2), esp. for his now lost elegiac *Demeter* (Knox 1993; Spanoudakis 2002: 223–43). Was St. perhaps influenced by Philitas' learned approach to this archetypal myth of bereavement and consolation?   **dirumque Acheronta:** M reads *durumque*, which very closely echoes *duri* (of Charon). Though close repetition is a feature of the *Siluae* (2.1.47–8n.), *dirum*, a solemn epithet for Underworld deities and places (*TLL* v 1.1270.31–72), is slightly more appropriate.

82 quo domini clamate sono! '[Philetos], lamented with what a cry from your master!', an emotionally compressed climax.

82–3 non saeuius atros | nigrasset planctu genetrix tibi salua lacertos 'your mother, if she had outlived you, would not more savagely have made her arms black with bruises for you'. Bruising one's arms – and thus assuming the colour of mourning – was a conventional feminine gesture of grief, here adopted by Ursus; cf. *Theb.* 7.475–6 (Jocasta) *bracchia planctu | nigra ferens*; *Ach.* 1.132 (Thetis) *nunc planctu liuere manus*; 2.1.23n. In the sense 'to make black and blue' *nigrare* occurs in classical Latin poetry elsewhere only at Lucr. 2.733, there with intransitive use; but St. does sometimes use formerly intransitive verbs with transitive sense (Van Dam). Juxtaposition with *atros*, which has negative emotional connotations (2.3.12–13n.), reinforces the idea of savage grief.   **tibi salua** 'if she had survived you', a generally accepted emendation for M's senseless *tibi saeua. salua* is ἀπὸ κοινοῦ with *pater*, both parents being dead (99).

85 erubuit uinci '[your brother] blushed at being outdone'; on competitiveness at the funeral pyre see 2.1.23n. *erubuit* parallels *nigrasset* in initial line position and perhaps anticipates the flames of the funeral pyre; cf. *Aetna* 635 *erubuere pios iuuenes attingere flammae.*

85–93 Philetos' funeral, like Glaucias', was lavish, with an abundance of exotic perfumes and spices. Yet Ursus is comparatively restrained in his grief; unlike Melior (2.1.25, 162–5), he does not try to throw himself, or all his wealth, on the pyre.

85–6 sed nec seruilis adempto | ignis 'but there was nothing servile about the pyre for the one taken from us', a compliment to Ursus for providing a grand funeral, an occasion for displaying wealth and social status to the public as well as *pietas* to the deceased. *seruilis* conflates two meanings, 'belonging to a slave' and 'ignoble' (*OLD* 1 and 2), and alludes to the opening theme of what constitutes a true slave. *ademptus* is a common euphemism for 'dead' (N–H on Hor. *Carm.* 2.9.10).

86 odoriferos: first in Roman poetry at Prop. 2.13.23 (a denunciation of a costly funeral) *desit odoriferis ordo mihi lancibus*; see Bömer on Ov. *Met.* 4.209. Here it is ἀπὸ κοινοῦ with *Sabaeos | et Cilicum messes* (86–7). On compound adjectives in *-fer* see 2.1.181n.   **Sabaeos** refers to a region of south-west Arabia associated with myrrh ([Sen.] *Her. O.* 376) and frankincense (Virg. *A.* 1.416). Both fragrances are probably meant here.   **exhausit** 'devoured'; cf. 2.1.164–5, where the fire cannot consume all the offerings.

87 et Cilicum messes: i.e. saffron (2.1.160 n.).

87–8 Phariaeque exempta uolucri | cinnama: St. refers to the phoenix, a symbol of longevity and renewal appropriate for consolation (2.4.36–7n.). It used cinnamon to build its nest (Ov. *Met.* 15.399), thus a very rare spice indeed! It is called 'Egyptian' because it flew from Arabia to dedicate its father's remains at the Temple of the Sun in Heliopolis, Egypt (Hdt. 2.73), hence it is a symbol of filial devotion (Ov. *Met.* 15.405 *pius*).

88 et Assyrio manantes gramine sucos: SB adopts Heinsius' emendation *germine* ('bud'), on the grounds that cardamon, if this is what is meant (2.4.34n.), comes from a shrub, not a herb (*gramen*); see Coleman on Virg. *Ecl.* 3.89. But as Courtney 2004: 452 points out, St. uses *gramen* of a small tree or shrub. Mention of liquid unguents (*sucos*) anticipates the surprising final item in the gifts to the pyre, Ursus' tears.

89 et domini fletus: cf. 5.3.45–6 *sume... | et lacrimas, rari quas umquam habuere parentes;* Ov. *Pont.* 1.7.29 *lacrimas, supremum in funere munus.* On the poetic tradition of the gift of tears at the pyre see N–H on Hor. *Carm.* 2.6.23.

89–90 hos tantum hausere fauillae, | hos bibit usque rogus 'these [*sc.* Ursus' tears] the ashes alone drained, these the pyre drank to the last drop'. St. plays on the contrast between water and fire; paradoxically the pyre 'drinks' rather than 'burns'.

90–3 nec quod tibi Setia canos | restinxit cineres... | ...miseris acceptius umbris | quam gemitus 'nor was the fact that Setian wine extinguished your grey ashes... more welcome to your wretched shade than groans of lamentation'. As a literary topos, the practice of extinguishing the funeral ashes with wine derives from Homer (*Il.* 23.236–8); cf. Virg. *A.* 6.226–7 *postquam conlapsi cineres et flamma quieuit, | reliquias uino et bibulam lauere fauillam,* with Austin. Setian was a fine Latian wine which Plin. *Nat.* 14.61 places in the first rank; a favourite of Augustus and subsequent emperors, it was valued esp. as a *digestif.* Ursus' use of a connoisseur's wine displays his wealth.

91–2 gremio nec lubricus ossa | quod uallauit onyx: a second noun clause, also dependent on *acceptius* (*erat*), but with *nec* postponed (2.1.140n.); the postponement of *quod* to the third position is unusual. Onyx, metonymy for the funerary urn, was an expensive marble admired for its spiral patterning (1.2.149 *flexus onyx*) and used mainly for small, exquisitely wrought objects such as unguent jars (Plin. *Nat.* 36.59). *lubricus* suggests marble's gleaming smoothness, in contrast with the rough bones it contains.

93–102 A turn to direct consolatory arguments with a series of short questions chiding Ursus for indulgence in his sorrow: anaphora of *quid* (93, 94, 96) is varied by *ubi* (95).

93 sed et ipse uetat: an emphatically abrupt sentence to announce the change in tack: the emendation *uetat* for M's *iuuat* introduces the consolatory convention of the deceased's prohibition against mourning, placed here shortly before the poem's end (cf. 2.1.153).

93–4 quid terga dolori, | Vrse, damus? 'why, Ursus, do we give way to grief?'; cf. *Theb.* 5.698 *dolor dat terga timori.* The metaphorical *terga dare* suggests a possible pun on Ursus' name that lightens the poem's mood in the move away from grief; see 2.5.18–19n.

94–5 quid . . . pectore iniquo | uulnus amas?: cf. *Theb.* 12.45 *amant miseri lamenta malisque fruuntur. iniquus* 'turbulent' expresses restlessness of the mind or heart (*OLD* 7); cf. Sen. *Con.* 9.1.3 *non iste iniquiore animo filiam amisit quam ego uxorem.* St. briefly acknowledges the philosophical tradition that condemned pleasure in grief (2.1.15n.; Markus 2004: 107–9, 130); cf. the endorsement of Ursus' *uulnera* at 6–8. Such recall, with change, facilitates the poem's move towards consolation.

95 ubi nota reis facundia raptis? 'where is that eloquence well known to defendants suddenly called away to court?' Ursus seems to have been a lawyer. But *rapere* in the sense of 'summon to court' otherwise always appears with an adjunct such as *in ius* (*OLD rapio* 7b; cf. Hor. *S.* 1.9.77). Van Dam thus proposes taking *rapere* in its sense of 'to snatch away by death' (2.1.1n.) and emending *reis* to *aliis*, with the idea that since Ursus was skilled in consolation 'when others had been snatched away by death', he should now do a better job of consoling himself. But this sense is strained and invalidates St.'s role as consoler. *raptis* pinpoints the difference between the living and the dead by a play on the two meanings – not those snatched away by death but those snatched off to court have now to be Ursus' proper concern. The call to resume one's duties is typical of consolatory literature; cf. 2.1.233–4; *Epic. Drusi* 473–4, a reminder to Livia of her responsibility to her spouse.

96 quid caram crucias . . . umbram?: cf. 5.1.180 (a wife's final request) *nec crucia fugientem coniugis umbram.* The metaphor has additional resonance here from the torture routinely applied to slaves, e.g. for criminal information (Bradley 1994: 165–73).   **tam saeuis luctibus:** cf. *saeue nimis,* of the person who would set a limit to grief. Now Ursus is castigated for not doing so.

97 eximius licet ille animi, (*sc. sit*) 'though he is matchless of mind'; *animi* is gen. 'of the sphere in which', as often with this noun (L–H–S 74–5); cf. Virg. *A.* 4.529 *infelix animi Phoenissa* ('Dido with doom in her heart', Austin).

98 soluisti: enjambment with the absolute use of the verb lends blunt finality to consolation: Ursus has paid his dues to Philetos with his grief and the lavish funeral. *soluere* 'to pay one's debts' plays on the common epitaphic theme that life is a 'loan' (Lattimore 1962: 71; Horsfall on Virg. *A.* 7.5 *exsequiis . . . solutis*). This financial metaphor leads Ursus back to the 'real' world that, as a rich property owner (61–8) and lawyer (95), he surely well understands.

98–102 The reception of Philetos in Elysium combines the elegiac model of the lovers' paradise (e.g. Tib. 1.3.57–66) with the poet's innovation, an Elysium where family welcomes the deceased (2.1.194–207, 3.3.205–7). The topos is treated in a reassuring way, without mention of the conventional horrors of the Underworld; cf. 2.1.183–8.

98 subit ille pios: cf. 2.1.155 *manesque subibit*; on *subire* as a term for descent to the Underworld see Gibson on 5.1.258. *pios* refers to the 'virtuous dead' (*OLD* 1b) who inhabit Elysium; cf. Hor. *Carm.* 2.13.23 *sedesque discretas piorum*; Virg. *A.* 8.670 *secretosque pios*; it also stresses Philetos' particular loyalty to Ursus (*OLD* 3d); cf. 10 *famulum . . . pium*. Likewise Propertius' Cynthia shares Elysium with faithful women (4.7.59–70); cf. Ov. *Am.* 2.6.51. The pointed repetition of *ille* (97) in the same metrical position in the line associates Philetos' virtue with his eternal reward, Elysium.

98–9 carpitque quietem | Elysiam 'and he enjoys the peace of Elysium'. Grimly used of Nemesis at 78, *carpere* now assumes the positive connotations of enjoying sleep or rest; cf. Sil. 17.160 *grauis curis carpit dum nocte quietem*; see Pease on Virg. *A.* 4.522 for poetic parallels. Prop. 4.7.60 seems to have introduced the adjective *Elysius* to Roman poetry.

99 clarosque . . . parentes: a return to earlier hints about Philetos' origins (21n., 22–3n.). If he is of noble stock, he will know for certain in the afterlife.   **illic** 'there in the Underworld' (McKeown on Ov. *Am.* 2.6.53).

100 amoena silentia Lethes: cf. 2.4.8 *aeterna silentia Lethes*. Silence is a particular feature of St.'s Underworld (2.1.204n.). The juxtaposition of *silentia* with Lethe emphasises the river's association with quiet and forgetfulness (λήθη); see 2.1.194n. *amoena* characterises the Elysian fields through which the river Lethe flowed (Virg. *A.* 6.705); cf. Virg. *A.* 6.638 *locos laetos et amoena uirecta*.

101–2 Auernales alludunt . . . | Naides: Lake Avernus, situated between Cumae and Naples and known since Hellenistic times as an entrance to the Underworld, was supposedly uninhabitable due to its exhalation of poisonous fumes (Lucr. 6.338–48; Virg. *A.* 6.238–41). 'Avernal Naiads' then are nymphs of the Underworld, introduced to poetry by Ovid; cf. *Met.* 5.540 *Auernales . . . nymphas*, with Börner. From Ovid on *Auernus* (or adjectival *Auernalis*) generally designates the Underworld, rather than the lake. *alludunt* creates a playful atmosphere; Philetos will have nothing to fear.

102 obliquoque notat Proserpina uultu: Proserpina's 'sidelong glance' is enigmatic. Vollmer assumes she envies the Naiads, since *obliquus* often has the sense of 'ill-omened' or 'with ill intent' (cf. Sil. 2.621). But the sidelong glance can also be flirtatious; cf. Ov. *Am.* 3.1.33 (of Lady Elegy) *limis . . . ocellis*, with Hunter 2006: 40–1; Snijder on *Theb.* 3.266 (of Venus) *uultumque obliqua*; cf. *Ach.* 1.766 (Ulysses' covert gaze upon Achilles) *obliquo lumine*. Proserpina's sidelong glance at Philetos is probably both amorous and guarded (to maintain her regal dignity); *notat* suggests she singles him out for his beauty.

103 pone, precor, questus: a renewed, final exhortation to Ursus to cease mourning; cf. the similar injunctions at 2.1.183 *pone metus*; Sil. 9.350 *pone, precor, lacrimas*.

103–104 alium tibi Fata Phileton, | forsan et ipse dabis: cf. Virg. *Ecl.*
2.73 *inuenies alium . . . Alexin*, with Clausen; Virgil alludes to Theocr. 11.76. St. thus
acknowledges the distinguished literary pedigree of his poem on a slave. The
echo of the end of *Ecl.* 2 also reinforces the injunction to Ursus to return to work
(95); cf. *Ecl.* 2.71–2. The idea of a replacement for the deceased was not regarded
as insensitive in consolations; Glaucias provided consolation for Blaesus' death
(2.1.201); cf. *Theb.* 6.49–50 *nunc aliam prolem mansuraque numine dextro | pignora*; Sen.
Ep. 63.11 *satius est amicum reparare quam flere.* SB tightens the parallel with *Ecl.* 2
by changing third person *dabit* to *dabis* (also *monstrabis* and *docebis* 105), claiming
(Appendix p. 391) that the idea that Philetos himself might find a replacement
is unparalleled and well in excess of the topos of the return of the deceased
in dreams (cf. 2.1.227–34); *dabit* requires us to imagine that Philetos grooms his
replica and sends him to Ursus from Elysium. *dabis* on the other hand stresses
the need for Ursus to look to the future now that Philetos has been laid to rest.

104 moresque habitusque: cf. (in reverse order) 21 and 23 (Philetos'
attributes).

105 monstrabis: in the sense of 'teach' see 2.4.31–2n.   **similemque
docebis amorem:** M has the impossible *amori.* Courtney reads *amari*, which
suggests that Ursus will teach a boy like Philetos (*similemque*) how to be loved.
amorem is an early correction endorsed by SB and Van Dam; Ursus, following
SB's shift to the second person, will teach the boy a love similar to the one that he
enjoyed with Philetos. This reading has the advantage of reinforcing the elegant
pun with which the poem ends: Philetos' name is synonymous with 'love' (81n.).

Siluae 2.7

2.7 is our earliest source for the life and non-extant work of Lucan (hereafter
L.). The two major ancient prose lives, Suet. *Vita Lucani* (*poet.* 33) and Vacca, *Vita
Lucani*, along with some fragments of L.'s poetry, are printed in Hosius' edition of
the *Bellum ciuile* (used in ref. here for the 'lives'). Other significant ancient sources
are Suet. *Vita Persi* (*poet.* 32 and 33); Tac. *Ann.* 15.49, 56–7, 70–1, 16.17. Unlike
these lives, 2.7 provides a brief critical synopsis of many of L.'s works, esp. the
Bellum ciuile. Discussion of the sources is found in Ahl 1976: 35–47, 333–57; see
also *N–P* vii 829–32 for an overview of L.'s life and works.

Romans customarily celebrated the birthday of the deceased; but the special
veneration accorded L. on his birthday also follows the Greek precedent *Ecl.*
according posthumous tribute to rulers and outstanding people such as Plato
and Epicurus (*OCD* s.v. 'birthday') and ties in with the development of a poetic
cult. 2.7 was written in response to a request from L.'s widow Polla for a birthday
poem (2 *pr.* 22–4); Mart. 7.21, 22, 23 were written for the same occasion (Buchheit
1961; Vioque 2002: 168–79). Birthday poems became an important genre in the

Augustan age, inspired by the regularisation of the calendar (Feeney 2007: 148–60); but 2.7 is a new poetic form, the *posthumous* birthday poem. As in 2.3 St. innovates with the *genethliacon*, combining the joy attendant on a birthday with commemoration of the deceased; his poem is an offshoot of the *exitus* literature popular at the time (introd. to 2.5) and contributes to L.'s rehabilitation as a major Roman poet after his political disgrace (see 101 n.; 2 *pr.* 23–4 n.). References to L.'s family, esp. Seneca, throughout 2.7 are a reminder that Nero annihilated the entire Annaei family. 2.7 may also reflect contemporary controversy over L.'s merits as a poet, with Martial and Quintilian judging him more an orator than a poet (Mart. 14.94; Quint. *Inst.* 10.90.1). The Muse of epic poetry authoritatively asserts that L. is to be judged as a poet, and she singles out the *Bellum ciuile* as the pre-eminent Roman historical epic.

The metre is hendecasyllabic, which was rare in actual epitaphs but is also used by St. with closural force for the final poems 1.6 and 4.9. A popular Catullan metre, hendecasyllables suggest the joy of the occasion; in addition, the short lines allow for terse, elegant expression, with many lines self-contained and sententious; enjambment is infrequent, so that the poem has a lapidary quality; see 2 *pr.* 25–6n.

The poem falls into three main sections: two encomiastic parts of roughly equivalent length focused on the birthday celebration (1–35, 107–35) frame Calliope's prophecy of L.'s career (36–106).

Further reading: on Roman birthday rites see *RE* VII 1.1142–49; on birthday poems Argetsinger 1992; Feeney 2007: 156–200. On the poem's structure see Buchheit 1960. Ahl 1976: 336–43, Hardie 1983: 115–18, Quint 1993: 132–5 and Malamud 1995 offer stimulating approaches to 2.7. On St.'s frequent allusion to the *Bellum ciuile* in the *Siluae* see Michler 1914; on allusions to L. in the *Thebaid* Venini 1971. On the significance of 2.7 as the closural poem of book 2 see Newlands 2006.

1–23 Proem, describing a sacral occasion; St. acts as master of ceremonies and 'priest'. Birthdays in the Roman world were religious occasions; but instead of invoking the traditional birthday genius (e.g. Tib. 2.2.1), St. summons an elite audience of inspired poets (1–4), Muses, and gods associated with both poetry and Thebes (5–11), thus making poetics central to 2.7. The frequent Graecisms of this elevated opening distance St. from the Roman poetics of L.

1 Lucani proprium diem: St. avoids the phrase *dies natalis*, a convention of the birthday poem (Van Dam); the opening echo of *lux* ('day', 'light') in L.'s name indicates St.'s double theme, the special commemoration of L. held on his birthday, and his elevation as object of poetic cult. For similar wordplay on L.'s name see also 19n. and 120n., each time with the suggestive proximity of *dies*; Maltby s.v. *Lucanus*; also Maltby s.v. *Lucina*; *OLD antelucanus* 'before daylight'. Such punning on proper names usually occurs towards the start or end of a work (2 *pr.* 1n.); Mart. 7.21, 22, 23 also play with the etymology of L.'s name (Vioque on

Mart. 7 p. 168). *proprium* indicates perpetual ownership (Austin on Virg. *A.* 1.73) and suggests perhaps that L.'s birthday (3 November), like Virgil's (Plin. *Ep.* 3.7.8), was a special day in the calendar.   **frequentet** 'let him come celebrate' (*OLD* 7, of a sacred occasion), a fairly grand word first used in this sense by Ovid; cf. *Met.* 3.691 *accessi sacris Baccheaque sacra frequento*, with Bömer.

2–4 quisquis . . . bibit: a conventional metaphor for the poet as drinker at a poetic spring, varied by St. in topographical and symbolic detail; see notes on 2.2 lines 36 through 40.

2 collibus Isthmiae Diones: i.e. Acrocorinth, the acropolis of Corinth with its famous temple of Aphrodite (2.2.35n.). *collibus* is topographically exact, as the Corinthian acropolis has two summits. Dione is fairly common in Roman poetry as a name for Aphrodite (McKeown on Ov. *Am.* 1.14.33). The Acrocorinth also boasted the poetic spring Pirene (Plin. *Nat.* 4.11); see 4n.

3 docto pectora concitatus oestro 'roused in their hearts by the learned gadfly', a bold paradox. The Greek loan word *oestrus* ('a gadfly') was introduced to Roman poetry by Virgil; cf. *G.* 3.147–8 *cui nomen asilo | Romanum est, oestrum Grai uertere uocantes*, with Mynors. First used at Hom. *Od.* 22.300 in a simile to describe the suitors' panic, *oestrus* became associated with madness and frenzy; cf. A. R. 1.1265–9. St. uses *oestrus* as a metaphor for poetic inspiration here and at *Theb.* 1.32–3 (its only other occurrence in St.) *tempus erit, cum Pierio tua fortior oestro | facta canam. docto*, a complimentary catchword of Hellenistic poetics (N–H on Hor. *Carm.* 1.1.29), suggests that St. summons poets like L. who combine passion with cultured learning, *ingenium* with *ars*; cf. Quint. *Inst.* 10.1.90 *Lucanus ardens et concitatus et sententiis clarissimus.*

4 pendentis . . . ungulae liquorem 'the water of the dangling hoof' (*OLD pendeo* 8a) would normally suggest Hippocrene, the Muses' spring on Mount Helicon, formed by the hoof of the winged horse Pegasus, but the Corinthian setting requires Pirene on the Acrocorinth (2.2.37–8n.). The close connection of Corinth in St.'s poetry with the myth of Ino and Palaemon (2.1.179–80n.) places the celebration on familiar Statian territory.

5 ipsi quos penes est honor canendi 'you yourselves who possess the honour of poetry', i.e. the Muses, Mercury, Bacchus and Apollo. *quos penes* is an elevated expression used in addressing deities or divinely appointed persons; cf. 1.4.16; McKeown on Ov. *Am.* 2.2.1. At the start of his epic L. blatantly dispensed with gods and divine agency, esp. Apollo and Bacchus (Luc. 1.63–6; Rosati 2002: 243–4). St. thus asserts his poetic independence here too; see 1–23n.

6 uocalis citharae repertor Arcas: elevated description of Mercury, born in Arcadia. The *cithara* is properly Apollo's lyre (hence his title *Citharoedus*) as distinct from the tortoiseshell lyre (*chelys*) invented by Mercury (N–H on Hor. *Carm.* 1.10.6), but the two types were often conflated in Roman poetry (D–S III

2.1437–48). *uocalis* = 'tuneful'; cf. *uocales* (of lyre strings) at Tib. 2.5.3; N–H on Hor. *Carm.* 1.12.7. St. uses *repertor* 'inventor' only here; cf. Ov. *Am.* 1.3.11 *at Phoebus comitesque nouem uitisque repertor*; Luc. 9.661 *Arcados auctoris citharae*; see Malamud 1995: 173–5. Mercury in the *Thebaid* helped foment the hatred between the two brothers (*Theb.* 2.1–57).

7 Bassaridum: cf. Sen. *Oed.* 432 *Bassaridum cohors*, possibly the first use in Latin literature of *Bassaris*, a rare Greek term for the Thracian Maenads, associated with a cult name of Bacchus 'Bassareus' (Βασσαρεύς); N–H on Hor. *Carm.* 1.18.11.   **rotator:** a unique title for Bacchus, patron deity of Thebes, coined from *roto*; Bacchus 'causes to whirl' (*OLD roto* 1) his followers, thus filling them with frenzy (Coleman on 4.3.121). Cf. *Theb.* 7.170–1 *nectere fronde comas et ad inspirata rotari | buxa.*   **Euhan:** a Greek cult title for Dionysus, derived from εὐάν, the Bacchantes' ritual cry. Euhan is found first for Bacchus at Lucr. 5.731; it is a favourite of St. (Carter s.v. *Liber*).

8 Paean: rare in St. for Apollo, patron deity of Argos (Thebes' rival city), found in the *Thebaid* only at 1.636 and 10.343, in the *Siluae* only here and at 1.2.2, both instances where St. draws on its association with *paean*, a laudatory song honouring other deities, heroes and mortals (*OLD* 2; cf. *Theb.* 4.157, 8.224, 10.306). St. excluded Apollo from 2.3 as too grand a deity for a modest birthday poem (6–7); but 2.7, despite its humble metre, is on a higher register.   **Hyantiae sorores** 'Boeotian sisters', i.e. the Muses, dwellers on Mount Helicon in Boeotia, *Hyantes* being an ancient name for the Boeotians (Plin. *Nat.* 4.28), who occupied the southern part of Theban territory. The short *i* of *Hyantiae* is for metrical convenience; hexameter poets write *Hyanteus*; cf. *Theb.* 1.183 *Hyanteos . . . per agros*; Ov. *Met.* 5.312 *Hyantea Aganippe*, a spring on Helicon. Prop. 3.10.1–4 summons the Roman Muses, the *Camenae*, to a birthday celebration, but St. summons to L.'s rites his own Theban Muses; cf. Mart. 7.22.2 *Aonidum turba, fauete sacris*, with Vioque. Roman poets adopt from Hellenistic practice reference to the Muses as 'sisters' rather than the traditional 'daughters'; cf. Virg. *Ecl.* 5.65 *una sororum*, with Clausen.

9 laetae purpureas uittas nouate 'joyfully renew the purple headbands'; the nom. pl. fem. adjective has adverbial force. The address shifts to the Muses alone who are ordered to attend to the birthday rites; cf. Ov. *Tr.* 3.13.14–18.   **purpureas . . . uittas:** *uittae* were strips of cloth or wool used as ritual headbands or as adornments to sacred places (*OLD* 2); they were usually white (Virg. *G.* 3.391), but cf. Cat. 64.309 (of the *Parcae*) *roseae uittae*; Prop. 4.9.27 (of the *Bona Dea*) *puniceae uelabant limina uittae*. *purpureus*, a colour with a range of shades on the 'red' spectrum (*OLD* 1), was associated with both nobility and mourning; roses and violets, emblems of grief, were common at funerals and gave their names to festivals of the dead, the Rosaria and Violaria (Champlin 1991: 163–4). The Muses' *uittae* express the poem's tension between celebration and mourning.

The renewal or replacement of headbands is an appropriately symbolic gesture for a day devoted to renewal of memory; the verb also draws attention to the novelty of St.'s poem, a feature esp. prized in Callimachean discourse (Call. *Aet.* I fr. 1.25–8 Pf.).

10 crinem comite: St. suggests a festive mood by inviting the Muses to tidy their hair (as opposed to loosening it in mourning). Cf. Prop. 3.10.14 (inviting Cynthia to fix her hair for the birthday party) *nitidas presso pollice finge comas.* **candidamque uestem:** white was traditionally worn at celebrations, including birthdays, to express happiness and symbolise good fortune; cf. Tib. 1.7.63–4 *at tu, Natalis multos celebrande per annos,* | *candidior semper candidiorque ueni,* with Maltby; Ov. *Tr.* 3.13.14 on the white clothing (*uestis . . . alba*) to be worn on his birthday.

11 perfundant hederae: garlands adorned hair and altars at the birthday rites; cf. Tib. 2.2.6 *decorent sanctas mollia serta comas*; Ov. *Tr.* 3.13.15 *cingatur florentibus ara coronis*; Courtney on Juv. 5.36–7. Ivy was the sacred plant of Bacchus (Hor. *Carm.* 3.30.15–16), and is esp. appropriate for a poet's birthday. The unusual enjambment (with *uestem*) emphasises the notion of profusion; the ivy does not 'dangle (everywhere) on' as Van Dam suggests but 'spreads all over' (the white garment), suggesting a miraculous growth. Ivy is esp. suited to the 'lighter genres' (N–H on Hor. *Carm.* 1.1.29). Yet *perfundant* suggests a wide-ranging poetic capacity. **recentiores** 'fresher' as it replaces last year's garland but with a suggestion again of poetic novelty; see 9n.

12–18 St. sets L.'s birthday celebration in an imaginary poetic grove that also incorporates Theban topographical features, a reminder of St.'s epic authority and his claim to be L.'s successor (introd. 16–17). He combines here the idea of the sacred grove dedicated to a poet's cult with the grove's symbolic function as a metaphor for refined poetic inspiration (2.3.1–5n.; N–H on Hor. *Carm.* 1.1.30; Fedeli on Prop. 3.1.2). The silvan setting is esp. appropriate for the final poem of *Siluae* 2; it symbolically accommodates epic to the poetics of the *Siluae.*

12 docti largius euagentur amnes: another striking expression of epic grandeur and neoteric sophistication; cf. 3 *docto . . . oestro*; 1.2.259 *et sociam haurimus doctis ab amnibus undam.* amnis is a grand poetic word (2.3.5n.); *largius* and *euagentur,* the latter used of rivers overflowing (*OLD* 2a), suggest the fuller tide of epic inspiration (cf. 11 *perfundant*); *docti* suggests meticulous composition. The rivers Permessus and Olmeius flow at the foot of Mount Helicon (Hes. *Th.* 5, 6; Wallace 1974: 14–21; Clausen on Virg. *Ecl.* 1.64). The landscape of Helicon, the source of poetic inspiration since the Muses appeared there to Hesiod (*Th.* 1–23), was part of Theban topography (8n.).

13 et plus, Aoniae, uirete, siluae: cf. Luc. 1–2 *bella per Emathios plus quam ciuilia campos* | *. . . canimus; plus* 'more than usual' emphasises that St.'s *Siluae* must adopt a higher style in honour of an epic poet. St. possibly alludes also to Virg. *Ecl.* 4.3 *si canimus siluas, siluae sint consule dignae*, a command to heighten the register of pastoral poetry; there too *siluae* means 'woods' both as natural growth and a body of poetry. But *uirete*, a command for greater fertility (or 'greenness'), suggests a different poetics from L.'s 'thundering' verse (66n.), implying the flowering of memory and L.'s rehabilitation.   **Aoniae:** a synonym for 'Boeotian' or 'Theban' that first appears in Roman poetry at Cat. 61.27 *perge linquere Thespiae | rupis Aonios specus*, drawn from Callimachean usage (Call. *Del.* 4.75 and fr. 572 Pf.; Fedeli on Cat. 61 pp. 38–9). Thereafter *Aonius* often refers specifically to the Muses or their springs (*OLD* 2b) as well as Thebes, since Mount Helicon was in Boeotia; cf. Ov. *Fast.* 3.456 (the Hippocrene) *leuis Aonias ungula fodit aquas*; *Met.* 7.763 *Aoniis . . . Thebis*. St. conflates both senses here and at *Theb.* 1.33–4 (a programmatic definition of his epic) *arma . . . Aonia*; cf. *Ach.* 1.10 *neque enim Aonium nemus aduena pulso*. 'Aonian woods' thus symbolise St.'s own literary territory, encompassing his two major works to date, the *Thebaid* and *Siluae.*

14–15 et, si qua patet aut diem recepit, | sertis mollibus expleatur umbra 'or if the shade anywhere has gaps or has let daylight enter, let it be filled with soft garlands'. St. plays here on the etymological connection of *lucus* ('grove') with absence of light; cf. Don. *Gramm.* 4.402.4 *lucus eo quod non luceat*; Maltby s.v. *lucus.* Thick, unbroken shade signalled the presence of divinity; cf. Sen. *Ep.* 41.3 *illa proceritas siluae et secretum loci et admiratio umbrae in aperto tam densae atque continuae fidem tibi numinis faciet*; St. creates a sacral, literary setting. Garlands were worn at Roman birthdays (11n.) and are also a traditional metaphor for poems or poetry books; cf. Mart. 8.82.4, with Schöffel. *mollibus*, a literary term associated with 'lighter' genres, offsets *expleatur*, a term for giving fullness of style to writing (*OLD* 4e).

16–17 centum . . . | stent altaria uictimaeque centum: a hecatomb, generally understood in Roman poetry as the sacrifice of one hundred oxen (Fitch on Sen. *Her. F.* 299–300), with here one victim for each of the hundred altars; *altaria*, etymologically associated with *altus* 'high' (*TLL* 1 1725.17–19; Maltby s.v. *altare*), emphasises the grand nature of the sacrifice, as does the framing of these two lines by *centum*. Birthday offerings were traditionally bloodless; Ov. *Tr.* 3.13.15–17 mentions an altar crowned with garlands, incense, cakes (*libaque . . . proprie genitale notantia tempus*); cf. Censorinus, *DN* 2.2; Argetsinger 1992: 186–8 on the anomaly of Hor. *Carm.* 4.11. The sacrifice here can be understood as a metaphor for poetic genre: the large, rich offerings symbolise epic poetry and fittingly honour L.; cf. Call. *Aet.* 1. fr. 1.23–4 Pf.; Hor. *Carm.* 4.2.53–4. On St.'s use of sacrifice as a sign of literary/ethical/social status see Henderson 1998: 101 on 1.4.127–31; on sacrifice as part of a poet's cult see Clay 2004: 81.

16 Thespiacis . . . lucis: *Thespiacus* is a learned epithet unique to St.; cf. *Theb.*
7.341 *Thespiacis . . . in agris*; the more usual but also rare *Thespius* first appears in
Latin poetry at Cat. 61.27 *Thespiae rupis*, a neoteric neologism modelled on Hes.
fr. 310.2 M–W θέσπιον ('divinely sounding'); see Fedeli on Cat. 61 p. 38. Thespia
was a region at the foot of Mount Helicon famous for its sacred grove to Hesiod's
Muses and for its festival in their honour (Paus. 9.31.3; Clay 2004: 95–6, 135–6).
lucis (< *lucus* 'grove') is an etymological antonym (14–15n.) that sustains the poem's
play between L.'s name and light (1n.).   **odora** modifying *altaria* (17) is rare;
its few instances in Latin poetry (*OLD* 1a and 1b) suggest an intense scent, as at
at *Theb.* 6.104 (the pine tree's sap).

18 Dirce: a famous Theban spring, named in St.'s epic proems; cf. *Theb.* 1.38
caerula cum rubuit Lernaeo sanguine Dirce; *Ach.* 1.12 *Dircaeus ager*. Dirce was a Theban
queen who was punished by dismemberment for her maltreatment of Antiope;
her mutilated body was either thrown into a spring or transformed into the
spring that bears her name (Hyg. *Fab.* 7 and 8; Apollod. 3.5.5; Prop. 3.15.11–42;
Fedeli on Prop. 3.15.13–16). She is a recurrent symbol in the *Thebaid* of Theban
crime (Berlincourt 2006: 134–8). The poetic landscapes of the *Thebaid* and the
Bellum ciuile overlap in their violent associations.   **lauat:** cf. Virg. *G.* 2.146–7
hinc albi, Clitumne, greges et maxima taurus | uictima saepe tuo perfusi flumine sacro, with
Thomas. Washing precedes sacrifice.   **Cithaeron:** a mountain in the south
of Boeotia near Thebes, regularly associated in St. with Dirce (Dewar on *Theb.*
9.679). It was the site of Bacchic revels, esp. the triennial celebrations of Dionysus'
birthday (Pease on Virg. *A.* 4.305; Ov. *Met.* 2.223 *natusque ad sacra Cithaeron*); here too
Pentheus' *sparagmos* took place (Eur. *Bacch.* 62–3; Ov. *Met.* 3.702–3) and the murder
of Ino's son Learchus (*Theb.* 3.186–7). The cattle are washed in Dirce's (troubled)
waters and nourished on Thebes' most violent landmark, acts appropriate to the
passionate style and violent theme of L.'s epic.

19–23 St. requests the Muses for inspiration for the poem.

19 Lucanum canimus: the second naming of L., in the same metrical *sedes*
as in the opening line (see also 30), and with the suggestive association with *dies*
(20); see 1n.

19–20 fauete linguis; | . . . fauete, Musae: this traditional prayer formula
(N–R on Hor. *Carm.* 3.1.2 *fauete linguis*) indicates the sacred nature of the occasion
and of the space in which it is held; St. displays his vatic role. On the association
of verbal gemination with divine revelation and ritual see Wills 61–2. Editors
generally put a semicolon after *linguis* to indicate that, despite the repetition of
fauete in the same metrical *sedes*, St. addresses two different audiences, first the
birthday celebrants, and then the Muses; he also uses *fauete* in two different senses:
first enjoining silence upon a general audience for the correct performance of
a religious rite; and next, asking for the Muses' favour (*OLD* 1b); cf. Mart. 7.22.2

Aonidum turba, fauete sacris, with Vioque. The Muses are not abruptly silenced (Malamud 1995: 170–2); *fauere linguis* sometimes commands well-omened words; cf. Ov. *Fast.* 1.71–2 (on 1 January) *linguis animisque fauete;* | *nunc dicenda bona sunt bona uerba die*; *Tr.* 3.13.18 (his birthday prayer) *concipiam bonas ore fauente preces*; Mart. 10.87.3–4 *linguis omnibus et fauete uotis;* | *natalem colimus.*

20 uestra est ista dies: the day is also the Muses' (cf. 1n.) since L. was dedicated to them at birth and was the foster child of Calliope (36–41).

21 qui: i.e. L.   **geminas . . . per artes:** poetry and prose, explained at 22 as metrically 'bound' and 'unbound' arts. Vacca (Hosius p. 336.17–22) lists as L.'s prose works two declamations, letters from Campania, and *De incendio urbis*, though the latter may have been a poem; see 60–1n.   **uos . . . tulit:** cf. Virg. *G.* 2. 475–6 *Musae,* | *quarum sacra fero*, with Thomas; Prop. 3.1.3–4 *primus ego ingredior puro de fonte sacerdos* | *Itala per Graios orgia ferre choros*, with Fedeli. *tulit* represents the poet as a priest conveying sacred objects, here the Muses as both goddesses and metonyms for poems.

22 et uinctae pede uocis et solutae: cf. 5.3.101–3 *siue orsa libebat* | *Aoniis uincire modis seu uoce soluta* | *spargere.* The juxtaposition of *pede* and *uocis* may suggest the sound of the Muses' dancing feet and their voices, two elements of the chorus.

23 Romani colitur chori sacerdos: cf. Hor. *Carm.* 3.1.3 *Musarum sacerdos*; Prop. 3.1.3–4 (cited at 21n.); Ov. *Am.* 3.8.23. The 'chorus' are the Muses, in this sense first at Virg. *Ecl.* 6.66 *Phoebi chorus . . . omnis*; see Clausen ad loc. L., like St. in the solemn role of priest, was both in charge of the Muses' worship and inspired by them to produce elevated poetry. They are specifically 'Roman' because of the *Bellum ciuile*, a poem of recent Roman history; cf. Luc. 1.66 *Romana . . . carmina*; Mart. 7.23.2 *Latiae . . . lyrae*, with Vioque. *colitur* is somewhat paradoxical: the priest in charge of worship is now himself worshipped. *colitur* also acknowledges the birthday's double function, to honour the deceased with offerings and to promote his posthumous reputation through poetic cult; see 126n. Alliteration and assonance mark the proem's solemn close.

24–35 Praise of Spain, where L. was born. Roman poets attributed great importance to local patriotism (Fränkel 1957: 304–5; Citroni on Mart. 1.61). St. sets the encomium within a competitive geographic context; see 2.2.93n.

24 felix heu nimis et beata tellus: cf. Mart. 1.61.2 *Marone felix Mantua est*, with Citroni; L. made his home region proud. But *heu* interjects a tragic note; this land, fortunate in its agriculture and poets, has also suffered loss. *nimis*, by postposition modifying both adjectives, hints that prosperity invites tragedy; cf. Virg. *A.* 4.657–8 *felix, heu nimium felix, si litora tantum* | *numquam Dardaniae tetigissent nostra carinae.*

25–6 quae pronos Hyperionis meatus | summis Oceani uides in undis: St. addresses Spain, the most western land known to the ancient Mediterranean world (*summis* = 'furthest'). Sunset was therefore believed to be very vivid there, imagined as a downward plunge of the solar chariot, its flames reflected on the waves; cf. Ov. *Met.* 2.67 *ultima prona uia est*. In hendecasyllabic verse caesura normally occurs after the fifth or sixth syllable. The unusual caesura after the eighth syllable (also 93n.; after the seventh at 32) highlights *Hyperionis*, a Homeric term for the Sun (Bömer on Ov. *Fast.* 1.385).

27 stridoremque rotae cadentis audis: a striking image of the solar chariot hissing as it plunges into the ocean; *rotae* cunningly conflates the meaning 'wheel', synecdoche for chariot, and 'disc of the sun' (*OLD* 4b). Since ancient chariot wheels had iron rims, they became very hot when driven at speed (N–H on Hor. *Carm.* 1.1.4). St. may allude to the belief that at sunset in Spain the sea seemed to sizzle (Str. 3.1.5).

28–9 Tritonide fertiles Athenas . . . | . . . prouocas: *Tritonis*, a learned cult title for Pallas Athena (2.2.117n.), here a striking metonymy for the olive, one of the goddess's emblems. Ironically Athens cannot claim the deity's exclusive patronage.

29 unctis . . . trapetum: Virg. *G.* 2.519 introduced *trapetum*, a Greek borrowing for 'olive press', to Roman poetry. 'Smeared with oil' (*unctis*) suggests high productivity. Like Spain, Athens was famous for its agriculture and its authors.   **Baetica:** the southernmost province of Spain after Augustus' reorganisation in 27 BCE (*OCD* s.v. *Baetica*), and one of the most Romanised of the imperial provinces (Str. 3.2.15).

30 Lucanum potes imputare terris 'you can count the world in your debt for L.'; cf. Mart. 7.22.3 *cum te terris, Lucane, dedisset. imputare* means 'to charge something as a debt or credit' (*OLD* 1); here it metaphorically suggests that as olives bring economic credit, so poetry brings literary credit, or possibly both. See 2 *pr.* 24n.

31 hoc plus: sc. *est.* **Senecam:** perhaps a conflation of the two Senecas, the elder (L.'s grandfather), author of *Controuersiae* and *Suasoriae*, and the younger (his son and L.'s uncle), the philosopher and tragedian; in St.'s judgment L. surpasses both; cf. Mart. 1.61.7 *duosque Senecas unicumque Lucanum*, with Citroni.

32 dulcem . . . Gallionem: the delayed caesura emphasises L.'s other uncle, eldest son of Seneca the Elder, called by adoption L. Iunius Gallio Annaeanus. Seneca the Younger dedicated to him *De ira* and *De uita beata. dulcis* suggests perhaps Gallio's pleasant declamatory style (Quint. *Inst.* 9.2.9; *OLD* 7c) and personality (Sen. *Nat.* 4 *pr.* 10–12).

33–5 The climax of the encomium: the river Baetis (modern Guadalquivir), which flowed by Corduba (L.'s birthplace), surpasses in fame the home regions of Homer and Virgil; cf. Mart. 12.98.1–2 *Baetis oliuifera crinem redimite corona* | *aurea*, playing on the river's poetic and agrarian associations. Roman poets often referred to their native regions by their rivers (N–H on Hor. *Carm.* 3.30.10).

33–4 attollat refluos in astra fontes | . . . Baetis 'may Baetis flow backwards, raising its sources to the stars', an 'adynaton' (a highly stylised impossibility) that unites 'the ideas of miracle and exaltation' (SB 159 n.6) by combining two images, stars as symbols of poetic immortality (N–H on Hor. *Carm.* 1.1.36 *sublimi feriam sidera uertice*), and springs as symbols of poetic inspiration (N–R on Hor. *Carm.* 3.4.25). The rare *refluus* 'flowing backwards' (usually of the sea's ebb) is found first at Ov. *Met.* 7.267 (Bömer), and then in post-Augustan poetry. Rivers flowing backwards are usually a negative phenomenon; cf. Sil. 5.624 (an earthquake) *reflui pugnarunt fontibus amnes*; Ov. *Ep.* 5.29–30 (a lover's faithless vow) *cum Paris Oenone spirare relicta* | *ad fontem Xanthi uersa recurret aqua*, with Knox. But here they also flow heavenwards; cf. Prudent. *Tituli* 15.1 *in fontem refluo Iordanis gurgite fertur*. The sources of the Bactis lay in the 300 metre-high Sierra Nevada; the adynaton has a basis in reality (Buchheit 1960: 232 n.1)

34 Graio . . . Melete: the Ionian river Meles flows near Smyrna, one of Homer's reputed birthplaces; cf. 3.3.60–1; Vioque on Mart. 7.22.4; Graziosi 2002: 72–7.

35 Baetim, Mantua, prouocare noli: praise of Spain culminates with L.'s greatest literary rival, Virgil, who was born in Mantua; cf. Sil. 8.593–4 *Mantua, Musarum domus. . .* | *et Smyrnaeis aemula plectris*. Repetition with place of origin was a regular feature of neoteric poetry, given here new syntactic expression with polyptoton (*Baetis, Baetim*; Wills 149–53). *noli* is rare in serious poetry; St. adopts a confrontational style in the first of several 'agonistic comparisons' (Quint 1993: 131) between L. and Virgil, forbidding the latter's town to challenge Spain's supremacy. *prouocare* echoes *prouocas* (29).

36–40 At birth L. is dedicated to the Muses, becoming the protégé and foster-son of Calliope, the chief Muse (Hes. *Th.* 79; Hor. *Carm.* 3.4.1 *regina*) in charge of epic poetry; cf. *Theb.* 8.373–4 *sed iam bella uocant: alias noua suggere uires,* | *Calliope, maiorque chelyn mihi tendat Apollo.*

36–8 natum protinus atque humum per ipsam . . . | blando Calliope sinu recepit 'at once and while he was still down on the ground Calliope received him in her welcoming lap'; cf. 5.3.121–2 (the Muses' adoption of St.'s father) *protinus exorto dextrum risere sorores* | *Aonides. protinus* should be taken with *recepit* to show that the Muse favoured him from birth. St. domesticates the scene of poetic dedication: Calliope acknowledges the infant L. as her foster son, as Melior

immediately acknowledged Glaucias at birth (2.1.79n.).   **blando ... sinu:**
cf. 5.5.84; *Ach.* 1.767–8.

37 dulce uagientem: *uagire* is the conventional word for a baby's crying (*OLD*
1a); but L. wails 'sweetly' in anticipation of his poetic promise; Vacca (Hosius p.
335.1–7) tells of bees flying around L.'s cradle, settling on his mouth and drinking
in his 'sweet spirit' (*dulcem ... spiritum*), thus marking out the future poet. On the
literary sense of *dulcis* see 32n.

39 posito ... luctu 'having set aside her grief' (*OLD pono* 10). L. provides
compensation for the death of Orpheus (98–9n.), who was generally agreed to
be Calliope's son (Coleman on Virg. *Ecl.* 4.57).

40 longos Orpheos ... dolores 'her long sorrow for Orpheus', objective
gen.

41–106 Calliope's song combines the theme of the Muse looking with favour
upon a child from birth (Hes. *Th.* 81–3; Hor. *Carm.* 3.4.9–20; N–R on Hor. *Carm.*
3.4.9) with the prophecy of a child's brilliant career (Cat. 64.303–83, the song
of the Fates for Achilles; Virg. *Ecl.* 4). The prophecy at birth was normally the
privilege of the Fates, not the Muses; cf. [Tib.] 3.4.45–6 *sed proles Semelae Bacchus
doctaeque sorores | dicere non norunt, quid ferat hora sequens*; Buchheit 1960: 243. But
the epic Muse sings with special authority of an epic poet. As foster mother,
Calliope's voice is also tempered by lament; like the Muses of Greek tragedy
(Segal 1993: 21), she registers the horror and injustice of L.'s fate.

41 dixit: used of formal song in Catullus and Horace (*TLL* v 1.977.65–
70).   **puer o dicate Musis:** the solemn religious connotations of *dicate* (*OLD*
2) cast L. in the role of 'priest of the Muses' from birth (23n.). On the postposition
of *o* for emotional effect, frequent in poetic commands and appeals, see Pease on
Virg. *A.* 4.578.

42 longaeuos cito transiture uates: a poignant juxtaposition of *longaeuos*
with *cito*. L. is 'destined to surpass' (predicative future part.) other poets in genius
and also in his early death at age twenty-six.

**43–4 non tu flumina nec greges ferarum | nec plectro Geticas moue-
bis ornos:** on 'Getic' see 2.2.61n. L. will be as great as Orpheus, but his talents
will move in a different direction, towards Roman themes. On the power of
Orpheus' poetry to influence nature see e.g. [Sen.] *Her. Oe.* 1035–60. Trees, wild
beasts and rocks were the traditional elements; rivers appear first at A. R.1.26–7;
see N–H on Hor. *Carm.* 1.12.9.

45 sed septem iuga Martiumque Thybrim: *Martius* means not simply
'Roman' (thus *OLD* 3) but 'of or belonging to Mars' (*OLD* 1; Luc. 7.146 *Martius ... ensis* 'the sword of Mars'); cf. 1.2.243 *Martia fluminea posuit latus Ilia ripa*,

where *Martia* refers to Ilia's rape by Mars on the Tiber bank. Calliope evokes L.'s Roman audience with allusion to a major founding myth.

46 et doctos equites: a sophisticated audience; cf. *greges ferarum* (43).

46–7 eloquente | cantu: the striking enjambment between the normally self-contained lines demonstrates St.'s eloquence also.

47 purpureum trahes senatum: the play upon the two meanings of *trahere* 'physically draw' (*OLD* 1) and 'charm' (*OLD* 10b) further identifies L. as the counterpart to Orpheus. The scenario is probably a public recitation of L.'s poetry; cf. 5.3.215–19, where St. prides himself on a comparably distinguished audience. Senators wore a toga with a broad purple stripe which also suggested their wealth and social distinction.

48–53 A priamel rejecting the famous topics of mythological epic as hackneyed; cf. Virg. *G.* 3.3–9. L. is original in writing historical epic. On the use of the priamel in encomia see N–H on Hor. *Carm.* 1.7.1. The brief hendecasyllable is an effective metre for pointed summaries of poetic themes.

48 nocturnas alii Phrygum ruinas: the nocturnal sack of Troy; *Phrygum* is gen. pl. of *Phryx*, a common, largely poetic, term for 'Trojan'. The anonymous pl. *alii* (subject of *sequantur* (51)) often suggests veiled contempt for individuals (Skutsch on Enn. *Ann.* fr. 206); but Calliope may be targeting not specific poets but rather the overuse of traditional themes; on the other hand, Troy's fall is the theme of Virg. *A.* 2.

49 tardi reduces uias Vlixis: the wanderings of Ulysses. In the *Siluae* Odysseus is typically characterised as *tardus* (2.1.118n.). *redux* normally applies to people (4.2.4 *reducem . . . Ulixem*) or to objects that move, such as ships (Ov. *Ep.* 6.1 *reduci carina*); hence some commentators favour *reducis*, gen. qualifying *Vlixis*, with adverbial *tarde*. But with the unusual *uias* St. perhaps alludes to the bold usage of the Annaei family at Sen. *Tro.* 167 *reduces quis deus claudat uias?*, and at Luc. 9.408 *irreducemque uiam*.

50 et puppem temerariam Mineruae: the voyage of the Argo. Although the Republican Varro of Atax had translated Apollonius Rhodius' *Argonautica* (77n.), Calliope may also target the *Argonautica* of the Flavian Valerius Flaccus; see Gibson 2004: 153. As the first sea-faring ship the Argo is 'rash'; cf. Ov. *Am.* 2.11.2–3 *pinus . . . | quae concurrentes inter temeraria cautes*, with McKeown; Cat. 64.4–6 *cum lecti iuuenes . . . | ausi sunt uada salsa cita decurrere puppi.*

51 trita uatibus orbita 'on the track well worn by poets', a familiar Calli-machean metaphor for epic poetry, or poetry that does not cultivate the new and recondite (9n.; 2.2.12–13n.); cf. Virg. *G.* 3.292–3 *iuuat ire iugis, qua nulla priorem | Castaliam molli deuertitur orbita cliuo*; *G.* 3.4, with Thomas.

52 tu carus Latio memorque gentis 'you dear to Latium and mindful of its people'. Though L. was from Spain, Rome adored him, and he in turn recorded its history. *memor* was etymologically linked with *mens*; Hardie 2005b: 80, 89 thus sees *carus* and *memor* as a two-part etymological play upon *carmen* (53); see 2.1.12–13n. On St.'s appreciation of L.'s interest in 'memory' see Gowing 2005: 95–6.

53 carmen fortior exseres togatum 'stronger, you will unsheath a Roman poem', i.e. when older, stronger, and thus more courageous, L. will tackle an original, historical theme, Roman civil war. Calliope suggests that the poet of martial epic – and of controversial Roman politics – must be of a martial disposition, an epic hero, in contrast to poets who write on escapist mythological themes. **exseres** describes the composition of the *Bellum ciuile* as the 'unsheathing' of a sword; cf. Ov. *Fast.* 3.814 (Minerva) *ensibus exsertis bellica laeta dea est*. The military metaphor is apt for an epic where 'violence and death characterise L.'s dealings with the past' (Hardie 1993: 109). The descriptive verb matches the theme and style of the poem also at 55 *ludes*, 57 *reserabis*, 66 *detonabis*, 71 *deflebis*, 77 *duxit*, 78 *transfigurat*; on the poet doing what he describes being done see McKeown on Ov. *Am.* 2.18.2. **carmen . . . togatum:** a bold coinage for the *Bellum ciuile*, modelled on *fabula togata*, comedy on Roman themes and in Roman dress (*OLD togatus* 4), with the hint that L. will write his masterwork when old enough to wear the toga.

54–72 A catalogue in possible chronological order of L.'s other works. This list does not square entirely with Vacca's, which adds the *Saturnalia*, an unfinished *Medea, Salticae fabulae, Epigrammata, Octauius Sagitta pro et contra* (prose declamations), *Epistulae ex Campania*, and, notably, ten books of *Siluae* (p. 336.17–22); see 21n. Suet. *Poet.* 33 (Hosius p. 333.5–6) also mentions a scurrilous poem against Nero. Vacca is generally now dated to the fifth century CE, so his list's authority is questionable (Ahl 1976: 333–4).

54 primum teneris adhuc in annis: L. was a child prodigy, writing epic poetry 'in his tender years' (*OLD tener* 2; 2.1.40n.). The marking out of different stages for the child's career, beginning with *primum*, loosely follows Virg. *Ecl.* 4, also a prophecy for a miraculous child; cf. *Ecl.* 4.18 *at tibi prima, puer, nullo munuscula cultu.*

55 ludes Hectora: a paradoxical reference probably to L.'s *Iliacon*. Van Dam proposes that *ludes* suggests not epic but a collection of short scenes from the *Iliad*, or of libretti for mimes. But the point is surely that L. was an epic poet from the start. St. challenges the Virgilian paradigm of the poetic career with its trajectory from light verse to serious epic (Farrell 2002); L. will begin with mythological epic, but it will be just child's play. *ludere* suggests early, 'minor' but polished, poetry (1 *pr.* 10 *praeluserit;* Virg. *Ecl.* 1.10, with Clausen; *G.* 4.565 (with the acc. as here)); cf. 66 *detonabis*, of L.'s mature epic. Scholia to the *Thebaid* preserve two fragments of

L.'s *Iliacon* (Hosius, fr. II, pp. 329–30). **Thessalosque currus:** an offhand reference to Hector's death, his body dragged by Achilles' chariot around the walls of Troy (Hom. *Il.* 23.395–405; Virg. *A.* 1.483–7); cf. Ov. *Tr.* 4.29–30 *cruentum | Hectora Thessalico . . . ab axe rapi*. Achilles was conceived and raised in Thessaly (*Ach.* 1.99–118; Hor. *Carm.* 2.4.10; Ov. *Am.* 2.8.11).

56 et supplex Priami potentis aurum: the great emotional climax of the *Iliad*, Priam's petition of Achilles for the right to bury his son Hector (Hom. *Il.* 24.485–506); cf. Virg. *A.* 1.484 *exanimumque auro corpus uendebat Achilles*. Here the transfer of *supplex* to *aurum* poignantly suggests that the gold, not Priam, was powerful, the plosives conveying the king's humiliation.

57 et sedes reserabis inferorum 'and you will unbar/reveal in poetry the dwelling places of the dead', a riddling reference to the *Catachthonion*, a poem on the Underworld; two lines are preserved in the scholia (Hosius, fr. III, p. 330); cf. Sen. *Ag.* 756 (of the Underworld) *reserate . . . terga nigrantis poli*. The entrance to the Underworld is imagined as a barred gate to which Cerberus was chained (2.1.230n.). *reserare* is etymologically derived from *sera* (Maltby s.v. *resero*) and is a favourite word of Ovid, often used metaphorically in the sense of 'reveal'; cf. Ov. *Met.* 15.145 *augustae reserabo oracula mentis*, with Bömer; 2.2.38n. St. here conflates its literal and metaphorical meanings; the poet again does what he describes (53n.).

58 ingratus Nero: probably a reference to the *laudatio* L. recited in Nero's honour at the quinnquennial games (Neronia) of 60 CE; the main verb is *proferetur* (59n.). Although Nero crowned L. on that occasion, he soon turned against him (Vacca (Hosius p. 335.21–6)), hence *ingratus*. Cf. 3.5.32–3 *saeuum ingratumque | . . . Iouem*, an artful blend of flattery and criticism of Domitian for failing to reward St. at the Capitoline games. **dulcibus theatris:** abl. of place with *proferetur* (59). The Neronia were held in Pompey's theatre, a complex which included an attractive (*dulcis*) portico famous for its fine works of art and beautiful garden (Kuttner 1999). *dulcis* also suggests the crowd's favour towards L. as well as the sweetness of his poetry (37n.).

59 et noster tibi proferetur Orpheus 'and my Orpheus will be produced by you' (dat. of agent); *noster* because Calliope speaks and Orpheus is her son. *proferre* means 'bring (a literary work) before the public' (*OLD* 6). We know virtually nothing of the *Orpheus* except that it was improvisational (Vacca (Hosius p. 335.23–4) *et ex tempore Orphea scriptum*); for the scattered references to the work see Hosius pp. 328–9.

60–1 dices . . . | infandos . . . ignes: the *De incendio urbis* on the fire of Rome in 64 CE, a work of uncertain genre; *dices* does not rule out a poem (41 n.; Ahl 1976: 335–52). *dices* contrasts with *infandos* 'unspeakable', also in initial line position, thus emphasising L.'s brave but dangerous frankness.

60 culminibus Remi: a curious periphrasis for Rome. The substitution of Remus for Romulus may well be *metri causa* (Ahl 1976: 339), yet the name of the murdered brother resonates with the repetition of ancient crime: the city founded through a brother's murder is destroyed through a descendant's treachery. Cf. Virg. *G.* 2.533 *olim hanc ueteres uitam coluere Sabini | hanc Remus et frater*, with its poignant suggestion that even in the 'good old days' the seeds of contemporary civic discord were sown.

61 domini nocentis: the pejorative language suggests the negative tone of the *De incendio urbis*, which may have contributed to L.'s fall from favour (Ahl 1976: 342–3). Although *dominus* as an *official* title for the emperor does not appear in public inscriptions until the time of Antoninus Pius (Ferri on [Sen.] *Oct.* 367), Nero was often called *dominus* after his death for treating the Romans like slaves (Roller 2001: 261); *nocentis* strengthens the negative connotations. Most ancient sources blame Nero directly for the fire (e.g. Plin. *Nat.* 17.1.1.5 *Neronis principis incendia quibus cremauit urbem*), though vary on his motivation: Nero wished to build a finer city (Suet. *Nero* 39); or he wished the theatrical pleasure of seeing Rome burn (Dio 62.61.1); see Ferri on [Sen.] *Oct.* 831. The demonisation of Nero as murderer, matricide, incendiary of Rome and defiler of the gods became firmly established in the Flavian period; see Griffin 1984: 15, 235–7; Beagon 1992: 3, 17–18; Degl'Innocenti Pierini 2007: 148–55; Vioque on Mart. 7.21.3–4.

62–3 hinc castae titulum decusque Pollae | iucunda dabis allocutione 'next, in a pleasant address, you will bestow fame and honour upon chaste Polla', our only mention of the *Allocutio Pollae*, an address to L.'s wife, which perhaps influenced St.'s poem to his wife (3.5); Vollmer ad loc. suggests that the *Allocutio* represents an allusion to L.'s *Siluae*, but it seems unlikely that one poem would stand for a ten-book collection; see Bright 1980: 34–7. The chiastic structure of 62 parallels that of 61: Polla's virtue is contrasted with Nero's vice. On *titulus* as a metaphor for fame see 2.2.146n.

64 coepta generosior iuuenta 'more noble-spirited in early manhood'; cf. 54 *primum teneris adhuc in annis*.

65 albos ossibus Italis Philippos: cf. Virg. *A.* 12.36 *campique ingentes ossibus albent*; Ov. *Fast.* 3.707–8 *testes estote, Philippi, | et quorum sparsis ossibus albet humus*. The juxtapostion of *Italis* with *Philippos* emphasises the tragedy of civil war that denies proper burial to those far from home. L. favours such emotive, geographic contrasts; cf. Luc. 7.473 (of the first weapon thrown) *primaque Thessaliam Romano sanguine tinxit*; also Luc. 7.164, 8.596. Philippi, Octavian's and Antony's decisive victory over Brutus and Cassius in 42 BCE (N–H II 106–7), is here a code word for the final political ruin of the Republic; cf. Luc. 7.872 *et Mutina et Leucas puros fecere Philippos*. There is no need to conjecture that L. had planned to finish his epic with Philippi. Although Pharsalia took place in 48 BCE, six years before Philippi, the two battles were often paired or conflated in poetic discourse about civil war (Mynors on Virg. *G.* 1.490; Ahl 1976: 314–15).

66 Pharsalica bella detonabis 'you will thunder out Pharsalian wars', i.e. an epic about the civil wars; cf. Mart. 7.23.1 *bella tonanti*, with Vioque. Pharsalia is a code word for L.'s epic (Leigh 1997: 74 n.72). *Pharsalicus* first appears at Cic. *Lig.* 9, *Deiot.* 29; L. introduced the epithet to poetry at 5.391. 'Thundering' was a literary-critical metaphor for the high style of epic and tragedy and a definitive term in the *recusatio*; cf. Call. *Aet.* 1 fr. 1.20 Pf. βροντᾶν οὐκ ἐμόν, ἀλλὰ Διός; Prop. 2.1.39–40 *neque Phlegraeos Iouis Enceladique tumultus | intonet angusto pectore Callimachus*, with Fedeli. Here it aptly describes the powerful style and matter of the *Bellum ciuile*; see 53n. *detonare*, with *de* expressing completed action, is a rare compound (not in L.) first found in Virgil of the 'thunder of war' (Harrison on Virg. *A.* 10.809); only Sil. 17.201 and St. here use it for powerful speech. *detonabis* aligns L. as narrator with Caesar the 'thunderbolt' (67n.). On the conflicting impulses within L.'s narrative technique dramatised by the thunderbolt see Masters 1992: 9–10; Bartsch 1997: 90–100.

67–9 In apposition to *Pharsalica bella*, Calliope celebrates the three protagonists of L.'s poem, Julius Caesar, Cato and Pompey, with snapshot characterisations; the sequence is regularised by the emphatic appearance of names or titles at line ends.

67 quo fulmen ducis inter arma diui 'where in the midst of war the captain-thunderbolt, who was deified', an allusion to L.'s first simile comparing Julius Caesar to the thunderbolt, an image of swift, destructive and indiscriminate power (Luc. 1.151–7); Lucretius probably was the first to use *fulmen* of a famous general rather than of Jupiter; cf. Lucr. 3.1034 *Scipiadas, belli fulmen*, with Kenney; Thomas on Virg. *G.* 4.560–1. Courtney, followed by SB, posits a lacuna of one line after 67; while Cato and Pompey are in parallel, accorded one line each, as *diuus* and victor Caesar could well claim an extra line. Alternatively, the possible ellipsis of a verb of action after *quo* would stress the swiftness of Caesar as thunderbolt and the terrifying uncertainty of his aim. *fulmen ducis* presents a further problem: either the gen. is possessive as at 4.7.50, where *Caesaris fulmen* simply means 'Caesar's thunderbolt' (Coleman), or it is explanatory, part of a descriptive phrase for Caesar ('the captain-thunderbolt', SB); cf. 5.1.133 *Caesarei . . . fulmen equi* ('Caesar's horse the thunderbolt').   **diui:** Julius Caesar was deified after his assassination in 44 BCE, the first of the Roman *diui*; cf. 1.1.24 *primus iter nostris ostendit in aethera diuis*.

68 libertate grauem pia Catonem 'Cato stern in his devotion to freedom', object of *detonabis*; cf. Virg. *A.* 1.151 *pietate grauem . . . uirum*, the ideal statesman whom commentators often identify with Cato Uticensis, leader of the Republican forces after Pompey's murder (Austin). *pia*, a transferred epithet, elevates freedom as an important civic principle. St. encapsulates L.'s characterisation of Cato as devoted to Liberty (also Sen. *Ep.* 104.29–33) while recognising that it was essentially defunct in his times; cf. Luc. 2.302–3 *tuumque | nomen, Libertas, et inanem prosequar umbram.* SB argues that *grauem* means 'irksome', for the high principles of Cato made him unpopular in some quarters, in contrast to Pompey who was well liked; but St.'s description of Pompey suggests his popularity was a weakness (69n.).

69 et gratum popularitate Magnum: an ironical juxtaposition of the strikingly prosaic *popularitate* (not found elsewhere in poetry) with *Magnum*, Pompey's *cognomen.* Van Dam argues for taking *popularitas* in a positive sense; but Calliope's thumbnail sketch conforms with L.'s ambiguous representation of Pompey as courter of popular favour; cf. Luc. 1.129–43, esp. 1.131–3 *famaeque petitor | multa dare in uolgus, totus popularibus auris | impelli, plausuque sui gaudere theatri.* L. often uses Pompey's *cognomen* with a sense of deep contradiction; cf. Luc. 1.135 *stat magni nominis umbra.*

70 Pelusiaci scelus Canopi: Pompey's murder in Egypt; cf. Luc. 8.542–4 *o superi, Nilusne et barbara Memphis | et Pelusiaci tam mollis turba Canopi | hos animos?* Canopus was situated at the west mouth of the Nile, Pelusium at the east, but both could refer to Egypt as a whole (Mynors on Virg. *G.* 1.228). L. repeatedly calls Pompey's murder *scelus*; e.g. Luc. 9.248 *Pompeio scelus est bellum ciuile perempto.*

71 deflebis: a strong word for mourning, corresponding to *detonabis* (66), the two verbs encapsulating the dominant modes of L.'s divided narrative voice 'that both thunders and weeps' (Malamud 1995: 179). Used earlier in prose, *deflere* was probably introduced to Roman poetry by Lucretius; cf. Lucr. 3.906–7 *horrifico cinefactum te prope busto | insatiabiliter defleuimus,* with Kenney. In subsequent poetry it is often associated with untimely, tragic death; cf. Luc. 9.169–70 *exemploque carens et nulli cognitus aeuo | luctus erat, mortem populos deflere potentis;* Horsfall on Virg. *A.* 11.59.   **pius:** Calliope aligns L. with Cato (68n.); writing the *Bellum ciuile* as lament (*deflebis*) is a final act of homage to the dead Republic. L.'s poem thus is also reinterpreted as a devout funerary offering, in line with 2.7. For Bartsch (1997: 146–9) the association between Cato and L. goes deeper; in joining the Pisonian conspiracy L. practised the message of his own poem and 'opted for Cato's choice' (148), engaging in political action despite his despair.

71–2 Pharo cruenta | Pompeio dabis altius sepulchrum: cf. Luc. 9.1080–1 *cruentam | . . . Pharon.* Pharos was an island off Alexandria famous for its lighthouse (*OLD Pharos* 2a), a necessary signal for sailors since the low-lying Nile delta lacked significant landmarks. It was one of the traditional 'wonders of the world' (e.g. *AP* IX 656.17–18), but is here 'bloody' because Pompey was murdered off the nearby coast, his body buried in an unmarked grave (Luc. 8.712–872). *Pharo cruenta* is abl. of comparison with *altius* (72), which conveys both physical size and grandeur; L.'s poem will form a loftier and more enduring memorial. St. pointedly varies Horace's famous boast at *Carm.* 3.30.1–2 that with his poetry

he has made a monument higher than the Egyptian pyramids (*monumentum . . .* |
regalique situ pyramidum altius; N–R on Hor. *Carm.* 3.30.1–5).

73–4 When he composes the *Bellum ciuile*, L. will be younger than Virgil when
he produced his *Culex*. According to the 'Life of Virgil' transmitted by Donatus,
Virgil was sixteen when he wrote the *Culex* (Donat.–Sueton., 18 Diehl). But
the *Bellum ciuile* was the work of L.'s final years; thus Donatus' figure has been
generally emended to twenty-six, L.'s age when he died. According to Suet. *Poet.*
33 (Hosius p. 332.5–6), L. made a similar boast (*quantum mihi restat ad culicem*).
The *Culex* was regarded in this period as a genuine work of Virgil (1 *pr.* 7; Mart.
8.55.20; *EV* I 948–9).

74 Maroniani: formed from Virgil's *cognomen*, an ironically grandiose hapax for
the lightweight *Culex* ('the Gnat'); cf. 4.4.54 for the more modest hapax *Maroneique*.

75–80 Calliope lists in succinct pairs four Roman epic poets whom L. surpasses.
Drawing on the formula of Prop. 2.34.65–6 (*cedite Romani scriptores, cedite Grai!* |
nescio quid maius nascitur Iliade), she makes a provocative inversion in that Virgil,
the poet to whom Propertius would have others 'yield', here does obeisance to L.
(79–80). The passage is also indebted to Ovid's catalogues of immortal poets (*Am.*
1.15.9–30; *Tr.* 2.421–70), a reminder of another great poet whose works survived
political disgrace.

75 cedet Musa rudis ferocis Enni: *rudis* plays upon Ennius' rural origins
in Rudiae, Calabria (Gibson on Ov. *Ars* 3.409–10) and his perceived primitive
quality at the start of Roman poetry; cf. Ov. *Tr.* 2.424 (where Ennius likewise
heads Ovid's 'list') *Ennius ingenio maximus, arte rudis*; Sil. 12.395–7, with Casali
2006; Quint. *Inst.* 10.1.88. On Ennius' reputation as talented but unsophisti-
cated poet see McKeown on Ov. *Am.*1.15.19 *Ennius arte carens.* As an epithet for
a poet, *ferox* is unique to St.; cf. 5.3.154 *Stesichorusque ferox.* Horace's Ennius is
fortis (*Ep.* 2.1.50); *ferocis* assimilates the epic poet to the military hero in spirited
style.

76 et docti furor arduus Lucreti: as at Ov. *Tr.* 2.423–6 Lucretius is paired
with Ennius, his important poetic model (Lucr. 1.117 *Ennius . . . noster*; Skutsch on
Enn. *Ann.* p. 12). The close relationship between the two poets is emphasised by
a similar syntactic pattern of interlocking nouns and adjectives with the proper
names in the gen. at line end; *furor* thematically echoes *ferocis.* Its juxtaposition
with *docti* makes a striking oxymoron that pinpoints the key features of Lucretius'
style, neoteric (and Epicurean) learning and epic passion, *ars* united with *ingenium*
(3n.), a long-standing judgment about Lucretius. *arduus*, a thematic word in 2.7
with a range of meanings (cf. 91, 101, 108), has the fig. sense of 'elevated' or
'sublime' (*OLD* 6), with the idea of the poet's striving for philosophical heights; cf.
Lucr. 1.659 *ardua dum metuunt*; Ov. *Am.* 1.15.23 *sublimis . . . Lucreti*, with McKeown.
(Did a mistakenly literal reading of *furor* contribute to the legend of Lucretius'

madness found in the brief notice in Jerome's *Chronicle* for 95 BCE *amatorio poculo in furorem versus?*; see Bailey 8–12).

77 et qui per freta duxit Argonautas: *uariatio*, with the next pair alluded to in relative clauses. The Republican poet Varro of Atax must be meant (Ov. *Tr.* 2.439 *is quoque, Phasiacas Argon qui duxit in undas*; Quint. *Inst.* 10.1.87), not the Flavian Valerius Flaccus, since the list of L.'s epic predecessors seems to be chronological; see 50n. The final quadrisyllabic noun gives the short line epic weight as at 74. *duxit* suggests that the poet of the *Argonautica* resembles the ship's helmsman (53n.).

78 et qui corpora prima transfigurat: a gloss on Ov. *Met.* 1.1–2 *in noua fert animus mutatas dicere formas | corpora. transfigurare*, impossible in dactyls and used elsewhere only in post-Augustan prose, is technically precise; again the poet is characterised as doing what he describes. The pres. tense too suggests that metamorphosis is a constant process. *prima* refers to the original physical shapes that are transformed, with a possible further echo of Ovid's proem stressing the bold scope and originality of his endeavour; cf. Ov. *Met.* 1.3 *primaque ab origine mundi*. Though the two mythological poets are linked, *corpora prima* is also a key Lucretian concept; St. melds Lucretius and Ovid, thus highlighting L.'s originality in the epic genre.

79 quid maius loquar? 'what greater thing shall I utter'? SB (Appendix p. 391) argues that Courtney's *quid? maius loquar* violates the rule that *quid* thus used should be followed by a question, not a statement. His adoption of *quin*, however, dilutes the ironic echo of Prop. 2.34.66 *nescioquid maius nascitur Iliade*, a reference to the *Aeneid* – which the *Bellum ciuile* in turn here surpasses as the 'greater' work. On *maius* as a programmatic, competitive term for elevated poetry see Casali 2006: 589 n.41.

79–80 ipsa te Latinis | Aeneis uenerabitur canentem: a bold inversion, marked by rare enjambment, of Latin literary history (as codified in Prop. 2.34.65–6); the *Aeneid*, personified as a female figure (cf. *Theb.* 12.816), will here revere L.'s talent, not vice versa. Martial more modestly places L. second to Virgil; cf. Mart. 7.23.2, with Vioque. Van Dam (on 35) argues that encomium demanded false flattery. Rather, Calliope's claim of L.'s poetic supremacy fits with the poem's consistent depiction of L. as a literary rebel who, like an epic hero, seeks to surpass all others. *Latinis* is rare poetic usage for 'Romans or Italians' (*OLD* 4); cf. 2.6.24.

81–8 L.'s wedding to Polla (the poem's addressee) occasions her praise, forming an 'interlude' that lowers the emotional temperature before the injustice of L.'s early death. 'Love interest' is often a feature of the Latin *genethliacon* (Hardie 1983: 116). Marriage also suggests L.'s maturity, despite the brevity of his life (Quint 1993: 131).

81 carminum nitorem 'poetic brilliance'. *nitor* has both social and rhetorical usage (*OLD* 4), like *lepos* in Catullus, suggesting sophistication of manners and of literary style; *nitidus/a* describes Melior (2.3.1) and Polla (2.2.10). *nitor* is an appropriate quality for a poet whose name is associated with 'light'. See 105–6n.

82 taedis genialibus 'wedding torches' (*OLD genialis* 2).   **dicabo:** a ritual term of marriage; cf. Virg. *A.* 1.73 *conubio iungam stabili propriamque dicabo*, with Austin. The dedication of Polla to L. parallels his to the Muses (41n.).

83 doctam atque ingenio tuo decoram: a line with double elision, rare in hendecasyllables. The alliterative adjectives emphasise Polla's intelligence: she is learned in her own right and complements (*decoram*) L.'s genius. *doctam*, the fifth appearance of this adjective in 2.7 (3, 12, 46, 76), associates Polla with the *docta puella*, the elegiac poet's inspiration; it also implies 'an enthusiastic preoccupation with literature and litterateurs' (White 1975: 283) and assimilates Polla to the literary culture of L. and St. In the *Siluae* the only other woman praised as *docta* is Polla, wife of Pollius Felix; see 2.2.153–4n.

84 qualem blanda Venus daretque Iuno 'a bride such as kindly Venus and Juno might grant', relative clause of characteristic. These goddesses were the tutelary deities of weddings (1.2.11–15, 1.2.239, 3.5.23), but Calliope here plays Juno's traditional part of *pronuba* (82). *blandus* connotes love and affection; cf. 38 *blando Calliope sinu*; 1.2.19 *blandus Amor*.

85–6 forma . . . | . . . decore: an asyndetic list of Polla's virtues, abl. nouns of description dependent on *qualem*. Hemelrijk 1999: 137 argues that Polla is praised differently from a male patron, for traditional female virtues that overshadow her patronal role (though 'chastity' is not cited). Certainly words for beauty frame the list; but property and lineage (86) give her cultural weight. The asyndetic list (cf. 1.6.44 also in hendecasyllables) is a feature of Senecan drama and imparts a stately, archaising note; cf. [Sen.] *Oct.* 176 *dolor ira maeror miseriae luctus dabunt*, with Ferri; Sidon. Apoll. *Carm.* 23.457 (of a friend, Magnus of Narbonne) *forma, nobilitate, mente, censu.*

85 simplicitate: the only appearance of this word in St., here in the sense not of 'simplicity' (SB; *OLD* 4a), for Polla is 'learned', but 'candour' (*OLD* 5), a quality much admired by St.; cf. 2.2.153, 2.3.15–16, 2.3.69–71, 3.1.32–3.

86 censu 'wealth'; see 2.1.163n. Polla's patronage of the arts had financial muscle; she also had the intellectual and economic resources to organise the cult of L.'s memory.

87 hymenaeon 'wedding song' (Quinn on Cat. 61.4).   **uestros . . . ante postes:** wedding songs were traditionally sung outside the groom's door by the party escorting the bride; cf. 1.2.237–8 *poste reclinis | quaerit Hymen thalamis intactum dicere carmen. uestros* emphasises Polla's new status as L.'s wife.

88 ipsa personabo: as a tribute to L.'s poetic genius and the excellence of his bride Calliope herself will 'loudly sing' (*OLD persono* 4b) the wedding song.

89–104 Calliope's speech ends with an emotional lament for L.'s untimely death.

89–90 o saeuae nimium grauesque Parcae! | o numquam data longa fata summis!: anaphora of initial *o* adds vehemence to this double exclamation against the Fates for L.'s death, though Calliope implicates Nero later (100n.). That fate refuses long life to greatness is a consolatory commonplace; cf. Luc.1.70–1 *inuida fatorum series summisque negatum | stare diu. saeuae* and *graues* stress the inexorability of the *Parcae* (2.1.120n.).

91 cur plus, ardua, casibus patetis? 'why, great heights, are you more vulnerable to sudden fall?'; *casibus* incorporates the idea of 'malignant chance' (*OLD* 5). *ardua* as a neut. pl. noun is common (Williams on *Theb.* 10.230), but the apostrophe of an abstraction is highly unusual. Apostrophe is a prominent feature of L.'s impassioned style; e.g. Luc. 7.551–6 addresses Caesar, *mens* and *Roma* in turn; see Leigh 1997: 307–10; Bartsch 1997: 93–8; D'Alessandro Behr 2007.

92 cur . . . non senescunt?: repetition of initial *cur* with a second rhetorical question stresses fate's injustice. That the best die young was a commonplace; cf. Ov. *Am.* 2.6.39–40 *optima prima fere manibus rapiuntur auaris; | implentur numeris deteriora suis.* **saeua uice** 'by a cruel lot'; cf. 89 *saeuae . . . Parcae.*

93–106 Calliope turns to a recurrent encomiastic strategy of the *Siluae*, legendary comparisons (introd. 24), citing here Alexander the Great, Achilles and Orpheus, men of exceptional talent who died young. Warriors are a fitting figure for L., who 'makes war' in his poetry (53n., 66n.). Repeated initial *sic* (93, 96, 98, 100, 105) structures this section.

93 natum Nasamonii Tonantis: a recondite allusion to Alexander the Great evoking the episode at Luc. 9.511–86 when Cato follows in Alexander's footsteps through the Libyan desert. The 'Thunderer' is the North African Jupiter Ammon (Luc. 9.511–30, 544–5; cf. Cat. 7.3–5), from whom Alexander claimed descent; unlike Cato, who virtuously refused to ask Jupiter Ammon's advice, Alexander consulted the oracle to receive confirmation of his divinity (Arr. *An.* 3.3.1–2). *Nasamonii*, highlighted by caesura after the eighth syllable, is a rare epithet for 'North African' first occurring in imperial poetry and derived from the Nasamones, who inhabited an inhospitable part of Libya (Luc. 9.438–44). L. is hostile to Alexander but St. is more ambivalent, in keeping with contemporary assessments (Spencer 2002). The comparison suggest that L., like Alexander, was an ambitious young man intent on pushing and transgressing boundaries, whether literary or geographical, and tragically too daring for his own good; see Malamud 1995: 183.

94 post ortus obitusque fulminatos 'after east and west had been struck by lightning'; cf. Luc. 10.34–5 (of Alexander) *terrarum fatale malum fulmenque quod omnes | percuteret pariter populos*. The idea of the lightning bolt associates Alexander with Julius Caesar as a brilliant but dangerous leader (67n.; Spencer 2002: 169–70). Virgil is the first to use *fulminare* of a person (Octavian) instead of Jupiter; cf. Virg. *G.* 4.561, with Thomas. *post* is temporal, marking the conclusion of a period of time (*OLD* 3). *obitus* fig. 'the west' (*OLD* 3b) usually describes the setting of heavenly bodies, and is less common than *occasus* in such expressions (cf. 4.6.61).

95 angusto Babylon premit sepulchro: cf. Luc. 8.798–9 (of Pompey's humble grave) *Romanum nomen et omne | imperium Magno tumuli est modus*, a commonplace contrast for a man of great gifts (N–H on Hor. *Carm.* 1.28.2). L. makes Alexander's subjection to the levelling power of death a moral and political lesson for tyrants (Luc. 10.20–52); the 'narrow tomb' framing this line makes the same point more starkly; *premit* 'covers over' (*OLD* 14b) also suggests the constriction of the grave for the world conqueror. Alexander died in Babylon (Luc. 10.46), but his body was later moved to a grand tomb in Alexandria (Curt. 10.10.20). St. ignores the move to Alexandria (though mentions it at 3.2.117–18), for the great city named after Alexander could not make the moral point of tragic downfall; cf. Juv. 10.168–72 *unus Pellaeo iuueni non sufficit orbis . . . | cum tamen a figulis munitam intrauerit urbem | sarcophago contentus erit*, with Courtney.

96–7 sic fixum . . . | Peliden: Achilles, identified by his Greek patronymic 'son of Peleus'; cf. *Ach.* 1.721; Ov. *Met.* 12.605, with Bömer.

96 Paridis . . . trementis: traditionally Paris kills Achilles with Apollo's aid; cf. Hom. *Il.* 10.359–60; Virg. *A.* 6.56–8 *Phoebe . . . | Dardana qui Paridis derexti tela manusque | corpus in Aeacidae*, with Norden. Already in Homer Paris is effeminate and weak in war (Rosati 1999: 148–9, 157–8; N–H on Hor. *Carm.* 1.15.13–20; Pease on Virg. *A.* 4.215). Here, without Apollo's intervention, Paris is an esp. unworthy opponent, and Achilles' death is thus ignominious; cf. Ov. *Met.* 12.608–9 *ille igitur tantorum uictor, Achille, | uictus es a timido Graiae raptore maritae*.

97 Thetis horruit: Achilles' mother Thetis is conventional in poems of lament (e.g. Ov. *Am.* 3.9.1). But here her maternal anguish anticipates Calliope's grief for Orpheus and L.

98 sic . . . ego: the shift to the first person introduces the Muse's own experience. The comparison with Orpheus is esp. pointed: Calliope is his mother and L.'s foster mother; he died young (Virg. *G.* 4.522); L. wrote a work called *Orpheus* (59n.).

98–9 sic ripis ego murmurantis Hebri | non mutum caput Orpheos sequebar: for the tradition that Orpheus' severed head sang Eurydice's name as it rolled down the Hebrus cf. Virg. *G.* 4.523–7; Ov. *Met.* 11.50–3. Calliope's following of the head is a new feature of the Orpheus myth that adds personal pathos. *murmurantis* suggests that the murmur of the river, which wept for Eurydice at Virg. *G.* 4.463, is combined with that of the head, whose tongue murmurs lament at Ov. *Met.* 11.52–3 *flebile lingua | murmurat exanimis*.

100 sic et tu: with an echo of *sic . . . ego* (98) Calliope adduces L. as the tragic climax.   **rabidi nefas tyranni:** a parenthetical exclamation, explained in the following line: L.'s enforced suicide is an 'outrageous crime' (*nefas*) of Nero. *rabidi*, generally used of wild animals or creatures who behave like wild animals (e.g. giants, Luc. 7.145; Maenads, *Theb.* 2.81), suggests Nero's savage, tyrannical thirst for blood. Mart. 7.21.3–4 likewise condemns Nero for L.'s death but in less virulent terms (*heu! Nero crudelis nullaque inuisior umbra | debuit hoc saltem non licuisse tibi*). On anti-Neronian sentiment under the Flavians see 61n. On the influence upon St. of the 'tyrant' in Seneca's tragedies and in L. see Venini 1971: 55–67.

101 iussus praecipitem subire Lethen 'ordered to plunge headlong into Lethe', a poetic, pointed expression for Nero's order of L.'s death after his part in the Pisonian conspiracy (Tac. *Ann.* 15.70 *exin M. Annaei Lucani caedem imperat Nero*), for Lethe, the Underworld river of forgetting, implies the threat of oblivion for L.'s works; cf. Luc. 9.355–6 *Lethon tacitus . . . amnis | . . . trahens obliuia. praeceps*, an epithet for swiftly moving rivers (*TLL* x 2.417.6–22; cf. Hor. *Carm.* 1.7.13 *praeceps Anio*), is odd for the silent, calm Lethe (Luc. 6.778 *tacitae . . . ripae*), and is best understood as a transferred epithet expressing the sudden haste and violence of L.'s end (*TLL* x 2.416.17–30); cf. Suet. *Poet.* 33 (Hosius p. 333.15–18); Vacca (Hosius p. 336.7–10).

102 dum pugnas canis: temporal *dum* suggests that L.'s great epic, which breaks off abruptly in book 10, was left incomplete, despite critical claims that the fractured ending was deliberate (e.g. Masters 1992: 224–7). Nero is blamed not only for the death of a great poet but also for the interruption of his masterpiece.   **arduaque uoce:** a unique use of *arduus* for an elevated poetic voice (see 76n.), in contrast with *subire* (101), the downward movement to oblivion. Poetry transcends death.

103 das solacia grandibus sepulchris 'you give consolation to the tombs of the mighty', i.e. as a consolatory epic for the great Republican heroes and citizens of Rome's past the *Bellum ciuile* replaces funerary offerings and monuments; see 2.1.157–8n. As such it is assimilated to a major preoccupation of *Siluae* 2; cf. Virg. *G.* 2.497 *grandiaque . . . sepulchris*, likewise in the context of civil war. But whereas Virgil looks with melancholy from a troubled present to a diminished future, Statius/Calliope sees in the past – and Lucan's poem – the possibility of consolation, of memorialising greatness in the present. On *solacia* see 2.1.30–2n. The collocation of *sepulchris* with *uoce* in the same metrical position may suggest a play on Calliope's name, 'fair-voiced' (ὀπὶ καλῆι), (*se-*)*pulcher* being a common etymology of *sepulchrum* (Maltby s.v. *sepulcrum*). But she is fair-voiced no longer, for she weeps as she sings in the lower metre of hendecasyllables.

104 (o dirum scelus, o scelus!) tacebis: cf. Luc. 7.556 *quidquid in hac acie gessisti, Roma, tacebo*, a key moment of poetic subjectivity revealing the narrator's struggle between the need to document the *nefas* of civil war and the voluntary desire to turn away in shocked, grieved silence; see Masters 1992: 148. Calliope's speech ends on an emotional note heightened by exclamation and repetition (cf. 89–90) as she expresses her fear of oblivion for L.; by contrast Orpheus continues to speak even in death (98–9). 2.7 thus rehabilitates L. and his poetry and restores joy to the Muses (cf. 9 *laetae*).

105–6 leuiterque decidentes | abrasit lacrimas nitente plectro: an original, metapoetic gesture of closure, the wiping away of tears with her plectrum; Calliope has been singing with the lyre. The plectrum (West 1992: 64–70) was often made of expensive material such as ivory (e.g. 5.5.31); Apollo's was golden (*h. Ap.* 185). Its shine thus suggests poetic excellence (*OLD niteo* 6) as well as material value, a fit instrument for the Muse who has endowed L. with *carminum nitorem* (81); cf. 1.2.92–3, where Cupid dries his eyes with his soft wing feathers. The topos of the Muses in mourning derives from Hom. *Od.* 24.60, where they lament the dead Achilles. Pindar (fr. 128c) and the epigrammatists (*AP* VII 8.10) refer to the Muses' grief for their own sons (Hardie 2005a: 20–2). But the striking parodos of the *Rhesus* attributed to Euripides, where an unidentified Muse mourns her young warrior son (890–982), seems to be the only precedent for a Muse's actual song for her dead son; see Pavlock 1985: 220; Said 2007: 42–4. Gel. 1.24.2 cites an epitaph (supposedly by Naeuius) claiming it was 'unlawful' for the Muses to lament a mortal poet (*immortales mortales si foret fas flere | flerent diuae Camenae Naeuium poetam*); but St. has made L. semi-divine, like Orpheus a 'child' of Calliope.

105 leuiterque: critics have differed over whether to take *leuiter* by position with *decidentes* (e.g. Mozley) or with *abrasit* (106) (Van Dam, SB). 'Lightly falling tears' does not suit the emotional climax of Calliope's loss of her two children. *radere* is fig. associated with stylistic refinement (2.2.65–6n.); *leuis* is a programmatic term for elegy or non-epic poetry (see 2 *pr.* 15n.); cf. Hor. *Carm.* 2.1.40 *leuiore plectro*, with N–H; Ov. *Am.* 1.1.19–20, with McKeown. *leuiter* suggests the epic Muse's alignment here with *Siluan* poetics; in 'light' hendecasyllables she celebrates as well as mourns her 'foster son'. *abradere*, which connotes particular vigour (Luc. 6.545), marks a decisive but polished finish to Calliope's song.

107–23 A cletic address to L. imagining his privileged afterlife modelled on Pompey's, ascending either to heaven aloof from mortal cares (107–10; Luc. 9.1–14) or residing in Elysium (111–19; Luc. 6.802–5), conventional consolatory alternatives; St. hopes for the same choices for his father (5.3.19–27, with Gibson;

Setaioli 2005). Some editors posit a third alternative for L., a visit to Tartarus; see 116–17n.

107 at tu: cf. 100 *sic et tu. at* introduces a new theme with muted reference to the contrast with L.'s former state; see 2.4.11n. An exceptionally long parenthesis (107–22) separates hymnic *tu* from its main verbs (*adsis, exores,* 120, 122); Wills 361–2). The repetition of *seu . . . seu* (107, 111) is also characteristic of prayer; see Gibson on 5.3.19.   **rapidum poli per axem** 'through the rapid vault of heaven' (SB); cf. *Theb.* 1.197 *rapidi . . . caeli.* The ancients viewed the sky as endlessly rotating: *polus* often means the whole sky, as here (cf. Ov. *Met.* 2.295, with Bömer), *axis* either the vault of the sky (*OLD* 5) or the axle on which the heavens swiftly turn (*OLD* 3); cf. Luc. 6.464–5 (the power of witches to alter nature's laws) *axibus et rapidis impulsos Iuppiter urguens | miratur non ire polos.* The ascent of Pompey's soul to the spheres is influenced by Cicero's *Somnium Scipionis.* L. will follow in Pompey's footsteps, after death recuperated as a Stoic hero; on the Stoic philosophical background in general see Housman's critical apparatus on Luc. 9.4, 5, 6, 9. This passage also has close parallels with Sen. *Dial.* 6.25, where Marcia's son is imagined as enjoying a Stoic afterlife in the heavens among the virtuous Roman dead. See also Narducci 2002: 335–49 on the influence of Senecan drama as well.

108 famae curribus arduis leuatus 'raised on the lofty chariots of fame', the fourth and final appearance of *arduus* in 2.7 (76n.), in an appropriately triumphal image for an epic poet; cf. Prop. 3.1.9 *quo me Fama leuat terra sublimis,* with Fedeli. St. also draws on the concept of apotheosis; see Bömer on Ov. *Met.* 14.818–28, where Romulus' immortal soul ascends heavenwards in Mars' chariot. The soul of St.'s father likewise after death ascends on high *in ardua* (5.3.19), but to reach a new level of knowledge, not of fame (5.3.19–20).

109 qua surgunt animae potentiores: *qua* refers to *rapidum poli per axem* (107), the way by which souls rise who are 'more powerful' through virtue and poetic genius, not secular authority; polysyllabic *potentiores* emphasises this special sense; cf. Hor. *Carm.* 3.2.21–4 *uirtus, recludens immeritis mori | caelum, negata temptat iter uia | coetusque uulgaris et udam | spernit humum fugiente penna,* with N–R. Ascent is also a common image of *poetic* immortality; cf. Hor. *Carm.* 1.1.36, 2.20; Thomas on Virg. *G.* 3.9.

110 terras despicis et sepulchra rides: cf. Luc. 9.14 *risitque sui ludibria trunci.* L.'s soul acts like Pompey's, mocking his body's humble fate from the starry spheres.

111–12 seu pacis merito nemus reclusi | felix Elysii tenes in oris 'or whether through your merit you are blessed in inhabiting the grove of peace, on the shores of Elysium now open to you'. The clause is recondite; see Van Dam on doubts about the text. *pacis* is best taken as descriptive gen. with *nemus,* not with *merito* – L. did not gain his reputation as poet of peace. *reclusi* does not mean a 'retreat' (SB); Elysium has 'opened up' to admit L.; cf. *Theb.* 5.156 *Acheronte* *recluso*; Hor. *Carm.* 1.24.17 *fata recludere*, with N–H; *Carm.* 3.2.21 cited above. Like Virgil, St. envisages Elysium as a 'grove'; cf. *A.* 6.638–9 *locos laetos et amoena uirecta | fortunatorum nemorum sedesque beatas.*

112 felix: cf. Virg. *A.* 6.669 *felices animae*; Luc. 6.784 *felicibus umbris.*   **oris:** Elysium was intersected by the rivers Eridanus (Virg. *A.* 6.658–9; cf. *A.* 6.674) and Lethe (Virg. *A.* 6.705), hence it has 'shores'.

113 Pharsalica turba: those who fell on behalf of the Republic; on *Pharsalicus* see 66n. L. mingles with the Republican heroes of the past – and of his poem. St.'s Elysium is influenced also by L.'s image of the Underworld as severely divided along partisan lines (Luc. 6.776–819). See 115n., 117n.

114 nobile carmen: the *Bellum ciuile*. Tibullus, followed by Ovid, set the precedent for assigning the deceased poet to Elysium; cf. Tib. 1.3.57–66; Ov. *Am.* 3.9.60–6; St. imagines his father in Elysium, composing poetry with Homer and Hesiod (5.3.24–7). But L. is in the company not of poets but of historical figures 'created' by his poetry.   **insonantem:** a resonant verb, expressive of loud noise and thus of grand epic style, here with rare transitive use (*OLD insono* 2); cf. Virg. *A.* 7.451 *uerberaque insonuit*, with Horsfall.

115 Pompei 'the Pompeys' (nom. pl.), i.e. Pompey and his two sons, Gnaeus Pompeius and Sextus Pompeius, who were executed after their respective defeats at Munda in 45 BCE and Naulochus in 36 BCE. The fate of the three men, scattered over three continents, was a popular epigrammatic theme; cf. *Anth. Lat.* 1 396–9, 452–4; Mart. 5.74, with Howell. St. here follows Luc. 6.804–5 *regnique in parte serena | Pompeis seruare locum.*   **Catones:** Cato the Elder, statesman and author, and his grandson, a major protagonist of L.'s poem (68n.), who committed suicide after the battle of Utica in 46 BCE; cf. Luc. 6.789–90 *maior Carthaginis hostis | non seruituri maeret Cato fata nepotis*; Sen. *Dial.* 6.25.1 *excepit illum coetus sacer, Scipiones Catonesque.*

116 tu magna sacer et superbus umbra 'you sacred and proud in your great shade'. With play upon Pompey's *cognomen Magnus* and the dual meaning of *umbra* ('shadow' and 'shade/ghost') St. rewrites in positive terms Luc. 1.135 *stat magni nominis umbra* (on L.'s ambivalent image of Pompey here see Masters 1992: 9–10).   **sacer** suggests the poet's semi-divinity through the Muses' protection and inspiration (*OLD* 8a; 23n.); it also anticipates the reference to Polla's private cult of L. (124–31). *sacer* may also have political connotations here, for it is esp. associated with Cato as Republican martyr; cf. Sen. *Dial.* 6.25.1 cited 115n.; *Anth. Lat.* 1 395.1–2 *iussa manus sacri pectus uiolasse Catonis | haesit.* Degl'Innocenti Pierini 2004: 143–4 argues that St. presents L. as a poetic martyr, equal to Cato in resolution before tyranny; Bartsch 1997: 146–9 suggests that L.'s part in the Pisonian conspiracy also made him a political martyr.   **superbus:** we might expect Nero rather than L. to be called 'proud'. Yet in addition to its common meaning of overweening pride, *superbus* can have the positive sense of rightful pride in achievements; cf. 2.1.108 *gressuque superbo*; *Theb.* 6.647 (of athletic

prowess) *uiris . . . superbas*; Luc. 6.807–8 *properate mori magnoque superbi | . . . animo.*
St. may have been influenced by Virg. *A.* 6.817 (of Brutus) *animamque superbum*,
where, Austin argues, both senses of *superbus* seem to be in play – admiration for
Brutus' overthrow of the tyrant Tarquin and horror at his execution of his own
sons. St. has perhaps a like ambivalence, expressing admiration for L.'s poetic
achievements, reservations about his political lack of caution; see Degl'Innocenti
Pierini 2004: 141.

116–17 tu . . . | nescis Tartaron 'you do not get to know Tartarus' (*OLD
nescio* 2). Courtney takes 116–19 as parenthetical after the 'either/or' sequence,
though this leaves *adsis* at 120, with *exores* at 122, rather isolated. But Virg. *G.* 1.36–
9 offers a similar, rather abrupt, parenthesis in its proemic hymn to Octavian,
who is to have no interest in ruling over Tartarus. SB however follows Heinsius
by admitting a third option for L.'s shade, an actual visit to Tartarus; he reads
seu in place of *tu*; and follows Haupt and others in reading *noscis Tartaron* ('you
get to know Tartarus'). But a visit to Tartarus, where the damned were eternally
punished (Virg. *A.* 6.548–627, with Norden), is alien to St.'s consolatory theme of
L.'s reception in Elysium (111–12n., 113n.). Moreover, while virtuous shades see
and hear the torments of Tartarus, divine law bars them from entry; cf. Virg. *A.*
6.563 *nulli fas casto sceleratum insistere limen*; *Theb.* 3.108–9 *nunc quoque Tartareo multum
diuisus Auerno | Elysias, i, carpe plagas.*

117 Tartaron: St. follows L. in dividing the Underworld along party lines,
with the Republican heroes of Pharsalus occupying Elysium, the guilty victors
Tartarus; cf. Luc. 6.782–3 *Elysias Latii sedes ac Tartara maesta | diuersi liquere duces*,
a division anticipated by the political separation between Tartarus and Elysium
depicted on Aeneas' shield (Virg. *A.* 8.666–70). St. updates the two regions to
include L. and Nero respectively. On L.'s partisan vision of the Underworld see
Ahl 1976: 137–45.

117–18 et procul nocentum | audis uerbera: like Aeneas, L. hears the
torments of Tartarus at a safe distance; cf. Virg. *A.* 6.557–8 *hinc exaudiri gemitus
et saeua sonare | uerbera, tum stridor ferri tractaeque catenae*; *A.* 8.666–8 *hinc procul addit
| Tartareas etiam sedes, alta ostia Ditis, | et scelerum poenas.* St. may refer here to the
sentence the Senate passed on Nero, death by flogging (Suet. *Ner.* 49.2; [Sen.]
Oct. 619–21, with Ferri).

118–19 pallidumque . . . | . . . Neronem: Underworld shades are pale
through lack of light and life-blood; cf. Lucr. 1.123 *simulacra modis pallentia miris*;
Virg. *A.* 6.480 *Adrasti pallentis imago.* Paleness is also the colour of fear, χλωρὸν
δέος (e.g. Hom. *Il.* 8.77; *TLL* x 1.129.69–130.5); Nero is terrified of his mother.
On the negative connotations of *pallidus* see Pease on Virg. *A.* 4.644 (Dido) *pallida
morte futura.*　　**uisa | matris lampade:** abl. abs. In Tartarus Nero grows
pale at the sight of his mother's torch, which was a key attribute of a Fury; cf.
Theb. 4.133 *Furiarum lampade nigra.* On Nero's matricide see [Sen.] *Oct.* 310–76;

Suet. *Nero* 34.14.3–12; Tac. *Ann.* 14.3–12; the image of his mother pursuing him with lash and torch haunted Nero even in his lifetime; cf. Suet. *Nero* 34.4 *saepe confessus exagitari se materna specie uerberibusque Furiarum ac taedis ardentibus.* St. was perhaps influenced here by Agrippina's depiction as a vengeful Fury in the near-contemporary play *Octauia*; cf. [Sen.] *Oct.* 23–4 *illa, illa meis tristis Erinys | thalamis Stygios praetulit ignes*, with Boyle; *Oct.* 594 *Stygiam cruenta praeferens dextra facem.* The apparition of Pompey's widow Julia as a Fury provides another probable model (Luc. 3.8–40); see 130–1n. Underpinning the image is the mythic paradigm of Orestes and Clytemnestra, the murderous son pursued by his vengeful mother as a Fury, a story popular on the stage and played by Nero (Suet. *Nero* 21.3, 39.2; Degl'Innocenti Pierini 2004: 142–5); cf. Virg. *A.* 4.471–3 *Orestes | armatam facibus matrem et serpentibus atris | cum fugit*, with Pease.

119 respicis: cf. Virg. *A.* 6.548 *respicit Aeneas.* The gesture expresses the moral as well as physical distance between the poet-hero, modelled on Aeneas, and the criminal emperor tortured in hell. St. may refer also to the backward glance of Orpheus (L.'s foster brother) at Eurydice, which commits her for ever to the Underworld; cf. Virg. *G.* 4.491 *uictusque animi respexit*; *Culex* 268–9 *quid, misera Eurydice, tanto maerore recesti, | poenaque respectus et nunc manet Orpheos in te?*; Ov. *Met.* 11.66 *Eurydicenque suam iam tuto respicit Orpheus.* But in consigning Nero to hell for ever, L.'s backward glance is positive. *respicis* also has a literary sense (Gale 2003) and ends the review of L.'s 'history'; now St. looks forward to the establishment of poetic cult.

120 adsis lucidus: a hymnic formula for summoning a deity that ends the cletic address (cf. 107 *tu*) and marks the poem's move towards closure; cf. 2.1.227. *lucidus*, an epithet for a god (*OLD* 1d; cf. *Theb.* 5.675 *lucidus Euhan*), is esp. apt here, given the allusion of L.'s name to *lux* (1n.); *diem* follows in the next line as at 19–20. L. shines in contrast to *pallidus* Nero, consigned to the darkness. St. emphasises L.'s new status as 'immortal' poet and object of poetic cult. On the importance of poets' cults in the Hellenistic and Roman imperial world see Clay 2004: 63–98.

120–2 uocante Polla | unum, quaeso, diem deos silentum | exores 'when Polla summons you, beg, I urge you, one day of the gods of the silent ones', a complicated tripartite plea. Polla summons L. instead of the conventional birthday Genius (Buchheit 1960: 238). But though she summons her husband, he in turn is to petition the gods – according to St.'s wishes. *quaeso* is coordinated with jussive subj. *exores* (*NLS* 134), conveying urgency. The Underworld deities rule 'the silent dead' (*OLD silens* 2); cf. Luc. 3.29 *regesque silentum.* In a compliment to Polla, St. evokes the exemplary couple of conjugal love, Laodamia and Protesilaus, allowed by the gods to see one another for three hours after he was killed on disembarking at Troy (5.3.273; Hom. *Il.* 2.695; Ov. *Ep.* 13; Hyg. *Fab.* 103, 104). The juxtaposition of *diem* and *deos* in a double acc. evokes the common etymological association between *dies* and *deus* (Isid. *Etym.* 5.30.5 *dies dicti a diis*; Michalopoulos 71–3).

122 hoc ... limen: the 'threshold' of the Underworld (2.1.227–8n.).

122–3 patere ... | ad nuptas redeuntibus maritis: cf. Virg. *A.* 6.127 *noctes atque dies patet atri ianua Ditis*; but St. rewrites Virgil's grim sentiment and imagines that the Underworld benevolently opens to allow husbands to be reunited with their wives. Since *redeuntibus* does not specify direction, St. may have in mind not only Protesilaus, who ascended to Laodamia, but also Orpheus, who descended to Eurydice; L. is thus implicitly linked again with his symbolic brother.

124–31 Polla keeps an expensive portrait bust of L. above her bed; Laodamia, a model wife, worshipped a statue of her deceased husband; cf. 3.3.195–204; Ov. *Ep.* 7.99 (Dido) *est mihi marmorea sacratus in aede Sychaeus*; Virg. *A.* 4.457, with Pease. On private cults of the deceased see 2.1.191–2n.; on the poet's house as the centre of private literary cult see Clay 2004: 82.

124–5 haec te non thiasis procax dolosis | falsi numinis induit figura 'she does not endow you with the form of a counterfeit deity, wantonly revelling in deceptive Bacchic worship'. The deceased was sometimes represented in sculpture as a deity; the statues of Abascantus' wife had the features of Ceres, Ariadne, Maia and Venus (5.1.231–5, with Gibson), but Polla prefers a realistic portrait of her husband. Her refusal of the *thiasus*, a riotous dance honouring Bacchus (*OLD* 1), emphasises her chastity, modesty and 'Romanness'; St. may have in mind Eur. *Bacch.* 317–18 'the chaste woman will not be corrupted even in ecstatic worship of Bacchus' (cf. Plut. *Mor.* 609a; also Ov. *Ep.* 13.151–8, where Laodamia (by contrast) handles the statue of her husband in a highly sexualised manner. Critics (e.g. Van Dam) argue that St. here alludes to a tradition that Protesilaus' statue portrayed him as Bacchus and that Laodamia worshipped it in a maenadic frenzy. But the evidence is slight, largely based on these lines and on 3.5.49 *quam tam saeui fecerunt maenada planctus*, a reference perhaps to Laodamia (Nisbet 1995b: 43–4) but equally to Ariadne (Laguna ad loc.); moreover, the statue of Ovid's Laodamia is the exact image of her husband, not of Bacchus (Ov. *Ep.* 13.149–50). See further Hardie 2002: 134–7.

125 falsi 'counterfeit' (*OLD* 5) both because the god takes the form of an artistic image, and because he does not accurately represent the deceased.

126 ipsum sed colit et frequentat ipsum: cf. Mart. 7.23.3–4 *tu, Polla, maritum | saepe colas et se sentiat ille coli*, with Vioque. Framing of the line with *ipsum* emphasises that Polla worships and commemorates (*OLD colo* 6d) L., not a false image. *frequentat* echoes the poem's first line in the slightly different sense of 'cherish the memory of' (*OLD* 6c); the public celebration is recalled in Polla's private cult. On verbal repetition as a closural strategy see 2.1.208n. St. perhaps alludes here also to Sen. *Ep.* 79.13–18, a discourse on posthumous fame which claims that virtue will eventually come to light, even for the persecuted; cf. esp. *Ep.* 79.17 *ad nos quidem nihil pertinebit posterorum sermo; tamen etiam non sentientes colet ac frequentabit.* On the neoteric postposition of *sed* see 2.1.78–9n.

127 imis altius insitum medullis 'planted deeply in her inmost marrow', the seat of the emotions (*OLD medulla* 2b); the comparative adverb is for metrical reasons (L–H–S 168–9).

128–9 at solacia uana subministrat | uultus: a surprising change of thought: L.'s portrait provides only 'vain consolation'. To avoid the possible slight to Polla, SB emends M's *ac* to *nec*, translating 'not idle the solace'. But Slater's *at*, adopted by Courtney, provides a conventional reference to the limitations of the visual arts, here in implicit contrast to the literary 'portrait' of L.; St. too may have in mind Admetus' famous reference to his deceased wife's statue as 'cold pleasure' (Eur. *Alc.* 353). *uana* thus incorporates two senses: 'devoid of physical substance', like ghosts (*OLD* 1; cf. Hor. *Carm.* 1.24.15 *uanae . . . imagini*, with N–H); and 'futile' (*OLD* 2). The portrait cannot restore the 'flesh and blood' poet, only his fleeting likeness; the prosaic *sumministro* (*OLD* 1a) occurs only here in classical Latin poetry and adds a down-to-earth note; cf. 5.1.1–15, which compares the commemorative statue to the more enduring poem of consolation; Tacitus' *Agricola* ends with a spirited defence of literature over the visual arts: physical portraits, no matter how fine, will perish, whereas mind and character when commemorated in literature are eternal (Tac. *Agr.* 46.3). For Ovid's Laodamia, her husband's statue would be as good as the living person if his voice could be added; cf. *Ep.* 13.154 *adde sonum cerae, Protesilaus erit*, a sly hint at the verbal power of poetry.

129 uultus 'face' as seen in the portrait, realistic but not real; cf. Ov. *Tr.* 4.3.19 *uultibus illa tuis tamquam praesentis inhaeret.*   **simili notatus auro** 'delineated in resembling gold', an oxymoron, for gold suggests artifice, but *simili* a close likeness (2.1.193n.). Gold here has metaphorical value, a brilliant metal for the poet of *carminum nitorem* (81); it also reflects Polla's wealth and her love. By the imperial period portrait busts, traditionally wax, could be made of more expensive mediums such as bronze, silver and gold; cf. 3.3.202 *nunc ebur et fuluum uultus imitabitur aurum*, with Laguna; Plin. *Nat.* 35.6–9. Propertius desecrated Cynthia's memory by melting down her gold portrait bust; cf. 4.7.47–8, with Hutchinson.

130 stratis praenitet 'shines very brightly before her couch'. The Romans kept wax portrait busts of their ancestors in the atrium (Flower 1996: 32–59), but in the imperial period portraits of family members or famous men were displayed also in other rooms of the house such as a library, peristyle or bedroom, as here. *praenitere*, rare in poetry, again plays on the association of L.'s name with 'light'; see 120n.

130–1 incubatque somno | securae: cf. Luc. 3.25 (the appearance of Julia's malevolent ghost to her ex-husband Pompey) *non securos liceat mihi rumpere somnos;*

Luc. 5.750. Malamud 1995: 185–7 suggests that L.'s *imago* 'haunts Polla like an incubus'. But although *incubare* 'to keep strict watch over' (*OLD* 5) often has sinister connotations (Thomas on Virg. *G.* 2.507), here it suggests benevolent protection; see 2.3.55n. Julia exemplifies perverted conjugal devotion for she aims to make Pompey's slumbers *not* free from care; L.'s portrait by contrast guarantees Polla a safe sleep; *securae* (gen.), emphasised by enjambment, is proleptic. At the poem's end L. is transformed from a violent epic poet to consolatory work of art, rehabilitated within the *Siluae*.

131–5 A celebratory conclusion to the poem and to book 2.

131 procul hinc abite, Mortes: an apotropaic inversion of the formal summoning of festive deities at the poem's start. Pl. *Mortes* is unusual (cf. *Theb.* 8.24 *uariaeque . . . Mortes*; Mart. 11.6.6 *pallentes procul hinc abite curae*), but it is an appropriate closural reference for a book largely preoccupied with untimely deaths.

132 haec uitae genitalis est origo 'this is life's birth and its beginning!' (SB); a jubilant expression for 'happy birthday': *uitae origo* is a variation of *uitae dies* ('birthday'; cf. *CIL* vi 20674.10, with Courtney, *Musa lapidaria* p. 373); *genitalis* means 'connected with one's birthday' (*OLD* 3; 2.3.62–3n.). The variant *genialis* (82n.), a reference to L.'s Genius (Mozley), diminishes the strong final contrast between birth and death, festive joy and grief. St. alludes here to a Lucretian phrase *genitalis origo* 'creative beginning' (Lucr. 5.176, with Costa; Lucr. 5.324, 1212). St. ends book 2 by acknowledging one of his most significant poetic models (76n.), and by suggesting a new beginning for L. as object of cult.

133 cedat luctus: a play on the etymological link between *luctus* and *lux* (Isid. *Diff.* 1.227 *lugentes . . . dicti, quasi luce egentes, unde et luctus*; Michalopoulous 112; for similar play with antonyms see 14–15n.). Grief will give way to 'light' and L.'s special day. **manent:** hortatory subj. < *mano* 'flow'.

134 iam dulces lacrimae, dolorque festus: oxymoronic: this special *genethliacon* is both lament and celebration. *dulces lacrimae* is the subj. of *manent*, *dolorque festus* of *fleuerat*, *adoret*; Courtney's comma after *festus* should be removed.

135 quicquid fleuerat ante, nunc adoret 'whatever [grief] once wept for, let it now [festively] adore'; a pointed close based on an antithesis between 'then' and 'now', lament and worship. *adoret* resolves the theme of mourning through the joy of L.'s annual commemoration, which transcends his tragic death. *adorare* appears also at the end of the *Thebaid* in the injunction to the epic to worship the path set by the *Aeneid* (*Theb.* 12.817 *semper adora*). As a closural word of St.'s poetry, *adoret* suggests a pattern of reception in which St., following Virgil and L., should be properly included as a major Roman poet; see Hardie 1993: 110; Lovatt 1999: 127.

BIBLIOGRAPHY

1. ABBREVIATIONS

Abbreviations of ancient authors and works and of modern collections mostly follow the conventions of the *Oxford Latin Dictionary* for Latin and Liddell and Scott, *Greek–English Lexicon* for Greek; abbreviations not found in *OLD* or LSJ are given as in the *Oxford Classical Dictionary*. However, the following list might be helpful.

CIL   *Corpus inscriptionum Latinarum* (Berlin 1863–)

D–S   C. Daremberg and E. Saglio, eds. *Dictionnaire des antiquités grecques et romaines* (Paris 1875–1912)

EV   *Enciclopedia Virgiliana* (Rome 1984–91)

K–S   R. Kühner and C. Stegman. *Ausführliche Grammatik der lateinischen Sprache, Zweiter Teil* (Hanover 1966)

L–H–S   M. Leumann, J. B. Hofmann and A. Szantyr, eds. *Lateinische Grammatik, Zweiter Teil* (Munich 1965)

LIMC   *Lexicon iconographicum mythologiae Classicae* (Zürich and Düsseldorf 1981–99)

LTUR   E. M. Steinby, ed. *Lexicon topographicum urbis Romae* (Rome 1993–2000)

N–H   R. Nisbet and M. Hubbard. *A commentary on Horace: Odes book 1, book 2* (Oxford 1975, 1978)

NLS   E. C. Woodcock. *A New Latin Syntax* (London 1959)

N–P   H. Cancik and J. Schneider, eds. *Der neue Pauly* (Stuttgart 1998–)

N–R   R. Nisbet and N. Rudd. *A Commentary on Horace: Odes book 3* (Oxford 2004)

OCD   S. Hornblower and A. Spawforth, eds. *Oxford classical dictionary*, 3rd edn (Oxford 1996)

OLD   P. G. W. Glare, ed. *Oxford Latin dictionary* (Oxford 1982)

RE   A. F. von Pauly, ed., rev. G. Wissowa *et al. Real-Encyclopädie der klassischen Altertumswissenschaft* (Stuttgart 1893–1980)

SB   D. R. Shackleton Bailey. *Statius: Siluae, Thebaid, Achilleid*, 3 vols. (Cambridge, MA 2003)

TLL   *Thesaurus linguae Latinae* (Leipzig 1900–)

2. EDITIONS, COMMENTARIES AND WORKS OF REFERENCE

References to works in this section are by name of author only, to distinguish them from entries in section 3 of the Bibliography, which are cited by name of author and date of publication.

Anderson, W. S. 1997. *Ovid's Metamorphoses, books 1–5*, Norman, OK

Austin, R. G. 1971. *Aeneid 1*, Oxford

    1964. *Aeneid 11*, Oxford

    1955. *Aeneid 1v*, Oxford

    1977. *Aeneid v1*, Oxford

Axelson, B. 1945. *Unpoetische Wörter: ein Beitrag zur Kenntnis der lateinschen Dichtersprache*, Lund

Bailey, C. T. 1947. *Lucreti Cari De rerum natura libri sex*, Oxford

Barchiesi, A. 2005. *Ovidio: Metamorfosi*, vol. 1, Rome and Milan

Barchiesi, A. and Rosati, G. 2007. *Ovidio: Metamorfosi*, vol. 11, Rome and Milan

Bömer, F. P. 1957–8. *Ouidius Naso: die Fasten*, 2 vols., Heidelberg

    1969–86. *P. Ouidius Naso: Metamorphosen*, 6 vols., Heidelberg

Boyle, A. J. 2008. *Octavia attributed to Seneca*, Oxford

Brink, C. O. 1971. *Horace on poetry: the 'Ars Poetica'*, Cambridge

Carter, J. B. 1902. *Epitheta deorum quae apud poetas Latinos leguntur*, Leipzig

Citroni, M. 1975. *Martialis Epigrammaton liber primus*, Florence

Clausen, W. 1994. *Virgil: Eclogues*, Oxford

Coleman, K. M. 1988. *Statius: siluae 1v*, Oxford

    2006. *Liber spectaculorum M. Valerii Martialis*, Oxford

Coleman, R. 1977. *Vergil: Eclogues*, Cambridge

Costa, C. D. N. 1984. *Lucretius De rerum natura v*, Oxford

Courtney, E. 1980. *A commentary on the Satires of Juvenal*, London

    1992. *P. Papinii Stati Siluae*, Oxford

    1995. *Musa lapidaria: a selection of Latin verse inscriptions*, Atlanta, GA

Dewar, M. 1991. *Statius: Thebaid 1x*, Oxford

Dilke, O. A. W. 1954. *Statius: Achilleid*, Cambridge

Durry, M. 1950. *Éloge funèbre d'une matrone romaine (éloge dit de Turia)*, Paris

Eden, P. T. 1984. *Seneca: Apocolocyntosis*, Cambridge

Fantham, E. 1998. *Ovid: Fasti book 1v*, Cambridge

Fedeli, P. 1972. *Il carme 61 di Catullo*, Friburg

    1980. *Il primo libro delle Elegie Sesto Properzio*, Florence

    2005. *Properzio: Elegie libro II*, Cambridge

    1985. *Properzio: Il libro terzo delle Elegie*, Bari

Ferri, R. 2003. *Octavia: a play attributed to Seneca*, Cambridge

Fitch, J. G. 1987. *Seneca's Hercules furens*, Ithaca, NY

Gibson, B. 2006. *Statius: Siluae liber 5*, Oxford

Gibson, R. 2003. *Ovid: Ars amatoria book 3*, Cambridge

Gow, A. S. F. and Page, D. L. 1965. *The Greek anthology: Hellenistic epigrams*, Cambridge

Gransden, K. W. 1976. *Aeneid book VIII*, Cambridge

Green, S. 2004. *Ovid: Fasti 1*, Leiden

Grewing, F. 1997. *Martial Buch VI (ein Kommentar)*, Göttingen

Hardie, P. 1994. *Virgil book IX*, Cambridge

Harrison, S. 1991. *Aeneid 10*, Oxford

Hellegouarc'h, J. 1963. *Le Vocabulaire latin des relations et des partis politiques*, Paris

Henriksén, C. 1998–9. *Martial book IX: a commentary*, 2 vols., Uppsala

Hine, H. M. 2000. *Seneca: Medea*, Warminster

Hopkinson, N. 2000. *Metamorphoses book 13*, Cambridge

Horsfall, N. 2000. *Aeneid 7*, Leiden
    2003. *Aeneid 11*, Leiden

Hosius, C. 1913. *M. Annaei Lucani Belli ciuilis libri decem*, Leipzig

Housman, A. E. 1926. *Lucan: Belli ciuilis libri decem*, Oxford

Howell, P. 1980. *A commentary on book one of the epigrams of Martial*, London
    1995. *Martial: The epigrams book 5*, Warminster, England

Hunter, R. 1989. *A commentary on Apollonius Rhodius book 3*, Cambridge

Hutchinson, G. 2006. *Propertius: Elegies book IV*, Cambridge

Kaster, R. A. 1995. *Suetonius: De grammaticis et rhetoribus*, Oxford

Kenney, E. 1971. *Lucretius De rerum natura book 3*, Cambridge
    1996. *Ovid: Heroides XVI–XXI*, Cambridge

Knox, P. E. 1995. *Ovid: Heroides. Select epistles*, Cambridge

Laguna, G. 1992. *Estacio: Siluas III*, Madrid

Leary, T. J. 2001. *Martial book XIII: the Xenia*, London
    1996. *Martial book XIV: the Apophoreta*, London

Lightfoot, J. L. 1999. *Parthenius of Nicaea*, Oxford

Maltby, R. 1991. *A lexicon of ancient Latin etymologies*, Leeds
    2002. *Tibullus: Elegies*, Cambridge

Mankin, D. 1995. *Horace: Epodes*, Cambridge

Martin, R. H. and Woodman, A. J. 1989. *Tacitus: Annals book 4*, Cambridge

Mayer, R. 1994. *Horace: Epistles 1*, Cambridge

McKeown, J. C. 1987, 1989, 1998. *Ovid: Amores*, Liverpool

Michalopoulos, A. 2001. *Ancient etymologies in Ovid's Metamorphoses*, Leeds

Micozzi, L. 2007. *Il catalogo degli eroi: saggio di commento a Stazio Tebaide 4, 1–344*, Pisa

Mozley, J. H. 1928. *Statius*, vol. 1, Cambridge, MA

Mulder, H. M. 1954. *Publii Papinii Statii Thebaidos liber secundus*, Groningen

Mynors, R. A. B. 1990. *Virgil: Georgics*, Oxford

Nisbet, R. G. 1939. *M. Tulli Ciceronis De domo sua*, Oxford

Norden, E. 1957. *P. Vergilius Maro: Aeneis Buch VI*, Stuttgart

Ogilvie, R. M. and Richmond, I. 1967. *Cornelii Taciti De uita Agricolae*, Oxford

Pease, A. S. 1967. *Publi Vergili Maronis Aeneidos liber quartus*, Darmstadt

Pederzani, O. 1995. *Il talamo, l'albero e lo specchio*, Bari

Pfeiffer, R. 1949. *Callimachus*, vol. I, Oxford

Pollmann, K. F. L. 2004. *Statius, Thebaid 12: introduction, text, commentary*, Paderborn

Quinn, K. 1973. *Catullus: the poems*, London

Raven, D. S. 1965. *Latin metre*, London

Rudd, N. 1989. *Horace: Epistles book II and Epistle to the Pisones*, Cambridge

Russell, D. A. and Wilson, N. G. 1981. *Menander Rhetor*, Oxford

Schöffel, C. 2002. *Martial Buch 8*, Stuttgart

Schoonhoven, H. 1992. *The Pseudo-Ovidian Ad Liviam de morte Drusi*, Groningen

Sherwin-White, A. N. 1966. *The letters of Pliny: a historical and social commentary*, Oxford

Skutsch, O. 1985. *Annals of Q. Ennius*, Oxford

Smolenaars, J. J. L. 1994. *Statius: Thebaid VII. A commentary*, Leiden

Smyth, H. W. 1972. *Greek Grammar*, rev. G. M. Messing, Cambridge, MA

Snijder, H. 1968. *P. Papinius Statius: Thebaid. A commentary on book III*, Amsterdam

Spanoudakis, K. 2002. *Philitas of Cos*, Leiden

Thomas, R. F. 1988. *Georgics*, 2 vols., Cambridge

Van Dam, H.-J. 1984. *P. Papinius Statius: Siluae book II. A commentary*, Leiden

Vioque, G. G. 2002. *Martial book VII: a commentary*, trans. J. J. Zoltowski, Leiden

Vollmer, F. 1898. *P. Papinii Statii libri*, Leipzig

Wacht, M. 2000. *Concordantia in Statium*, Hildesheim

Watson, L. and Watson, P. 2003. *Martial: Epigrammata*, Cambridge

West, M. L. 1966. *Hesiod: Theogony*, Oxford

Williams, R. D. 1962. *P. Vergili Maronis Aeneidos liber tertius*, Oxford

    1960. *P. Vergili Maronis Aeneidos liber quintus*, Oxford

    1973. *The Aeneid of Virgil, books 7–12*, London

    1972. *P. Papini Stati Thebaidos liber decimus*, Leiden

Wills, J. 1996. *Repetition in Latin poetry: figures of allusion*, Oxford

Woodman, A. J. 1977. *Velleius Paterculus: the Tiberian narrative (2.94–131)*, Cambridge

    1983. *Velleius Paterculus: the Caesarian and Augustan narrative (2.41–93)*, Cambridge

Zetzel, J. E. G. 1995. *Cicero: De republica. Selections*, Cambridge

3. OTHER WORKS CITED

Adams, J. N. 1982. *The Latin sexual vocabulary*, London

Ahl, F. 1976. *Lucan: an introduction*, Ithaca

Anderson, H. 2000. *The manuscripts of Statius*, Washington, DC

Anderson, W. S. 1963. 'Multiple change in the *Metamorphoses*', *Transactions of the American Philological Association* 94: 1–27

Ando, C. 2003. 'A religion for the Empire', in Boyle and Dominik 2003: 323–44

Argetsinger, K. 1992. 'Birthday rituals: friends and patrons in Roman poetry and cult', *Classical Antiquity* 11: 174–94

Arnott, W. G. 1977. 'Swan songs', *Greece and Rome* 24: 149–53

2007. *Birds in the ancient world from A to Z*, London

Ash, R. 1999. *Ordering anarchy*, Ann Arbor

Asmis, E. 1996. 'Epicurean poetics', in D. Obbink, ed. *Philodemus and poetry: poetic theory and practice in Lucretius, Philodemus, and Horace* (Oxford) 15–34

2004. 'Epicurean economics', in J. T. Fitzgerald, D. Obbink and G. S. Holland, eds. *The New Testament world* (Leiden and Boston) 133–76

Augoustakis, A. 2007. 'Taming the lion and *Siluae* 2.5', in Augoustakis and Newlands 2007: 207–21

Augoustakis, A. and Newlands, C., eds. 2007. *Statius' 'Siluae' and the poetics of intimacy* (*Arethusa* 40)

Baltussen, H. 2009. 'Personal grief and public mourning in Plutarch's *Consolation to his wife*', *American Journal of Philology* 130: 67–98

Barchiesi, A. 1997. *The poet and the prince: Ovid and Augustan discourse*, Berkeley

2005. 'The search for the perfect book: a PS to the new Posidippus', in Gutzwiller 2005: 320–42

Barney, R. 1998. 'Socrates Agonistes: the case of the *Cratylus* etymologies', *Oxford Studies in Ancient Philosophy* 16: 63–98

Bartman, E. 1991. 'Sculptural collecting and display in the private realm', in Gazda 1991: 71–88

Bartsch, S. 1997. *Ideology in cold blood*, Cambridge, MA

Bartsch, S. and Elsner, J. 2007. 'Introduction: eight ways of looking at an ekphrasis', *Classical Philology* 102: i–vi

Bausi, F. 1996. *Angelo Poliziano: Siluae*, Florence

Beagon, M. 1992. *Roman nature: the thought of Pliny the Elder*, Oxford

Beard, M. 1998. 'Imaginary *horti*: or up the garden path', in M. Cima and E. La Rocca, eds. *Horti Romani* (Rome) 23–32

Beard, M. and Henderson, J. 2001. *Classical art: from Greece to Rome*, Oxford

Beloch, J. 1879. *Campanien: Topographie, Geschichte und Leben der Umgebung Neapels im Alterthum*, Berlin

Bergmann, B. 1991. 'Painted perspectives of a villa visit: landscape as status and metaphor', in Gazda 1991: 49–70

2001. 'Meanwhile, back in Italy . . . Creating landscapes of allusion', in S. Alcock, J. F. Cherry and J. Elsner, eds. *Pausanias: travel and memory in Roman Greece* (Oxford) 154–66

Berlincourt, V. 2006. 'Queen Dirce and the Spartoi: wandering through Statius' Theban past and the *Thebaid*'s early printed editions', in Nauta, Van Dam and Smolenaars 2006: 129–45

Bernstein, N. 2005. 'Mourning the *puer delicatus*: status inconsistency and the ethical value of fostering in Statius, *Siluae* 2.1', *American Journal of Philology* 126: 257–80

2008. *In the image of the ancestors: narratives of kinship in Flavian epic*, Toronto

Bing, P. 1981. 'The voice of those who live in the Sea: Empedocles and Callimachus', *Zeitschrift für Papyrologie und Epigraphik* 41: 33–6

Bloomer, M. 2006. 'The technology of child production: eugenics and eulogics in the *De liberis educandis*', *Arethusa* 39: 71–99

Bodel, J. 1997. 'Monumental villas and villa monuments', *Journal of Roman Archaeology* 10: 5–35

    1999. 'Death on display: looking at Roman funerals', in B. Bergmann and C. Kondoleon, eds. *The art of ancient spectacle* (New Haven) 259–81

Boyle, A. J., ed. 1995. *Roman literature and ideology: Ramus essays for J. P. Sullivan*, Victoria, Australia

Boyle, A. J. and Dominik W. J., eds. 2003. *Flavian Rome: culture, image, text*, Leiden

Bradley, A. 1969. 'Augustan culture and a radical alternative: Vergil's *Georgics*', *Arion* 8: 347–58

Bradley, K. 1984. *Slaves and masters in the Roman Empire: a study in social control*, Brussels

    1994. *Slavery and society at Rome*, Cambridge

Braund, S. and Gilbert, G., 2003. 'An ABC of epic *ira*: anger, beasts, and cannibalism', *Yale Classical Studies* 32: 250–85

Brelich, A. 1937. *Aspetti della morte nelle iscrizioni sepolcrali dell'impero romano*, Budapest

Bright, D. 1980. *Elaborate disarray, the nature of Statius' Siluae*, Meisenheim am Glan

Buchheit, W. 1960. 'Statius' Geburtstagsgedicht zu Ehren Lucans (Silu. 2.7)', *Hermes* 88: 231–49

    1961. 'Martials Beitrag zum Geburtstag Lucans als Zyklus', *Philologus* 105: 90–6

Burrow, C. 1999. 'Ovid on imitating and on the imitation of Ovid', in P. Hardie, A. Barchiesi and S. Hinds, eds. *Ovidian transformations* (Cambridge) 271–87.

Caldelli, M. L. 1993. *L'agon capitolinus: storia e protagonisti dall'istituzione domizianea al IV secolo*, Rome

Cancik, H. 1965. *Untersuchungen zur lyrischen Kunst des P. Papinius Statius*, Hildesheim

    1968. 'Eine epikureische Villa', *Die altsprachliche Unterricht* 11: 62–75

    1971. 'Amphitheater: zum Problem der "Gesamtinterpretation" am Beispiel von Statius, *Siluae* II 5: Leo mansuetus', *Die altsprachliche Unterricht* 14: 66–81

Carcopino, J. 2003. *Daily life in ancient Rome*, New Haven and London

Carey, S. 2003. *Pliny's catalogue of culture: art and empire in the natural history*, Oxford

Casali, S. 2006. 'The poet at war: Ennius on the field in Silius' *Punica*', *Arethusa* 39: 569–93

Cawsey, F. 1983. 'Statius: *Siluae* II iv. More than an ex-parrot?', *Proceedings of the African Classical Association*, 17: 69–84

Champlin, E. 1991. *Final judgments: duty and emotion in Roman wills, 200 BC–AD 250*, Berkeley and Los Angeles

Chevallier, R. 1976. *Roman roads*, London

Clauss, M. 1999. *Kaiser und Gott: Herrscherkult im römischen Reich*, Stuttgart and Leipzig

Clay, D. 2004. *Archilochus heros: the cult of poets in the Greek polis*, Cambridge

Clinton, K. 1973. 'Publius Papinius St[—] at Eleusis', *Transactions of the American Philological Association*, 103: 79–82

Coffee, N. 2006. 'Eteocles, Polynices, and the economics of violence in Statius' *Thebaid*', *American Journal of Philology* 127: 415–52

Coleman, K. 1986. 'The emperor Domitian and literature', in *Aufstieg und Niedergang der Römischen Welt* II 32.5: 3087–115

  1998. 'The *liber spectaculorum*: perpetuating the ephemeral', in Grewing 1998: 15–36

  2000. 'Latin literature after AD 96', *American Journal of Ancient History* 15: 19–39

  2003. 'Recent scholarship on the *Siluae* and their context: an overview', in SB 11–21

Colini, A. M. 1944. *Storia e topografia del Celio nell' Antichità*, Vatican City

Colton, R. E. 1967. 'Parrot poems in Ovid and Statius', *The Classical Bulletin* 43: 71–8

Connolly, J. 2007. *The state of speech: rhetoric and political thought in ancient Rome*, Princeton

Connors, C. 2000. 'Imperial space and time: the literature of leisure', in O. Taplin, ed. *Literature in the Greek and Roman worlds: a new perspective* (Oxford) 492–518

Conte, G. 1994. *Latin literature*, trans. J. B. Solodow, Baltimore

Corbier, M. 1989. 'Usages publics du vocabulaire de la parenté: *patronus* et *alumnus* de la cité dans l'Afrique romaine', *L'Africa Romana* 7: 815–54

Courtney, E. 1966. 'On the *Siluae* of Statius', *Bulletin of the Institute of Classical Studies* 13: 94–100

  1968. 'Emendations of Statius' *Siluae*', *Bulletin of the Institute of Classical Studies* 15: 51–7

  1971. 'Further remarks on the *Siluae* of Statius', *Bulletin of the Institute of Classical Studies* 18: 95–7

  1988. 'Problems in the *Siluae* of Statius', *Classical Philology* 83: 43–5

  2004. 'On editing the *Siluae*', *Harvard Studies in Classical Philology* 102: 445–53

Courtney, J. and James, P., eds. 2006. *The role of the parrot in selected texts from Ovid to Jean Rhys*, Lampeter

Criado, C. 2000. 'Statius: a reflection upon the application of mannerism and historical baroque concepts in Roman literature', *Germanisch-Romanische Monatsschrift* 50: 299–331

Curtius, E. R. 1953. *European literature and the Latin Middle Ages*, trans. W. R. Trask, New York

D'Alessandro Behr, F. 2007. *Feeling history: Lucan, Stoicism and the poetics of passion*, Columbus, OH

D'Ambra, E. 1993. *Private lives, imperial virtues: the frieze of the Forum Transitorium in Rome*, Princeton

Damon, C. 2002. 'The emperor's new clothes, or, on flattery and encomium in the *Siluae*', in Miller, Damon and Myers 2002: 174–87

D'Arms, J. 1970. *Romans on the Bay of Naples: a social and cultural study of the villas and their owners from 150 BC to AD 400*, Cambridge, MA

1974. 'Puteoli in the second century of the Roman Empire: a social and economic study', *Journal of Roman Studies* 64: 104–24.

Darwall-Smith, R. 1996. *Emperors and architecture: a study of Flavian Rome*, Brussells

Davis, G. 1967. '*Ad sidera notus*: strategies of lament and consolation in Fortunatus' *De Gelesuintha*', *Agon* 1: 118–34

Degl'Innocenti Pierini, R. 2007. '*Pallidus Nero* (Stat. *silu.* 2, 7, 118 s.): il "personaggio" Nerone negli scrittori dell'età flavia', in A. Bonadeo and E. Romano, eds. *Dialogando con il passato* (Florence) 136–55

Delarue, F. *et al.*, eds. 1996. *Epicedion: hommage à P. Papinius Statius 96–1996*, Poitiers

Dewar, M. 1996. 'Episcopal and Epicurean villas: Venantius Fortunatus and the *Siluae*', in Delarue *et al.* 1996: 297–313

2002. '*Siquid habent ueri uatum praesagia:* Ovid in the 1st–5th centuries AD', in B. Boyd, ed. *Brill's companion to Ovid* (Leiden) 383–412

Dietrich, J. 2002. 'Dead parrots society', *American Journal of Philology* 123: 95–110

Dixon, S. 1992. *The Roman family*, Baltimore

Duckworth, G. E. 1967. 'Five centuries of hexameter', *Transactions of the American Philological Association* 98: 77–150

Dufallo, B. 2003. 'Propertian elegy as "restored behaviour": evoking Cynthia and Cornelia', *Helios* 30: 163–79

Eck, W. 1983. 'Die Gestalt Frontins in ihrer politischen und sozialen Umwelt: Organisation und Administration der Wasserversorgung Roms', in W. Eck and G. Garbrecht, eds. *Wasserversorgung im Antiken Rom: Sextus Iulius Frontinus, curator aquarum* (Munich) 47–62

1997. 'Rome and the outside world: senatorial families and the world they lived in', in Rawson and Weaver 1997: 73–99

Edwards, C. 2007. *Death in ancient Rome*, New Haven and London

Elsner, J. 1995. *Art and the Roman viewer: the transformation of art from the pagan world to Christianity*, Cambridge

Fantham, E. 1999. '*Chironis exemplum:* on teachers and surrogate father in *Achilleid* and *Siluae*', *Hermathena* 167: 59–70

Farrell, J. 2002. 'Greek lives and Roman careers in the classical *Vita* tradition', in P. Cheney and F. A. de Armas, eds. *European literary careers: the author from Antiquity to the Renaissance* (Toronto) 24–46

Feeney, D. 1982. 'A commentary on Silius Italicus: Punica 1', DPhil Oxford

2007. *Caesar's calendar: ancient time and the beginnings of history*, Berkeley and Los Angeles

Fishwick, D. 1987. *The imperial cult in the Latin West*, Leiden

Fitzgerald, W. 2000. *Slavery and Roman literary imagination*, Cambridge

Flower, H. I. 1996. *Ancestor masks and aristocratic power in Roman culture*, Oxford

2006. *The art of forgetting: disgrace and oblivion in Roman political culture*, Chapel Hill

Forbes, C. A. 1955. 'The education and training of slaves in Antiquity', *Transactions of the American Philological Association* 86: 321–60

Fowler, A. 1982. 'The silva tradition in Jonson's *The Forrest*', in M. Mack and G. de Forest Lord, eds. *Poetic traditions of the English Renaissance* (New Haven and London) 163–80

1994. *The country house poem: a cabinet of seventeenth-century estate poems and related items*, Edinburgh

Fowler, D. 1995. 'Martial and the book,' in Boyle 1995: 199–226

2002. *Lucretius on atomic motion*, Oxford

Fowler, H. N. and Stillwell, R. 1941. *Corinth*, vol. I. *Introduction, topography, architecture*, Cambridge, MA

Fraenkel, E. 1957. *Horace*, Oxford

Frazer, A., ed. 1998. *The Roman villa: villa urbana*, Philadelphia

Frederiksen, M. 1984. *Campania*, London

Futtrell, A. 1997. *Blood in the arena: the spectacle of Roman power*, Austin, TX

Gale, M. R. 2000. *Virgil on the nature of things: the Georgics, Lucretius, and the didactic tradition*, Cambridge

2003. 'Poetry and the backward glance in Virgil's *Georgics* and *Aeneid*', *Transactions of the American Philological Society* 133: 323–52

Ganiban, R. T. 2007. *Statius and Virgil: the Thebaid and the reinterpretation of the Aeneid*, Cambridge

Garin, E., ed. 1952. 'Oratio super Fabio Quintiliano et Statii Syluis', in *Prosatori latini del Quattrocento* (Milan and Naples) 867–85

Garvey, J. J. 1989. '*Siluae* 2.5 and Statius' art', *Latomus* 48: 627–31

Gazda, E. K. ed. 1991, *Roman art in the private sphere: new perspectives on the architecture and décor of the domus, insula, and villa*, Ann Arbor

Gibson, B. 2004. 'The repetitions of Hypsipyle', in M. Gale, ed. *Latin epic and didactic poetry* (Swansea) 149–80

Gleason, M. 1995. *Making men*, Princeton

Gnoli, R. 1988. *Marmora Romana*, 2nd edn, Rome

Gombrich, E. 1996. 'Architecture and rhetoric in Giulio Romano's Palazzo del Tè', in R. Wood, ed. *The essential Gombrich: selected writings on art and culture* (London) 401–10

Gowing, A. 2005. *Empire and memory: the representation of the Roman Republic in imperial culture*, Cambridge

Graziosi, B. 2002. *Inventing Homer*, Cambridge

Grewing, F., ed. 1998. *Toto notus in orbe: Perspektiven der Martial-Interpretation*, Stuttgart

Griessmair, E. 1966. *Das Motiv der mors immatura in der Griechischen metrischen Grabinschriften*, Innsbruck

Griffin, M. 1976. *Seneca: a philosopher in politics*, Oxford

1984. *Nero: the end of a dynasty*, London and New Haven

Grimal, P. 1943. *Les jardins romains*, Paris

Gutzwiller, K., ed. 2005. *The new Posidippus: a Hellenistic poetry book*, Oxford

Habinek, T. 1998. *The politics of Latin literature: writing, identity and empire in ancient Rome*, Princeton

Håkanson, L. 1969. *Statius' Siluae: critical and exegetical remarks, with some notes on the Thebaid*, Lund

1982. 'Homoeoteleuton in Latin dactylic poetry', *Harvard Studies in Classical Philology* 86: 87–115

Hallett, J. 1970. 'Over troubled waters: the meaning of the title *pontifex*', *Transactions of the American Philological Association* 101: 219–27

Hardie, A. 1983. *Statius and the Siluae: poets, patrons, and epideixis in the Graeco-Roman world*, Liverpool

1997. 'Philitas and the plane tree', *Zeitschrift für Papyrologie und Epigraphik* 119: 21–36

2003a. 'Poetry and politics at the games of Domitian', in Boyle and Dominik 2003: 125–47

2003b. 'The statue(s) of Philitas', *Zeitschrift für Papyrologie und Epigraphik* 143: 27–36

2005a. 'Sappho, the Muses, and life after death', *Zeitschrift für Papyrologie und Epigraphik* 154: 13–32

2005b. 'The ancient etymology of *carmen*', *Papers of the Langford Latin Seminar* 12: 71–94

2008. 'An Augustan hymn to the Muses (Horace *Odes* 3.4)', *Papers of the Langford Latin Seminar* 13: 55–118

Hardie, P. R. 1987. 'Ships and ship-names in the *Aeneid*', in M. Whitby, P. Hardie and M. Whitby, eds. *Homo uiator: classical essays for John Bramble* (Bristol) 163–71

1993. *The epic successors of Virgil*, Cambridge

1997. 'Closure in Latin epic,' in D. H. Roberts, F. M. Dunn and D. Fowler, eds. *Classical closure: reading the end in Greek and Latin literature* (Princeton) 139–62

2002. *Ovid's poetics of illusion*, Cambridge

2005. 'Statius' Ovidian poetics and the tree of Atedius Melior (*Siluae* 2.3)', in Nauta, Van Dam and Smolenaars 2006: 207–21

Harrison, S. J., ed. 1995a. *R. G. M. Nisbet, collected papers on Latin literature*, Oxford

1995b. 'Horace, Pindar, Iullus Antonius and Augustus: Odes 4. 2', in S. J. Harrison, ed. *Homage to Horace: a bimillenary celebration* (Oxford) 108–27

Hemelrijk, E. A. 1999. *Matrona docta: educated women in the Roman elite from Cornelia to Julia Domna*, London and New York

Henderson, J. 1998. *A Roman life: Rutilius Gallicus on paper and in stone*, Exeter

2002. *Pliny's statue: the letters, self-portraiture and classical art*, Exeter

2004. *Morals and villas in Seneca's letters: places to dwell*, Cambridge

Henriksén, C. 1998. 'Martial und Statius', in Grewing 1998: 77–118

Herrlinger, G. 1930. *Totenklage um Tiere in der antiken Dichtung*, Stuttgart

Heslin, P. 2005. *The transvestite Achilles: gender and genre in Statius' Achilleid*, Cambridge

Heuvel, H. 1936–7. 'De inimicitiarum, quae inter Martialem et Statium fuisse dicuntur, indiciis,' *Mnemosyne* 4: 299–330

Hill, D. E. 2002. 'Statius' *Nachleben*: the first few hundred years', *Schede Umanistiche* 16: 5–28

Hinds, S. 1985. *The metamorphosis of Persephone: Ovid and the self-conscious Muse*, Cambridge

1987. 'Generalising about Ovid', *Ramus* 16: 4–31

1998. *Allusion and intertext: dynamics of appropriation in Roman poetry*, Cambridge

2000. 'Cinna, Statius, and "immanent literary history" in the cultural economy', *L'Histoire Littéraire Immanente dans la Poésie Latine*. *Entretiens sur l'Antiquité Classique* 47: 221–65.

2002. 'Landscape with figures: aesthetics of place in the *Metamorphoses* and its tradition', in P. Hardie, ed. *The Cambridge companion to Ovid* (Cambridge) 122–49

2005. 'Dislocations of Ovidian time', in J. P. Schwindt, ed. *Zur Poetik der Zeit in augusteischer Dichtung* (Heidelberg) 203–30

Hopkins, K. 1978. *Conquerors and slaves*, Cambridge

1983. *Death and renewal*, Cambridge

Hopman, M. 2003. 'Satire in green: marked clothing and the technique of *indignatio* at Juvenal 5.141–5', *American Journal of Philosophy* 124: 557–74

Howell, A. and Shepherd, B. 2007. *Statius: Siluae. A selection*, London

Hunter, R. 2006. *The shadow of Callimachus*, Cambridge

Huskinson, J. 1996. *Roman children's sarcophagi: their decoration and social significance*, Oxford

Hutchinson, G. O. 1993. *Latin literature from Seneca to Juvenal*, Oxford

James, P. 2006. 'Two poetic and parodic parrots in Latin literature', in Courtney and James 2006: 1–32

James, R. and Webb, L. 1991. 'Ekphrasis and art in Byzantium', *Art History* 14: 1–17

Janson, T. 1964. *Latin prose prefaces: studies in literary conventions*, Stockholm

Jennison, G. 1937. *Animals for show and pleasure in ancient Rome*, Manchester

Johannsen, N. 2006. *Dichter über ihre Gedichte: die Prosavorreden in den Epigrammaton Libri Martialis und in den Siluae des Statius*, Göttingen

Jolivet, V. 1987. 'Xerxes togatus: Lucullus in Campania', *Mélanges de l'École Française de Rome, Antiquité* 99: 875–904

Jones, B. 1992. *The emperor Domitian*, London

Kassel, R. 1958. *Untersuchungen zur griechischen und römischen Konsolationsliteratur*, Munich

Kaster, R. A. 1988. *Guardians of language: the grammarian and society in late antiquity*, Berkeley

2005. *Emotion, restraint and community in ancient Rome*, Oxford

Kaufmann, T. D. 1993. *Mastery of nature: aspects of art, science, and humanism in the Renaissance*, Princeton

Keith, A. M. 1992. *The play of fictions: studies in Ovid's Metamorphoses book 2*, Ann Arbor

2000. *Engendering Rome: women in Latin epic*, Cambridge

Kenney, E. J. 1964. 'Erotion again', *Greece and Rome* 11: 77–81

Kleijwegt, M. 1991. *Ancient youth*, Amsterdam

Knox, P. 1993. 'Philetas and Roman poetry', *Papers of the Leeds International Latin Seminar* 7: 61–83

Konstan, D. 1973. *Some aspects of Epicurean psychology*, Leiden

Koortbooijan, M. 1995. *Myth, meaning and memory on Roman sarcophagi*, Berkeley and Los Angeles

Krevans, N. 2005. 'The editor's toolbox: strategies for selection and presentation in the Milan epigram papyrus,' in Gutzwiller 2005: 81–96

Krüger, A. 1998. *Die lyrische Kunst des P. Papinius Statius in Silue II.2*, Frankfurt

Kuttner, A. 1998. 'Prospects of patronage: realism and *Romanitas* in the architectural vistas of the 2nd style', in Frazer 1998: 93–107

1999. 'Culture and history at Pompey's museum', *Transactions of the American Philological Association* 129: 343–73

Kyle, D. 1998. *Spectacles of death in ancient Rome*, London and New York

Laes, C. 2003. 'Desperately different? *Delicia* children in the Roman household', in D. L. Balch and C. Osiek, eds. *Early Christian families in context* (Grand Rapids, MI) 298–324

La Penna, A. 1996. 'Modelli efebici nella poesia di Stazio', in Delarue *et al.* 1996: 161–84

Lattimore, R. 1962. *Themes in Greek and Latin epitaphs*, Urbana, IL

Leach, E. 2004. *The social life of painting in ancient Rome and on the Bay of Naples*, Cambridge

Leigh, M. 1997. *Lucan: spectacle and engagement*, Oxford.

Leiwo, M. 1994. *Neapolitana: a study of population and language in Graeco-Roman Naples*, Helsinki.

Linderski, J. 1989. 'Garden parlors: nobles and birds', in R. I. Curtis, ed. *Studia Pompeiana et classica*, vol. II. *In honor of Wilhelmina F. Jashemski* (New York) 105–27

Lomas, K. 2003. 'Public building, urban renewal, and euergetism', in K. Lomas and T. Cornell, eds. *Bread and circuses: euergetism and municipal patronage in Roman Italy* (London and New York) 28–45

Lonsdale, S. 1990. *Creatures of speech: lion, herding, and hunting similes in the Iliad*, Stuttgart

Lorenz, S. 2002. *Erotik und Panegyrik: Martials epigrammatische Kaiser*, Tübingen

Lovatt, H. 1999. 'Competing endings: re-reading the end of the *Thebaid* through Lucan', *Ramus* 28: 126–51

2005. *Statius and epic games: sport, politics and poetics in the Thebaid*, Cambridge

2007. 'Statius, Orpheus, and the post-Augustan *uates*', in Augoustakis and Newlands 2007: 145–63

MacMullen, R. 1980. 'Romans in tears', *Classical Philology* 75: 254–5

Malamud, M. 1995. 'Happy Birthday, dead Lucan: (p)raising the dead in *Siluae* 2.7', in Boyle 1995: 169–98

Manning, C. E. 1978. 'Grief in Statius' Epicedia', *Journal of the Australasian Universities Language and Literature Association* 50: 251–60

Markus, D. 2000. 'Performing the book', *Classical Antiquity* 19: 138–79
    2004. 'Grim pleasures: Statius's poetic *consolationes*', *Arethusa* 37: 105–35

Martinelli, L. C. 1978. *Angelo Poliziano: commento inedito alle Selve di Stazio*, Florence

Marx, F. A. 1937–8. 'Tacitus und die Literatur der exitus illustrium uirorum', *Philologus* 92: 83–103

Masters, J. 1992. *Poetry and civil war in Lucan's Bellum ciuile*, Cambridge

Mayer, R. 1982. 'Neronian classicism', *American Journal of Philology*, 305–18

McNelis, C. 2002. 'Greek grammarians and Roman society during the early Empire: Statius' father and his contemporaries', *Classical Antiquity* 21: 67–94

Mellor, R. 2003. 'The new aristocracy of power', in Boyle and Dominik 2003: 69–101

Michler, W. 1914. *De P. Papinio Statio M. Annaei Lucani imitatore*, Breslau

Millar, F. 1977. *The emperor in the Roman world, 31 BC–AD 337*, London

Miller, J. F., Damon, C., Myers, K. S., eds. 2002. *Vertis in usum: studies in honor of Edward Courtney*, Munich and Leipzig

Miller, S. G. 2004. *Ancient Greek athletics*, New Haven

Mohler, S. L. 1940. 'Slave education in the Roman Empire', *Transactions of the American Philological Association* 71: 262–80

Montiglio, S. 2008. '*Meminisse iuuabit*: Seneca on controlling memory', *Rheinisches Museum für Philologie* 151: 168–80

Morales, H. 2004. *Vision and narrative in Achilles Tatius' Leucippe and Clitophon*, Cambridge

Morgan, T. 1998. *Literate education in the Hellenistic and Roman worlds*, Cambridge

Morris, I. 1992. *Death-ritual and social structure in classical antiquity*, Cambridge

Myers, K. S. 1990. 'Ovid's *Tecta Ars*: *Amores* 2. 6, "Programmatics and the parrot"', *Echos du Monde Classique* 34: 367–74
    2000. '*Miranda fides*: poet and patrons in paradoxographical Landscapes in Statius' *Siluae*', *Materiali e Discussioni per L'analisi dei Testi Classici* 44: 103–38
    2002. '*Psittacus redux*: imitation and literary polemic in Statius, *Siluae* 2.4', in Miller, Damon and Myers 2002: 189–99
    2005. '*Docta otia*: garden ownership and configurations of leisure in Statius and Pliny the Younger', *Arethusa* 38: 103–29

Nagel, R. 2000. 'Literary and filial modesty in *Siluae* 5.3', *Ramus* 29: 47–59

Nagle, B. R. 2004. *The Silvae of Statius*, Indiana

Narducci, E. 2002. *Lucano, un'epica contro l'impero*, Rome

Nauta, R. R. 2002. *Poetry for patrons: literary communication in the age of Domitian*, Leiden
    2008. 'Statius in the *Siluae*', in Smolenaars, Van Dam and Nauta 2008: 143–74

Nauta, R. R., Van Dam, H.-J. and Smolenaars, J. J. L., eds. 2006. *Flavian poetry*, Leiden

Neudecker, R. 1988. *Die Skulpturenausstattung Römischer Villen in Italien*, Mainz
  1998. 'The Roman villa as a locus of art collections', in Frazer 1998: 77–91

Newlands, C. 1988. 'Jonson's "Penshurst" and Statius' villa poems', *Classical and Modern Literature* 8: 291–300
  1991. '*Siluae* 3.1 and Statius' poetic temple,' *Classical Quarterly* 41: 438–52
  2002. *Statius' Siluae and the poetics of Empire*, Cambridge
  2005. 'Animal claquers: Statius *Silu.* 2.4 and 2.5', in W. Batstone and G. Tissol, eds. *Defining genre and gender in Latin literature* (New York) 151–73
  2006. 'Book-ends: Statius' *Siluae* 2.1 and 2.7', *Ramus* 35: 63–77
  2009a. 'Statius' prose prefaces', *Papers in honour of Elaine Fantham (Materiali e Discussioni per l'Analisi dei Testi Classici* 61): 91–104
  2009b. '*Statius: Siluae. A selection*. Versions by Anthony Howell and Bill Shepherd', *Translation and Literature* 18: 110–16

Newmyer, S. T. 1979. *The Siluae of Statius: structure and theme*, Leiden

Nielsen, H. S. 1987. '*Alumnus*: a term of relation denoting quasi-adoption', *Classica et Mediaevalia* 38: 141–88
  1997. 'Interpreting epithets in Roman epitaphs', in Rawson and Weaver 1997: 169–204
  1999. 'Quasi-kin, quasi-adoption and the Roman family', in M. Corbier, ed. *Adoption and fosterage* (Paris) 249–62

Nisbet, R. G. M. 1995a. 'The oak and the axe', in Harrison 1995a: 202–12
  1995b. '*Felicitas* at Surrentum (Statius, *Siluae* II.2)', in Harrison 1995a: 29–46

Noy, D. 2000. 'Building a Roman funeral pyre', *Antichthon* 34: 30–45

O'Hara, J. 1996. *True names*, Ann Arbor.

Oliensis, E. 2002. 'Feminine endings, lyric seductions', in T. Woodman and D. Feeney, eds. *Traditions and contexts in the poetry of Horace* (Cambridge) 93–106.

Pagán, V. E. 2010. 'The power of the epistolary preface from Statius to Pliny', *Classical Quarterly* 60: 194–201

Patterson, A. 1984. *Censorship and interpretation: the conditions of writing and reading in early modern England*, Madison, WI

Pavlock, B. 1985. 'Epic and tragedy in Virgil's Nisus and Euryalus episode', *Transactions and Proceedings of the American Philological Association* 115: 207–24

Pavlovskis, Z. 1965. 'Statius and the late Latin epithalamia', *Classical Philology* 60: 164–77
  1973. *Man in an artificial landscape: the Marvels of civilization in imperial Roman literature*, Leiden

Peachin, M. 2004. *Frontinus and the curae of the curator aquarum*, Stuttgart

Perry, E. 2005. *The aesthetics of emulation in the visual arts of ancient Rome*, Cambridge

Pitcher, R. A. 1990. 'The emperor and his virtues: the qualities of Domitian', *Antichthon* 24: 86–95

Pollini, J. 2003. 'Slave boys for sexual and religious service,' in Boyle and Dominik 2003: 149–66

Pond, C. 2006. 'The scientific background to parrots in literature', in Courtney and James 2006: 175–219

Potter, D. 1999. 'Entertainers in the Roman Empire', in D. S. Potter and D. J. Mattingly, eds. *Life, death and entertainment in the Roman Empire* (Ann Arbor) 256–325

Price, S. 1987. 'From noble funerals to divine cult: the consecration of Roman emperors', in D. Cannadine and S. Price, eds. *Rituals of royalty: power and ceremonial in traditional societies* (Cambridge) 56–105

Purcell, N. 1987. 'Town and country and country in town', in E. B. MacDougall, ed. *Ancient Roman villa gardens* (Dumbarton Oaks) 187–203

Quint, D. 1993. *Epic and empire: politics and generic form from Virgil to Milton*, Princeton

Ramsby, T. 2005. 'Striving for permanence: Ovid's funerary inscriptions', *Classical Journal* 100: 365–91

Rawson, B. 1997. 'The iconography of Roman childhood', in Rawson and Weaver 1997: 205–38

    1999. 'Education: the Romans and us', *Antichthon* 33: 81–98

    2002. 'The express route to Hades', in P. McKechnie, ed. *Thinking like a lawyer: essays on legal history and general history for John Crook on his eightieth birthday* (Leiden) 273–88

    2003. *Children and childhood in Roman Italy*, Oxford

Rawson, B. and Weaver, P., eds. 1997. *The Roman family in Italy: status, sentiment, space*, Oxford

Reeve, M. D. 1977. 'Statius' *Siluae* in the fifteenth century', *Classical Quarterly* 27: 202–25.

    1983. 'Statius', in L. D. Reynolds, ed. *Texts and transmission* (Oxford) 394–9

Richlin, A. 1992. *The garden of Priapus: sexuality and aggression in Roman humor*, 2nd edn, Oxford

Riggsby, A. 2003. 'Pliny in space and time', *Arethusa* 36: 167–86

Rimell, V. 2008. *Martial's Rome*, Cambridge

Roberts, M. 1989. *The jeweled style: poetry and poetics in Late Antiquity*, Ithaca, NY

    2009. *The humblest sparrow: the poetry of Venantius Fortunatus*. Ann Arbor

Rodgers, R. H. (ed.) 2004. *Frontinus: De aquaeductu urbis Romae*, Cambridge

Roller, M. 2001. *Constructing autocracy: aristocrats and emperors in Julio-Claudian Rome*, Princeton

    2006. *Dining posture in ancient Rome: bodies, values and status*, Princeton

Rosati, G. 1999. 'La Boiterie de Mademoiselle Élégie: un pied volé et ensuite retrouvé (les aventures d'un genre littéraire entre les Augustéens et Stace)', in J. Fabre-Serris and A. Deremetz, eds. *Élégie et épopée dans la poésie ovidienne (Héroïdes et Amours): en hommage à Simone Viarre* (Lille) 147–63

    2002. 'Muse and power in the poetry of Statius', in E. Spentzou and D. Fowler, eds. *Cultivating the Muse* (Oxford) 229–51

2006. 'Luxury and love: the encomium as aestheticisation of power in Flavian poetry', in Nauta, Van Dam and Smolenaars 2006: 41–58

Rose, G. P. 1979. 'Odysseus' barking heart', *Transactions of the American Philological Association* 109: 215–30

Ross, D. O. 1969. *Style and tradition in Catullus*, Cambridge, MA
 1975. *Backgrounds to Augustan poetry: Gallus, elegy, and Rome*, Cambridge

Rühl, M. 2006. *Literatur gewordener Augenblick: die Silven des Statius im Kontext literarischer und sozialer Bedingungen von Dichtung*, Berlin

Said, S. 2007. 'Les transformations de la Muse dans la tragédie grecque', in F. Perusino and M. Colantonio, eds. *Dalla lirica corale alla poesia drammatica* (Pisa) 23–48

Saller, R. 1982. *Personal patronage under the early Empire*, Cambridge

Sanna, L. 2008. 'Dust, water and sweat: the Statian *puer* between charm and weakness, play and war', in Smolenaars, Van Dam and Nauta 2008: 195–214

Sauter, F. 1934. *Die römische Kaiserkult bei Martial und Statius*, Stuttgart and Berlin

Schröder, B.-J. 1999. *Titel und Text*, Berlin and New York

Scott, K. 1936. *The imperial cult under the Flavians*, Stuttgart and Berlin

Scourfield, J. H. D. 1993. *Consoling Heliodorus: a commentary on Jerome, Letter 60*, Oxford

Segal, C. 1993. *Euripides and the poetics of sorrow*, Durham

Sens, A. 2002–3. 'Grief beyond measure: Asclepiades 33 Gow-Page (*AP* xiii.23) on the troubles of Botrys', *Hermathena* 173–4: 108–15

Setaioli, A. 2005. 'The fate of the soul in ancient "Consolations": rhetorical handbooks and the writers', *Prometheus* 31: 253–62

Shackleton Bailey, D. R. 2004. 'On editing the *Siluae*: a response', *Harvard Studies in Classical Philology* 102: 455–9

Shaw, B. 2001. 'Raising and killing two children: two Roman myths', *Mnemosyne* 54: 31–77

Shearman, J. 1967. *Mannerism*, London

Slater, W. J. 1974. 'Pueri, turba minuta', *Bulletin of the Institute of Classical Studies* 21: 133–40

Small, J. P. 1997. *Wax tablets of the mind: cognitive studies of memory and literacy in classical antiquity*, London and New York

Smolenaars, J. J. L., Van Dam, H.-J. and Nauta, R. R., eds. 2008. *The poetry of Statius*, Leiden.

Spencer, D. 2002. *The Roman Alexander: reading a cultural myth*, Exeter

Steiner, D. 2007. 'Feathers flying: avian poetics in Hesiod, Pindar and Callimachus', *American Journal of Philology* 128: 177–208

Stroh, W. 1971. *Die römische Liebeselegie als werbende Dichtung*, Amsterdam

Strubbe, J. 1998. 'Epigrams and consolation decrees for deceased youths', *L'Antiquité Classique* 67: 45–75

Syme, R. 1930. 'The imperial finances under Domitian, Nerva, and Trajan', *Journal of Roman Studies* 20: 55–70

Szelest, H. 1972. 'Mythologie und ihre Rolle in den *Siluae* des Statius', *Eos* 60: 309–17

Tandoi, V. 1969. 'Il ricordo di Stazio "dolce poeta" nella Sat. VII di Giovenale', *Maia* 21: 103–22

Thévenaz, O. 2002. '*Flebilis lapis?* Gli epigrammi funerari per Erotion in Marziale', *Materiali e Discussioni per l'Analisi dei Testi Classici* 48: 167–91

Thomas, R. 1998. '"Melodious tears": sepulchral epigram and generic mobility', in M. A. Harder, R. F. Regtuit and G. C. Wakker, eds. *Genre in Hellenistic poetry* (Hellenistica Groningana III) (Groningen) 205–23.

Thompson, D'A. 1936. *A glossary of Greek birds*, Oxford

Toynbee, J. M. C. 1971. *Death and burial in the Roman world*, Ithaca, NY
   1973. *Animals in Roman life and art*, London

Tybout, R. A. 2001. 'Roman wall-painting and social significance', *Journal of Roman Archaeology* 14: 33–55

Van Dam, H.-J. 1996. 'The coming of the *Siluae* to the Netherlands', in Delaure *et al.* 1966: 316–25

Venini, P. 1971. *Studi staziani*, Pavia

Vermeule, E. 1979. *Aspects of death in early Greek art and poetry*, Berkeley and Los Angeles

Vessey, D. W. T. 1973. *Statius and the Thebaid*, Cambridge
   1981. 'Atedius Melior's tree: Statius *Siluae* 2.3', *Classical Philology* 76: 46–52
   1986. 'Style and theme in Statius' "Siluae"', in *Aufstieg und Niedergang der Römischen Welt* II 32.5: 2754–802
   1996. 'Honouring Statius', in Delarue *et al.* 1996: 7–24

Vout, C. 2007. *Power and eroticism in imperial Rome*, Cambridge

Wallace, P. W. 1974. 'Hesiod and the Valley of the Muses', *Greek, Roman, and Byzantine Studies* 15: 5–24

Wallace-Hadrill, A. 1998.'The villa as a cultural symbol', in Frazer 1998: 43–53

Watson, P. 1995. *Ancient stepmothers: myth, misogyny and reality*, Leiden

Weaver, P. R. C. 1991. 'Children of freedmen (and freedwomen)', in B. Rawson, ed. *Marriage, divorce, and children in ancient Rome* (Canberra) 166–90

Webb, R. and James, L. 1991. '"To understand ultimate things and enter secret places": ekphrasis and art in Byzantium', *Art History* 14: 1–17

West, M. 1992. *Ancient Greek music*, Oxford

White, P. 1974. 'The presentation and dedication of the *Siluae* and *Epigrams*', *Journal of Roman Studies* 64: 40–61
   1975. 'The friends of Martial, Statius, Pliny and the dispersal of patronage', *Harvard Studies in Classical Philology* 79: 265–300
   1978. '*Amicitia* and the profession of poetry in early imperial Rome', *Journal of Roman Studies* 68: 74–92
   1993. *Promised verse: poets in the society of Augustan Rome*, Cambridge, MA

Wilcox, A. 2005. 'Sympathetic rivals: consolation in Cicero's letters', *American Journal of Philology* 126: 237–55

Wilkinson, L. P. 1963. *Golden Latin artistry*, Cambridge

Williams, C. 1999. *Roman homosexuality: ideologies of masculinity in classical antiquity*, Oxford

Williams, G. D. 2005. 'Seneca on winds: the art of anemology in *Natural Questions* 5', *American Journal of Philology* 126: 417–50

Williams, R. 1973. *The country and the city*, London

Williams, R. D. 1951. 'The local ablative in Statius', *Classical Quarterly* 45: 143–6

Wilson, L. M. 1938. *The clothing of the ancient Romans*, Baltimore

Wilson, M. 1997. 'The subjugation of grief in Seneca's "Epistles"', in S. Braund and C. Gill, eds. *The passions in Roman thought and literature* (Cambridge) 48–67

Wray, D. 2007. 'Wood: Statius' *Siluae* and the poetics of genius', in Augoustakis and Newlands 2007: 127–43

Yates, F. A. 1966. *The art of memory*, Chicago

Zablocki, S. 1966. 'De antiquorum epicediis', *Eos* 56: 292–310

Zaganiaris, N. J. 1977. 'Le Roi des animaux dans la tradition classique', *Platon* 29: 26–48

Zanker, P. 1998. *Pompeii: public and private life*, trans. D. L. Schneider, Cambridge, MA

2004. *Mit Mythen leben: die Bilderwelt der römischen Sarkophage*, Munich

Zeiner, N. 2005. *Nothing ordinary here: Statius as creator of distinction in the Siluae*, New York

Zetzel, J. 1982. 'The poetics of patronage in the late first century BC', in B. Gold, ed. *Literary and artistic patronage in ancient Rome* (Austin, TX) 87–102

2003. 'Plato with pillows', in D. Braund and C. Gill, eds. *Myth, history, and culture in Republican Rome* (Exeter) 119–38

INDEXES

1. SUBJECTS

Single-number references are to pages of this book; three-number references are to lemmata in the commentary.
Page numbers precede references to lemmata.
The index is selective; the addresses of book 2 are not listed.

2. LATIN WORDS

3. WORDS OF GREEK ORIGIN